A New History
of Redemption

The Work of Jesus the Messiah
through the Millennia

Gerald R. McDermott

IB
Baker Academic
a division of Baker Publishing Group
Grand Rapids, Michigan

To my beloved wife, Jean,

whose love and support during these years of writing
have brought a new beauty to our union

© 2024 by Gerald McDermott

Published by Baker Academic
a division of Baker Publishing Group
Grand Rapids, Michigan
www.bakeracademic.com

Printed in the United States of America

Library of Congress Cataloging-in-Publication Data
Names: McDermott, Gerald R. (Gerald Robert), author.
Title: A new history of redemption : the work of Jesus the Messiah through the millennia / Gerald R. McDermott.
Description: Grand Rapids, Michigan : Baker Academic, a division of Baker Publishing Group, [2024] | Includes bibliographical references and index.
Identifiers: LCCN 2023029023 | ISBN 9780801098543 (cloth) | ISBN 9781493444434 (ebook) | ISBN 9781493444441 (pdf)
Subjects: LCSH: Redemption—Christianity—History of doctrines. | Jesus Christ—Person and offices—Biblical teaching.
Classification: LCC BT775 .M34 2024 | DDC 234/.3—dc23/eng/20230821
LC record available at https://lccn.loc.gov/2023029023

Unless otherwise noted, Scripture translations are the author's own.

Scripture quotations labeled ESV are from The Holy Bible, English Standard Version® (ESV®), copyright © 2001 by Crossway, a publishing ministry of Good News Publishers. Used by permission. All rights reserved. ESV Text Edition: 2016

Scripture quotations labeled KJV are from the King James Version of the Bible.

Baker Publishing Group publications use paper produced from sustainable forestry practices and postconsumer waste whenever possible.

24 25 26 27 28 29 30   7 6 5 4 3 2 1

Contents

Part Five: From Christ's Resurrection to the End of the World

Part Six: The Eschaton

Detailed Contents

Preface

I wrote this book because I was inspired by what Jonathan Edwards (1703–58) was trying to do at the end of his life. He was working on a massive *summa* that would show the beauty of the Triune God in a new, historical way. Edwards, who was fixated on God's beauty more than anyone else in the history of Christian thought,[1] was convinced that because God is a God of history—revealing himself not in one blinding flash but successively through history—history must be the best way to talk about God and the world. He was also convinced that God used the world's cultures, which at root are religious, in his design to use history to show his beauty. Since I had already written a book about his fascination with religions outside the Judeo-Christian tradition—plus other books on his system of spiritual discernment, his typological view of reality, his public theology, and then with Michael McClymond a big survey of his thought—and had myself written seven books on world religions, I wanted to see if I could finish what he started in his 1739 sermon series, A History of Redemption, which was to have become a theological story using a historical method.

More than twenty years ago I had my own Copernican revolution when I realized that I had previously missed the profound Jewishness of Jesus and the gospel. Since then I have put out three books and many articles on this subject. Not too long into this new research I discovered that Edwards also realized that Israel is the center of history, the world, and the gospel. Then when I returned to his 1739 sermon series, I was delighted to discover that these insights were very close to

---

1. Edward Farley, *Faith and Beauty: A Theological Aesthetic* (Burlington, VT: Ashgate, 2001), 43; Patrick Sherry, *Spirit and Beauty: An Introduction to Theological Aesthetics* (Birmingham, UK: SCM, 2002).

the major themes of that series. So I determined to pick up where Edwards left off and to continue his narrative using recent scholarship to track an Israel-centered history of redemption through biblical and church history until the new heavens and new earth. This book became my attempt to connect the dots surrounding Israel, redemption by the Jewish Messiah, secular and sacred history, the world religions, and Jewish-Christian worship through liturgy and sacraments. I have tried to argue that it is only through this historical method tracing the Messiah's redemption amid the turmoil of the world and the worship of his people that one can best see God's beauty.

Readers who were formed by the Enlightenment and its historical-critical method will be frustrated and perhaps impatient when I launch immediately into biblical interpretation without considering questions of historical fact in and behind the biblical story. To them I would advise patience. Let them listen to the narrative for four or more chapters before they conclude whether all of this hangs together. At its heart this book is biblical theology. It is a big picture in which every part is connected to every other part, with the whole being more than the sum of its parts. In an important book published recently, neurologist/philosopher and literary scholar Iain McGilchrist argues that most scientists and philosophers in the last few hundred years have restricted knowing to the left brain, which apprehends and manipulates, without attending to the right brain, which comprehends the big picture.[2] I think the same has happened in biblical and theological studies. When considering the meaning of redemption through the Jewish Messiah, we need to listen to Fichte on method: "It will be necessary first to obtain a view of the whole before any single proposition therein can be accurately defined, for it is their interconnection that throws light on the parts; a method which certainly assumes willingness to do the system justice, and not the intention of merely finding fault with it."[3]

This book is biblical theology carried up through the last two thousand years, applying the big picture to some of the big events of these last two millennia. It is not a book privileging the methods of religious studies. I ask how, for example, Genesis makes sense of human origins, not whether anthropology can tell us about the relations of prehominids to Adam and Eve. I don't quarrel here with the Genesis account of long life spans and its numbers of generations, and I don't

2. Iain McGilchrist, *The Matter with Things: Our Brains, Our Delusions, and the Unmaking of the World*, 2 vols. (London: Perspectiva, 2021), 431–500.

3. J. G. Fichte, preface to *The Foundations to the Entire Science of Knowledge*, in *The Science of Knowledge*, ed. and trans. P. Heath and J. Lachs (Cambridge: Cambridge University Press, 1991 [1774]), 90, quoted in McGilchrist, *Matter with Things*, 16.

think its writer(s) were being anything but literal in their intentions. I want to explore what all this meant to them and to their billions of readers and listeners over the last three millennia. In other words, I am trying to map the logic of the Bible and the Great Tradition that has given us a way to interpret the Bible. I am not interested in what religious studies claims for what is behind the Bible or is the actual story of human origins. Those claims change every few decades. Instead, I have tried to decipher what the biblical authors, and then their traditional interpreters, have meant by human origins and ultimate reality, which means the God of Israel and the working of his redemption through history. These have remained much more stable over the last few millennia.

This means, among other things, that I also accept the Scriptures that the Church has passed down to us as its governing canon without detailing the development of that canon (which was long and sometimes messy) and the nature of their authority. Discussion of that process involves questions for historical criticism, consideration of which would make this a much longer and very different book. What matters for me is that the universal Church has used the biblical canon and its accompanying traditions through which to see all of reality and to live and worship accordingly. Just as the Great Tradition (something close to what C. S. Lewis called "Mere Christianity") has not sought to justify its existence by Enlightenment criteria, neither do I try to argue for the validity of either the biblical canon or the Great Tradition. I presume the coherence and beauty of the Christian vision of the Triune God as passed down to us through Scripture and tradition, and in this book I seek to explain its coherence in ways that I have not seen previously.

All the biblical quotations in this book are my own translations unless indicated otherwise.[4] Readers might be surprised to find that I have transliterated the Tetragrammaton, God's sacred name, as YHWH, in order to reproduce in English form what is in the Hebrew text and in the Jewish Siddur (prayer book). I have done so in order to signal that we worship not an amorphous Lord but the very particular God of Israel. Jews keep the Tetragrammaton in print in their Bibles and prayer books but when reading out loud replace it with Adonai (Lord) or HaShem (the Name) out of reverence for the Creator and obedience to the commandment (Exod. 20:7).[5] We Christians might want to do the same.

For similar reasons I have translated *Christos* (Greek for "the anointed one") in the New Testament as "Messiah," since this is what came to mind for first-century

---

4. Any italics in Scripture quotations are added for emphasis.
5. Thanks to Jewish theologian Pesach Wolicki for helping me think through this.

readers and listeners, who knew immediately that "the anointed one" is a Jewish term for their Messiah. I have used caps for both Jews and Gentiles since they are coequal but distinct sorts of people in the Messiah's Body. Fairly early in this book, following Edwards's example, I have referred to "the Jewish Church," indicating the continuity between God's people in the First (Old) Testament and the Second (New) Testament. Instead of "Old Testament" I frequently use the Jewish term Tanach (an acronym for its three parts, Torah/Pentateuch, Nevi'im/Prophets, and Ketuvim/Writings) in order to remind readers that these are Jewish Scriptures delivered to us by a Church founded by a Jewish Messiah and his Jewish apostles. Jesus and the apostles used these Hebrew words for its parts.

I have used the masculine pronoun for God, for a number of reasons that I have summarized in a previous book as follows:

> I must explain why I use the masculine pronoun for God when some Christians argue that such use renders God sexual and diminishes the worth of females. On the one hand, it is true that masculine language for God should not be used to the exclusion of all feminine imagery. The Bible itself uses feminine imagery (Num 11:12; Ps 22:9–10; 71:6; 139:13; Is 49:15; 66:9, 13; Mt 23:37); use of feminine imagery and language in prayer can enrich our apprehension of God's self-giving l ove.
>
> But when it is suggested that the masculine pronoun for God be excised because of women's oppression by men, the cure proves worse than the disease. Avoidance of the masculine pronoun for God often forces us to use ungainly expressions like "Godself," which is not only awkward but also theologically problematic because it undermines the notion that God is a person. It is particularly important to highlight God's personhood when discussing religions that deny it. Philosophical Hindus and Buddhists, for example, insist there is no personal God because there is no final distinction between God and the cosmos.
>
> Second, . . . the problem with "Godself" is that "it" is too inoffensive, and as a result assumes too much. It runs the risk of avoiding the scandal of particularity (the Christian God is the Father Who sent His Son to die on Pilate's cross), and it suggests that we can know the divine essence behind the biblical Father, Son and Holy Spirit. But Scripture tells us that we know the Father truly only through the Son, and the creeds inform us that God is known first not as some amorphous essence but as Father. In other words, we don't know anything about any god but the God Who has revealed Himself as Father, Son and Holy Spirit. We don't know a supposed divine essence behind the Father and Son that can be named without the name Father and Son. All we know is that God has given us His name as Father,

Son and Holy Spirit. And when God alone is invoked by Scripture, that God is the "Father." Hence "Father" and "Son" are not simply metaphorical but literal names—indeed proper names—of the deity.[6]

As my sons (and now some of our grandchildren) know, I could not have written this book without my beloved wife, Jean, who not only discussed much of this with me but also cleared space in our home and lives so that I could think and write. This book was started at Beeson Divinity School under Timothy George's wise direction and continued during Doug Sweeney's first year at the helm. But most of it has been written while I served as teaching pastor at St. John Lutheran Church in Roanoke during the first summer of COVID-19, teaching at Nashotah House for a semester, and while I helped homeschool six grandchildren in Pittsburgh for nearly five months. It resumed with intensity in 2022, when I battened the hatches and tried to look neither left nor right.

I am grateful to all those who have read part or all of the manuscript and made suggestions: Dan Juster, Malcolm Lowe, Mark Graham, Alan Pieratt, Michael Giere, Blake Johnson, Drew Thomas, Mike McClymond, Bruce Ashford, Os Guinness, Sean Rubin, and Briane Turley. My deep appreciation goes to Dave Nelson, who encouraged this project from its first mention at Baker and gave valuable advice in early and later stages. Bob Hosack helped me negotiate later bottlenecks, and James Korsmo and Robert Banning provided prodigious polishing to a penultimate text. All my failures to take their suggestions, and of course all my other mistakes, are my responsibility alone.

Pentecost 2023

Select Bibliography

Fichte, J. G. Preface to *The Foundations to the Entire Science of Knowledge*. In *The Science of Knowledge*, edited and translated by P. Heath and J. Lachs, vii–xviii. Cambridge: Cambridge University Press, 1982. First published 1774.

McDermott, Gerald. "Appendix: God and the Masculine Pronoun." In *God's Rivals: Why Has God Allowed Different Religions? Insights from the Bible and the Early Church*, 169–73. Downers Grove, IL: IVP Academic, 2007.

6. Gerald McDermott, "Appendix: God and the Masculine Pronoun," in *God's Rivals: Why Has God Allowed Different Religions? Insights from the Bible and the Early Church* (Downers Grove, IL: IVP Academic, 2007), 169–70. Used by permission of InterVarsity Press, P.O. Box 1400, Downers Grove, IL 60515, USA. www.ivpress.com.

McGilchrist, Iain. *The Matter with Things: Our Brains, Our Delusions, and the Unmaking of the World*. 2 vols. London: Perspectiva, 2021.

Sherry, Patrick. *Spirit and Beauty: An Introduction to Theological Aesthetics*. Birmingham, UK: SCM, 2002.

1

What Is Redemption?

Jonathan Edwards (1703–58) is widely regarded as the greatest Christian theologian in the history of North America. He is becoming increasingly known for having made *beauty* more central to his vision of God than any other thinker in the history of Christian thought. In 1739 he preached a sermon series on the history of God's work of redemption that he intended eventually to expand so that it would include other religious and cultural phenomena in human history. He wanted it to unfold "the grand design of God, and the *summum* and *ultimum* of all the divine operations and decrees," which, "beginning from eternity," encompassed "the chief events coming to pass in the church of God, and revolutions in the world of mankind, affecting the state of the church and the affair of redemption."[1] Reaction to a smallpox vaccine, however, cut Edwards down in his prime and prevented the completion of this project. This book is an attempt to imagine what would have resulted if Edwards had had more time and the benefit of later scholarship.

> Fear ye not the reproach of men,
>   neither be ye afraid of their revilings.
> For the moth shall eat them up like a garment,
>   and the worm shall eat them like wool:
> but my righteousness shall be for ever,
>   and my salvation from generation to generation. (Isa. 51:7b–8 KJV)

---

1. Edwards, letter to the Princeton trustees, quoted in Jonathan Edwards, *A History of the Work of Redemption*, vol. 9 in *The Works of Jonathan Edwards* (New Haven: Yale University Press, 1989), 62. From here forward, this Edwards volume will be abbreviated as *HWR*.

In these verses from the King James Version of the Bible, Edwards found the key themes for his *History of the Work of Redemption*: while today's Church is suffering and persecuted, her people need to remember that the prosperity of her enemies is temporary, and God will constantly be merciful and faithful to her. He will continue "to work salvation for her, protecting her" from the attacks of her enemies and "carrying her safely through all the changes of the world" until her final "victory and deliverance."[2]

These verses appear in a portion of Isaiah's prophecy where the eighth-century-BC prophet is comforting his distressed people. They are defeated. Many have been killed and driven into exile. But Isaiah gives them hope. Since they are God's people, "in whose heart is [his] law," their future is "joy and gladness" (Isa. 51:3, 7). God's righteousness, which is God's faithfulness to his promises to save his people (Neh. 9:8; Pss. 36:10; 51:14; Dan. 9:16), is drawing near for them (51:5a). His salvation has already gone out on its way to work (51:5b). It will continue to save and succor his people through all of history and into eternity.

But this will not be the case for those who despise righteousness. Those who "reproach" and "revile" God's people in this life will be "eaten up" just as a moth eats a garment and a worm eats wool (51:8). They will die and be no more, just as clouds in the sky "vanish like smoke" and clothing "wears out" (51:6). God will pour out his wrath on the Church's "tormentors." He will punish those who have stepped on his people and make them "stagger" in the same way they persecuted the saints (51:22–23).

Theology as History

These are the overall themes of Edwards's *History*, and they are also the themes of this *New History*: the "happiness" of the Church and the destruction of her enemies.[3] This book will follow much of Edwards's historical outline for its first fourteen chapters but stop at more places in the history to reflect on the theological meaning of what has happened. Edwards did little, for example, with the world religions; I will do more. Edwards spoke more than many of his predecessors about the Jewish roots of Christianity, but I will go further. Edwards did relatively little with liturgy and sacraments in the history of redemption; I will go a bit deeper.

The upshot is that while this is a history of God's saving work in his creation, it is not a systematic theology that proceeds by loci or topics (such as God, creation,

2. Edwards, *HWR*, 113.
3. Edwards, *HWR*, 113.

sin, etc.). It starts with the counsels of redemption in which the three divine Persons conspire to create a world. It proceeds with God's work of redemption immediately after the fall, the chaos of the first generations until Babel, the flood of judgment on those generations, and the calling of Abraham to start over with a family. Then it moves through the history of Israel and its surrounding world and the coming of the Jewish Messiah and his establishment of a Church. It touches on important moments in two thousand years of Church (and world) and ends eventually in the new heavens and new earth.

Topics will be treated as they arise in history. For example, I won't discuss the sources and nature of Scripture until it starts to be produced after the rise of Moses in the thirteenth century before Christ. But along the way I will discuss not only the history of God's people in Israel and the later Christian Church as we know them in the Scriptures but also their relation to the rise of other civilizations and religions such as those of the Far East. So Islam will be treated not as a religion in the abstract or a recent phenomenon but as a new heresy within the Christian world of the seventh century. I will also try to think about the relation between secular and sacred history. For example, what import did the history of Israel and the Church have for the great kingdoms of the ancient Near East—and medieval and modern Europe?

Of course this is a book of theology and not history or politics. Its goal is to think *theologically* about the meaning of Israel and Christ (Messiah) for the nations, even those not directly affected by Jews and Christians. This will force us to consider questions about the salvation of those who did not hear of revelation from the God of Israel, the Father of Messiah Jesus. It will also require us to think about the material content of redemption. In other words, not just the *fact* of redemption from sin, death, and the devil but the *manner and means* by which that redemption is carried out over the whole lives of saints. That is, what have been the *vessels* of redemption through life for the billions of Jews and Christians? *How* has the life of the Triune God sustained them through the course of life with its ups and downs? How have they received new faith and love and joy? For most of these billions, growing in God was unthinkable apart from liturgy and sacraments. We will trace—briefly of course—their development in the history of redemption.

Righteousness and Redemption

But before we start all this history, we must define some important terms. I have already used the words "redemption" and "salvation." This book will show that while most Christians think of "salvation" as rescue from eternal death, "redemption" for Scripture (and Edwards) meant more, as we shall see below. But what is the relation of "righteousness," which I have defined as God's acting to fulfill his promises, to "salvation" or "redemption"? One is the cause of the other. God's righteousness, which could also be called his covenant mercy, is the cause of redemption. God made a covenant or determination to redeem his people, and he has been faithful through history to fulfill his promises to redeem them through all of their lives and for eternity. It is his righteousness—his commitment to fulfill those promises—that causes him to redeem. Redemption is the sum of all his works for his people by which he showers them with love and mercy.

The Scope of Redemption

So how much history is involved in the history of redemption? Scripture sometimes uses the word "redemption" for simply the *purchase* of salvation by the life, death, and resurrection of the Messiah, particularly by his death (Isa. 44:22; Rom. 3:24–26; Gal. 3:13; Eph. 1:17; Heb. 9:12). In these uses, we say that his resurrection is when he *finished* the work of redemption.

But Scripture also uses the word to refer to all of God's works that contribute to the end of the salvation of his people (Luke 21:28; Rom. 3:24; 8:23; Eph. 4:30; Titus 2:14). That means not only the purchase of redemption but also everything God arranged to *prepare* for that purchase and also everything that applied the *fruit* of the purchase to the people of God. So all of the preparation in history for the incarnation plus the imputation (assigning to a person's account) and application and success of the Messiah's redemption are summed up as the work of redemption. This involves not only Messiah in his offices as Prophet, Priest, and King but also what the Father and the Holy Spirit have done in their united plan (with the Son) to redeem sinful men and women. This is the meaning I use in this book for "history of redemption": all of history as means through which the three divine Persons brought sinful human beings back to their Creator and filled them with the divine character.

This means even history before the fall of humanity and creation itself. For there was a planning for the world before the creation in what theologians call the "counsels of redemption" among the three divine Persons. It was their covenant to redeem a world that they knew would go awry. They agreed, as we shall see in the next chapter, that the best Person to procure redemption would be the Son of God. Because this covenantal planning by the divine Persons took place in eternity, where there is no time, we can say that God's electing love had no beginning. His love for his people always was.[4]

The creation itself was for the purpose of redemption. For the *building* of a house is only for the purpose of the *use* of that house, which use is therefore greater in value than its building process. Jesus told the sheep in Matthew 25 that "the kingdom" was prepared for them "from the foundation of the world" (v. 34). The foundation—or creation—of the world was designed for the purpose of God's kingdom, where God applies to his people the purchase of Christ's redemption.

If the history of redemption includes planning for the creation, it includes the long history of humanity before the incarnation of the Messiah. All of that history helped pave the way for the incarnation. And the history of the Church until the new heavens and new earth is the history of the Triune God's *applying* redemption to his people. The work of redemption is ongoing insofar as it administers the *fruits* of the Messiah's redemption to men and women throughout the long history of the Church. At the end of the world, the work of redemption will be finished. But after the end of the world, when the Body of the Messiah (his Church) will continue on the renewed earth, she will continue to enjoy those fruits forever. In that sense the *fruits* of the work of redemption will have no end.

The Parts of Redemption

For the sake of clarity, I will make a few other distinctions. There are parts of the *fruit* of redemption and parts of the *work* of redemption.[5] We can see parts of the fruit when we think about the Israelites being redeemed under Moses. They were redeemed first *from* slavery in Egypt. But then forty years later the next generation was brought by God *into* the promised land. In the individual Christian's life, the first part of the fruit corresponds to being saved *from* eternal punishment for sin, eternal death, and the power of the devil through the life, death, and resurrection of Messiah Jesus. This is what most Christians mean by "salvation." But "redemption" involves more, and specifically this second part of the fruit—the Spirit's enabling each soul gradually to grow in holiness (sanctification) and then to be glorified in heaven. So the whole work of redemption means far more than what is commonly called "salvation." It means all of the following: God regenerates a dead soul to give it new life, justifies it by blotting out its sins and accepting it

---

4. Edwards, *HWR*, 118–19.
5. Edwards, *HWR*, 119–20.

as righteous in his sight through the righteousness of Jesus Messiah, fills it with his Spirit and gradually conforms it to the likeness of Messiah, comforts the soul with the consolation of his Spirit, and finally after death bestows upon the soul eternal glory (Rom. 8:30).[6]

The work of redemption can also be divided into two parts—*individual* redemption, which takes place in each soul by the process we just described, and *corporate* redemption of the whole people of God, which is carried out through history. Individual redemption is done in much the same way for billions of souls in every age of history—sinners deserving hell are forgiven and given the Spirit and Word to grow into the Messiah. But corporate redemption is an infinitely complex process consisting of innumerable stages and phases, each one fitted to make its contribution to the whole. Some of this fittingness is explained in Scripture, such as the ways that Judaism prepared the way for the Messiah and his Church. Other things in history such as the radical evils of the Holocaust and Gulag are far from clear. Yet we are taught that every part of history is used in God's mysterious sovereignty for the ultimate redemption of his people (Rom. 8:28).

The Purposes of Redemption

Finally, let us look briefly at the purposes of redemption. These will show us not only God's ultimate designs but also the meaning of redemption. Each of these purposes will show one depth-dimension of this cosmic phenomenon of redemption.

First, redemption is the defeat of evil. God sent his Messiah to "reign until he has put all his enemies under his feet" (1 Cor. 15:25). Jesus the Messiah came to "destroy the works of the devil" (1 John 3:8). He was sent as "the seed of the woman" to "bruise" the head of the serpent (Gen. 3:15). After the creation and fall of humanity, Satan set himself up as god of this world instead of the God who had made it. He enticed the first man to sin, which brought guilt and death and all kinds of misery into this world. But the Father sent his Son by the Spirit to defeat all these works of evil. Because of his resurrection the Messiah's own being can heal human corruption, blot out human guilt, reverse human demerit from sin, and prevent eternal death. He triumphed over the devil and his principalities at the resurrection and his ascension, and this triumph will be displayed to all the

6. Edwards, *HWR*, 121.

cosmos at his second coming. This demolition of the prince of evil and all his works will be gloriously visible through all of eternity.

Second, redemption means the restoration and renewal of all that was ruined by the fall. Because of sin, the human soul was ruined and the image of God in man was blighted. Human nature was corrupted, and every new human being born in history came into life dead in sin. Creation itself was "subjected to futility" and given over to "bondage to decay" (Rom. 8:20–21). But in the long work of redemption the Triune God comes to billions of souls through history and brings them out of death into life. He restores their souls, renews in them the image of God, gives them new bodies at the general resurrection, and renews the face of the earth itself. The end of the work of redemption is the new heaven and new earth (Isa. 65:17), when the New Jerusalem, which was fashioned in heaven, comes down to the renewed earth for God's elect people (Rev. 21:1–5). Redemption is restoration of not only God's people but God's world.

Third, redemption means uniting all things together in the Messiah, things in both heaven and earth (Col. 1:20). This world is plagued by division and conflict. Nature is often at odds with humanity, nations go to war against nations, cultures are sometimes at each other's throats. Even nations are often internally divided. So are families. But redemption means harmony among God's people, reconciling all the divides among nations and tribes and cultures and families. By the history of redemption God's elect people are joined to the Messiah by the Spirit, and he brings them to the Father as one Body under one head. Because of the work of redemption even the powers of nature serve God's people, united in history's grand purpose, the worship of the Triune God. This work began after the fall, continues through all of human history, and will be finished at the end of the world.

Fourth, redemption is the work of perfecting the glory and beauty of God's elect people, the Church. God wants not only to forgive the Church of its sins but also to share his divine nature with his people (2 Pet. 1:4). He intends them to shine with spiritual beauty, and he intends to fill them with the pleasure and joy that spiritual beauty brings (Dan. 12:3; Zeph. 3:14–17). God wants his human creatures to share the glory and joy of the angels at their "highest pitch" under their common head, the Jewish Messiah. Measures of that beauty and joy can be seen in most saints during history, but the fullness of that joy and beauty will be seen on the renewed earth after the end of history. Toward this end of the perfection of their beauty God began to work immediately after the fall and has kept on working throughout the history of redemption. It will be perfected at the end of the world.

Fifth, redemption means the glory of God. God designed the history of redemption in order to glorify himself in all three of his Persons. In other words,
not only is God's glory a purpose of the work of redemption, but it is brought
about by every part of that work. Edwards wrote that God first decided to glorify
himself, and then selected this history and work as the best means to accomplish
his purpose of self-glorification. Both the Son and the Father were glorified by
redemption's climax at the cross: "Now is the Son of Man glorified, and God is
glorified in him. If God is glorified in him, God will also glorify him in himself"
(John 13:31–32). "Father, the hour has come; glorify your Son that the Son may
glorify you" (17:1). All of this was accomplished by the Holy Spirit, and Christ's
resurrection was by the Spirit (Rom. 8:11). So the Spirit too was glorified in those
fateful three days of redemption in the first century AD. But those three days were
(only) the means of all the work of redemption that started after the fall and will
continue until the end of this world.

Select Bibliography

Edwards, Jonathan. *A History of the Work of Redemption*. Edited by John F. Wilson. Vol. 9 in
    The Works of Jonathan Edwards. New Haven: Yale University Press, 1989.
———. *The Works of Jonathan Edwards*. 26 vols. New Haven: Yale University Press, 1957–2008.
———. *The Works of Jonathan Edwards Online*. Edited by the Jonathan Edwards Center at
    Yale University. An additional 47 vols., for a total of 73 vols. http://edwards.yale.edu/.
McClymond, Michael, and Gerald McDermott. "The Concept of a History of Redemption."
    In *The Theology of Jonathan Edwards*, 181–90. New York: Oxford University Press, 2012.

Part One

From Eternity
to the Dispersal
of the Nations

2

Redemption Planned from Eternity

God is infinitely happy and always has been. The Father has always loved the Son with infinite love, and the Son has always rejoiced in that love: "I was beside the master Craftsman, delighting him day after day, rejoicing before him at all times"; "Father, I wish those you have given to me . . . would see my glory which you gave me because you loved me before the foundation of the world" (Prov. 8:30; John 17:24). The Father has always been delighted by the Son: "This is my beloved Son, in whom I am well-pleased" (Matt. 3:17). He "loves the Son and shows him everything he is doing" (John 5:20). And the Son has always loved the Father with perfect love: he surrendered in love to the Father's plan "before the foundation of the world" (1 Pet. 1:20) and wanted "the world to know that I love the Father. I do whatever he commands me" (John 14:31).

The love between the Father and the Son is, and always has been, so perfect that it is a third divine Person, the Holy Spirit. He is love itself, the divine Person who *is* the energy of love between the Father and Son: "God is love"; "I have made known to them your name, and will continue to make it known, so that the love with which you have loved me might be in them and I in them"; "Hope does not disappoint us because the love of God has been poured out within our hearts through the Holy Spirit that has been given to us" (1 John 4:8; John 17:26; Rom. 5:5). Scripture never says that either the Father or the Son loves the Spirit; this is a principal reason why the Western tradition has thought of the Spirit as the Person who *is* the love between the Father and the Son.

This perfect love in the Trinity, which is another way of speaking about the beauty of God in his inner life, has always been perfect and boundless. The divine society that the Christian tradition has called the Trinity has always been infinitely happy and full of joy. And this was the case, if we can think of it that way, in the eons and eons before the creation. But this infinite happiness begs the question of the time of the creation.

Creation and Time

Since, as Augustine most famously put it, time as we know it started with the creation of the world, eternity before the creation is a realm that we cannot probe with our finite conception of time.[1] Yet Scripture suggests that the Trinity made plans for the creation "during" that time-that-was-not-our-time and that that planning came before the creation. Even if there was no "before and after" as we think of it, there was nevertheless planning *for* the creation and so, as far as we can imagine it while recognizing that our sense of "before" does not hold then, *before* the creation.

Mention of creation will cause some readers to wonder if we will wrestle with questions posed by modern cosmology and anthropology to biblical chronology. As I indicated in the preface, those are matters for a different sort of book. This volume seeks to understand the logic of the chronology that we have in the text, the same logic that the tradition has interpreted for upward of three thousand years. However, readers might want to flip forward to chapter 25 for discussion of modern scientific questions about the *how* of creation rather than the *when*.

But if we can say just a bit about the "when," the bigger question is the "why." If God was already infinitely happy in eternity before the creation, why would he create a world that he knew would bring excruciating pain, both physical and spiritual, to his beloved Son? Why would he create a world of creatures, both angelic and human, many or most of whom he knew would be ungrateful and defiant across millennia?

I should add that speaking about God's pain is problematic theologically. The Christian Fathers of the first seven centuries emphatically repudiated the idea that God in his essence suffers pain, arguing that the deity per se does not suffer but that the *human* (as opposed to the divine) nature of one of the Three suffered. So we can speak about God's pain but remember that it is restricted to the human nature of one of the three Persons in God.

---

1. Augustine, *Confessions* 11.13, trans. Henry Chadwick (Oxford: Oxford University Press, 1991), 230.

Then Why?

Now back to our principal question, Why did God create the world? Scripture teaches that the short answer to this question is that God created the world for himself: "All things were created by him and for him"; "From him and through him and to him are all things. To him be the glory forever!" (Col. 1:16; Rom. 11:36). That last verse by Paul at the end of Romans 11 illustrates what Scripture means by God making the world for himself—that he creates and administers the cosmos for his glory. Another example of this is in Isaiah chapter 48: doing something for himself means getting glory for himself. He told Isaiah that he was refining Israel: "For my sake I am doing it, for *my* sake. How can I let [Israel be] polluted? I will not give the glory to anyone else!" (Isa. 48:11).

The rabbis taught the same in the Mishna, which was the first major collection of Jewish commentary on Torah (the Pentateuch). They argued that the creation was for God himself, which means for his glory: "Whatever the Holy One, blessed is he, created in his world, he created it only for his glory, as it is written, *Everything that is called by my name and that I have created, I have formed it, yea, I have made it* [Isa. 43:7]" (Avot 6:11, Danby trans.).

Seven Components

That is the most simplistic answer to the question of why God created the world: for his own glory. But what does that mean? Scripture suggests that the meaning has seven different components: that God created the physical cosmos (1) and all human beings (2) but especially the saints (3) for the purpose of demonstrating his goodness and greatness and beauty. This was the purpose of his work of redemption (4) and even the virtues (5) that he put into his people. The apostles (6) made this their purpose. Finally, even God's judgments on evil and its perpetrators (7) were for the purpose of demonstrating the divine glory—in this case, his justice.

Let us look a bit more at each of these. God says that he created *this cosmos* so that it would testify in all its parts to his glory. "The heavens recount the glory of God and the sky above declares his handiwork" (Ps. 19:1). God created so that his human creatures would exclaim that his "majesty" could be seen in "all the world" (Ps. 8:1, 9). They would see that majesty radiating from the heavens with their sun, moon, and stars (8:3); in marvelous works of nature—clouds, springs in the mountains, grass and plants that feed livestock and human beings, trees, birds, mountains, oceans, and the marvelous renewal of the "face of the ground" every spring (104:3, 10, 17, 24, 30); and in the ways he uses the cosmos to "satisfy the desire of every living thing" (145:16).

But it is not only his human creatures that God moves to praise him for the wonders of the physical world. God calls on angels and inanimate creation itself to give him glory. "Praise YHWH . . . , all you [angel] armies. . . . Praise him, O sun and moon, praise him all stars that give light, praise him O heaven of heavens, and you waters that are above the heavens. . . . Praise YHWH you sea creatures and deep waters, fire and hail, snow and mist, storms that obey his word, mountains and hills, fruit trees and all cedars, wild animals and all livestock, reptiles and birds. . . . Let them all praise the name of YHWH" (Ps. 148:2–4, 7–10, 13). One gets the sense that the physical world was created by God not only because its beauty and wonder would evoke praise from angels and humans but also because in some way that we cannot yet perceive, those lifeless (to most eyes and ears) parts would give living praise to their Creator. Perhaps they already do.

God's *human* creatures were also created for his glory. They were created as his image-bearers, which means their purpose was to show God's beauty and goodness to all who could see (Gen. 1:27). Solomon and Jesus agreed that humans have a duty to "fear God" and keep his commandments (Eccles. 12:13; Luke 12:5; Matt. 19:17). In other words, humans' purpose is to live not for themselves but for God. As Paul put it, like all the rest of creation they not only came "from" God but exist "for" him (Rom. 11:36). This is why they are to "give to YHWH the glory *due* his name" (1 Chron. 16:29). Because God made them, glory to him is their due. They are to do what most fail to do, "glorify him as God and give thanks to him" (Rom. 1:21).

But if *all* human beings are created to glorify him, this is especially true of those he has called to himself and filled with his Spirit—*his saints*. Ancient Israel, where God first formed his people after the flood and Babel, is said to have been raised up by God to glorify him. David said that Israel was "the one nation on earth that God went to redeem for himself" so that they would be a people for him and so that he might make a "name" for himself (2 Sam. 7:23). Here "name" was a biblical synonym for "glory," since it was the exaltation of God's name through which were displayed his glorious perfections and by which God won praise for himself (Pss. 23:3; 79:9; 1 John 2:12; Rom. 1:5; Matt. 19:29; Isa. 43:21; 1 Chron. 16:8; Rom. 3:25–26; Eph. 2:4, 7; Job 37:6–7). God said through Isaiah that he formed Israel so that she might "declare my praise" (Isa. 43:21). The people of Israel were his sons and daughters; they are referred to as those "called by my name, whom I created for my glory" (43:6–7). One day they would all be righteous, the branch of his planting, "so that [he] might be glorified" (60:21). The servant of the Lord was anointed to bring good news to the oppressed who mourned in Zion by replacing their "spirit of fearfulness" with a "mantle of praise." But why? So that they would be "trees of righteousness, the planting of YHWH, for the sake of his glory" (61:3). Both Israel and Judah would cling to YHWH as a loincloth clings to a man, so that "they might be for me a people, a name, praise, and glory" (Jer. 13:11). This is how YHWH would be glorified in and through Israel (Isa. 44:23; 49:3).

The New Testament repeats this theme of God raising up his people for the sake of glorifying himself. Jesus said he was glorified through the apostles he had called and trained (John 17:10). Paul wrote that when Jesus returns, he will be "glorified in his saints and marveled at by those who have believed" (2 Thess. 1:10). Peter told his churches that they were a "holy nation, a people for his possession, *so that* you might proclaim the excellencies of the one who called you out of darkness into his wondrous light" (1 Pet. 2:9). He told the Church's first council at Jerusalem that God was calling out a people from the Gentiles (which was a bit surprising to all his Jewish hearers) "for his name" (Acts 15:14). These New Testament passages sound a common biblical theme, that the purpose of God raising up a people throughout the ages was primarily for his own sake, that his beauty and perfections might be displayed to them and the rest of the cosmos.

The "How" of God's Glory

This raises the question of how precisely God's perfections would be displayed through his people. The answer is what constitutes the principal theme of the Bible—*the history of redemption*. It was through this history of God's working to save his people from sin, death, and the devil that his beauty and glories are displayed. God himself says this throughout his Scripture. He redeemed the people of Israel from slavery in Egypt not primarily for their sake but to make a name for himself. As we saw above, David says God raised up Israel to make a name for himself (2 Sam. 7:23). His redemption of Israel from slavery in Egypt was for the same reason: "He saved [our fathers in Egypt] for the sake of his name, to make known his power"; God "divided the waters before them so as to make for himself an everlasting name" (Ps. 106:8; Isa. 63:12). Solomon prayed that God would maintain the cause of Israel "so that all the peoples of the earth would know that YHWH is God and no other" (1 Kings 8:59–60). When Hezekiah prayed that God would save his people from the Assyrian king Sennacherib, he seemed to sense that God's purpose was not merely to rescue his people but to win glory for himself in the eyes of the nations: "And now, O YHWH our God, save us, we pray, from his hand, so that all the kingdoms of the earth would know that you, YHWH, are the only God" (2 Kings 19:19). During the Babylonian exile, God told the prophet Ezekiel that he had scattered his people Israel among the nations because they had shed innocent blood and worshiped idols. He would eventually save them from exile and bring them back to their own land, he promised, but it would not be for their sake: "Not for your sake am I working, O house of Israel, but for my holy name, which you have polluted among the nations to which you came. I will vindicate my great name, which has been profaned among the nations. . . . The nations will come to know that I am YHWH, says the Lord YHWH, when I vindicate my holiness through you before their eyes" (Ezek. 36:22–23). It is clear that the God of Israel makes known his glories through the repeated acts of saving his people and that his own glory is the reason why he saves them even when they have been unfaithful.

In the New Testament we find the same pattern: God has worked redemption in order to demonstrate the riches of his glory. In anticipation of what would be worked through the little baby at Bethlehem, the angels announced that this would bring "glory to God in the highest [levels of heaven]" (Luke 2:14). Jesus, the primary agent of redemption, declared that God's glory was why he came to earth: "For this [reason] I came to this hour. Father, glorify your name" (John 12:27–28). As he forecast his death and resurrection on the eve of the crucifixion, Jesus predicted that the next three days would glorify the Father and himself: "Now the Son of Man is glorified, and God is glorified through him" (13:31). All that he did in his life and death were for the purpose of glorifying the Father: "He who speaks from himself seeks his own glory. But he who seeks the glory of the one who sent him, it is he who is truth and there is no unrighteousness in him" (7:18).

Paul reiterates this theme. God put Jesus forward as a propitiation of wrath for sin, for the purpose of "showing [God's] righteousness because he had let previous sins go unpunished" (Rom. 3:25). Hence redemption through Jesus manifested or glorified God's justice. God rewarded Jesus for his humble submission to death on a cross by giving him a name before which every knee will bow and every tongue confess that he is Lord. But to what end? "To the glory of God the Father" (Phil. 2:11). Paul told the Ephesian church that they were chosen in Messiah Jesus before the foundation of the world and predestined for adoption through Jesus Messiah for a purpose—"for the praise of the glory of his grace" (Eph. 1:6). Just a few verses later Paul said again that they were predestined to obtain an inheritance, and again there is a reason: "So that we might be for the praise of his glory" (1:12). In chapter 2 of his epistle to the same church, Paul adds that they were raised up to sit with Messiah in the heavenly places. Why? "So that it might be *shown* in the coming ages the surpassing riches of his grace in kindness toward us in Messiah Jesus" (2:7). Again, the purpose of God's redemption of the Ephesians was to glorify God and his grace. In chapter 3 Paul goes further, asserting that God wants to be glorified not only to human beings but to the cosmic powers. Paul was made a minister of the gospel, he writes, so that "the mystery hidden for ages might come to light [and] . . . the manifold wisdom of God be made known to the [angelic] rulers and authorities in the heavenly places" (3:9–10). God saved his human creatures through the work of his Messiah not only because of his love for the world (John 3:16) but also in order to display his wisdom to the heavenly powers. Finally, the spread of the gospel for Paul was all about glorifying God: "For all these things are for your sake, so that the grace that has multiplied because of the multiplication of thanksgiving might overflow *to the glory of God*" (2 Cor. 4:15).

When God redeems a people, he fills them with his own life. This life is displayed in the Christian *virtues*. Scripture attests that these virtues are given so that God might be glorified. In John's Gospel Jesus says that we prove that we are his disciples and thereby glorify his Father if we bear fruit (which in this Gospel refers to obedience and love; John 15:10, 12): "In this is my Father *glorified*, that you bear much fruit and so prove to be my disciples" (15:8). In the Sermon on the Mount he told his followers that God would be glorified by their good works: "Let your light shine before others so that they might see your good works and *glorify your Father who is in the heavens*" (Matt. 5:16). Paul prayed for the Philippians that God would fill them with the "fruit of righteousness that comes through Jesus Messiah [and is] for the *glory* and praise of God" (Phil. 1:11). Paul wrote to the Romans that his gift of apostleship was for the purpose of promoting "the obedience of faith among the Gentiles *for the sake of his name*" (Rom. 1:5). Again, Paul's overall purpose was not evangelism or discipleship or even obedience in his disciples. These were penultimate ends that served the ultimate end—God's glory. Peter was another apostle who suggested that the purpose of Christian virtue was the glory of God: "Maintain good behavior among the Gentiles so that . . . they might see your good works and *glorify God* on the day of [his] visitation" (1 Pet. 2:12). Jesus commends the church in Ephesus for its patience: "You have borne up patiently *for my name*" (Rev. 2:3). The implication is that the value of their endurance is that it gives glory to Jesus's name.

The apostles seem to have made God's glory the aim of their lives. Paul repeatedly prayed that God and his Son Jesus would be glorified through Paul's ministry.

After explaining to the Galatians that Jesus gave himself for our sins to deliver us from this present evil age according to the will of God our Father, he exclaimed, "To him be glory forever and ever! Amen" (Gal. 1:4–5). Paul was so grateful to God that he burst out with praise. After his prayer for the Ephesians in chapter 3 of his letter to them, he exclaimed with praise for God's glory, but this time prayed that the church would glorify God and that it would continue doing so among all generations of families: "To him is the *glory* in the Church and in Messiah Jesus for all the generations in age after age. Amen" (Eph. 3:21). In his letters to the Romans and Philippians and Timothy he prayed similarly (Rom. 11:36; 16:27; Phil. 4:20; 2 Tim. 4:18). Peter, the author of Hebrews, and Jude do the same (2 Pet. 3:18; Heb. 13:21; Jude 25). In Revelation John is like Paul: he cannot describe redemption without breaking out in praise for God: "To him who loves us and freed us from our sins by his blood, and made us a kingdom [of] priests to God his Father, to him be *glory* and power to the ages. Amen!" (Rev. 1:5–6).

Glory Manifested in God's Justice

Finally we must consider one other aspect of God's administration of his kingdom, the justice that issues from his holiness. We find here that in Scripture God's *judgments* are also said to be administered for the purpose of his glory. God hardened the hearts of the Egyptians so that they would "go in after [the Jews]" and he "would get *glory* over Pharaoh and all his army and chariots and horsemen" (Exod. 14:17). God told Ezekiel that he would defeat Israel's enemy Gog and there would be so many dead that it would bring Israel "renown on [that] day that I show my *glory*" (Ezek. 39:13). Paul tells us that God will be *glorified* on the day when he comes in wrath to judge the world (Rom. 2:5; 2 Thess. 1:9–10). God continues to endure the "vessels of wrath made for destruction"—those who reject his truth—so that he might "make known the riches of his *glory* toward vessels of mercy"—those who accept the truth of the gospel (Rom. 9:22–23). But one day he will "show his wrath and make known his power" when he pours out judgment on those who want nothing of him (9:22). Then he will be *glorified*, as he carries out his holy and just judgments.

The Second Reason for Creation

So the first and primary reason that God created the world was to demonstrate his perfections through the glories of the creation and his redemption of that creation. This is clear from the Scriptures. But that was not the only reason Scripture gives us for the creation. There was another significant one—that he might *share his goodness and beauty with his creatures.* This too was an ultimate end for the creation. In other words, God wanted it because it was good in itself. It was not a secondary end, serving some other, higher purpose. To create the world for himself—demonstrating his perfections for his own glory—was a good that brings God joy in itself. But so does imparting himself to his human creatures—in all his love and beauty and truth—bring joy to God because that too is good in itself. If creating the world for himself was first and giving himself to his creatures second, these are first and second in numerical order but not order of importance. Both are all-important because both are ends in themselves for God. Both delight him. We shall see that these two ends or purposes for creation are one and the same. But for now, let us examine the biblical evidence that God delights in giving good to his human creatures.

No Joy in Wrath

One way of seeing God's joy in giving good is to see that he exercises his wrath only reluctantly. To see his human creatures in a state of misery does not delight him in itself. God told Ezekiel that he was asking Israel, "Why do you want to die? . . . I have no pleasure in the death [of anyone]" (Ezek. 18:31–32). Later in Ezekiel God insisted this was true even for the death of those who oppose him: "I have no pleasure in the death of the wicked one, but only in [his] turning from his path" (33:11). Jeremiah proclaimed that God "has not afflicted [people] *from his heart* and does not [willingly] grieve the sons of men" (Lam. 3:33). Peter brought this vision of God's heart into the New Testament: God is not "wishing that any be lost but that all would go forward to repentance" (2 Pet. 3:9).

So the God of the Bible does not seem to enjoy exercising his wrath. Judgment is often necessary because justice demands it. He is slow to anger and delights in showing mercy. Nehemiah confessed that Israel was stiff-necked and refused to obey her Maker but reminded God in prayer that he was "a God of forgiveness and grace [and] compassion, slow to anger, and abundant in loving-kindness—and you did not forsake us!" (Neh. 9:17). The psalmist recalled the same: "YHWH is merciful and gracious, slow to anger and full of loving-kindness" (Ps. 103:8). Micah rings the changes on this theme: "Who is a God like you, pardoning guilt and passing over rebellion . . . ? He does not keep his anger forever because he *delights in* loving-kindness" (Mic. 7:18).

Delight in Lovingkindness

God's delight in showing lovingkindness is particularly manifested in his work of redemption in history. All of that work is motivated by God's *love* for his human creatures, as if what chiefly motivated him was care for those creatures as an end in itself. "God so *loved* the world that he gave his only son [for it], so that whoever trusts in him might not perish but have eternal life" (John 3:16). "By this was the *love* of God shown among us, that God sent his son, his only [one], to the world so that we might live through him. In this is *love*, not that we loved God, but that he *loved* us and sent his son as a sin offering for our sins" (1 John 4:9–10). "But God, being rich in mercy, because of the great *love* with which he *loved* us, even when we were dead in our sins, made us alive in Messiah—by his gift of grace you are saved" (Eph. 2:4–5). These passages show us the all-consuming motivation of God's heart—love for his human creatures that drove him to give his all for them, his only Son whom he loved infinitely. One gathers that this love for them was as ultimate in his reasons for creating the world as anything else. It was the love of his heart for his people and their future good.

Jesus Messiah showed the same love. Paul reported that he lived "by the faithfulness of the Son of God, who *loved* me and delivered himself up for me" (Gal. 2:20). The Messiah Jesus "*loved* the Church and gave himself for her" (Eph. 5:25). Jesus consecrated himself because of his love for his Church: "I set myself apart *for their sake*, so that they too might be set apart in truth" (John 17:19). The love that the Father and Jesus showed God's people by the Son's suffering was prophesied by Isaiah: "YHWH was willing to crush him and put him to grief [in order to make] his soul an offering for sin" (Isa. 53:10).

But even if his passion brought great grief to the Son, he endured it because of "the joy that was set before him," the joy he would share with his disciples: "I have told you these things so that my joy might be in you and your joy would be full" (Heb. 12:2; John 15:11). The fact that the Trinity planned such a painful work of redemption shows that the three divine Persons created the world as much for the joy they could share with the Church as for the glory it would give God. The Spirit of God prophesied this intent to fill the Church with joy in several places in the Old Testament. Isaiah wrote, "You have increased [your people's] joy; they rejoice before you as with joy at the harvest" (Isa. 9:3). Nehemiah declares that the righteous will have a "joy" from God that will be their "strength" (Neh. 8:10). The psalmist adds that for the righteous there may be weeping at night, "but rejoicing comes in the morning" (Ps. 30:5).

Forgiveness because of Love

The Bible speaks of God's forgiveness as something God grants because of his love for his people. David prays, "Remember not the sins of my youth or [my] acts of rebellion, [but] in your loving faithfulness remember me *for the sake of your goodness*, O YHWH" (Ps. 25:7). David seems to be asking God to draw upon his deep goodness and faithfulness to his chosen, of whom David is one. The presumption is that God's heart is full of faithful love for his people, and it is this love that moves him in his relations to his people. Nehemiah makes a similar plea. While confessing the sins of his people and acknowledging that YHWH continually showered them with love and deliverance despite a long history of "arrogance" and ingratitude, Nehemiah appealed again to God's love and mercy: "In your abundant loving feelings you have not annihilated or abandoned [Israel] *because you are a gracious and compassionate God*" (Neh. 9:31). In other words, God has love and compassion for his people. That is an objective part of God's character that moves him in all his work of redemption. If he redeems for his glory, he also redeems because he wants to shower his people with his goodness.

God's love for his people as the driving force behind his creation and redemption takes on a stunning color when we consider what Jesus says about the sabbath: "The sabbath was made *for man*, not man for the Sabbath, so the Son of Man is Lord even of the Sabbath" (Mark 2:27–28). This is remarkable, not only because Jesus here implies that because he is Lord, he is governor of all the world, including the administration of God's commandments for his people. It is also remarkable because he suggests that all of these commandments are given not for the sake of God but for the sake of his people ("man"). We have already seen that God created and redeemed for his own sake, for his glory. But in these stunning words "for man" we also see that God created and redeems because sharing his goodness with humanity is for him a good in and of itself.

Judgments for Love

Even God's judgments are for the sake of his people. YHWH tells Israel that he gave up "Egypt as *your* ransom, Cush and Seba [regions to the south of Egypt] in exchange *for you*" (Isa. 43:3–4). He "struck down the firstborn of Egypt" as a sign of his "steadfast love" (*hesed*) for Israel, which will last forever (Ps. 136:10). Hence his judgment of Egypt was for the sake of his people Israel, even if it was also for his own glory. Later in Psalm 136 we read that his judgments of "Pharaoh and his army in the Red Sea," his killing various "kings," and his striking down "Sihon, king of the Amorites" and "Og, king of Bashan" were all because of his "steadfast love" (*hesed*).

We hear a similar note in Romans, where Paul tells us that God has endured "vessels of wrath" for the sake of "vessels of mercy" for whom he has been preparing glory (Rom. 9:22–23). One day the vessels of wrath will suffer "destruction," but in the meantime God is patiently enduring their sin. Although we have previously seen that God will glorify himself one day when he makes known his wrath and power in their destruction, we also see here that God in his love has been preparing his own people from "beforehand for glory" (9:23). So the damnation of some is somehow for the purpose of blessing others with goodness. That is not to say that God created the vessels of wrath in order to damn them. We have already seen that God does not relish the death of anyone, even the wicked who spend their lives defying him. But he uses their hatred to fulfill his love for his elect.

If we have seen several astonishing revelations of God's intent and character, there are more, including the staggering peek into God's intent for the creation that we see in 1 Corinthians 3:21–22. There Paul wrote to Corinthian Christians who were divided into fan groups that jealously exalted one Christian leader over another, as if one leader would make his followers better than fans of another leader. Paul rebuked them by pointing to what they were missing—that because they were in Messiah and he rules the cosmos, all the cosmos was theirs. "All things are yours, whether Paul or Apollos or Cephas [Peter] or the cosmos or life or death or things that are or things that will be—all are yours." This is a mysterious statement that deserves far more reflection, but a part of what it means is certainly this—that Messiah is administering all these leaders and things for the sake of his Body. Therefore, nothing happens to his Body from any of these people or things that will not be for their good. Again, God creates and his Messiah rules because of their desire to share their goodness with God's people. And this has been in God's heart since "the foundation of the world" (Matt. 25:34). God has been preparing a kingdom for the Messiah and his disciples from the very beginning.

Two Purposes Become One

Let's take stock now of what we have seen in the biblical vision of God's purposes for creating the world. The Triune God created the world for himself, which means for his glory—that is, to demonstrate the beauty of his character and excellencies to the cosmos. But he also created the world because he wanted to share himself with his human creatures. He desired to bring them into his own beauty and goodness and truth. In two words, God created for both glory and love—to glorify himself and to impart his goodness to his people. Both of these goals were ultimate, which means they were both ends in themselves rather than being for the purpose of something else. Both gave God pleasure in themselves and were worth doing in the absence of any other result. The glory of God is an ultimate end in itself, and so is sharing his goodness with others.

But how do these two ultimate goals of creation relate to each other? Part of Edwards's genius was to see that the two are one. The two ends of creation are one and the same. God created both for himself and for his people, and the two are one because his people are the Body of his Son by the Spirit. The Father wants to glorify and love the Son, which includes his Body (the Church). Thus, what God does for his own glory will also benefit his people, who have been joined to himself through the Messiah his Son.

We see the conjoining of the two in Isaiah 43 and 60. In chapter 43 God declares his love for Israel in moving words: "Because you were precious in my eyes and honored and I loved you, I gave men for you and peoples in exchange for your life" (Isa. 43:4). But then he says that they are now his witnesses and chosen servant so "that you might know me and trust me and understand that I am he, before whom there was no god [ever] formed and after me there [will be] none" (43:10). He loves Israel and wants them to see his glory. The same pattern is in chapter 60. God tells Israel to "rise and shine," for he has sent his glory upon her. He will bring her sons and daughters from afar, and the wealth of the nations shall come to her, because "in my favor I have shown love for you" (60:10). He will make her "majestic forever, a joy from age to age," but for his glory: "You shall know that I am YHWH your savior and redeemer, the Mighty One of Jacob" (60:15–16). He loves Israel so that they might see his glory.

The two are one because of God's nature. He is the quintessentially giving God, who is ever giving himself in love to others. In eternity the three Persons give themselves infinitely in love one to another. This is why the Scriptures say not that God *has* love but that he *is* love. It is his inner nature to give his beauty, goodness, and truth to others, that they might be filled with him in all of his excellencies. His nature is to display his own beauty and goodness, and so it is called his glory. Because his nature gives to others, it is called love.

Edwards observed that God looks on the giving of himself as though he were not in his most glorious and complete state without that sharing. The Church is called the "fullness of Messiah" (Eph. 1:23), as if Messiah is not in his most "complete state" without her, as Adam was in a defective state without Eve ("It is not good that the man should be alone"; Gen. 2:18).[2] This is why the Church is called the "glory of Messiah" and woman the "glory of man" (1 Cor. 11:7).

So the two are together and always will be. The Church is Christ's Body, whom he "nourishes and cherishes" (Eph. 5:29), and the Church in turn glorifies him. When the Son of God is glorified for both the creation and redemption, his body is also blessed. His disciples are in him, so all glory that goes to him brings love and goodness to them. And for him to glorify the Father by sharing in the creation and effecting the redemption is to bring love and goodness and beauty to God's people, his Body.

How It Works

Let's close by looking at how this works. Edwards detected three parts in the divine fullness: knowledge, holiness, and joy. We are able to know, be holy, and have joy only to the extent that we share in *God's* knowledge, holiness, and joy. Let's look at the first, knowledge. Because only God knows God, all our knowledge of God comes by our *participation* in God's knowledge of himself, when the Son shares his knowledge of himself and the Father with us by the Spirit (Luke 10:22). Edwards likens this to the beams of the sun, which participate in the light and glory of the sun itself. We are like those beams that share in the sun, having the light of knowledge only to the extent that we share in the Son's light of knowledge.

Another part of the divine fullness is holiness. We can have virtue only if we share in divine holiness. This comes by participation in the holiness of God's Son as mediated by the Spirit (1 Cor. 1:30).

The third part of the divine fullness is God's happiness, with which we started this chapter. True happiness comes only by sharing in Jesus's joy, the joy in the Spirit that he shares with the Father (John 15:11).

These are the three fundamental ways in which God gives himself in love to people—by sharing with them ever-increasing knowledge of himself, his own holiness, and his own joy. This is also the way God is most glorified in the creation—by his human creatures knowing, loving, and rejoicing in him. This knowledge, love, and joy come only by participation in the inner life of the Trinity. And it is also the only real way for human beings to be happy.

---

2. Jonathan Edwards, *End of Creation*, in *Ethical Writings*, ed. Paul Ramsey, vol. 8 of *The Works of Jonathan Edwards* (New Haven: Yale University Press, 1989), 439.

These are the reasons why God created the world—to glorify himself and to make his people happy. They are one and the same thing.

Select Bibliography

Edwards, Jonathan. *A History of the Work of Redemption*. Edited by John F. Wilson. Vol. 9 in *The Works of Jonathan Edwards*. New Haven: Yale University Press, 1989.

McClymond, Michael, and Gerald McDermott. "The End of God in Creation." In *The Theology of Jonathan Edwards*, 207–23. New York: Oxford University Press, 2012.

3

Redemption after Eden

Did God wait for thousands of years before he started saving sinners? Was it not until the incarnation in the first century, so that redemption was unavailable until the Word was then made flesh (John 1:14)?

We know from Hebrews that God was saving sinners from the very beginning, since in its eleventh chapter we are told that Abel was "commended as righteous" (v. 4). And we know that God chose Abraham and his progeny to be his chosen people and that many of these Jews loved the God of Israel and found his salvation for their lives and eternity (Pss. 139:17; 23:6).

But how did redemption work back then? And what about those who lived before Abraham? How could they have been redeemed when there was no Israel from which would come salvation (John 4:22)?

Prophecy and Mediation

These were times of light from God's revelation, but it was not the bright light that we find in the times of Jesus and his Jewish apostles. Edwards compares it to the light on a clear night from the moon and the stars—a dim light but light nonetheless.[1] Just as the light of the moon is a reflection of the light of the sun, redemption and revelation after Eden and before the cross were reflections of the light that was shining *back* from the future of what God would eventually do in Israel and Jesus.

---

1. Edwards, *HWR*, 129.

How could that be? One answer is prophecy. The Old Testament is full of predictions of the coming Messiah and the redemption he would bring. One of these predictions, we shall see, was made immediately after the fall in the garden. Another answer is typology. This is the history of living symbols that God put into history from the very beginning to point forward to the redemption that would come through the Messiah and his kingdom. The best-known type is the exodus of the Jews from slavery in Egypt, which pointed to the deliverance that Messiah Jesus would bring from slavery to sin, death, and the devil.

But there is still another remarkable answer to the question, one that was put by the early fathers of the Church and picked up by Edwards and others: that the Son of God was the mediator between the holy Father and sinful human beings from just after the fall until the full incarnation of the Son thousands of years later. This was because the Father is all-holy and cannot abide in the direct presence of sin or sinners. So he appointed a mediator after the fall, his only Son, to represent him before sinners. This is the reason, Edwards wrote, that wrath did not break out to destroy Adam and Eve after they defied God's commands. This is why they did not immediately suffer the full penalty of the curse that they had brought on themselves.

There are other lines of evidence that run throughout the Bible. Consider the repeated theme that God the Father is invisible and yet he is said to have been seen, even in the Old Testament. Jesus declared that "no one has seen God *at any time*" (John 1:18), yet Jacob said he saw God "face to face" when wrestling with the angel (Gen. 32:30), and Moses talked to God "face to face as a man speaks with his friend" (Exod. 33:11). The seventy elders at Sinai "saw the God of Israel" (24:10). Whom were they seeing if God the Father has *never* been seen?

The Angel of the Lord

Consider also that the "angel of the Lord" in the Old Testament is often said to be God himself. After the angel of the Lord told Hagar that her offspring would be so many that they could not be numbered, she told him, "You are a God of seeing" (Gen. 16:10, 13). After wrestling with the angel of the Lord, Jacob said he had seen "God" (32:30). The angel of the Lord appeared to Moses in the burning bush and then told him, "I am the God of your father, the God of Abraham, Isaac and Jacob" (Exod. 3:6). After the angel of the Lord appeared to Manoah, he told his wife, "We shall surely die, because we have seen God" (Judg. 13:22).

The pattern seems to be that this *messenger* from God—which the Hebrew word usually translated "angel" can also mean—is somehow God himself. But if not the Father, who is invisible and cannot be seen, then who? We are given another clue in the stories of Israel in the wilderness. God—the Father, presumably—told the people of Israel, "I am sending before you an angel/messenger to guard you on the way and to bring you to the place that I have prepared. Pay careful attention to him and obey his voice; do not rebel against him, for he will not pardon your transgression, for my name is in him. But if you carefully obey his voice and do all that I say, then I will be an enemy to your enemies and an adversary to your adversaries" (Exod. 23:20–22).

God sent this angel/messenger to guard and guide the children of Israel through the wilderness. They were to obey him, and he had the authority to pardon their sins. Jews knew that they were to obey God alone and that only God could pardon their sins. So this angel/messenger, as in the other stories we have just seen, was somehow separate from God and yet the same as God. He was the angel who stood at the Red Sea between Israel and Pharaoh's army (Exod. 14:19–20), the "angel of his presence" that saved them in "all the days of old" (Isa. 63:9). This was the same angel to whom the author of Ecclesiastes said we cannot say our unperformed vow was a mistake, for "God" would be angry at our voice (Eccles. 5:4, 6). Again, the angel of the Lord is distinct from the high God yet somehow also God.

This odd distinction within God is given more shape by Scripture's use of the "name" of God. It speaks of YHWH reigning above the heavens (Ps. 99:2; 113:4) but putting his name on earth, especially in the temple (2 Sam. 7:13; 1 Kings 3:2; 5:3–5; 8:16–20, 29, 43, 48; 9:3, 7; 2 Kings 21:4, 7; 1 Chron. 22:7–10; 2 Chron. 33:7). God's people were told to fear his name (Mic. 6:9; Mal. 4:2), desire and love his name (Isa. 26:8; Ps. 5:11), and seek and wait for his name (Pss. 83:16; 52:9). All of these expressions suggest that the name of YHWH was a person, somehow within God and yet distinct from YHWH himself. They were to pray for the sake of the name (25:11) and ask for guidance for the sake of the name (31:3). They asked God for pardon "for your name's sake" (79:9), as if it were only because of the name of God that YHWH could forgive their sins. Proverbs 18:10 suggests something very similar, that God's people could find protection by fleeing to God's name: "The name of YHWH is a strong tower; the righteous man runs into it and is safe." We also know that in the ancient world the name of a person expresses his identity and character. So this name that protects a man or woman of God is a part of God that expresses his inmost identity and character.

In his "Controversies Notebook" section on justification, Edwards wrote that God distinguished between YHWH and his name to prevent Old Testament believers from thinking that there were two gods within YHWH but also to show that YHWH and his name shared the same nature and substance—a unity with difference that the later Church would agree is fundamental to the relationship between the Father and the Son.[2]

So God sent his angel, who is also called his name and glory (Isa. 3:8; 59:19; Ezek. 8:4; 9:3; 10:18–19; 11:22; 43:2), to deal with sinners directly as his mediator. This is why the "angel of the LORD" in so many Old Testament stories is also called "God" himself. That it was the Second Person of the Trinity, another person within God, is suggested by the distinction between God and these messengers. God sent the angel or messenger, so the God who sent and the angel who was also God are distinct persons. The "commander of the army of YHWH" who appeared to Joshua was sent from YHWH but somehow was distinct from him (Josh. 5:13–15). The author of Proverbs distinguishes YHWH, who "established all the ends of the earth," from "his son" (30:4). The angel of the Lord who appeared as a glorious man to Abraham, Isaac, Jacob, Manoah, Joshua, Moses, and the seventy elders—and as the glory of God to Isaiah (John 12:41)—was divine and therefore in God but mysteriously distinct from the first in the Godhead.

First-century Jews understood that there would be a mediator between them and God. Philo (ca. 20 BCE–50 CE), the great Jewish philosopher who was a contemporary of Paul the apostle, wrote of the *Logos* or Word who stood as a middle person between God and his creatures. Many referred to this middle person as the "son of God" who was often mentioned in the Old Testament. Caiaphas the high priest knew that the Messiah would be this Son of God, for he demanded of Jesus: "Tell us if you are the Messiah, the Son of God" (Matt. 26:63). The Sanhedrin understood that Daniel's "one like a son of man" who was with the Ancient of Days and given everlasting dominion (Dan. 7:13–14) was not YHWH himself but a divine figure. When Jesus told them that they would see the "Son of Man seated at the right hand of the power of God"—clearly citing Daniel's prophecy—these chief priests and scribes connected the dots: "Are you then the Son of God?" (Luke 22:69–70).

There was also compelling evidence in the Old Testament that the Israelites' sacrifices for sin were never enough by themselves to make atonement, but that the Messiah would somehow make an end of their liability for sin. The rabbis taught

2. Edwards, "Controversies Notebook," in *Writings on the Trinity, Grace, and Faith*, ed. Sang Hyun Lee, vol. 21 of *The Works of Jonathan Edwards* (New Haven: Yale University Press, 2003), 377.

that the Messiah would be a priest "after the order of Melchizedek" (Ps. 110:4), and Jews knew that priests helped them deal with their sins. They also knew that the psalms and prophets often said that God did not delight in sacrifices and burnt offerings that were not accompanied by a broken spirit (Pss. 50:5, 14–15; 40:6; 51:17; Isa. 1:11; Hosea 6:6; Mic. 6:6–8; Jer. 7:22–23; Isa. 66:1–3). They read that God would send his servant the Branch, who would remove iniquity in a single day (Zech. 3:8–9). He would be a humble king who would set prisoners free by the blood of the covenant (9:9–11), a servant of the Lord who was a man of sorrows thought by humans to be smitten by God but in reality wounded for their own transgressions (Isa. 53:4–5). His soul was to make an offering for their sins (53:10). He would bear the sin of many (53:12).

Jesus thought that the Old Testament Scriptures taught this so clearly that he berated his disciples for not understanding these things (Luke 24:25–26; Matt. 16:11).

First Glimmers of Hope

Let's take stock of what we have seen so far. Even if revelation of redemption was not as clear in the Old Testament as the New, there was plenty there. Readers found profuse and interlocking themes of a mediator between YHWH and the people of God who was referred to as the angel of the Lord, the name of the Lord, the messenger of the covenant, and even the glory of the Lord. This mediator appeared to have been a separate person within God who was also God. It was because of him that there would be pardon for sins, even while Old Testament sacrifices brought temporary pardon if accompanied by repentance. There were prophecies and types of the coming redemption by that mediator, and he made real appearances to God's people after Eden. Through him they learned about redemption through sacrifice, as we shall see, and through him the first souls were saved.

But first, there was an immediate declaration of coming redemption within minutes of God's condemnations after the fall. At that point all light had been extinguished. It was darker than before the beginning of the world, when "darkness was on the face of the deep" (Gen. 1:2). God had just asked, "What is this that you have done?" The first couple must have been filled with shame and terror. What hope or comfort could be given to a couple who had been given everything and then turned against the One who had given it all?

Yet God's first words of condemnation—to the serpent!—were the first glimmers of light and hope. He told the tempter that Eve's "seed will crush your head"

(Gen. 3:15). Eve's offspring would one day destroy the devil. This was, as Edwards put it, like the early dawn in the east that signaled the approach of morning.[3] It was the promise of a Messiah, the seed of the woman, who would defeat the enemy of God's people.

These were the words not of God in general but of that person in God called the mediator. He had sprung into action immediately after the fall, taking up his role as the image of God before a sinful people. In time he would take on the roles of prophet, priest, and king. But at this point he started serving as prophet, foretelling the redemption that he would win in the future.

This gave hope and comfort to the devastated couple who had slunk around in the darkness trying to cover their shame with fig leaves. The mediator was giving hope and comfort to Adam and Eve in their despair. It was as if he was saying, in the idiom of a writer thousands of years later, "Don't give up. Aslan is coming!"

If this was a first word of hope to the first sinners, it was also a first type of redemption after Eden. God showed the way that redemption would be provided by teaching about, and then putting into practice, sacrifice. We are shown this by Abel's sacrifice soon after the fall. Genesis tells us that God was pleased with Abel's sacrifice of the firstborn of his flock (Gen. 4:4), and the Letter to the Hebrews adds that God testified that Abel was "righteous" by accepting his gift (Heb. 11:4). This remarkable event demonstrates two things. First, that sacrifice was accepted by God as an expression of faith ("By faith Abel offered to God a better sacrifice than Cain"; Heb. 11:4). And second, that sacrifice was already an established institution.

Taught by God

But how could this have originated? As Edwards observed, it did not come from the light of nature. Reason alone does not tell us that animals must be slain in order to please God. It is also doubtful that the first humans could have conceived of it as a way to commend themselves to God. Scripture is adamant that God detests religion "taught by men" that is not commanded by him (Isa. 29:13; Matt. 15:7–9). So he would not have been pleased by a religious rite concocted by human beings. Therefore, it must have been taught by God himself to his first human creatures soon after the fall.

3. Edwards, *HWR*, 132–33.

But when would God have taught this? We are told in Genesis 3 that when Adam and Eve were hiding their nakedness after their sin, God made for them "garments of skin and clothed them" (Gen. 3:21). The Hebrew word for "skin" refers to the hides of animals that are slain to get their skins. They were not slain for their meat, because men and women were not eating animal meat until after the flood (Gen. 3:18; 9:2–3).

Why would God use animal skins? He could have clothed Adam and Eve with other kinds of plant products. Perhaps, as many theologians ever since have observed, God was showing them that sin causes death, and justice demands that the life taken by sin must be replaced by another life (Rom. 3:25–26). As Satan later put it in the book of Job, "Life for life, skin for skin" (Job 2:4). A living being's life would substitute for the sinner's life. It was God, then, who taught them to make a sacrifice for sin. This institution of animal sacrifice for sin would prepare later generations for the ultimate sacrifice of God's Son for the sins of all. These animal skins that covered the first couple's nakedness were also a type of the righteousness of the Messiah that would cover the naked unrighteousness of all of us sinners (Rom. 5:17; 2 Cor. 5:21).

Notice what was happening here. If we are right to surmise—with many of the fathers of the Church—that God taught the first couple to make a sacrifice for sin, God was ordaining sacrifice to himself! But why would God need to do that? God does not need anything. Yet he showed on the cross of Jesus at Calvary that one Person of the Trinity was making a sacrifice to another Person of the Trinity for the sake of human sinners. The Son was making a sacrifice of himself to the Father. His sacrifice was a "propitiation" that saves sinners from the Father's "wrath to come" (Rom. 3:25; 1 Thess. 1:10; 5:9). God is *holy* love that in justice demands punishment of sin because sin destroys the creation he loves. So he sent the Son to make a propitiatory sacrifice that was just punishment for our sins. One divine Person made sacrifice to another Person for the sake of the justice that the Two taught and that One embodied. God was willing to make his own sacrifice for our sins is typified (shown in symbolic form) in this first sacrifice after the fall.

The First Redeemed Souls

So God was saving souls through Jesus's redemption right after the fall. Adam and Eve were his firstfruits. First he gave them a promise of redemption (Gen. 3:15), and then he clothed them with what he no doubt told them were types of the Messiah's righteousness to come. Both of these redemptive actions brought comfort to our first parents in their despair.

We have evidence that they believed these promises. After Cain's birth, Eve said, "I have gotten a man by YHWH" (Gen. 4:1). She knew that YHWH was her God and helper. But her faith probably started long before. When she and Adam were ashamed with guilt after their fall, they realized they were naked and sewed fig leaves together to cover their nakedness. Like us, they thought they could do something by themselves (establishing their own righteousness, as Paul put it in Rom. 10:3) to cover their sin.

But then they were further terrified when they heard the voice of God as he was walking in the garden. They realized that the fig leaves would not cover their sin, so they tried to hide. They stood trembling after God called them to account: "Where are you? . . . Have you eaten of the tree that I told you not to eat from?" (Gen. 3:9, 11).

It must have been the Son of God walking in the garden and talking to them, since God the Father is spirit (John 4:24) and does not have a body.[4] It was he who gave them the promise of redemption when they heard him telling the serpent that Eve's seed would crush the head of the serpent. Then when he comforted them further by using animal skins to clothe them, he surely explained to them what he was doing. For the Son is also the Word of God. By clothing them with these skins, the Son of God showed them that God the Father accepted their sacrifice for sin and that these skins that covered them were forerunners of the Messiah's righteousness, which would cover the sins of all their progeny.

These were the ways that the Son of God as Mediator rescued the first two captives of the devil. Adam and Eve believed these promises and started walking toward final redemption. The Mediator not only saved them but also harassed the devil immediately after his triumph. This was the first fulfillment of the promise that the seed of the woman would crush the head of the serpent.

The First Soul in Heaven

Another fruit of Jesus's redemption, retroactively as it were, was the glorification of Abel. This was the entrance into heaven by Abel, the first human being to do so. He was murdered by Cain but "commended as righteous" by God (Heb. 11:4).

---

4. This was a preincarnation incarnation of the Son of God. Since the incarnation in the first century AD was new and radically different, these appearances of the Son as Mediator must be understood as types of the great antitype when the Word became flesh (John 1:14).

Abel was the first human soul conducted by angels as "ministering spirits" (1:14) to glory. This was a reward greater than being restored to earthly paradise. For in heaven there was no sorrow or sighing and no more possibility of sinning. The angels in heaven saw in Abel the effect of the Messiah's future redemption—great honor and joy given to a human creature who had been plunged by the fall into the pit of sin and misery. Here was redemption after Eden.

Select Bibliography

Edwards, Jonathan. *A History of the Work of Redemption*. Edited by John F. Wilson. Vol. 9 in *The Works of Jonathan Edwards*. New Haven: Yale University Press, 1989.

———. "Question: In What Sense Did the Saints under the Old Testament Believe in Christ to Justification?" In *Writings on the Trinity, Grace, and Faith*, edited by Sang Hyun Lee, vol. 21 of *The Works of Jonathan Edwards*, 372–408. New Haven: Yale University Press, 2003.

McClymond, Michael, and Gerald McDermott. "The Person and Work of Jesus Christ." In *The Theology of Jonathan Edwards*, 244–61. New York: Oxford University Press, 2012.

4

The Spirit and Messiah
from Enosh and Enoch
to Noah and the Nations

The next step in the history of redemption after the fall was a fresh outpouring of the Spirit of God. It came in the life of Enosh, Seth's first son. Seth was the third son born to Adam and Eve, their first after Cain had murdered Abel. This was about 235 years after the creation, since Adam was 130 at the birth of Seth and Enosh was born when Seth was 105 years old (Gen. 5:3, 6).

Communal and Liturgical Worship

Moses (or a team among his disciples who were final editors of his text) tells us that "it was then that humans began to call on the name of YHWH" (Gen. 4:26b). Throughout the Old Testament, people "call on the name of YHWH" when they make a sacrifice to him and gather with others for liturgical worship. After God called Abraham and promised he would be given sons and a land, Abraham built an altar at Bethel and "called upon the name of YHWH" (12:8b). Abraham and Lot traveled to the same altar a bit later and "called upon the name of YHWH" (13:4). After sacrificing animals in order to cut a covenant with Abimelech in Beersheba, Abraham "called on the name of YHWH" (21:33).[1] When

---

1. For the image of "cutting a covenant," see "More Details about Redemption" in chap. 5.

God appeared to Isaac and renewed his covenant promises to him, Isaac built an altar and "called upon the name of YHWH" (26:25). Elijah prepared a sacrifice before the prophets of Baal, telling them he would "call upon the name of YHWH" to answer by fire and show that he is the true God (1 Kings 18:24). When David brought the ark up to his city, he told the crowd to "give thanks to YHWH, call upon his name" (1 Chron. 16:8). The psalmists repeated the cry in contexts of sacrifice and liturgical praise: "I will lift up the cup of salvation and call on the name of YHWH" (Ps. 116:13; see also Ps. 105:1; 116:4). Zephaniah prophesied that on the day of the Lord, God will lead people to bring him his offering and "call on the name of YHWH" (Zeph. 3:9–10).

So with Enosh began communal and liturgical worship, calling on YHWH for redemption. People had prayed for two hundred years, but it seems that with Enosh came the first communal and liturgical prayer. Perhaps it was accompanied by sacrifice. Since it was different from the spontaneous prayer of the two hundred years before, it must have been the result of a special outpouring of the Spirit of God. We will see that whenever there is a remarkable effusion of God's Spirit, there is always a marked jump in prayer. After the revival of Pentecost, the early Church gathered daily for "the prayers" (Acts 2:42). When the Spirit opened Paul's eyes to see that Jesus was the Messiah, he spent the next three days in prayer (9:9, 11).

The Spirit and Revivals

The work of the Spirit in Enosh's time was the first of what we see throughout the history of redemption—revivals occasioned by fresh outpourings of the Holy Spirit. That is not to say that the Holy Spirit is active only in revival. No, the Holy Spirit is at work whenever there is seeking God on a daily basis and particularly in liturgy and sacraments when participants come in faith. But beyond these ordinary works of the Spirit are extraordinary times of outpouring that initiate new phases in the history of redemption. There was redemption before this, but this was the first rainstorm of the Spirit to produce a harvest of souls. Their *gathering* for worship, the first in biblical history, is evidence that something new was happening in the history of redemption.

Enoch was probably a fruit of this harvest, and certainly its most glorious. He has stood out in the history of redemption for three reasons. First, his holiness was greater than had ever been to that time. Moses says he "walked with God for three hundred years after he fathered Methuselah" (Gen. 5:22), and the writer to the

Hebrews notes that he "was commended [by God] as having pleased God" (Heb. 11:5). This height of holiness showed believers then and ever after that redemption was possible in this life and to a degree never thought possible before—to walk with God in intimacy for hundreds of years.

Redemption of Bodies

Second, Enoch showed believers that God would redeem not only their souls but also their bodies. Moses wrote that "Enoch walked with God, and he was not, for God took him" (Gen. 5:24). Hebrews adds, "By faith Enoch was taken up so that he should not see death; he was not found because God had taken him" (Heb. 11:5). God had already shown Adam and Eve that he would crush the head of the serpent and save their souls, and he had already glorified Abel. Now he was showing a new generation that their *bodies* would be redeemed. If Enoch walked with God and then was taken up in body to heaven, the future was far more glorious than they had imagined. God also showed this redemption of the body centuries later when he took Elijah up without death (2 Kings 2) and then again after the Messiah's resurrection when saints from Old Testament days walked around in their bodies on the streets of Jerusalem (Matt. 27:53). But this was the *first* clear sign from God of bodily redemption that awaited all believers.

Third, Enoch was a special emissary from God announcing the future judgments of the Messiah against not only wicked human beings but also wicked angels. The book of Jude quotes the apocryphal 1 Enoch to tell readers (who apparently knew of 1 Enoch and considered it authoritative) that Enoch prophesied that God would judge the false teachers of Jude's day, who "pervert the grace of our God into sensuality" (Jude 4). But Jude also connects Enoch to the mysterious passage in Genesis 6 about the "sons of God" who "entered the daughters of man, [who] bore their children" (Gen. 6:4). Both first-century Jews and the Christian fathers in the first three centuries of the Church believed that this passage was about fallen angels who took on bodies in order to have sexual relations with women on earth. Jude put it this way: The "angels did not keep their own proper position but departed their own dwelling [above] . . . just as Sodom and Gomorrah . . . committed sexual sin and pursued strange flesh" (Jude 6–7). So Jude seems to have agreed with early Jewish and patristic interpretation that the "sons of God" in Genesis 6 were fallen angels who ignored God's instructions to stay within their boundaries and came down to earth to have intercourse with women. Jude says these lustful angels are being kept in "eternal chains" until the final judgment (Jude 6) and that Enoch announced not only their future judgment but also the coming judgments of the "ungodly." Both the fathers and Edwards thought that the coming judgments included Noah's flood. First Enoch proclaimed that the wickedness on earth that precipitated the flood was instigated by the children produced by these wicked "sons of God" (1 En. 10–15).

Sons of God and the Nephilim

This reading of the "sons of God" in Genesis 6 as fallen angels has not been widely shared in the modern era until recently. Many have thought it refers instead to the righteous sons of Seth or to kings. Even Edwards thought they were the "posterity of Seth." But there is no link to Seth's lineage either in Genesis 6 or anywhere else in Scripture. The real contrast, as Michael Heiser has demonstrated, is between two classes of beings, one human and the other semi-divine. With the rare exceptions where Israelite kings were called "sons of God" in Scripture, the majority of uses of "sons of God" are to divine beings rather than human kings (Job 1:6; 2:1; 38:7; Pss. 29:1; 82:1, 6; 89:6). For centuries a variation of the Hebrew text at places like Deuteronomy 32:8 read "sons of Israel," but the Dead Sea Scrolls have confirmed that the original Hebrew text was *bene elohim* ("sons of God").

So according to both Jude and 2 Peter (2:4–10), fallen angels sinned sexually against women on earth, and this provoked the judgment of the flood. Both 1 Enoch and Jude say that Enoch was sent to proclaim God's judgment against the angels and the people who were influenced by them.

But there is also the intriguing mention of giants and Nephilim. The word "Nephilim" probably comes from the Aramaic *naphilya*, which means "giant." The ten spies who brought back a bad report about Canaan said, "All the people whom we saw there were *of great stature*. And we saw there the Nephilim (the sons of Anak, who come from the Nephilim), and *we were* in our own sight *like grasshoppers*" (Num. 13:32–33). The prophet Amos testified that some of the Amorites (the biblical term for Canaanites who lived in the hill country) were unusually tall (Amos 2:9). Moses wrote that King Og was "left of the remnant of the Rephaim" (associated in the Bible with Nephilim) and that the Rephaim were as "tall as the Anakim" (Deut. 3:11; 2:21). Og, who fought Israel but was defeated, was tall enough for an iron bed that was thirteen feet long and six feet wide (3:11). First Enoch, whose authority we have seen was recognized by several

New Testament authors, states that the product of the unions between fallen angels and beautiful women was a race of giants. Joshua says that after his conquests "none of the Anakim [said by Num. 13:32 to be of the Nephilim] were left in the land" except in Gaza, Ashdod, and Gath—the home of Goliath, who was at least six feet six inches tall in an era when the average height of an Israelite man was five feet (Josh. 11:21–22; 1 Sam. 17:4).

These Anakim/Nephilim/Rephaim were frightening to the Israelites. Not only did they tower over them in height, but they were thought to be ferocious in battle and inspired by demons. The Genesis 6 passage calls them "mighty men," and Ezekiel says *nophilim* (which means "fallen" but according to scholars suggested to ancient readers the soundalike "Nephilim"), "mighty men," inspired "terror . . . in the land of the living" (Ezek. 32:27). Moses calls them "demons" (Deut. 32:17), which is close to what Enoch called the giants in the prophecy that Jude and 2 Peter cited—"evil spirits" (15).

In any event, the Nephilim worked against the purposes of the God of Israel. It is why Og tried to prevent Israel from entering the land, and it explains why Joshua "cut off the Anakim from the hill country of Hebron and Debir and Anab, and from the hill country of Judah, and from all the hill country of Israel" (Josh. 11:21a). Scholars have long concluded that Joshua did not devote all of the Canaanites to *herem* or destruction. But the text makes clear that he did devote the Anakim, sons of the Nephilim, to destruction: "Joshua devoted [the Anakim] to destruction with their cities" (Josh. 11:21b).

As we will see, a major plotline in the Old Testament story of redemption is that there is ongoing war between those descended from the Nephilim and those descended from Abraham, who fight for the God of Israel. It turns out that Nimrod, whose name is a variant of the Hebrew word for "rebellion," is at the headwaters of both Assyria and Babylon, Israel's two great ancient enemies. Moses tells his readers that Nimrod, who was a *gibbor*, or mighty man, just like the Nephilim of Genesis 6, started his kingdom with "Babel . . . in the land of Shinar" and from there went on to "build Nineveh," capital of the later Assyrian Empire (Gen. 10:9–11). In these suggestive ways, Moses signals to readers that the offspring of the fallen angels of Genesis 6 produced a progeny of larger-than-life warriors against YHWH's emerging kingdom. Thus, much of the story of redemption will be about how YHWH and his Messiah rescue their people from Babel and Assyria. But YHWH struck early for redemption by sending judgment against the first wave of corruption inspired by the Nephilim. This first massive judgment was the flood of Noah's day.

Noah and the Flood

Relatively speaking—compared to the millennia that followed—YHWH struck early by sending the flood. But it was actually after a few centuries and something of a population explosion. Adam and Eve's oldest child, Cain, was probably born soon after the fall. By the time Seth was born more than one hundred years later, Cain had plenty of time to have produced many children and grandchildren. Adam and Eve themselves "had other sons and daughters" in the "800 years after he fathered Seth," which means that by the time Adam died at the age of 930, his multiplied descendants could have been in the hundreds or thousands (Gen. 5:4). By all indications our first parents, newly redeemed, wanted to obey God's commandment to "be fruitful and multiply" (1:28). Each of their descendants probably produced their own multitudes after several hundred years. It is no wonder that Genesis 4:14 implies large numbers of people soon to appear on the earth: "Anyone who finds me will slay me." This is why YHWH set a mark on Cain—"lest anyone who found him might attack him" (4:15).

But while the population of the new human race seems to have mushroomed quickly, the number of those wanting to be righteous like Enosh and Enoch appears to have been tiny. Immediately after Moses tells us of the fallen angels breaking their bounds to pursue beautiful women, and of the giants they produced who wanted to make a name for themselves (Gen. 6:4; more on that in a bit), we are told that "YHWH saw that the wickedness of man on the earth was great, and that every intent of the thoughts of his heart was totally evil all the time" (6:5). Wickedness was all-pervasive. It broke through every would-be restraint. Violence was endemic: "The earth was filled with violence" (6:11). Evil spirits produced by the unholy liaisons between fallen angels and women had poisoned their descendants with hatred for God and one another.

Yet at this time when the Church was near its vanishing point, God showed that he is a God of great surprises. When Satan was licking his chops at the prospect of finally eliminating YHWH followers, the flood not only saved the Church but promoted the work of redemption. It fooled the devil by restoring the Church to a new concentrated purity in a little family. Here the seed of the future Lord Redeemer was preserved. Even if Satan had lopped off the branches and cut down the trunk of what had been a tree of YHWH worshipers after the Enosh revival, the root had been protected. God kept it alive in the family of Noah. Retroactively, the blood of the Messiah was effective long before it was actually shed, for he was "the lamb slaughtered from the foundation of the world" (Rev. 13:8).

Yet just before the flood, things looked hopeless for the Church. Its enemies were in a rage, set to destroy it with violence and hatred. It was clear that the Messiah had been right when he said in the garden to the serpent that he would put enmity between him and the woman's seed. God's Spirit had struggled in human consciences for 120 years (Gen. 6:3), but to no avail. Noah's preaching was utterly disregarded. God's people were reduced to one family. Their backs were up against a wall, just as the Jews would be at the Red Sea as Pharaoh's army was charging toward them (Exod. 14), and just as Jerusalem would feel hopeless as Sennacherib's giant army was surrounding the city (2 Kings 18).

But finally the flood came, just as God later opened up the Red Sea for his people and drowned the Egyptian soldiers, and just as God's angel later struck down 185,000 of Sennacherib's army in one night. The flood destroyed all the enemies of God's little flock. It was a type (God-planted symbol) of the redemption that the Messiah would bring later. Just as redemption by the Messiah was sealed later by the waters of baptism (1 Pet. 3:20–21), so too this redemption of God's tiny Church was effected by water. "Water . . . washed away the filth of the world" just as the blood of the Messiah washes away the worst enemies of God's people, their sins. There was enough water to cover mountain tops (Gen. 7:20), just as the Messiah's blood was sufficient to bury mountains of sin. The ark was "a refuge and hiding-place" from the judgment, just as the Messiah and his Church are the sinner's places of refuge from the wrath of God.[2]

The Noahic Covenant

God made a covenant with Noah and all his progeny after Noah's sacrifice (Gen. 8:20–9:17). Noah built an altar on which he sacrificed every clean animal and bird. When God smelled its "pleasing aroma," he made promises and imparted blessings. This was another type, in this case a type of the Messiah's covenant of grace. Just as YHWH cut this covenant with Noah and his sons and their descendants on the basis of the sweet aroma of this sacrifice, God established his covenant of grace after the Messiah's sacrifice on the cross, which exuded its own "fragrant aroma" (Eph. 5:2).

The promises and blessings of this covenant consisted of three things made new. First, God made a new promise never to destroy the whole earth again. This is extraordinary because the world since then has seen far more wickedness and

2. Edwards, *HWR*, 151–52.

violence despite having received greater light of revelation from God. Yet God has not wiped it out. This testifies to God's extraordinary patience: he is "not wanting anyone to perish but for all to reach repentance" (2 Pet. 3:9).

Second, God made a "new grant of the earth" to Noah's family and descendants.[3] They were to "fill the earth," just as God had told Adam and Eve. But whereas at that earlier time God's only explicit gift was of "every plant yielding seed" (Gen. 1:29), now God was giving to the new Adam (Noah) and his progeny "everything" (9:3).

Third, God gave this new humanity a new dominion over other creatures. Adam and Eve were given dominion over fish and birds and living things, but now God said he would give all creatures *fear* of human beings. And while our first parents were restricted to a vegetarian diet, now the new parents could eat the meat of animals. In fact, into the hands of Noah and his descendants all the creatures were delivered (Gen. 9:2).

Every covenant contains requirements for both parties. When God promises, he binds himself to keep the promises. He also binds his human creatures to keep the terms he sets for them. In his covenant with Noah and his sons and "the people of the whole earth" (Gen. 9:19), we see some of the terms. Noah and the future humanity were to be fruitful and multiply and fill the earth, not eat blood, and see that "whoever sheds the blood of man, by man shall his blood be shed" (9:1, 4, 6).

The Noahic Commandments

The rabbis, both before and after the New Testament era, saw these and other terms as having been set by God for all human beings to live by. They called these terms the Laws of Noah. There were seven, all taught in the book of Genesis and all of them given by God to Noah for all human beings (not just Jews): (1) not to worship idols; (2) not to curse God; (3) not to commit murder; (4) not to commit adultery, bestiality, or other kinds of sexual immorality; (5) not to steal; (6) not to eat flesh torn from a living animal; and (7) to establish courts of justice.

In this Jewish tradition of Noahic commandments aimed especially at Gentiles, those who kept the seven laws were called "righteous Gentiles" and were believed to have a "share in the world to come," the Jewish version of what Christians call "the new heavens and new earth."

How does this Jewish reflection on the Noah story help us understand the history of redemption? From Augustine and Aquinas to the present, Christians

---

3. Edwards, *HWR*, 152.

have taken these seven laws as not only taught by Scripture but also apparent to all human beings by the use of reason. Christians call these truths "natural law," laws taught by nature (in this case, rational human nature). We can say that these show God's justice in the history of redemption. When God judged sinners before Moses and Jesus, he was holding them to standards they had been shown by reason and tradition (taught by Noah's sons to their progeny). They could see his truths and had opportunity to find redemption by seeking to live by those truths (and realizing they could do so only by God's help). So when they refused those opportunities for redemption, God was not being unfair by withholding redemption. They had withheld it from themselves.

The Righteous Remnant

Second, the Jewish tradition of "righteous Gentiles" reinforces the Christian understanding that God always had a righteous remnant in Old Testament times, even before the revelation of Mosaic law, and that there was redemption then too, just as there was after Moses. Christians would say that these righteous Gentiles who followed the Noahic commandments were doing so only by grace, which means only by the help of the Messiah's blood and Spirit applied retroactively from the cross (Rev. 13:8).

This implies of course that there was plenty that needed redemption, even immediately after the flood. We will see that some of the fallen angels and the wicked creatures they inspired seem to have survived the flood. But how could that be if all of the little Church's enemies were destroyed?

There are two possible answers. The first is that the flood was regional and not universal. This is suggested by Psalm 104:9, where it seems that it was only at the creation that waters covered the whole earth.

The other answer is that perhaps fallen angels broke their bounds and sinned with women at other, later times. This is a possible reading of Genesis 6:4: "*Whenever* the sons of God went into the daughters of men . . ."

In any event, wickedness reappeared after the flood and the reestablishment of the Body of the Messiah in Noah's family. The influence of wicked spirits on human beings did not stop but continued. Jews at the time of the early Church were convinced that these demons came from the incident(s) described in Genesis 6 and the offspring of sons of God and women referred to there. And as we have seen, so did Jude and Peter.

The Nations and Other Religions

The Bible has more to say about other religions than most people imagine. To begin to understand what it says about the rise of religions that challenge the God of Israel, we have to start with the sons of Noah. Genesis tells us that Japheth, Ham, and Shem gave birth to what became seventy nations, which was a number that stuck with Jewish and early Christian imaginations for over a millennium. It was no coincidence that the Sanhedrin had seventy members and Jesus sent out seventy disciples. Moses tells us that the world that came from Noah's sons was divided into these seventy nations, collections of "peoples" who were in turn dispersed by their families or "tribes" and according to common languages ("tongues") and lands (Gen. 10:5, 20, 32). These are the same categories used by the author of Revelation to describe the Church of the redeemed on the renewed earth (Rev. 7:9; 11:9; 13:7; 14:6; 17:15). Significantly, as scholars have argued in *Race and Covenant*, the Bible does not divide people by race as defined by skin color, a category foreign to the world of Scripture and without basis in either biology or anthropology.[4] Race as skin color was invented in the early modern period to serve the interests of colonial slavers.

Moses interrupted his chronicle of the sons of Shem, just before he got to the line that produced Abraham, to explain why the peoples were dispersed with different languages. The explanation was rebellion and pride that culminated in the tower of Babel. Jewish readers picked up the hint in the genealogy coming from Ham that corruption set in quickly again after the flood: Nimrod's name suggests rebellion, and he was a *gibbor* just like the wicked Nephilim. Early Christian readers heard the same ominous tone because their Bible (the Greek Septuagint) translated the Hebrew *gibbor* as the Greek *gigas* or "giant," like the Nephilim.

Rebellion at Babel

These hints of spreading corruption so soon after the flood were confirmed in Genesis 11. People didn't want to "fill the earth," as God had commanded after the flood (Gen. 9:1), but to concentrate their power in one city so that they could "make a name" for themselves and build a tower that would reach to "the heavens," where God was. This would-be civilization was everything that YHWH's work of

---

4. Gerald McDermott, ed., *Race and Covenant: Recovering the Religious Roots for American Reconciliation* (Grand Rapids: Acton, 2020).

redemption was not: a concentration of power in only one part of the earth, pride in their own name rather than God's name, and trying to reach high to God by their own efforts rather than humbling themselves in lowliness and waiting for God's redemption. Babel was erecting its tower as an idol for its own glory while YHWH's people gloried in his beauty and power.

The Bible used this proud tower—and the proud civilization Babylon that it pointed to—as a symbol of later civilizations that were built on human autonomy and made war on the saints. The book of Revelation referred to the Roman Empire as Babylon the Great (Rev. 17:1–14). For these reasons—its pride and its hostility to YHWH's redemption—Genesis says that YHWH destroyed the tower. Without this destruction, Moses tells us, YHWH saw that its builders would spread their corruption exponentially ("nothing will be impossible for them"; Gen. 11:6). So he frustrated their plans as he frustrates Babel in every soul that accepts his redemption. The best-known part of YHWH's frustrating Babel was dividing their languages. But the other part—disinheriting them and dispersing the nations—is not so well known.

Disinheriting the Nations

Moses describes YHWH's disinheriting the nations in several passages in Deuteronomy. The clearest is Deuteronomy 32:8–9. "When the Most High caused the nations to inherit [their lands] and he divided the sons of Adam [from one another], he fixed the boundaries of the peoples according to the number of the sons of God. For YHWH's portion was his people Jacob; [this was his] line of inheritance." By "sons of God" Moses means the fallen angels we saw above. There were seventy nations and apparently seventy fallen angels for these purposes (if there were more of these angels, only this number seems to have had the capacity for governing a nation). In another passage in Deuteronomy Moses mentions this same event in which YHWH divided the governance of the nations between himself and these angels, members of what is called elsewhere his "divine council":

> [Watch out] lest you lift up your eyes to the heavens and behold the sun, moon, and stars and all the host of the heavens and be led astray and bow down to them, and serve them which YHWH your God assigned to all the peoples under the heavens. But YHWH took you and brought you out from the iron furnace of Egypt to be a people for him, his possession, as you are this day. (Deut. 4:19–20)

The idea here is that when God saw that after the punishment of the flood his human creatures did not learn, he gave them over to the fallen angels. They had continued to turn away from him as the source of all truth and goodness and beauty and had corrupted themselves like their predecessors before the flood into wickedness and violence. They were inspired by the evil spirits who had descended from the union of fallen angels and beautiful women. When God saw that the new human race was descending into pride and hatred like the first generations after Adam, and when they turned to themselves and other gods to worship, he gave them up to their desires and gods in the same way that Paul describes in Romans 1: "Although they knew God, they did not glorify God or give thanks [to him], but . . . they exchanged the truth about God for a lie and worshiped and served the creation rather than the Creator. . . . For this reason God gave them over to dishonorable passions and . . . to a debased mind, to do things that should not be done" (vv. 21, 25–26, 28).

Paul had suggested earlier in his career that when God gave people over to their desires, he was giving them up to the service of "principalities and powers," his terms for the fallen angels of the Old Testament (Eph. 6:12; Col. 1:16; 2:10, 15; Phil. 2:10; 1 Cor. 15:24). These were the powers behind the sun, moon, and stars of the Deuteronomy 4 passage above and "the creation," which Paul said people worshiped instead of God (Rom. 1).

Rule by Fallen Angels

So God punished the generations after the flood by giving them over to be ruled by fallen angels. He kept the people of Israel for his own rule. That is what is meant in both of these Deuteronomy passages above by God's giving the seventy nations their lands and inheritance "according to the number of the sons of God" while keeping the people of Jacob as his own inheritance. Heiser calls this the "disinheritance of the nations."[5] If we think this bizarre and unjust, the biblical rationale is as follows. God gave every generation of his human creatures plenty of grace to follow him and stay in his redemption, but the vast majority rejected his rule to follow other beings (fallen angels) masquerading as the true God. God said to them in effect, "If you don't want me and insist on following another god, then I will give you over to that other god—just as my servant Paul says I give sinners over to their desires and gods. Any other god but me will always lead its servants to destruction."

5. Michael Heiser, *The Unseen Realm: Recovering the Supernatural Worldview of the Bible* (Bellingham, WA: Lexham, 2015), 112–16.

The fallen angels masquerade as gods and in fact as the true god. (I purposely use the lowercase "god" to indicate the infinite difference between their pretensions and the true God of Israel.) Most readers will object that there are no other gods in the Bible and that all talk of "gods" there is of nonentities, subjects of human imagination. Yet scholars have recognized for a long time that the Bible does indeed recognize other supernatural powers as "gods." They are neither creators nor redeemers—there is only one Creator and Redeemer, and he is the God of Israel—and therefore are infinitely incomparable to the only one truly called God.

Yet the Psalms are full of other gods as real entities.[6] "There is none like you among the gods, O Lord" (86:8 NRSV); "For great is the LORD, and greatly to be praised; he is to be revered above all gods" (96:4 NRSV); "Our Lord is above all gods" (135:5 NRSV); "Ascribe to YHWH, [you] gods, ascribe to YHWH glory and strength" (29:1); "He is exalted above all gods" (97:9); "For YHWH is a great god, and a great king above all gods" (95:3). And so on.

But it's not just the Psalms. In Exodus YHWH predicts that he will execute judgments "on all the gods of Egypt" (12:12). The author of Numbers then declares that that is indeed what happened: "YHWH executed judgments against their gods" (33:4). There is no hint that YHWH is the only God. Instead it is clearly implied that Egypt has her own gods, and YHWH will defeat them. When YHWH gives his people the Ten Commandments, the first commandment implies the existence of other gods: "You shall have no other gods before me" (Exod. 20:3; see also Deut. 5:7). In Exodus 23:32–33 Israel is told not to covenant with or worship other gods; there is no suggestion that the gods of Israel's neighbors do not exist. Paul Hiebert has shown that the verse itself suggests that belief in the nonexistence of other gods owes more to our own prejudice than to the passage.[7]

Real Gods in Masquerade

Deuteronomy picks up this theme. Israel is told, "Do not follow other gods, any of the gods of the peoples who are all around you" (6:14 NRSV). YHWH predicts to Moses that after he dies, the Jewish tribes "will begin to prostitute themselves to the foreign gods in their midst, the gods of the land into which they are going" (31:16 NRSV). Again, "the gods" seem to have real existence.

6. The next five paragraphs are drawn from Gerald R. McDermott, *God's Rivals: Why Has God Allowed Different Religions? Insights from the Bible and the Early Church* (Downers Grove, IL: IVP Academic, 2007), 46–49. Copyright © 2007 by Gerald R. McDermott. Used by permission of InterVarsity Press, P.O. Box 1400, Downers Grove, IL 60515, USA. www.ivpress.com.

7. Paul G. Hiebert, "The Flaw of the Excluded Middle," *Missiology* 10, no. 1 (January 1982): 35–47.

So for the authors of the Old Testament, there are real gods who masquerade as the true god but who are neither Creators nor Redeemers. They learned enough from the time before their fall to project some knowledge of the true God, the God of Israel, and to keep their billions of slaves fooled. Some of the greatest of the early Christian theologians (Justin Martyr, Irenaeus, Clement of Alexandria, and Origen) recognized all this. They knew that it was to these biblical phenomena that the biblical authors attributed the rise of the world religions that competed with the God of Israel.

For example, in the book of 2 Kings we find the bizarre story of Israel's war with Moab, a people on the east shore of the Dead Sea. The kings of both Israel and Judah, along with the king of Edom, had attacked Moab with great success. All the Moabite cities but one had been overturned, and that last city was surrounded (2 Kings 3:21–25). But then, with his back against the wall, the king of Moab pulled out his ace in the hole, a card that only horrifies modern readers: "He took his firstborn son who was to succeed him, and offered him as a burnt offering on the wall. And great wrath came upon Israel, so they withdrew from him and returned to their own land" (3:27 NRSV). Once we get over our revulsion for this king's barbarism, we must recognize the other remarkable feature of this story: the author clearly seems to believe that Moab's god was real, was pleased with this grisly sacrifice, and as a result did something that actually prevented Israel from completing its victory. The text does not tell us exactly what happened at this point, but it nevertheless makes plain that Chemosh (the god of Moab) liked the smell of the poor boy's flesh and rewarded his father's unfeeling ruthlessness by obstructing the Israelite army. In short, the gods are real and have genuine power to affect what happens on earth. Behind this false religion that competed with faith in YHWH was a real god with some sort of existence.

After this second false start for the human race—Babel—God turned to an elderly couple in what is now southern Iraq to start again. True religion did not emerge from the first human couple despite their having every advantage. Nor did it develop from generations of nationalities after the flood. Now God would work redemption through one family.

Not a Backup Plan

Was God correcting his earlier mistakes? No. The big picture of Scripture makes clear that God does not do do-overs. He does not have backup plans in case his first plan fails. He knew from before the creation that Adam and Eve would fall and that the flood would be followed by further disaster. One might surmise that the first two human races—those after Adam and Eve and then Noah—were not failed plans but demonstrations for all the cosmos to see that God is just and loving to all his human creatures. He provided redemption for all the world from day one after the fall. If they failed to secure redemption, it was their fault—not God's. So too for the generations descended from Noah's sons. Noah had taught his sons great and beautiful truths about the Triune God that had been passed on to him from Adam and Eve and their faithful progeny. Shem, Ham, and Japheth passed these truths down to their children and grandchildren. God renewed awareness of these truths by the great miracles he did for Noah's family before, during, and after the flood. But these generations chose to turn away to wickedness and false gods.

Now God turned to a couple living in an idolatrous city near the Persian Gulf. From this man and woman would emerge a new family that would be an ark of the covenant protecting the Messiah.

Select Bibliography

Edwards, Jonathan. *A History of the Work of Redemption*. Edited by John F. Wilson. Vol. 9 in *The Works of Jonathan Edwards*. New Haven: Yale University Press, 1989.

Heiser, Michael. *The Unseen Realm: Recovering the Supernatural Worldview of the Bible*. Bellingham, WA: Lexham, 2015.

Hiebert, Paul G. "The Flaw of the Excluded Middle." *Missiology* 10, no. 1 (January 1982): 35–47.

McClymond, Michael, and Gerald McDermott. "The Angels in the Plan of Salvation." In *The Theology of Jonathan Edwards*, 273–94. New York: Oxford University Press, 2012.

McDermott, Gerald. *God's Rivals: Why Has God Allowed Different Religions? Insights from the Bible and the Early Church*. Downers Grove, IL: IVP Academic, 2007. See particularly chaps. 5–8.

McDermott, Gerald, ed. *Race and Covenant: Recovering the Religious Roots for American Reconciliation*. Grand Rapids: Acton, 2020.

Part Two

From Abraham to Moses

5

Abraham and the Patriarchs

God started a new chapter in the history of redemption when he called Abram (his name before God added a syllable) to leave his family and home and go to a new land. This is the transition that most Christians are familiar with: YHWH called Abram to go to an unknown land with the promise of a son who did not come till after Abraham (his new name) and his wife were past childbearing age. Yet most Christians are not aware of *why* God took this new approach to redemption. Nor are they familiar with the extraordinary revelations that God gave to Abraham of the future Redeemer and his work.

God Separates a Person

By the time of Abram, which was probably near the beginning of the second millennium BC, the inhabited world was overrun with idolatry. In the southeastern part of modern Iraq was the city Ur of Chaldea, where Abram's family lived. Here the people were polytheists dedicated to Nanna, the moon god who was thought to be the chief deity responsible for fertility in the fields and family. Scripture tells us that Abram's family had succumbed to this idolatry. Abram, his father Terah, and his brother Nahor "served other gods" (Josh. 24:2).

God saw that if Abram were left with his larger family in this land, whatever faith in YHWH he possessed would be corrupted by this idolatry and eventually extinguished in his posterity. Like most people in the world who acknowledge the true God along with others, Abram and his children would have soon discovered that false gods choke allegiance to the true God. Humans cannot serve two masters. The only way for true religion to survive would be to remove from corrupt society the person who was to be the father of the family of the Messiah. So YHWH came to Abram when he was seventy-five years old and said, "Get out from your land and from your clan and from the house of your father, and go to the land which I will show you" (Gen. 12:1). Separation was necessary for redemption.

The Center of Idolatry

Abram's home was Ur of the Chaldees, and Chaldea is associated in the Bible with Babylon. Jeremiah wrote that YHWH sent the exiles from Judah to Babylon, "the land of the Chaldeans" (Jer. 24:5; 50:1). As we saw in the last chapter, Babylon is most famous for its idolatry of the human self. The rest of the Bible depicts it as the center for the dissemination of idolatries of all sorts. After all, once the human self is made the source of worship, it is easy to transfer worship to whatever god promises to exalt the self and its desires. So Babylon became known as "a land of images" that was made "insane because of their idols" (50:38).

Because of the danger to the messianic family that Ur of the Chaldees presented, YHWH called Abram out. This was a new way of redemption. Until this point the true Church was mixed with the rest of the world. But a problem kept repeating. Those with true faith would marry those without that faith, and the faith would be corrupted or die. God's people were almost brought to nothing, over and over again. So at first God resorted to drowning the wicked world and saving the only faithful family in an ark. But then after the flood the world became corrupt again, and once again the future messianic family was jeopardized. This time God did not destroy the wicked world and save Abram and Lot and their families in a boat but called them out of the wicked world to live apart from that world.

A New Foundation

Because the world had become idolatrous, the seed of the woman had to be separated from that world in order to protect it. Moving it to a new land and starting a new nation would preserve that seed until the Messiah would come. One advantage of a separate nation was its ability to preserve God's oracles until the coming of the Messiah. Only a nation would have the personnel and structure to safeguard the history of God's great works of creation and providence. This history was necessary to create and preserve the people who would give birth to the Messiah. From there the life of the Messiah and his gospel would be sent to the rest of the world. These things could not have occurred if God's people had lived and married among the pagan world.[1]

So the Church was given a new foundation. It was a new nation that was necessary for producing the redeemer whose redemption could be delivered to the nations. Abraham was therefore the father of all the Church, which was made up of all the faithful starting with Adam and Eve and Abel. The Church was enlarged by Enosh and Enoch and all their faithful families through Noah and his sons and their descendants who remained faithful to the traditions passed down by Noah and his sons. Once it was restarted with Abraham and his family, Abraham became the root of the tree of Israel, which became distinct from all other nations. When the Messiah came approximately two thousand years after Abraham, some natural branches of the tree of Israel were broken off and wild branches of Gentiles were grafted in to share the nourishing root—redemption life that comes from the root of Abraham-like faith in the Messiah, his seed (Rom. 11:17). Abraham is therefore still the father of the faithful in the Messiah's Body, both Jews and Gentiles, the root of the olive tree called Israel. This is the tree that has spread its branches all over the world and that some day will fill all the earth with knowledge of the glory of YHWH (Hab. 2:14).

New Revelations of Redemption and the Redeemer

We saw the original promise of redemption after the fall when God promised that Eve's seed would crush the head of the serpent (Gen. 3:15) and clothed our first parents with animal skins that were types of the Messiah's righteousness to come. Then after the flood we saw that God renewed his covenant by promising Noah that he would never again send a general flood but was giving him a "new grant of the earth" with new dominion. Now in Abraham there are new revelations of a Messiah, his origins, and his reach. There would be a Messiah who would come from Abraham and would be a blessing for all the families of the earth.[2]

God made these promises repeatedly in Genesis. In chapter 12, after telling Abram to leave his family and land, God promised that he would make him into a great nation and that by him all the families of the earth would bless themselves

---

1. Edwards, *HWR*, 159–60.
2. Edwards, *HWR*, 152, 160–63.

(12:2–3). Also, God promised, to Abram's seed would be given the land of Canaan (12:7). Then after Abram told Lot he could have whatever part of this new land he wanted, God promised that Abram's seed would be like the dust of the earth and that God would give to Abram's seed forever all the land that he could see in every direction (13:14–16).

When Abram was eighty-five, God promised that his seed would be as numerous as the stars and God would give to that seed land "from the brook of Egypt" (probably Wadi El-Arish in Sinai) to the Euphrates (Gen. 15:5, 18–20).

At ninety-nine Abram and his wife Sarai still had no son. Yet God promised again that God would multiply him greatly. In fact, he would not be Abram any longer but Abraham, which means "father of a multitude," and kings would be among his progeny. Their land would be "all the land of Canaan for [their] possession forever" (Gen. 17:1–8).

Years later, after Isaac had become a young man, God promised yet again that he would multiply Abraham's seed as the stars of heaven and that by his seed all the nations of the earth would be blessed (Gen. 22:16–18).

More Details about Redemption

These repeated promises in a relatively short time greatly enlarged the Jewish Church's emerging understanding of God's redemption. First, they showed that the future Messiah would come from Abraham: by Abraham's seed (recall God's first promise after the fall that Eve's *seed* would crush the head of the serpent) all the nations of the earth would be blessed. Second, the Gentiles would be included in God's blessing of Abraham's family, for Abraham would be the father of a multitude of nations. Third, God would call into his Jewish Church people from all the nations, since "all the nations" would be blessed by Abraham's seed. Fourth, this blessing would reach not only people from every nation but members of every genealogy ("family"). Fifth, the condition of the covenant was faith, which means allegiance to the Messiah: Abraham "trusted in YHWH, and [YHWH] counted it to him for righteousness" (Gen. 15:6).

So the covenant was given much more particular shape by these extraordinary revelations. YHWH would save the world through the family of Abraham— through Abraham's seed the Messiah—and the Messiah's blessing would include Gentiles from every nation and family.

In these same remarkable revelations, YHWH gave to Abraham a stunning series of confirmations of this covenant. The first was a sacrament—that is, an outward sign of an invisible grace. The outward sign was circumcision, and its inner grace was inclusion in the family that would produce the Messiah. When God changed Abraham's name and told him he would be the father of whole nations, he said that circumcision would be "a mark of the covenant" between YHWH and all those in Abraham's family (Gen. 17:11).

Because this sacrament was not merely an outward sign, Paul emphasized that the intention of the sign was to authenticate the inward grace of faith: Abraham "received the sign of circumcision as an authentication [or seal] of the righteousness of faith" which is in the uncircumcised as well as the circumcised (Rom. 4:11). The outward circumcision was to represent the inner circumcision of the heart (2:29), which Torah had taught many centuries before Paul (Lev. 26:41; Deut. 10:16; 30:6). At this point in the history of redemption, circumcision was the principal wall of separation between Abraham's family and the outside world. Even if some pagans had circumcised their sons, only *this* circumcision pointed to trust in the God of Israel and membership in his family.

God gave a second confirmation to Abraham of his covenant with him and his family, victory over a powerful coalition of kings and their armies. The leader of this coalition was Chedorlaomer, a king from Elam, more than one thousand miles distant in what is now southwest Iran. Abraham's victory over this formidable army with only 318 men was astonishing and must have confirmed to Abraham that YHWH would do what he had promised.

Melchizedek drew the same conclusion. He was the mysterious Canaanite king and priest who praised God to Abraham for delivering "your enemies into your hand" (Gen. 14:20). Melchizedek, whose name means "king of righteousness" and who was king of Salem (the later Jerusalem in which King Jesus would be crucified), gave to Abraham bread and wine. The fathers took this to be a type of the Eucharist, which means that Messiah Jesus, whose Spirit inspired this text, signaled that he would give his people his body and blood for their redemption and that this divine humanity would be communicated through bread and wine. As Augustine put it in his *City of God*, "Then first appeared the sacrifice which is now offered to God by Christians in the whole wide world."[3] So in this beautiful story about the one into whose eternal priesthood the Messiah would be consecrated (Heb. 6:20–7:3), we are given the type of a second sacrament. The first, circumcision, was a type of baptism (Col. 2:11–12). Two sacraments, then, were given to Abraham as a third confirmation of the covenant—circumcision and a proto-Eucharist.

---

3. Augustine, *City of God* 16.22, trans. Marcus Dods (New York: Modern Library, 1950), 545.

A fourth confirmation was the vision God gave to Abraham of a smoking furnace and burning lamp that passed between the halves of slaughtered animals (Gen. 15:12–21). This was the sacrifice for the covenant that God "cut" with Abraham. YHWH used the practice common in the ancient Near East for two parties making a solemn agreement. Animals would be cut in half, and the parties would pass between them as a sign that they too could be cut in half if they did not fulfill the terms of the covenant. In this case God himself passed between the animal halves to indicate his promise to fulfill his side of the agreement, to be God to Abraham's family in all the ways he said he would. Since fire was a common sign of God's presence, the fathers took the furnace and lamp to symbolize various aspects of the Godhead. For Chrysostom, they represented "the indissolubility of the covenant and the presence of the divine energy."[4] For Edwards, the furnace represented the sufferings of the Messiah, and the lamp the glory that his sufferings earned.[5]

A fifth confirmation of the covenant was the miracle child Isaac, born to Abraham when he was one hundred years old and Sarah ninety. Abraham's body was "as good as dead," but he and his wife conceived a child anyway, the child through whom the Messiah would come (Rom. 4:19; Heb. 11:18).

A sixth corroboration of the covenant was God's delivering Isaac from the dead, as it were, after Isaac had been strapped down for sacrificial slaughter at God's command. The author of Hebrews notes that Abraham was being tested and knew that the God who had promised progeny through Isaac was able to raise Isaac from the dead, from which he was raised "figuratively" (Heb. 11:18–19). Because Abraham passed the test, God promised that he would multiply his seed to become like the stars of heaven and the grains of sand on the seashore. Furthermore, God promised, Abraham's seed would not be oppressed by their enemies because they would "possess [their] gate" (Gen. 22:17).

These spectacular sacraments and events took the Old Testament Church in Abraham and his family a quantum leap forward in their understanding of the Messiah's future redemption. They had a much clearer vision of the fact that Abraham's family would produce a Messiah and of the great blessings that the Messiah would give to God's people. Because of all these things that YHWH showed Abraham in visions and personal appearances (Gen. 15:1; 17:1; 18:1), and because it was

4. John Chrysostom, *Homilies on Genesis*, in *Catena on Genesis*, Patristic Bible Commentary (website), accessed May 12, 2023, https://sites.google.com/site/aquinasstudybible/home/genesis/catena-on-genesis/catena-chapter-15.

5. Edwards, *HWR*, 164.

probably the Son of God who made these appearances, Jesus told the Judean leaders that Abraham rejoiced to see his day (John 8:56). Jesus was affirming what the rabbis of his era taught, that Abraham saw the future of the Messiah and his age.[6] Jesus probably was referring to these visions when he told his opponents that when Abraham saw God, he was seeing Messiah Jesus and his day.

God's Protection of His People

One of the most encouraging things to see in the story of God's redemption is the repeated work of God to protect his people. God's purpose was to preserve the family that would produce the Messiah and his redemption.

When God told Abraham that his seed would sojourn in a foreign land for four hundred years, he suggested the wickedness of the Canaanites when he told the patriarch that the sins of the Amorites had not reached their full measure (Gen. 15:16). Their sins were great but would be allowed to increase to the point where they deserved expulsion under Joshua.

This wickedness is why Abraham and Isaac were grieved when Esau married several daughters of the pagans in the land, and it is why Isaac and Rebecca sent Jacob away to find a wife from people related to the patriarchs (Gen. 26:34–35; 28:1–5, 8). Abraham's family sometimes committed their own grievous sins against their pagan neighbors, but God repeatedly protected them from destruction at the hands of their hostile neighbors.

For example, Scripture makes clear the great wickedness of Sodom and its hostility to the little family of the patriarchs. This was a fulfillment of the prophecy that God would put enmity between Eve's seed and Satan's seed (Gen. 3:15). Abraham's family were strangers in the land, and natives are always more disposed to be hostile to strangers, especially when those strangers rebuke the natives. So when Lot was "oppressed by the lawless sensuality" of the men of Sodom and told them not to "act so wickedly," they took offense (Gen. 19:7; 2 Pet. 2:7). Just as Cain was offended because his own deeds were evil and Abel's were righteous, so too the Sodomites were enraged by Lot's suggestion that their plans were wicked. Lot rebuked them gently, but all they heard was a stranger who had come to judge them (Gen. 19:9).

---

6. C. H. Dodd: a rabbinic tradition held that Abraham was allowed a vision "of all the 'days,' or periods of time to come, [including] the parting of the Red Sea and the giving of the Law. . . . [This] would justify the statement that Abraham [also] saw the day of the Messiah." See Dodd, *The Interpretation of the Fourth Gospel* (Cambridge: Cambridge University Press, 1953), 261, cited in Frederick Dale Bruner, *The Gospel of John: A Commentary* (Grand Rapids: Eerdmans, 2012), 557.

Yet God protected Abraham and Lot and their families, as Psalm 105 reports: "When they were few in number, of little account, and strangers there, wandering from nation to nation . . . [God] allowed no one to oppress them. He rebuked kings for their sake, saying, 'Do not strike my anointed ones, do no evil to my prophets'" (vv. 12–15). Even after Simeon and Levi murdered all the males in Shechem to avenge Dinah's rape so that Jacob became a "stink" to his neighbors, they did not pursue Jacob and his family because "a terror from God" fell upon them (Gen. 35:5).

God continued to protect Jacob. When his uncle Laban was infuriated by Jacob's sudden and secret departure, God warned Laban in a dream not to speak to Jacob (Gen. 31:24). When his estranged brother, Esau, approached Jacob with an army of men, God turned Esau's heart and changed him from an enemy into a friend (Gen. 33). At all these times God protected this little root of the Messiah from dangers and enemies, just as God had earlier preserved the Church in the ark through a cataclysmic deluge.

Terrors of the Law

God has always used the terrors of the law in his work of redemption. By this is meant the frightening knowledge that we deserve to be damned because of our rebellion against God's law, and therefore we need redemption. People since the time of the cross have felt this terror, through preaching and Church tradition, because they have known that God poured out his wrath over their sin against his law upon his own Son at Calvary. But before the cross, God had to show his wrath toward sin against his law in other, more graphic ways.

This is the reason for the terrifying thunder and fire at Sinai. Before Sinai, stories of earlier terrors were passed down from generation to generation. Adam lived 930 years and told his descendants of God's fearsome threats at the fall. Those who talked with him lived, according to the Genesis accounts, until the flood.

Yet by the time of the destruction of Sodom, most had forgotten the flood, even if some of Noah's sons were still alive at this time (Gen. 11:10–26). But the demolition of Sodom and Gomorrah by a terrifying rain of lightning fire and sulfurous gases is probably why the cities of the surrounding plain did not dare touch Jacob and his family. It signaled to those with eyes to see and ears to hear that apart from divine redemption there was no escape from the terrors of divine judgment. Those visible terrors were an image of the hell that awaits all who ignore the terrors of the law.

Renewals of the Covenant of Grace

In many and various ways God renewed his promises of Messiah and redemption to Jacob and his sons. To Isaac God promised that all the nations would be blessed by his seed (Gen. 26:3–4). To Jacob he promised that peoples and nations would bow down to him, and those who cursed him would be cursed, and those who blessed him would be blessed (27:29). At Bethel God gave him the vision of a ladder to heaven with angels ascending and descending, which showed that through his seed there would be a way of redemption. The stone on which he rested his head became an altar upon which he poured oil and which opened up to another world: "This is nothing but the house of God, even a gate to the heavens" (28:17). Jacob saw that God would be with him and his seed and that there was a place where he and his family could find God and his heavenly kingdom. Many centuries later Jesus said that Jacob's stone altar marking the ladder was the Messiah himself connecting heaven and earth: the "angels of God [were] ascending and descending upon the Son of Man" (John 1:51).

This was a spectacular renewal of the covenant between God and the family of Abraham. Jacob heard again that his seed would be as numerous as the dust of the earth, that they would be given this land, and that by his seed all the families of the earth would be blessed (Gen. 28:13–15).

It was affirmed again at Penuel, where Jacob wrestled with the Messiah in human form and prevailed (Gen. 32:22–32). Then after Jacob left Paddan-aram and came to Bethel a second time, God appeared once more and renewed these promises (35:9–15).

Over and over, then, God renewed the covenant of grace. He did so more often than in previous stages of the history of redemption. Through these repeated visions and appearances the light of the gospel shone brighter and brighter as the time grew closer to the coming of the Messiah.

Joseph a Type of the Redeemer

At the end of the book of Genesis we find a remarkable image of the Redeemer himself in the person of Joseph. Just as Messiah Jesus redeems us from spiritual famine, Joseph saved his family from literal famine in Canaan. When a seven-year famine was approaching, God sent Jacob's family to Egypt to keep the holy seed alive. Just as God saved humanity from sin by the sins of the Romans and certain Judean leaders in the first century, God saved Jacob's family through the sin of Joseph's brothers who sold him into slavery. God told Joseph many years later that while his brothers meant it for evil, God meant it for good, to keep his family alive (Gen. 50:20). This was another example of the recurring theme we have seen, that every time the holy root was in danger of destruction, God acted miraculously to protect it.

Joseph was a type of the Messiah. As I just mentioned, both he and the Messiah saved their people from famine. Joseph forgave his brothers and so was not ashamed to call them his brothers, just as Jesus forgives sinners and is not ashamed to call them his brothers (Heb. 2:11). Joseph was hated at first by his brothers and delivered up to be killed, just as Jesus was hated and handed over to be crucified. Joseph was humiliated and cast into a dungeon, just as Jesus humbled himself and was cast into a grave. Joseph was lifted up to the king's right hand and from there distributed food to keep people alive, just as Jesus Messiah was raised to the right hand of the Father and from there gives the food of eternal life. Both Joseph and Jesus gave gifts to those who once despised them.

Locating the Messiah

Until this point no one knew where or when the Messiah would come. But during this burst of revelation light to the patriarchs, God started to indicate details of how and when he would appear. Whereas before this time God had indicated only that the Messiah would emerge from Noah's family and Shem's line (Gen. 11:10–26), descent became clearer with Abraham's family. God gradually narrowed the line of descent: the Redeemer would come through Isaac of Abraham's many sons (17:19), through Jacob of the two sons of Isaac (27:29), and then through Judah of the twelve sons of Jacob (49:10). The Messiah would be the lion of the tribe of Judah (Gen. 49:9; Rev. 5:5).

Jacob's prophetic blessing of Judah suggested the timing of the Messiah's coming. It would be when the Gentiles joined Israel in large numbers, for to Jacob's seed would come "the obedience of the peoples" (Gen. 49:10). Although Gentiles joined Israel throughout her history from Abraham to the Messiah, it was not until the early Church that whole peoples of majority Gentiles started coming to worship the God of Israel through his Messiah. The attraction of whole peoples to the God of Israel in the first century—and after—marked the time of the Messiah. The spectacle of large numbers from nations outside Israel worshiping the God of Israel was the fulfillment of prophecy from centuries before the Messiah's incarnation.

Early Hindu Tradition

It is helpful to observe the rise and development of other world religions in order to see the uniqueness of the God of Israel and the redemption he was offering the world. The only other major world religion for which we have extant texts close to the end of the patriarchal period (estimated between 1800 and 1500 BC) is Vedic religion, a precursor to classical Hindu traditions. The religion of the Rigveda (the earliest collection of Sanskrit hymns) is devoted to the pursuit of health, wealth, sons, and protection from evil spirits. The head of a household would make ritual sacrifices of animals (and sometimes human beings) to gods of the hearth, sun, war, and rain for the sake of those ends. The gods were believed to control history and nature, but were weak: they were neither creators nor saviors, and they depended on human sacrifices for their own strength. There was no love between them and their devotees, only a contractual relationship devoted to this-worldly goods. Belief in life after death with the gods came later in the Vedas, and transmigration of the soul (reincarnation) did not arise until the Upanishads, even later.

Therefore, the contrast between the religion of the early Hebrews and that of the earliest Hindus in northwest India (where the Rigveda was found) is stark. The God of Israel is one and not many. He is both creator and redeemer. He is concerned with all the peoples of the world and not just one people in one part of the world. He wants to have a relationship of love with people and not simply provide services. He invites people into an eternal covenant that transcends death. He showed Abraham that he would raise his people from the dead (Heb. 11:18–19). Jesus told the Sadducees, who denied the resurrection of the dead, that God indicated the resurrection of the patriarchs by telling Moses, "I *am* the God of Abraham and the God of Isaac and the God of Jacob" (Matt. 22:32).

Select Bibliography

Augustine. *The City of God*. Translated by Marcus Dods. New York: Modern Library, 1950.

Edwards, Jonathan. *A History of the Work of Redemption*. Edited by John F. Wilson. Vol. 9 in *The Works of Jonathan Edwards*. New Haven: Yale University Press, 1989.

John Chrysostom. *Homilies on Genesis*. In *Catena on Genesis*. Patristic Bible Commentary (website). Accessed May 12, 2023. https://sites.google.com/site/aquinasstudybible/home/genesis/catena-on-genesis/catena-chapter-15.

McClymond, Michael, and Gerald McDermott. "Edwards's Calvinism and Theology of the Covenants." In *The Theology of Jonathan Edwards*, 321–38. New York: Oxford University Press, 2012.

McDermott, Gerald. *World Religions: An Indispensable Introduction.* Nashville: Nelson, 2011.

McDermott, Gerald, and Harold Netland. *A Trinitarian Theology of Religions: An Evangelical Proposal.* New York: Oxford University Press, 2014.

Part Three

From Moses to the Incarnation

6

Moses to David

One of Jonathan Edwards's maxims was that God gets a people ready before he does a spectacular new thing for them. God might get them ready through extraordinary suffering, or he might give them unprecedented new revelations to prepare for a quantum leap in the history of redemption. In the period covered by this chapter, God gave his chosen people revelations of his redemption and redeemer like never before. This period contained a concentrated series of revelations of the Messiah and his ways to prepare God's people for his coming.

The preparation proceeded in four stages. First he redeemed the Jews from slavery in Egypt and separated them from all other peoples in the world. Then he formed their souls and consciousness by giving them the law and prophecies of the Messiah. Third, he brought the most dedicated Jewish generation into the land and gave them ways of worship that would reveal the ways of the Messiah and his redemption. Finally, he purified his people by personal appearances of the Messiah and sending a succession of early prophets.

Redemption from Egypt

God started this intense series of revelations at a time when the Egyptians were trying to destroy the people of Israel. First Pharaoh tried to reduce their numbers by subjecting them to cruel slavery. When that only increased the Jewish population, he tried to murder every newborn boy. Yet still the Jewish people multiplied.

At the same time the Jews were losing their faith by degrees. Most were so influenced by Egyptian society that they had taken up the worship of Egyptian gods. As the prophet Ezekiel put it, they had refused to throw out the detestable things their eyes feasted on and so kept "whoring after" the idols of Egypt (Ezek. 20:6–8; 23:8).

This was the third time that "God's church was almost swallowed up" by the world's corruption (the other two were before the flood and the call of Abraham).[1] But again God redeemed his nearly dead Church. Just as he had saved the little Church in an ark, so now he saved it again in an ark of bulrushes (Exod. 2:3). And just as God saved the Church because of Noah's obedience, so now he delivered the tiny Church because Moses's parents refused to obey Pharaoh's edict (Heb. 11:23).

This deliverance became the greatest of all the Old Testament types (God-designed symbols) of the Messiah's redemption. Pharaoh was a type of Satan, so when Israel was freed from slavery to Pharaoh, she was displaying the freedom that Messiah brings from slavery to sin and Satan. Scripture talks about Israel being liberated from the "iron furnace" (Deut. 4:20) of Egypt just as Messiah liberates us from the fires of hell. YHWH brought Israel out of Egypt with a strong hand and outstretched arm just as Jesus Messiah disarmed the principalities and the powers at the cross, crushing the serpent's head (Deut. 26:8; Col. 2:15; Gen. 3:15). Israel was saved by the paschal lamb's sprinkling of blood, just as the Church is "saved by the sprinkling of the blood" of Messiah while "the rest of the world is destroyed."[2] Pharaoh did everything he could to keep the Israelites in Egypt just as Satan tries his hardest to keep every sinner in his clutches, especially those who follow the Lamb to safety.

The Lamb's triumph was glorious. He went before the Israelites in pillars of cloud and fire. When Satan pursued them with Pharaoh's army, the Messiah-Lamb destroyed them by the waters of the Red Sea. Never again did Pharaoh and his army pursue YHWH's people. Scripture suggests they were baptized in the Messiah's blood when they were sprinkled by its *Red* Sea waters as they passed through it: they were "baptized into Moses in the cloud and in the sea" (1 Cor. 10:2). "In his love and his pity" the Messiah "redeemed his people and carried them . . . on eagles' wings" so that no enemy "could touch them" (Isa. 40:31).[3]

---

1. Edwards, *HWR*, 174.
2. Edwards, *HWR*, 176.
3. Edwards, *HWR*, 176. Although the Hebrew Torah generally uses *yam suph* or "Sea of Reeds" for the river/marsh which the Hebrews crossed, the Septuagint mostly used *erythra thalassa* or "Red Sea," and the New Testament authors followed the Septuagint (Acts 7:36; Heb. 11:29).

Few Christians realize that it was the Messiah at work in this greatest of all First Testament redemptions—even though Jude says this explicitly: "Jesus saved a people out of the land of Egypt" (v. 5). It was Jesus who spoke as the angel of the Lord at the burning bush (Exod. 3:2–3). When Moses stopped to look at the bush that burned without being consumed, he was seeing the Messiah's suffering, the fire of God's wrath, but without being destroyed. When the pillars of cloud and fire led God's people through their days and nights, they were unwittingly watching the Messiah lead them in some of his many interventions during their wilderness wanderings.

This marked a new turn in the history of redemption, and Moses knew it. He asked, Did any god ever deliver a whole people out of another nation with such terrifying power? (Deut. 4:32–35). This unprecedented deliverance was necessary for the later incarnation of the Messiah. The people who would bring this Messiah to birth had to be separated from every other nation for their own protection. Until the exodus this people had been strangers and sojourners in a variety of societies. But repeatedly they had run the risk of being overrun by the idolatry of their neighbors. Now they had to be isolated from the midst of these idolatrous societies and kept separate until the enfleshment of the Messiah. The revelations of Messiah through types and prophecies had to be protected. Only the separation of this nation from all others could ensure this protection.

Rejection of Other Peoples

God works in ways that confound the human intellect. His plan of redemption operates by a pattern of unbelief and jealousy that no human mind could have ever predicted. God revealed that he permitted every nation to reject him in unbelief so that he could have mercy on each and it would be clear that they had found him by his mercy and not their merit (Rom. 11:30–32). In each case unbelieving peoples looked with envy on those who walked with the God of Israel, and this jealousy led them to seek him.

In the centuries before and during the rise of Israel, the Gentiles progressed in their rejection of truth, even as the God of Israel was revealing his truth and beauty to Israel. Some Gentiles like Rahab and Ruth joined Israel because they saw the truth and beauty of her God. But over time the Gentile nations consolidated in their rejection of the God of Israel and his truth and goodness.

We don't know when this apostasy became common. It was not universal in Abraham's time because there was Melchizedek, the mysterious priest who recognized the true God in the One who had called Abraham. True religion persisted for some time in the family of Nahor, Abraham's brother. Job and his three friends with Elihu shared knowledge of the true God, and they were from Uz, the land of Nahor (Gen. 22:21). Elihu was born to Buz, son of Nahor, and Bildad the Shuhite was a son of Shuah, Abraham's son by Keturah (Job 32:2; 2:11; 8:1). So after Abraham the true religion persisted for a while outside Israel.

But not very long. By the time God separated Israel from Egypt, he seems to have given up on the Gentiles. Then at the time of the Messiah's incarnation, it had become clear that "the world did not know God through wisdom" (1 Cor. 1:21). There were shadows of truth in thinkers like Socrates and Confucius, but the word of the cross was folly to those who refused to move beyond them (1:18).

Tens—perhaps hundreds—of thousands of Jews put their faith in Jesus Messiah in the first century, but the majority did not (Acts 21:20; Rom. 10:3). In the mystery of God's plan of redemption, he shut up most Jews into unbelief in their Messiah so that he could make room in time for Gentiles (Rom. 11:28: "They are enemies for your sake"). At the end of the time of the Gentiles, he will then call all Israel (which does not mean every last Jew), who will have their own jealousy for life in Messiah after centuries of unbelief in Yeshua (11:25–26). In this way God works his special redemptive logic: he consigns all to disobedience so that he can have mercy on all (11:12). Both Gentiles and Jews have had their times of refusing God's revelation, so that each set of peoples can say that redemption came not by their achievement but by God's mercy.

Shortening of Human Life

Oddly, but logically, the diminution of human life spans was part of God's plan for redemption. In the first biblical era before written revelation, long life spans were needed for the transmission of God's truths from one generation to another. As we saw, it was because Adam lived more than nine hundred years that people who learned from him lived to tell Noah's generation of God's promised judgment of sin. But long lives also diminished the force of those threats. People reassured themselves that they had plenty of time to postpone thinking about those warnings.

So God reduced human life spans drastically, from more than nine hundred years in the first generation to about seventy-five by the time of Moses. God made the first reductions after the flood, in the first generation to six hundred years and in the next to somewhere between four hundred and five hundred years. The final average between seventy and eighty years came after the generation that left Egypt had died. This was the generation that rejected the good report of the two spies and refused to obey God's commandment to go up into the promised land. When their carcasses were left in the wilderness, God told Moses that the years of human life would be seventy, perhaps eighty for the strong, but full of toil and trouble. Soon they would be over and fly away (Ps. 90:10).

This was good for the work of redemption. Humans with short lives would be more ready to hear about everlasting life and a savior who would give it to them. This good news had a far better chance of bringing joy to those who knew that life is short.

If they had continued living for hundreds of years, they would have been tempted "to rest in the things of this world and to neglect any other life but this."[4] This is probably the reason for the great wickedness of the antediluvians. But now, even with the advances of modern medicine, we know that we will probably die at one-twelfth the age of those who lived before the flood. It helps us to think of death and what comes after.

The Law at Sinai

Christians routinely misunderstand what most Bibles translate as "law." The word is *Torah* in Hebrew and is better translated as the "teaching" of a wise and loving heavenly Father who wants to show his children how to have a happy and prosperous life. This means living in the joy of his beauty and truth by becoming one with his Messiah and following the Messiah's interpretation of Torah. When Jesus and Paul talk about "law" in the New Testament, they use the word *nomos*, which in the first century was used in medical manuals for the regimen of life which would best produce healing. This helps us understand why the psalmist exults, in Psalm 119:97: "Oh how I love your Torah!" It is why Paul declares in Romans that "the law [*nomos*] is holy, and the commandment is holy and righteous and good" (7:12).

The structure of the Pentateuch, which Jews call Torah, connotes the same. Rather than being dominated by rules, which the word "law" suggests, four of the five books are filled with stories, and magnificent ones at that. The only book that looks like a lawbook with rules is Leviticus, and its rules are set around a mysterious set of sacrifices and rituals—a far cry from what most think of as "law."

---

4. Edwards, *HWR*, 185.

Therefore, when God first gave to his people at Sinai his Torah, it was a rule of life that pointed to redemption by God's Messiah. But it was also awesome and frightening, for the reason I mentioned in the last chapter—that since the cross was in the future, God's people needed to see his wrath toward sin. Men and women needed to be convinced of their sin and helplessness before God's majesty and justice so that they would realize they needed a savior from sin. This is why Moses trembled with fear at the mountain on fire and the earth shaking, and the people begged that no further messages be given them (Heb. 12:18–21). They saw that they would need a mediator to come between their sinful selves and a holy God.

They also came to see that Torah (and its elaboration in the rest of the Old Testament) showed them a path they must follow without looking to the right or the left. It was a narrow way to life that required sincerity and obedience. Innumerable blessings would follow obedience, and horrible curses would fall on the disobedient (Deut. 28).

At the same time, this Torah was a schoolmaster that would show them the Messiah and his redemption (Gal. 3:24). Whereas before the Law at Sinai God had shown here and there intimations of redemption through a coming Messiah, now the Law was typological at every point. Its sacrifices and sacraments (such as circumcision) were types of the Messiah's sacrifice and sacraments, its rules for everyday living were types of Jesus's commandments for everyday discipleship, and its laws for life as a nation were types of the ways of the kingdom that are both now and not yet—realized partly in the kingdom of Jesus in the Church and messianic synagogues but fully manifest on the renewed earth to come. Its stories of the patriarchs and kings are thoroughly typical, illustrating the beauty, truth, and goodness of the Messiah's kingdom. Everything we see in Torah and Tanach (the Old Testament as a whole; it is an acronym from the first letters of the three Hebrew words for its three major parts, Torah/Pentateuch, Nevi'im/Prophets, Ketuvim/Writings) is a shadow of things to come (Heb. 10:1), veiled behind a provisional order as Moses's face was veiled to hide the glory (Exod. 34:35).

The Written Word of God

The first written word of God was either the book of Job or the ten words etched into stone by the finger of God at Sinai. Until this time the Word of God had come to human beings either by immediate revelation to the persons we have discussed so far in Genesis or by the passing-on of those words to later generations by tradition. Because of the long lives of these first generations, it is plausible that God's words were passed down to the generations just before Moses. Noah could have talked with Adam, and Noah lived till roughly Abraham's time. The sons of Jacob could have delivered these traditions to their grandchildren in Egypt.[5]

But by Moses's day the time from the beginning was so great and human lives were so short that it was necessary to commit God's words to writing.[6] God had prepared for this time by separating the nation of Israel from her neighbors so that she could be the womb in which to preserve God's oracles. Now the Word could be a steady light throughout the ages. It would also be a continuing "witness against" Israel (Deut. 31:26), placed beside the ark of the covenant in the tabernacle. The tablets with the "ten words" (4:13) were inside the ark, but the whole Torah was placed alongside the ark to warn and guide the Jewish Church throughout its pilgrimage in the land. Later, and especially after the return from exile in Babylon, the books of history and wisdom and prophecy were added to make the whole Tanach. After the incarnation of Jesus, his interpretation of Torah in the Gospels and then his inspiration of his apostles in the rest of the New Testament completed the written Word. These written revelations would be the undying light and rule for the Church throughout her time in the old heavens and earth.

The Journey to Canaan

The story of Israel's journey in the wilderness was an important part of that written word. It consisted of an extended series of types for the Church's journey through this world on the way to her eternal inheritance. As Paul put it, all the steps of "our fathers'" journey were "written as types [typikōs] for our instruction" (1 Cor. 10:11). Israel's bondage in Egypt represents our bondage to sin, death, and the devil before salvation. Her offering of the paschal [from the Hebrew word for "passing over"] lamb on the night God killed the firstborn in Egypt and the angel of death passed over Jewish houses was a type of the Messiah's offering of himself as the Lamb of God for our sins. When our households are joined to the Lamb by the allegiance of faith, we too are passed over by the angel of eternal death.

Israel's passing through the Red Sea was when the fathers of that generation "were baptized into Moses" (1 Cor. 10:2), converted to the God of Israel after

5. Edwards, *HWR*, 182–83.
6. Edwards, *HWR*, 182–83.

flirting with the gods of Egypt (Ezek. 20:6–8; 23:8). Their conversion, even if only temporary before their reversion to the golden calf, was a type of Christian conversion by attachment to the blood of the Messiah. Their journey through the wilderness, recounted in Exodus and Numbers, was full of lessons for the Church on pilgrims' progress through this evil world: they were led daily by the pillar of cloud and fire (as Jesus-believers are led by Word and Spirit), they were supported materially by manna and water from the rock (as believers are provided for materially and through sacraments by their heavenly Father, who cares for them), they were endangered by pests and fiery serpents (as God's people are threatened regularly by the devil and his temptations), and they warred with Amalekites and other enemies (as Jews and Christians are increasingly persecuted in these latter days). These and other events in the wilderness are images of what the Messiah's Body meets in all ages of the world.

Perhaps the most remarkable parts of this wilderness story, and its antitypes (the things to which types point) in the Church's story, are the uncanny ways in which God provided—and provides!—for his people. In a word, God's providence. The fact that upwards of two million people survived for forty years in a dry and barren wilderness without farming is nothing short of miraculous. In fact, one continuous miracle. Without food and drink people die in a month or less. Only daily bread coming out of heaven and water coming out of a rock that followed them (1 Cor. 10:4) kept them alive. Scripture tells us that their clothes did not wear out (Deut. 8:4; 29:5). No nation in history has ever been sustained for so long and in such spectacular ways. God was doing it to protect the people in whose loins was the promised seed of the great Redeemer of the world.

By the way, Torah nowhere says the rock followed the people in the wilderness. But the story was part of rabbinic midrash (retelling of biblical stories), which Paul apparently thought divinely inspired. Peter Enns and John Byron have shown that evidence of this midrash is found in several ancient Jewish texts as well as the contemporaneous Pseudo-Philo.[7]

Prophecies of the Messiah

In this period of history when God was ensuring the ongoing testimony to his redemption, he gave three prophecies of the Messiah that provided more specificity

---

7. John Byron, "Paul, Jesus and the Rolling Stone," *Biblical Archaeology Review* (September/October 2015): 28, 66; Peter Enns, "The 'Moveable Well' in 1 Cor 10:4," *Bulletin for Biblical Research* 6 (1996): 23–38. See also Pseudo-Philo, *The Biblical Antiquities of Philo* 10.7, trans. M. R. James (London: SPCK, 1917).

than ever before. The first came, ironically, through the pagan prophet Balaam. He told the Moabite king Balak that a star would come out of Jacob that would be a scepter from Israel, used by "one from Jacob" who would exercise dominion (Num. 24:17–19). Many rabbis interpreted this to point to a coming Messiah who would be a king of kings.

The second prophecy spoke of the prophetic ministry of the Messiah. YHWH told Moses that he would raise up a "prophet like you" from among his brothers. To this prophet like Moses all Jews were to listen, and God would "require it" of them. YHWH reminded his people that his own voice had been "too terrifying" when he had spoken to them earlier, and the fire on Sinai had been too terrible to see. So he would send this prophet as a mediator; he would put his words in his mouth so that this mediator would tell them everything that YHWH commanded him (Deut. 18:17–19). Apparently he would not be as terrifying as YHWH had been on Mount Sinai.

The third prophecy was of the future day when YHWH would call the Gentiles in large numbers to join the family of Israel. It came in the Song of Moses, which the great leader gave just before his death in Deuteronomy 32. YHWH told Moses that because Israel had made him jealous by their worship of what was no god, he would make them jealous of a people who previously had not been a people for the God of Israel (v. 21). He would make Israel angry by calling a nation that had previously always been "foolish"—the nations of Gentiles, whom he now referred to collectively as one nation.

Until this point in the history of redemption, almost all the prophecies of the Messiah and his redemption had been in figurative and typological language. The woman's seed would crush the serpent's head, and in the seed of the patriarchs all the families of the earth would be blessed. Even to Balaam the Messiah was called a "star." But now the Messiah is referred to with the utmost straightforwardness. He would be a prophet like Moses and would protect the people of Israel from fearsome sights and sounds by talking to them with a human face and in a human way. But he would also be a king who would one day rule all the kings of the world, especially the kings of Israel's traditional enemies.

Pouring Out the Spirit

As we have seen, the generation that escaped from Egypt was tainted with Egyptian idolatry. YHWH told the prophet Ezekiel that he warned that generation to cast off their idols, but "they rebelled against me" (Ezek. 20:8). They had Aaron make for them a golden calf, similar to the Egyptian goddess Hathor, who had cow horns and ears. YHWH was angered by them and swore they would not enter the land (20:15).

But the next generation was the polar opposite of that previous one. They were born in the wilderness or were under twenty when their parents left Egypt. This younger generation was raised with intimate knowledge of God's daily provisions. They were pious and did not murmur against God when under trial (Num. 14:31; Jer. 2:2–3; Deut. 8:2–3). So God poured out his Spirit on them—not as a reward but as a further blessing on top of Spirit-induced preparation. They had probably been moved by seeing the great judgments God poured out on Korah's rebellious company and on the twenty-three thousand killed by the plague in punishment for their Baal worship at Peor (Num. 16; 25).

So God poured out wonderful blessings on this younger generation, the vast majority of whom seem to have been savingly converted. He fought for them and gave them the land of Canaan. By faith they overcame the mighty kings Og and Sihon and giants in Canaan. Joshua commended them for cleaving to the Lord "as you have done until now" (Josh. 23:8). They had shown their zeal after being defeated at Ai by determining to root out the sinful cause of their defeat in Achan's coveting silver and gold (Josh. 7). Then they confronted the two and a half tribes that had set up an altar apart from the approved one, and they resolved the dispute peaceably (Josh. 22).

So God renewed the covenant with this younger and faithful generation (Deut. 29). This was a familiar pattern after a general reformation, such as we will see for Hezekiah and Josiah: covenant renewal. Here the people, led by the king, rehearsed the history of the covenant, renewed their pledges to it, and shared sacred meals (2 Chron. 29–30, esp. 30:21–27; 2 Chron. 34–35, esp. 35:17). This and other covenant renewals were types of the coming covenant renewal led by the Messiah in person at the Eucharist, the Church's participation in his paschal death and resurrection. Here the followers of the Messiah are joined to the death that continues to be the perfect sacrifice renewing YHWH's covenant with Israel and Gentiles attached to Israel by union with her Messiah.

This covenant renewal at Moab, just before Israel entered the land under Joshua, might have been the greatest flourishing of religion in the history of Israel. It was much like the revivals during the days of Hezekiah, Josiah, and Ezra and Nehemiah. It was akin to the zeal of the Church in the time of the apostles. Here, as in the days of the early Church, God was advancing the work of redemption by powerful outpourings of his Spirit.

Settlement in Canaan

The Jewish Church's entrance into the land is full of types. Joshua was a type of the Messiah, bringing his people into the land of promise. Not coincidentally, his name is the same as Jesus in Greek—*Iesous*—which can be seen in the Greek New Testament where Joshua is mentioned (Acts 7:45; Heb. 4:8).

Joshua brought God's people into Canaan, which was a type of the heavenly Canaan that the Messiah purchased with his blood (Heb. 9:24). He conquered the kings of Canaan and subdued the giants, just as Jesus Messiah conquered the devil and his demons to set us free (Josh. 11:18, 21; Col. 2:15). Joshua divided the Jordan, just as the Messiah divided the Red Sea for Moses and Israel (Josh. 3). Joshua caused the walls of Jericho to fall down at the sound of trumpets, just as preachers of the gospel cause the walls of Satan's kingdom to collapse (Josh. 6). Joshua bade YHWH to have the sun and moon stand still in order to fight his enemies, which demonstrated that God makes all nature serve the work of redemption (10:12–13). Since the Messiah created and governs nature, all things visible and invisible are his by right and purchase. So we should not be surprised that he manipulates them at will when needed. This is what Paul means when he says all things are "for him" (Col. 1:16) and "all things are yours . . . you are the Messiah's, and Messiah is God's" (1 Cor. 3:22–23). God has Messiah manipulate creation for the sake of his redeemed people. What a marvelous thing to realize!

We see this in graphic detail in Joshua 10. After being reminded that there was "a man" who commanded the army of YHWH (Josh. 5:13–14), we are told that YHWH helped Joshua as he was leading his men against the Amorites at Gibeon and then Beth-horon (10:6–11). Since we know that the Messiah is the only divine being who is also a man, it must have been he who threw the Amorites into a panic as they fled before Joshua's men, killing more with hailstones than with the sword (v. 11). Then Messiah made the sun and moon stand still until Joshua's men finished taking "vengeance on their enemies" (v. 13). YHWH "obeyed the voice of a man" on this remarkable day and showed that all of nature is at his beck and call. The Lord of nature is also the Lord Redeemer.

Liturgical Worship and Sacraments

As long as Israel was a nation of itinerants, a good part of the Law was not operational. Its feasts of firstfruits and ingathering, for example, made sense only for an agricultural people. So too the Law's cities of refuge and its tithes and offerings from the products of the soil.

So Israel's religious life could function properly only in the land of promise. That religious life seems strange to modern eyes, with its center spelled out in a mysterious system of sacrifices in Torah's most arcane book, Leviticus. This is the book most Christians have thought the most expendable from the Bible. Yet it is also the book that rabbis have said to be the hermeneutical key to Tanach. And if Tanach was Jesus's Bible, and he was both its author and meaning, then Leviticus is the secret to the riddles of all Scripture.

How could this be? Perhaps this is why it was the first book taught to young Jewish boys. It is the grammar that was necessary to know before one could understand the logic and rhetoric of God's ways and Word. It articulates the liturgy of worship in puzzling images that take a lifetime to comprehend. Its sacrifices signal both God's holiness and humanity's wretchedness. Like a storm whose power and beauty can be better seen and heard than told, Leviticus's sacrifices communicate God only in their performance: no verbal description of their meaning is capable of capturing their mysteries.

This is why the Letter to the Hebrews says the Torah is a shadow and its sacrifices are images of a heavenly pattern (Heb. 10:1; 9:23). It is why Pascal described its sacrifices as both pleasing to God and displeasing. They demonstrated a divine dialectic, a back-and-forth between human corruption and redemption. Just as we cannot know God without knowing our own wretchedness, we cannot catch a glimpse of the beauty of the Messiah's perfect sacrifice without knowing the sinfulness of the human beings it redeems.

The common denominator of the book of Leviticus is holiness—*qadosh* in Hebrew for "set apart." Its source and rationale are found in Leviticus 19, which is the secret to the inner mysteries of Scripture and redemption. The Messiah is the Son set apart, whose life and death set a people apart. The full meaning of the Son's holiness and therefore the mystery that is God the Father are seen in shadows here, the back of God's glory (Exod. 33:23).

We cannot see God's glory full-on because it would blind and kill us. But just as the tabernacle enforced a graduated and protected approach to the divine presence—through the outer court before the Holy Place and then the Holy of Holies—so too the sacrifices took sinners by steps into God's presence.

Sacrifices were usually of animals. While the priests sought to minimize the animal's pain by slitting its throat with a near-razor-sharp knife and causing unconsciousness by rapid loss of blood, nothing short of this disturbing procedure could impress on ancients the life-and-death consequences of sin. Only this graphic experience of blood and death could prepare a people to understand that sin kills and that another life must be offered in exchange for the life that was taken. Of course the death of an animal does not make up for the tragedy caused by serious sin. But the ancients were taught nevertheless that forgiveness of sins has a cost. They were being prepared for the message that ultimate forgiveness requires an ultimate cost, the death of the perfect man, the Messiah.

Leviticus details what is needed for a variety of sacrifices and offerings. There are many because the dimensions of atonement are many. Just as no single picture in an anatomy textbook can capture the complexity of a living organism, so too no one sacrificial offering could communicate all that is foreshadowed of the atonement on Calvary. Burnt offerings suggested our need to offer our whole selves to God; grain offerings expressed praise to God; peace offerings communicated gratitude; sin offerings provided cleansing of impurity caused by sin; and guilt offerings removed the guilt after unintentional sin.

Sacrifices provided worshipers a sense of spiritual connectedness. They understood that this costly act (either in kind or money) opened a line of communication with God. Rising smoke told them their prayers and offerings were going to God, so that despite their sin they could come near to the holy God. The Hebrew word for sacrifice, *korban*, means "to come near."

Moderns often dismiss Hebrew sacrifices as pagan. But biblical sacrifices were vastly different from those of pagans. Unlike pagan temples, the Holy of Holies contained no image of the deity. And while Mesopotamian religion was about the care and feeding of the gods, Hebrew sacrifices were on the outer altar in the open courtyard, removed from God's resting place in the inner sanctum. The bread of the presence was eaten by the priests, not their God. The Hebrew scriptures are clear that God does not consume the sacrifices, because he has no need for human food (see, for example, Ps. 50:9–13). Sacrifices instead represented the commitment of the worshiper to the God of Israel. The blood of animal sacrifices represented the life that his sin destroyed (Lev. 17:11).

Not all worshipers understood all of this, just as most Christians today understand only a portion of the Messiah and his redemption. Even the apostle Paul saw only dimly (1 Cor. 13:12). But representatives of Israel's twelve tribes understood most of this and more, and they led the little Church that was the reconstitution of Israel's tribes, the reconstituted olive tree (Rom. 11).

Preserving the Church and True Religion

Amazingly, true religion was preserved up through the time of David. God miraculously protected the Jewish Church three times a year when all the men went up to where the ark was, first Shiloh and then Jerusalem. Their enemies could have destroyed the people with their males absent, but they never did. In David's time there were still large numbers of Canaanites and other former inhabitants who were bitter enemies of Israel. The country was left defenseless each of these three times a year. Yet we never read of an enemy taking advantage of these opportunities. This was "no less than a continual miracle" in which God protected his plan of redemption.[8]

It is even more remarkable that this pattern persisted during the time of the judges. Even though the land was often overrun by idolatry, the true Church never went extinct. God never permitted true worship to be wiped out. The tabernacle stood throughout this tumultuous period. The ark was preserved, as were the Book of the Law and the priesthood. Whenever it looked like true religion was on its last legs, God sent revival and raised up a deliverer—an angel or prophet or other figure who brought redemption. This pattern persisted in Israel's struggles against the king of Mesopotamia (Judg. 3:8–9), the Moabites (3:12–30), Jabin the king of Canaan (Judg. 4), the Midianities (Judg. 6–7), Ammon (10:6–11:33), and the Philistines (Judg. 13:1; 1 Sam. 7:3–14).

All of Israel's deliverers during the time of the Judges were types of the coming Messiah, especially Barak, Jephthah, Gideon, and Samson.

Appearances of the Messiah

The Bible is full of mysteries that are impossible to systematize. One of these is the preincarnation incarnations of the Messiah. These are the times when the Messiah took on human form centuries before the Word became flesh in Jesus of Nazareth (John 1:14).

The most stunning of these appearances was to Moses, who was himself a type of the Messiah. Scripture tells us that Moses regularly met with YHWH in a tent outside Israel's camp in the wilderness (Exod. 33:7–11). There YHWH spoke to Moses "face to face" (33:11) and "mouth to mouth" (Num. 12:8), not in riddles but in "the form of YHWH" (12:8). Since Jesus said that when the disciples saw

---

8. Edwards, *HWR*, 195.

him they saw the Father (John 14:9), and that no one has seen the Father (6:46), the form of YHWH must have been the Messiah himself.

Intriguingly, this divine appearance was twofold. It came verbally or spiritually when the Messiah *told* Moses the meaning of his name, which was his character: "I will proclaim before you my name YHWH. I will be gracious to whom I will be gracious, and have compassion to whom I will be compassionate. . . . [I am] YHWH, YHWH, a God merciful and gracious, slow to anger, and abundant in goodness and truth" (Exod. 33:19; 34:6). He would show steadfast love to thousands, forgiving their iniquities and sins, but he would not clear the guilty (34:7).

After this conceptual revelation of his character, Scripture says YHWH showed Moses something of himself externally. Moses had asked to see his glory, and YHWH said he would put Moses in a cleft of a rock as that glory passed by. YHWH would cover Moses with his hand and Moses would see only his "back." Not his face. "For no one can see me and live" (Exod. 33:20).

This appearance of the back of his glory was the back of a radiant human "form." The Hebrew word can also be translated "image" or "likeness." This was probably the same dazzling human form that Jesus showed at his transfiguration and after his resurrection.

The Messiah also appeared to the seventy elders on Sinai. They were with Moses and Aaron and Aaron's sons Nadab and Abihu. Torah tells us "they saw the God of Israel . . . and ate and drank" in his presence (Exod. 24:10–11).

We saw earlier that the Messiah appeared to Joshua in his human nature as the "commander of the army of YHWH" (Josh. 5:13–15). Surprisingly, he told Joshua that he was neither for his band nor their enemies but for YHWH's cause. He allowed Joshua to worship him and ordered him to take off his sandals, "for the place where you are standing is holy" (5:15).

Messiah then appeared both to Gideon and to Manoah (Judg. 6:11, 14; 13:17–22). In both instances an angel of the Lord appears, and these Israelites say they "have seen God" (Judg. 13:22). As I argued in an earlier chapter, when God appears in visible form in the Old Testament, it is the Mediator, the Messiah. In his appearance to Manoah, "the angel went up in the flame from the altar" where a young goat had been offered in sacrifice (Judg. 13:20). For Edwards, this suggested the Messiah's incarnation and death: "For he appeared in an [sic] human form . . . and . . . intimat[ed] . . . the great sacrifice that must be offered up to God for a sweet savor in the fire of his wrath, as that kid was burned and ascended up in that flame."[9]

9. Edwards, *HWR*, 198.

Early Prophets

This was the beginning of the long history of the schools of the prophets. There had been occasional moments of prophecy in the times before this, but after Moses a spirit of prophecy descended on Israel and continued off and on until Malachi, after whom it ceased until the arrival of the Messiah at Bethlehem. The principal role of the prophets was to keep reminding Israel of a coming Messiah who would bring redemption. In hindsight it became clear, as Peter and other apostles preached centuries later, that the prophets were given words from "the spirit of the Messiah" that pointed to his "sufferings and subsequent glories" (1 Pet. 1:10–11).

The spirit of prophecy descended after Moses, first on Joshua and then on the judges in varying degrees. But this period of prophecy ended some time before Samuel, for when he was a young man "the word of YHWH was rare. . . . There was no vision bursting forth" (1 Sam. 3:1).

With Samuel began a string of prophets that stretched for centuries to Malachi. God raised up Nathan, Gad, Iddo, Heman, and Asaph. Under Rehoboam and Jeroboam there were Shemaiah and Ahijah. Under King Asa of Judah there were Elijah, Micaiah, and Elisha. Under Joash and Amaziah of Judah, Jonah, Amos, and Hosea prophesied. Then in the reign of Uzziah God raised up Isaiah and Micah. In the reigns of Hezekiah, Josiah, and their successors, the Spirit used Joel, Nahum, and Jeremiah. During captivity in Babylon, Ezekiel and Daniel prophesied, and after captivity there were Zechariah, Haggai, and Malachi.

After the first few prophets, schools emerged. Young men were trained under a great prophet, who taught them divine things and the practice of holiness. The students were called "sons of the prophets." Samuel might have been the first master of such a school. When Saul sent messengers to look for David, they came upon a group of prophets prophesying and Samuel standing over them as their "head" (1 Sam. 19:20).

Elijah and Elisha were also masters of schools of prophets. The "sons of the prophets" bowed to the ground before Elisha when they saw that the spirit of Elijah rested on him (2 Kings 2:15). Elisha cared for the student prophets in his school, performing miracles to feed them and building a bigger house when they outgrew a smaller one (2 Kings 4:38–44; 6:1–7). There were prophet schools in Bethel, Jericho, Gilgal, and Jerusalem. Under wicked King Ahab there were so many prophets that Obadiah hid one hundred of them in two caves (1 Kings 18:4).

Apparently God's usual way of appointing a prophet for the nation and its kings was to raise up a prophet from one of these schools. For when God called

Amos, Amos protested that he wasn't a student at one of these schools but was only a herdsman (Amos 7:14).

In any event, the early Church repeatedly proclaimed that, whether these prophets knew it or not, they were being led by the Spirit to bear witness to the coming Messiah. In his second speech in Jerusalem, Peter testified that "all the prophets from Samuel and after him proclaimed these days" of the Messiah's appearance (Acts 3:24). God "foretold through the mouth of all the prophets that his Messiah would suffer" (3:18). Later, in Cornelius's house in Caesarea, Peter preached that "all the prophets bear witness" to the Messiah and that forgiveness comes to all who trust in his name (10:43).

So this time of the First Testament was not the time of final redemption that came with full light in the early Church. In comparison, this was a time of night. But the prophets radiated their own light of prophecy, a reflected light that came from the sun of righteousness in the Messiah. They were like the stars and moon that shine their own reflected light on a clear night. They were "searching diligently" for when and in what manner the grace of redemption would come (1 Pet. 1:10). The Spirit of the Messiah was moving them to write, wittingly or not, of his passion and resurrection (1:11). This is why we are told that the Church of the Redeemer is built on the foundation of the apostles and the prophets, with the Messiah himself being the chief cornerstone (Eph. 2:20). The prophets foretold the Messiah and his redemption, and the apostles preached them.

Select Bibliography

Byron, John. "Paul, Jesus and the Rolling Stone." *Biblical Archaeology Review* (September/October 2015): 28, 66.

Edwards, Jonathan. *A History of the Work of Redemption.* Edited by John F. Wilson. Vol. 9 in *The Works of Jonathan Edwards.* New Haven: Yale University Press, 1989.

Enns, Peter. "The 'Moveable Well' in 1 Corinthians 10:4." *Bulletin for Biblical Research* 6 (1996): 23–38.

McClymond, Michael, and Gerald McDermott. "Providence and History." In *The Theology of Jonathan Edwards,* 224–43. New York: Oxford University Press, 2012.

Pseudo-Philo. *The Biblical Antiquities of Philo.* Translated by M. R. James. London: SPCK, 1917. Internet Sacred Texts Archive. https://www.sacred-texts.com/bib/bap/index.htm. See particularly 10.7.

7

David to the Captivity

We have been tracking the development of redemption by the Messiah through the Old Testament period, from the creation to the beginning of Israel's monarchy. Now we will see that God's work of redemption after the establishment of the monarchy was almost entirely related to David, Israel's greatest king and the Messiah's progenitor. We will trace David's call and anointing, God's repeated acts to protect him from danger and death, the Church's worship that was renewed and transformed by his psalms, God's choice of Jerusalem through David as the holy city, his covenant of grace with David and his seed, the fulfillment of the land promise under David, God's preservation of his visible people in the line of David's descendants, the glory of the Jewish Church under David's son Solomon, and its decline after Solomon. We will conclude the chapter by seeing the spectacular prophecies of the Messiah in a new development of prophecy, whole books of revelation by major and minor prophets.

Anointing of the King

Until this point we have been following the history of a *people* from whom the Messiah would come. Now God zeroes in on a *person* from whom the Messiah would come. Just as God improbably picked this people instead of others whom we might think more worthy, so God chose David out of thousands of men who seemed to have more going for them. His father was a mere sheep-breeder in a little village, and he was the youngest of eight sons, the one whom his father thought least likely to be chosen by Samuel.

This unlikely candidate for the most distinguished throne in world history was often identified with the Messiah (2 Sam. 23:1; Ezek. 37:24–25). Perhaps that is unsurprising since his family would give birth to the Messiah, and the Messiah was said to occupy David's throne forever. In this way God made the kingdom of the Messiah a visible phenomenon that would change world history. The Messiah would change hearts in ways *in*visible to the outside world, but those men and women would act *visibly* in ways that would eventually redirect the world's fortunes. The yeast was small and hidden for much of the time but would leaven big loaves over the course of history. And the huge loaf of the Messiah's kingdom would last forever.

Although the kingdom was from this point on associated with David's Jewish family, there were always Gentiles who attached themselves to it. Many of David's lieutenants were from Gentile tribes and lands but joined Israel by profession and marriage. After the Messiah came in the flesh and told his apostles to make disciples of all the Gentile nations, his Church slowly filled with Gentiles, by the hundreds at first and then the thousands and millions. But even when Gentiles reached a majority, they were still "wild olive shoots" grafted onto the root of the olive tree, Israel (Rom. 11:17). They were still associate members of "the commonwealth of Israel" (Eph. 2:12).

David was the greatest personal type of the Messiah in all the Old Testament. As we have already seen, there were personal, institutional, and providential types. Sacrifices were the greatest institutional types, the exodus from Egypt the greatest providential type, and David the greatest personal type of the Messiah. Just as David was called the "anointed one" or Messiah, so too the Messiah was often referred to as David. Two prophecies of the Messiah in Ezekiel, for example, do this. Centuries after the death of David, Ezekiel speaks of a future "David" who will be one shepherd for Israel and king over God's people (Ezek. 34:23–24; 37:24).

David's anointing is said in the Scripture to be the anointing of the Messiah himself. Long after David's death, the psalmist writes that with holy oil God anointed David and with his arm God *will* strengthen him (Ps. 89:21). The intent of the passage appears to be that David will act in or through the Messiah when he comes. Hence the Messiah is represented as the new King David.

The New Testament authors reiterate this identification of David with the Messiah by repeatedly saying that he would rule from David's throne. At the annunciation the angel told young Mary that God would give to Jesus the throne of David (Luke 1:32). In his Pentecost sermon Peter declared that God had sworn that he would place one of David's descendants on his throne (Acts 2:30).

This helps explain why God told Jeremiah that he would raise up the "branch of righteousness"—the Messiah—to execute judgment and righteousness in the land (Jer. 23:5). He would do this *for* David. So the Messiah's kingdom was an extension of David's kingdom.

God's choice of David showed the grace of the Messiah. His lifting a lowly shepherd from an undistinguished family was typical of the way he acted in all of history. David was short and Saul was tall, but God chose David. Israel was a little people with a checkered history, but God fixed his love on this little people in a tiny land, just as Jesus's band was his "little flock" (Luke 12:32). The Messiah was without outward beauty or majesty (Isa. 53:2), and his people were generally without power or nobility (1 Cor. 1:26), but God delights in choosing what seems foolish to the world in order to shame the so-called wise ones (1:27). In God's kingdom, the last in the world are often first, and the esteemed of the day are often last in the only kingdom that matters (Matt. 20:16).

So just as God often protected his less powerful people from their more powerful enemies, God repeatedly saved David—the premier personal type of the Messiah—from danger and death. God rescued David from a lion and bear as the teenager protected his sheep from the beasts' depredations, just as the Messiah rescues his lambs from the devil, who prowls around like a roaring lion to devour souls (1 Pet. 5:8). Goliath could have ripped David apart piece by piece and fed him to the birds, but God gave David a strategy to stun the giant and cut off his head—just as the Messiah "slew the spiritual Goliath with his weapon, the cross," and delivered his lambs.[1]

Time and again God saved David from Saul. Saul tried to get David killed by the Philistines when David took up the king's offer of his daughter at the price of one hundred enemy foreskins, but David won the foreskins without injury. Twice Saul, who was bigger and probably stronger than David, threw a javelin at David but missed. Saul commanded his son Jonathan and his servants to kill David, but God inclined Jonathan's heart to love David as his own soul and protect his friend from his own father—this despite the fact that Jonathan was in line for his father's throne and knew his friend David would probably take it instead. Saul sent messengers to kill David at his home with Michal, and then to Naioth at Ramah, where David was staying, but Saul was thwarted both times. Michal let David out through a window, and God's Spirit threw both Saul's messengers and Saul himself into a spirit of ecstasy. When Saul was pursuing David in the wilderness mountains at Maon and then in a cave at Engedi, God again delivered David each time. At Engedi

---

1. Edwards, *HWR*, 206.

God delivered Saul into David's hands, but David refused to kill Saul, snipping off his tassels instead. When the people of Keilah were about to surrender David to Saul even though David had previously saved the city from the Philistines, God allowed David to slip out of their hands. Twice David lived among the Philistines in safety even though the Philistines had suffered from his prowess in the past. Both times God moved Achish the Philistine king to befriend David and protect him.

In all of these perilous circumstances God preserved the precious seed that would birth the Messiah by foiling the best plans of his enemies and turning some of their hearts to befriend and protect him.

Enlargement of the Biblical Canon

It was largely through David that one of the most significant parts of the Bible was added, the Psalms. This book became the principal worship book for the Jewish and Christian Churches. It has been the mainstay of both public liturgy and private devotion for billions of Jews and Christians. It is no wonder that David was the author of so many psalms, for he had a spirit of prophecy. Peter called him a prophet at Pentecost (Acts 2:29–30), and the Spirit came on him even before he was a king, for many of his psalms were penned in the years of his troubles before he rose to the throne. When Samuel anointed David with oil for the kingship, the oil seems to have been both a type of the Holy Spirit and its antitype (fulfillment), for the Scripture says that the Spirit of YHWH came on David from that day forward, apparently with even more power than before the anointing (1 Sam. 16:13).

The psalms are thoroughly christological, which means messianic. For this reason they are quoted by the New Testament authors more than any other book of the Old Testament. David was inspired by the Spirit to write psalms that the early Church came to recognize were messianic at one level, even if David was not aware of that at the time. Their power has come from both these messianic undertones and the love for YHWH, which sweetens their words. Indeed, Scripture calls David "the sweet psalmist of Israel" (2 Sam. 23:1).

Of course David was not the only author of the psalms. Asaph, Heman, and Ethan are named (Pss. 50, 80, 88), and we know there were others who are unnamed. But the psalms generally represent a marked "increase of gospel light" in the history of God's work of redemption.[2] Whereas before this there were occasional prophecies of the Messiah that we have noted in this book, the psalms

---

2. Edwards uses this phrase in *HWR*, 144, 146. But the passage about the Psalms is in *HWR*, 209–11.

describe the Messiah and his work in profusion. The Spirit speaks through the psalms about the Messiah's incarnation, life, death, resurrection, ascension, satisfaction, and intercession—in other words, his work as prophet, priest, and king.

They also speak to the glory the Messiah gives to believers in this life and the one to come, his union with the Church and her resulting happiness, the calling of the Gentiles, the future glory of the Church at the end of the ages (even if accompanied by great persecution), and the Messiah's presidency at the final judgment.[3] All these and more are portrayed by these magnificent songs.

It seems clear that the Psalms were given by God to the Church for the purpose of praising God in public worship. The book has been used this way by Jews for three thousand years and by Christians in most churches through all of their history. Their musical intentions are suggested by the inscriptions of many to "the chief musician," and we have evidence that they were used this way after David's death. The Chronicler tells us that Hezekiah and his officials commanded the Levites to sing praises to YHWH with the words of David and Asaph (2 Chron. 29:30). The early Church told itself to use psalms for singing with the heart to God (Eph. 5:19; Col. 3:16). The people of God had always used song for praise to God, such as at the Red Sea with Moses's song (Deut. 32) and after Barak and Deborah's victory, but now with the Psalms God for the first time gave his people a *book* of songs for regular praise and joy.

Samuel's Role

We should not be surprised that David is so closely associated with the Messiah, since Samuel was a "prophet" and it was through Samuel that most of David's history came to us—at least in 1 and 2 Samuel. In his second sermon in Jerusalem Peter proclaimed that Samuel was a prophet who with other prophets proclaimed the days of the Messiah (Acts 3:24). So according to Peter, Samuel's records of David proclaimed the Messiah. First Chronicles tells us that all the history of David—"from first to last"—is written in "the records of the seer Samuel, and the records of Nathan the prophet, and Gad the seer" (1 Chron. 29:29). So there were contemporary records of these events, and Samuel played a role in them. According to the New Testament, it was Samuel who primarily saw the messianic significance of David and his reign. So even if the so-called Deuteronomic history (Deuteronomy, Joshua, Judges, 1–2 Samuel, 1–2 Kings) was given final shape

---

3. Edwards, *HWR*, 210–11.

after the exile, Samuel "the prophet," who foresaw the Messiah and his kingdom, played a chief role in giving us this history and its significance.

Jerusalem

Through David and his son Solomon we can see the fullest extent of the Jewish kingdom, which was an earthly vision or type of the messianic kingdom. One of its most visible characteristics is God's choice of Jerusalem as the center of this kingdom.

Setting Jerusalem as the center for orthodox worship was a new development in the history of redemption. Before this, the center of worship moved from place to place with the ark and the tabernacle. Then the worship center was Shiloh, and finally Jerusalem. Here, God said, was the place where he had told his people in the wilderness he would place his name (Deut. 12:5). To David, who was the first to conquer the city for God's people, YHWH showed the place in Jerusalem for the temple, the threshing floor of Araunah the Jebusite (2 Sam. 24:18–21). This is why Jerusalem was called "the holy city" (Isa. 52:1; Dan. 9:16, 20, 24; Matt. 4:5; 27:53; Rev. 11:2, 8; 21:10): God put his name there and ordered that worship be centered there. Even in New Testament times it was thought to be the center of both the existing world and the one to come. Jesus said that God still dwelled in the temple, even if its leadership was corrupt (Matt. 23:21). God chose Jerusalem to be the place of the first gathering of the Church after the resurrection (Acts 1:12–26; 2:42–47).[4] The resurrected Jesus told the apostles to send the gospel from Mount Olivet, overlooking Jerusalem, just as he sent the Law from Mount Sinai (Acts 1:8, 12). Not surprisingly, the ancient churches told their members to face east when they prayed because the Messiah would return to Jerusalem from the east. The Lamb in the future will return to Mount Zion (Rev. 14:1), the renewed earth will have its center in Jerusalem, and the New Jerusalem's twelve gates will be inscribed with the names of the twelve tribes of the sons of Israel (21:2, 12).

The Covenant of Grace

Jerusalem was connected to the messianic covenant that God made with David, a covenant characterized by grace. Jerusalem was David's city and the location

---

4. Edwards, *HWR*, 213.

of the house David wanted to build for God. God told David that he had taken him from following sheep to make him a prince over Israel. Rather than David building a house for YHWH, the LORD would make a house for David. Through David's seed, YHWH continued, David would be given a kingdom and throne that would last forever (2 Sam. 7:4–17). This is grace—not what David would do for God, but what God would do for David. It was a kingdom of grace that would pass down from David to his seed the Messiah and all those who received the Messiah throughout the succeeding ages. Isaiah fleshed out the *gracious* meaning of this covenant when he prophesied that by it YHWH was inviting every thirsty soul and everyone with no money to come and buy and eat and drink, for the wine and milk would be free (Isa. 55:1). The food was rich and satisfying (55:2). This was an invitation to the same "everlasting covenant" YHWH had made with David (55:3). Those who accepted could enjoy the same "love and faithfulness" YHWH had showered on David. To be more precise, they were being invited to participate in that same covenant of grace, David's covenant.

The covenant with David was actually the "fifth . . . establishment of the covenant of grace."[5] The first four were with Adam, Noah, the patriarchs, and Moses. In every instance God was showing his love to the unlovely. He was bestowing favor on those who did not deserve it. As David exclaimed, "Who am I, O Lord YHWH, and what is my house, that you have brought me to this point?" (2 Sam. 7:18). There were stipulations of course: the recipients of grace had to humble themselves by confessing and repenting their sins, and they were called to live in a way worthy of their gracious calling (Eph. 4:1; Phil. 1:27; Col. 1:10). But all stumbled. David committed both adultery and murder. Paul helped murder disciples of the Messiah. So the covenant of grace was God's commitment to sinners—humble and seeking sinners, but sinners nonetheless. David the sinner was given a kingdom and throne that would continue forever through his seed the Messiah. Its inner character was of grace, its members sinners who had been freed by God's love to live in his ways.

The Land

It was under David that the fullest extent of the land promise was realized. Much of the land was appropriated by Joshua, but not all, not by any means. Even after his conquests many of the old inhabitants were left unsubdued. Jebusites, Philistines,

5. Edwards, *HWR*, 215.

and Canaanites remained in control of portions of the land, particularly those parts of the land that belonged to the tribes of Judah and Ephraim. It was only by David and Solomon that all the seven nations of Canaan and the Philistines were subdued (1 Chron. 18:1; 1 Kings 9:20–22).

God originally promised to Israel all the lands "from the brook of Egypt" (probably Wadi El-Arish in Sinai) to the Euphrates (Gen. 15:18). The promise varied in its geographical reference points: from the Red Sea and Sinai desert to the Euphrates (Exod. 23:31), from the Mediterranean to the Euphrates (Deut. 11:24), and from the wilderness east of the Jordan to the Euphrates and from the land of the Hittites (near Hebron and west of the Dead Sea) to the Mediterranean (Josh. 1:3–4). These vast spaces were never possessed until David and Solomon, when their conquests included the lands of Moab and Ammon, the Amalekites, Edomites, and Syrians. In most of these lands David put garrisons in their cities (2 Sam. 8), and Solomon ruled over them (1 Kings 4:24; Ezra 4:20). So Joshua, who was a type of the Messiah, began the conquest of the lands of promise but left it to the much greater type, David, to complete it. In this David was typical of his seed the Messiah, who shall have dominion from sea to sea (Ps. 72:8).

Jewish Worship

Another way in which David is central to the history of redemption is the manner in which he transformed Israel's worship. This is important for Christians because of the influence of Israel's worship on the early Church and later Christian worship.

Israel's worship was not finalized by Moses. Under David new changes were made. For example, new responsibilities were given to Levites. Under Moses the Levites had duties to carry the tabernacle and its vessels (Num. 3–4), but in the Davidic dispensation Levites were told to cease and desist from those tasks (1 Chron. 23:26). Now they were given a variety of tasks in the "house of YHWH," with four thousand assigned to lead musical worship. Most of Israel's worship under Moses in the traveling tabernacle was conducted in silence, with the exception of trumpets at sacrificial offerings on feast days and at the beginning of each month (Num. 10:10). But when David brought the ark to Mount Zion in Jerusalem and put it under a tent, he appointed Levite choirs and orchestras to lead musical worship regularly (1 Chron. 23:5, 30; 25:1–31).

Under David, Levites were given additional responsibilities as porters, treasurers, officers, and judges. These roles were continued after the Babylonian captivity and into New Testament times when we see Zacharias, father of John the

Baptist, serving as a priest in "the division of Abijah" (Luke 1:5). This was one of the twenty-four groups of priests with regular duties organized for the temple by David (1 Chron. 24). The musical and other duties for Levites were parts of a new pattern shown by God to David that Solomon followed when he organized worship at the first temple (28:11–12, 19). Whereas Moses was shown a pattern for tabernacle worship in the wilderness (Exod. 25:40), David was given a new pattern (1 Chron. 28:11–19), and Jesus was given a further pattern for worship under his high priesthood (Heb. 8–9). Neither David's nor Jesus's pattern for worship abolishes everything related to the previous worship; each adds to and builds upon what came before (Matt. 5:17–19). Worship under Jesus as high priest is the antitype to which the types of Mosaic and Davidic worship pointed. Just as every type is a "shadow" of its antitype, with both continuity and discontinuity between them, so worship of the Trinity now that the Messiah has been revealed is a glorious affair to which the lesser glories of the tabernacle and temple point; and by pointing, each enhances the later glory.

Miraculous Preservation

In the last chapter we saw God's miraculous protection of Israel over a long history of threats from her many enemies. Here we see that God's protection was even more particular in relation to the Messiah's legal ancestors. The interesting thing is that the crown of Israel over its ten northern tribes changed from one family to another over its troubled history, while the crown of Judah remained "in the same family . . . with very little interruption."[6] The kings of Judah were sometimes wicked—as in Rehoboam, Abijam, Jehoram, Ahaziah, Ahaz, Manasseh, and Amon—but this line had God's blessing on it because it contained the legal ancestors of the Messiah. God said he preserved this line because of the covenant promise he had made to David (1 Kings 15:4; 2 Chron. 21:7).

Another way of seeing this is to observe that the Messiah was descended from the line that passed down through the two tribes of Judah and Benjamin in the south, not the ten tribes of the north, who worshiped golden calves and were eventually lost to history after their conquest and exile to Assyria in 721 BC. This is why God exercised extreme care over the course of many generations to keep the crown of Judah in a direct line following David, a line that lasted as long as Israel was an independent kingdom. Not coincidentally, the true worship of God

6. Edwards, *HWR*, 223.

was kept up in this line, with the Messiah's legal ancestor always on the throne, except for Jehoahaz and Zedekiah. Jeroboam led the ten northern tribes to rebel against Rehoboam and his Davidic line in the last third of the tenth century BC.

So Jesus the Messiah was descended *legally*, if not *naturally*, from the Davidic kings, but "both legally and naturally" from David himself.[7] He was not naturally descended from the Davidic kings because Luke tells us that his descent was through David's son Nathan, who never became king (Luke 3:31). Luke mentions this most likely because God told Jeremiah that the line coming from David through Solomon and Jeconiah would never sit on the throne of David (Jer. 22:24–30). Some speculate that Jesus's mother, Mary, was descended from David through this Nathan, so Jesus came from David himself if not all the Davidic kings.

Yet Jesus was descended legally from Davidic kings because according to Matthew's genealogy Joseph, Jesus's legal father, was descended from Solomon and Rehoboam (Matt. 1:7, 16). It was customary in Jewish law for a boy to be a legal if not natural heir of a man whose fatherhood is recognized in special situations such as a man marrying his deceased brother's wife and adopting his brother's sons. Jesus was Joseph's lawful son because he was conceived while Mary was his legally engaged wife. Hence Jesus was the legal heir of David's crown as Joseph's firstborn son since Joseph was a descendant of Davidic kings and Mary descended from David himself (Acts 2:29–36).

The Glorious Religion

It was in this Davidic line under Solomon that the religion of Israel reached its greatest glory. The apex of glory was achieved just after the completion of Solomon's temple, which was the great type of three things: the human nature of the Messiah, the Christian Church, and heaven.

In another chapter I have compared the religion of Israel to the moon, which reflects the light of the sun, just as Israel contains and points to the blazing brightness of the Messiah's kingdom. And just as the moon waxes and wanes in glory, so too the religion of Israel gradually increased in glory from Abraham's time. By Solomon's time it was at full moon and about halfway between Abraham and the incarnation. The people of the combined kingdoms of Israel and Judah were as many as the grains of sand at the seashore (1 Kings 4:20), the kingdom was in the family that would produce the Messiah, Jerusalem was the chosen city, Israel

7. Edwards, *HWR*, 221.

was in full possession of the promised land, and its dominion was held in peace from the Nile to the Euphrates. All of its former enemies were submitted to it.

Jewish worship was settled in all of its established ordinances. The temple was the most beautiful and magnificent structure the world had seen. It pointed as a God-ordained type to the perfect humanity of Jesus, the fullness of the Church that would spring from his side, and the glory of heaven, where the Messiah reigns amid the adoration of saints and angels who behold the perfect sacrifice of the Lamb (Rev. 4–5).

At this apex of Israel's history its people enjoyed peace and plenty. Every man sat under his vine and fig tree, eating and drinking with happiness (1 Kings 4:20, 25). The nation was at its height of earthly prosperity: silver was as plentiful as stones, the land was "full of gold and precious stones, . . . foreign commodities . . . were brought by Solomon's ships" from all over the ancient Near East, and its king was thought to be the wisest of men, rivaling the greatest princes of history for insight and wealth.[8]

In all of this God was pointing to the fullness of redemption through the Messiah. Just as the temple was a type of three dimensions of the messianic kingdom, David and Solomon were shadows of the Messiah, who would reign one day in visible glory. David was a type of the Messiah in his humiliation, at war with his enemies. Solomon was a representation of the Messiah exalted and triumphant in his kingdom of peace. The rule of Solomon at his height was a type of the new heaven and earth during the eschaton, when nation shall not lift up sword against nation and men will learn war no more (Isa. 2:4).

Decline of the Kingdom

But things started going downhill fast, and it all started with Solomon's idolatry (1 Kings 11:1–8). After his death, the ten northern tribes revolted and withdrew from the house of David and its true worship of God in the temple at Jerusalem. Jeroboam, the new king over the northern tribes, set up the golden calves at Bethel and Dan. When Jeroboam went to war with Abijah king of Judah, a half million men of Israel fell in battle. This was a turning point in Israel's history from which she never recovered.

It was also the beginning of the end religiously. Whereas under Jeroboam Israel pretended to worship the true God with calves, under Ahab the worship of Baal

8. Edwards, *HWR*, 226–27.

was introduced. Now Israel adopted "gross idolatry, ... the direct worship of false gods" in place of the true God, YHWH the God of Israel.[9]

Even Judah was corrupted for a time when Jehoram married Athaliah, Ahab's daughter, and the worship of Baal was introduced in the south (2 Kings 8:16–24). God began to judge both Israel and Judah for their idolatries by leading the Aramaean king Hazael to destroy and capture Israel east of the Jordan. Judgment culminated with Tiglath-Pileser's conquest of northern regions and taking their people as captives to Assyria, and then Shalmaneser's conquest of Samaria and dragging many of the remaining Israelites to Assyria (2 Kings 15–17) toward the end of the eighth century BC. The king of Judah was carried captive to Babylon less than 150 years later, along with many of its leading citizens. Most never returned. Those who did became vassals of the kings of Persia and Greece and Rome, except for one hundred years of independence under the Maccabees (165–63 BC).

So after a period of shining glory for Israel under David and his most illustrious son, things went south and ended in shame and disgrace. Yet God used these worldly defeats and religious compromises to prepare the way for the incarnation of the Messiah. The twinkling stars gave way to the dawn of glory in the sun. Colonization by Greece and then Rome heightened Jewish yearning for the Messiah. Corruption by the temple establishment inspired hunger for spiritual purity. Jews came to realize that God often works through a remnant rather than a majority. Just as God had to cull Gideon's army down to three hundred in order to separate those who trusted in themselves from those who looked to God, Jews hungering for the Messiah came to realize that God might work through a "little flock" that would reconstitute the twelve tribes (Luke 12:32). It is no wonder that large numbers of Jewish priests accepted Jesus as the Messiah and that within the first decades after the resurrection more than twenty thousand Jews in Jerusalem alone were following Jesus (Acts 6:7; 21:20),[10] not to mention tens of thousands more Messianic Jews in the diaspora across the Mediterranean world.

The Preservation of Judah

Despite Judah's own intermittent lapses into idolatry, the royal line returned to true worship repeatedly. And God preserved this southern tribe against

9. Edwards, HWR, 229.
10. James and the brothers told Paul in Acts 21:20 that there were *myriades* (plural of *myriad*) of Jews zealous for the Law who followed Jesus, and one *myriad* is ten thousand. So a minimum of twenty thousand Jewish Jesus-followers in Jerusalem alone.

repeated threats of annihilation. I say "this tribe" because it soon absorbed the tribe of Benjamin, since the latter was so small and the former so large. God preserved this amalgam known as "Judah" ever since because it was in this tribe that the visible Church of the Messiah was principally located after the time of Solomon. Benjamin was annexed by it just as the original Benjamin was taken under Judah's wing when Joseph's brothers went to Egypt to buy grain (Gen. 43). This is why God told Solomon, after the latter's idolatry, that he would tear away the kingdom from him and give it to his servant but leave "one tribe" for his son (1 Kings 11:11–13). It is also why all but the tribe of Judah were sent into exile to Assyria (2 Kings 17:18). And, significantly, the future of the Jewish people was contained in this one tribe, for the name "Jew" comes from the name of this tribe. The people over whom the Messiah's legal ancestors reigned and who were of the house of David were the people of the tribe of Judah.

This Messianic tribe was remarkably preserved by God's providence time and time again. When Shishak king of Egypt came to fight Rehoboam with an army "without number" (2 Chron. 12:3), the king and his princes humbled themselves before YHWH, apparently confessing their idolatries and God's just judgment. Shishak plundered Jerusalem but did not destroy the kingdom. YHWH's wrath was turned away (2 Chron. 12:12).

When Jeroboam brought eight hundred thousand soldiers against forces half that size from Abijah, Rehoboam's son, Abijah stood up on Mount Zemaraim and proclaimed to the army of Jeroboam that they were fighting against the kingship that YHWH had given to David and his sons. The army of Judah prevailed "because they trusted in YHWH, the God of their fathers" (2 Chron. 13:18). One half million men from the northern tribes perished that day. As we noted above, Israel never recovered from that devastating defeat.

When Zerah the Ethiopian came with a million men against Asa, Abijah's son Asa cried out to YHWH. His army was half the size of the Ethiopian host, but YHWH defeated the Ethiopians before Asa and the army of Judah (2 Chron. 14:12). When Jehoshaphat faced the combined forces of Moab, Ammon, and Mount Seir, Judah prevailed by listening to the Levite prophet who told them to "stand still and see the salvation of YHWH" (20:17). They sang praises. On the following day YHWH turned the armies of Ammon and Moab against those of Mount Seir, and they destroyed one another. None escaped (20:23–24).

In Ahaz's time, at the end of the eighth century BC and just before the ten northern tribes would be carried off to Assyria in 721, once again Judah was spared.

Ahaz was a wicked king over Judah, yet God defended him against the predations of Rezin king of Syria and Pekah the king of Israel (2 Kings 16:5).

Ahaz's son Hezekiah was miraculously delivered from Assyrian conquest at the very end of the eighth century, perhaps in 701 BC. Sennacherib the Assyrian king was besieging Jerusalem and had sent his messenger the Rabshakeh to insult and intimidate the people of Judah. "Don't think YHWH will deliver you. None of the gods of the other lands we have conquered delivered them," bellowed the Rabshakeh in Hebrew (2 Kings 18:32–33). "You will be forced to eat your own dung and drink your own urine" (v. 27). The people of Jerusalem trembled like lambs before a growling lion. Sennacherib's army had already taken the fenced cities of Judah and the ten tribes.

But Isaiah the prophet told Hezekiah not to worry, that YHWH had heard the words with which the messenger of Assyria had insulted him, and that YHWH would cause the Assyrian king's army to return to their land, where the king would fall by the sword (2 Kings 18:6–7).

And so it was. An angel of YHWH struck down 185,000 soldiers in one night, perhaps from a sudden plague. When the camp was filled with dead bodies the next morning, the Assyrian army departed. When the king was worshiping in the temple of his god back in Nineveh some time later, his own sons murdered him (2 Kings 19:35–37).

As the Church experienced innumerable times in this and later times, God's people were revived after being on the verge of destruction. The Body of the Messiah always has a secret life that sends roots down deep and invisibly and which eventually bear fruit upward.

The Prophets

One last feature of this Davidic age before the captivity of Judah in Babylon was the rise of the major and minor prophets. Their chief calling was to witness to the coming Messiah, just as the prophets before them had done. Before King Uzziah (ca. 783–742 BC), as we have seen, God raised up prophets like Samuel whose principal calling was to write histories, such as Nathan, Gad, Ahijah, Iddo, Shemaiah, and Jehu (1 Chron. 29:29; 2 Chron. 9:29; 12:15; 20:34; 1 Kings 16:1, 7). Even the major prophet Isaiah wrote history (2 Chron. 26:22).

But then with the rise of Uzziah God raised up a host of prophets to write whole books of prophecy. Hosea, for example, prophesied in the days of Uzziah, Jothan,

Ahaz, and Hezekiah—kings of Judah—and also under Jeroboam in Israel. Isaiah, Amos, Jonah, Micah, and Nahum also prophesied in these times.

All these prophets were forerunners of the greatest prophet, the Messiah. Their main business was to foreshadow him and teach about him and his kingdom. Their purpose was to give testimony to Jesus the Messiah, the great redeemer to come. This is why the angel told John that the "testimony [about] Jesus is the spirit of prophecy" (Rev. 19:10). Yet in another sense the spirit of prophecy was the spirit *of* Jesus, for it was his Spirit who spoke through the prophets: "Concerning this salvation the prophets who prophesied sought and inquired diligently about the grace that was to be yours, inquiring what person and time the Spirit *of Messiah* in them was predicting concerning the sufferings for the Messiah and the later glories" (1 Pet. 1:10–11). So the Messiah himself was moving the prophets to speak and write in all that we have of their words in the Scriptures. And their purpose, we are told, was to show us both his sufferings and the glories of his kingdom.

This was especially true of Isaiah, who was a favorite of the early Church. When the newly converted Augustine asked Ambrose what to read in preparation for baptism, Ambrose commended Isaiah. For Edwards, Isaiah "seems to teach the glorious doctrines of the gospel almost as plainly as the apostles did."[11] Paul praises Isaiah's "boldness" in teaching the good news of salvation being offered to the Gentiles (Rom. 10:20–21). The New Testament frequently quotes Isaiah 53 because of that chapter's extensive and detailed exposition of the nature and purpose of the Messiah's suffering (Matt. 8:14–17; John 12:37–41; Luke 22:35–38; 1 Pet. 2:19–25; Acts 8:26–35; Rom. 10:11–21). This is why Isaiah has often been called "the evangelical prophet."[12] He not only was the most careful to delineate the Messiah's suffering, but he also wrote expansively about the unspeakable blessings that the Messiah and his kingdom would bring. Perhaps the messianic fullness of this book of prophecy is due to the appearance that the Messiah made to the prophet in his human nature: "In the year of King Uzziah's death, I see the Lord sitting on a throne, high and lifted up, and the hem [of his robe] is filling the temple" (Isa. 6:1).

Among the things that the prophets saw were suffering and further exile in Babylon. In the next chapter I will discuss this exile and its impact on expectation for the messianic kingdom. We will also look at the rise of other world religions in this period such as Buddhism and the Chinese religions.

11. Edwards, *HWR*, 239.
12. Edwards, *HWR*, 239.

Select Bibliography

Augustine. *Confessions*. Translated by Henry Chadwick. New York: Oxford University Press, 1991.

Edwards, Jonathan. *A History of the Work of Redemption*. Edited by John F. Wilson. Vol. 9 in *The Works of Jonathan Edwards*. New Haven: Yale University Press, 1989.

Griffith, Sidney. *The Church in the Shadow of the Mosque: Christians and Muslims in the World of Islam*. Princeton: Princeton University Press, 2008.

McClymond, Michael, and Gerald McDermott. "Providence and History." In *The Theology of Jonathan Edwards*, 224–43. New York: Oxford University Press, 2012.

8

From the Captivity to the Messiah

This chapter covers a long period in which one of the kingdom's greatest mysteries is displayed. In these six hundred years we see that God used great tragedy to prepare for redemption. This was a period of massive bloodshed and recurring revolution. But through all these revolutions God was preparing the ground for the arrival of his Messiah, the King of Kings.

The Age of Revolutions

God intimated the coming of these wars and revolutions to his prophet Jeremiah. At the beginning of the sixth century BC God told Jeremiah that he was sending his "cup of the wine of wrath" (Jer. 25:15) to the nations of Jeremiah's world. First it would come to "Jerusalem and the towns of Judah" (25:18), then to Egypt, then to the Philistines, and eventually to all the nations that trekked across the Holy Land to seek their ends. "One after another," all "the kingdoms of the world that are on the face of the earth" (v. 26 NRSV) would drink the cup. They all would suffer revolution and conquest.

And suffer they did. First it was Judah's turn to be conquered by Babylon in 586 BC, its leading inhabitants dragged into captivity in Babylon. Then it was Babylon that was conquered by Cyrus II ("the Great") in 539 BC to create the Persian Empire—even bigger than Babylon's—stretching from Asia Minor in the west all the way to India. Two centuries later (330 BC) Alexander the Great overthrew the Persian king Darius in his lightning-fast conquest of greater territory than the Persians had held (334–329 BC). After Alexander's death at the age of thirty-two in 323, four of his generals divided his enormous empire; two of the generals—the Egyptian Ptolemy I Soter and the Greek Seleucus I Nicator—and their successors ruled empires that controlled Jewish Israel for much of the next two centuries. Finally it was Rome's turn. Between 200 BC and AD 14, Rome conquered Western Europe and Greece, the Balkans, the Middle East, and North Africa. In 63 BC the Roman general Pompey began the long Roman occupation of Israel.

Scholars debate the dates of Daniel's prophecies, but the fact remains that they track both the progress of these revolutions and their outcome in the incarnation of the Messiah. We see in chapter 2 of Daniel's prophecy four kingdoms represented by gold, silver, bronze, and iron. The first is Babylon and the last is Rome. Yet Rome's kingdom is said to be divided (as it came to be between its Eastern and Western realms) and would one day be broken in pieces before a kingdom set up by the "God of heaven" (Dan. 2:44), which we now know was the kingdom of the Messiah Jesus. The same succession of empires is prophesied in Daniel's vision of the four beasts in chapter 7, and Persia and Greece are depicted in Daniel's vision of the ram and goat in chapter 8. Chapter 11 sketches both Alexander's conquest of the Persians and the Seleucid persecution of the Jews in Israel.

The biblical prophets provided intriguing hints that these three great revolutions would follow the Babylonian captivity and that they would pave the way for the coming of the Messiah's kingdom. Ezekiel, who was a Jewish priest during the Babylonian captivity, predicted three vast "overturnings" that would take place before the coming of him "to whom judgment belongs" (Ezek. 21:27). During all these years of captivity and colonization by Babylon, Persia, Greece, and then Rome, Israel lost authority to rule itself—except for a one-century interlude under the Maccabeans. But God told Ezekiel that One was coming who would restore that authority, presumably after these three great overturnings (Persia, Greece, and Rome) had occurred. Then in the fifth century BC Haggai sounded a similar note, predicting that YHWH would "shake all nations, and then will come the chosen of all the nations" (Hag. 2:7 in the Septuagint). These are the words of the Septuagint, the Greek translation of the Old Testament, which was the principal Bible for the early Church.

Mysteriously, then, the prophets foretold three great empires that would rule the biblical world after the Babylonian captivity. They suggested that these three empires would somehow prepare the way for the Messiah. Even secular historians of these six hundred years agree that these empires created conditions that eventually helped spread the Christian message.

All these wars and bloodshed showed the world its need for a Prince of Peace who would deliver the world from its miseries. They helped demonstrate that a kingdom that could deliver freedom to the lowest slave was more glorious than the greatest temporal empires. They showed the best that Satan's kingdoms could offer. But as with Goliath's fearsome power, it took only one stone to bring them down. Each earthen kingdom was greater than the one before, yet each was overthrown by something greater still. The Messiah's kingdom, in overthrowing the Roman Empire, was "the one cut out by no human hand" that shattered into pieces the iron, clay, bronze, silver, and gold, so that they all became "like the chaff on the summer threshing floor" (Dan. 2:34–35).

The Messiah "came into the world to bring down the high things of Satan" that are "proud and lofty," all things that are high and lifted up, "the haughtiness of men and their lofty pride" (Isa. 2:12–17).[1] He came to warn of the day when YHWH of armies (the meaning of "the LORD of hosts") shall strike down everything that is proud and exalted. On that day the Messiah shall bring down everything that has lifted itself up.

So while all the world seemed out of control during these savage and bloody six centuries, in reality YHWH was superintending their histories to make way for the emergence of the Messiah's kingdom. One sign of this was the remarkable manner in which he preserved his people during these terrible revolutions. While the world was roiled for all these centuries by war after war, and so many men killed "by the sword of [their] brother" (Hag. 2:22), the Church was preserved despite being reduced to a remnant. It is particularly remarkable that Judea was preserved, since it was in the midst of all these empires and was often overrun and subdued. It was turned from one overlord to another, and its people were hated by this people and then that one. It was envied by all the pagans, many of its people were slain, and rulers sought to exterminate them. Yet God prevented the Jewish people from being eliminated.

Jews were taken captive to Babylon, were given over to the Persians, suffered greater indignities from the Greeks, and, like much of the world, were trodden under by the Romans. Never did they suffer as they did under Antiochus IV, whose depredations I will describe. But in all these centuries, while dominated by foreign powers, God's Jewish people learned the truths of Psalm 46, that "God is our refuge and strength, a certain help in adversities. Therefore we will not fear

1. Edwards, *HWR*, 249.

even when the earth changes and the mountains slip into the seas. Even when the
waters roar and the mountains shake with power" (vv. 1–3).

The Babylonian Captivity

The Babylonian captivity helped prepare the way for the Messiah by crippling
Israel's outward glory and therefore causing God's people to hunger for restoration. On the one hand, the captivity was a huge boon because it put an end to
future idolatry by the nation as a whole. As Isaiah predicted, one day the "idols
shall completely pass away" (Isa. 2:18). And pass away they did, once the exiles
returned to Jerusalem to rebuild. Isolated individuals fell back into this sin during
the persecution of Antiochus, but the people as a whole never again showed any
desire for this most detested of all defections from the God of Israel.

Yet while the captivity cured the Jewish nation of an itch for idolatry, it
greatly diminished Israel's outer glory. It marked the end of the house of David's
independence—except for a brief 102 years (165–63 BC) of revolution and independence under the Maccabees. For most of these six hundred years the kings who
were the types of the coming Son of David were forcibly withdrawn from control
of Israel until the ultimate Son of David began his public ministry in about AD 30.

Israel also lost the tables of the Law. These were the two stones of testimony
delivered to Moses, written with the finger of God (Exod. 31:18). Apparently
they were preserved in the ark until the Babylonian invasion: "There was nothing
in the ark but two slabs of stone which Moses put there at Horeb" (1 Kings 8:9).
But then, according to common Jewish testimony, they were lost.

Along with the tablets the Urim and Thummin also disappeared. These were the
instruments by which the high priest inquired of God to get immediate answers
to questions of discernment. Both Josephus and the Talmudic rabbis believed
they were jewels in the high priest's breastplate that were illuminated by the Holy
Spirit. The rabbis wrote that after the exile God no longer manifested his will by
Urim and Thummim, for they were among the five things missing from the Second
Temple, the others being the ark and its cover, the Cherubim, the fire, and the
manifest presence of God (Yoma 21B).

As the rabbis wrote, the manifest Shekinah glory was missing from the Second
Temple, which was first built by Ezra and Nehemiah. This was the cloud of glory
that descended on the tabernacle and then Solomon's temple (2 Chron. 7:2).
Perhaps it never came to the Second Temple because that would wait for God to
"fill with glory" the house of "the chosen of the nations" (Hag. 2:7). That would

explain the loss of the fire on the altar that came down to consume the burnt offerings in the wilderness and Solomon's sacrifices (Lev. 9:24; 2 Chron. 7:1). This fire was never to go out, and probably never did, until the Babylonians destroyed the first temple. This holy fire seems never to have returned to the Second Temple, so its fire had to start with common fire. This was God's sign that the first covenant's lights were dimming in preparation for their renewal at the Messiah's coming—the coming of the glorious "sun of righteousness" (Mal. 4:2).

Return of the Jews

If the glory of the Second Temple never reached that of the first, nevertheless God's administration of the Jewish return from Babylon was a remarkable affair. Next to the redemption out of Egypt, it was the most spectacular of all Old Testament redemptions. It was mind-boggling that a pagan emperor (Cyrus) would give Jews the liberty to return and rebuild their city and temple. What is more, this pagan ruler gave Ezra and Nehemiah silver and gold and beasts and goods (Ezra 1:4). But it didn't end there. God moved the heart of another Persian emperor, Darius, to give his own money to help build a house for the God of Israel. He commanded their bitter enemies the Samaritans to help, on pain of being impaled on a beam from their own houses (6:11). Still another Persian king, Artaxerxes, contributed to these efforts, donating silver and gold and ordering his treasurers beyond the Euphrates to provide silver, wheat, wine, and oil. Amazingly, he freed the Jews from taxes, tolls, and customs (7:11–26).

All of these extraordinary favors from pagan rulers demonstrate that "the king's heart is a river of water in the hand of YHWH" (Prov. 21:1). God moves the minds of the mighty to help his people while he turns aside the stratagems of their bitterest enemies. In this case he thwarted the Samaritans (Ezra 4–5) and Sanballat and Tobiah (Neh. 2; 4; 6). Of course there are plenty of times when God's people suffer ferocious persecution. But there were also these times in the history of redemption when God preserved the Jewish people and their city and temple, for the sake of the glory that the Messiah would bring to them, as Haggai and Zechariah suggested.

Outpouring of the Spirit

It is God's ordinary manner to pour out fresh effusions of his Spirit at every new juncture in the history of redemption.[2] There were new outpourings of the Spirit

---

2. As Edwards puts it, "'Tis observable that it has been God's manner in every remarkable new establishment of the state of his visible church, to give a remarkable outpouring of his Spirit." *HWR*, 266.

at the first establishment of God's Church in the land under Joshua—so too now at this second establishment in the land, after the return of the exiles. And, as we will see, at the establishment of the Jesus-centered Church after his resurrection. This outpouring in the time of Ezra and Nehemiah was the final cure not only for Israel's past history of national idolatry, as we have seen, but also for Israel's past history of marrying idolatrous pagans. Ezra put an end to this upon his return, and it has been officially frowned upon by Jews ever since.

But the Spirit's work was especially evident in the leadership of Ezra and Nehemiah. Their attempts to reform the ways of the returning exiles were successful. There was great repentance for their sins, and they agreed to a solemn covenant with their God. When Ezra prayed and made confession with tears, the people followed suit. They wept for their sins, confessing their unfaithful marriages to idolators and vowing to put an end to this (Ezra 10:1–5).

About the same time, the people listened to Ezra reading the Law from early morning to midday. All were attentive. Levites helped them understand the texts. The people wept, determined to obey, and promised to keep the Feast of Tabernacles (Neh. 8). They kept a seven-day fast, listened to more of Torah, made more confession of sins, and worshiped (Neh. 9). Then they formally renewed the covenant and took action to show their reformation. They expelled the wives who might lead them into idolatry, drove Tobiah out from his temple apartment, renounced work and trade on the Sabbath, and vowed not to give their children in marriage to pagans (Neh. 13).

All of these prodigious changes were signs of a deep work of the Spirit of God. The outpouring of the Spirit that accompanied this new beginning in the land was like what we saw under Enosh and Samuel and David. We will see a similar outpouring at every new turn in the history of redemption.

Diaspora

During and after the Babylonian captivity, Jews were dispersed around the ancient Near East and beyond. This too helped prepare the way for the spread of the good news of the Messiah.

Those who were exiled to Babylon built homes and accumulated possessions there. They followed God's command passed on to them by Jeremiah: "Seek the peace of the city where I have removed you, and pray for it to YHWH, for in its peace you will find peace" (Jer. 29:7). Many settled such deep roots there that when Cyrus let them return to Jerusalem, they preferred to stay. They were unwilling to trek hundreds of miles to a land none of the younger men had seen. Only a small number returned.

By the time of Zechariah, at least twenty years after the initial return in 539 BC, the Jews in Babylon were so disconnected from the Jewish community in Jerusalem that they had to send two messengers, Sharezer and Regemmelech, to ask if they were to keep the annual fast commemorating the destruction of the temple and city in 587. By this time more Jews had been dispersed beyond Babylon to many adjacent lands. By Esther's time, at some point in the Persian period (539–334 BC), Jews had been dispersed throughout the vast empire. As Haman put it to King Ahasuerus, "There is a people scattered through all the provinces of your dominion" (Esther 3:8).

This scattering of Jews continued in the succeeding centuries. By the first century five million Jews were living outside Palestine, far more than within Israel, and according to the *Encyclopaedia Britannica*, 40 percent of the Roman Empire's second-biggest city, Alexandria, was said to be Jewish.[3] The great Jewish philosopher of the first century AD, Philo, wrote that there were one million Jews in Egypt, one-eighth of that country's population.[4] Some historians report that in first-century Rome there were between forty thousand and sixty thousand Jews.[5]

Before the great persecution by Antiochus Epiphanes in the second century BC, his Seleucid predecessors had seen Jews as allies and helped them settle in new parts of the empire. According to the Jewish historian Josephus, Antiochus III (the Great)—father to the persecutor—established a Jewish community in Phrygia (Asia Minor) in the third century BC by transporting two thousand Jewish families from Babylon and Mesopotamia to Phrygia and adjacent Lydia. The Jewish settlers supported the Seleucid monarchy after Phrygia had risen in revolt, and Jews had helped the Seleucids put them down (2 Macc. 8:20). The Seleucids rewarded the Jews with land, tax exemptions, and permission to live by their own laws.[6] Jews also settled in this period in Pontus, Galatia, Pamphilia, and Ephesus. They migrated from these regions of Asia Minor (modern Turkey) to Athens, Corinth, and Rome.

---

3. *Encyclopaedia Britannica*, s.v. "Diaspora," https://www.britannica.com/topic/Diaspora-Judaism.

4. Philo, *Flaccus* 6–9 (§43), trans. Charles Duke Yonge, available at http://www.earlychristianwritings .com/yonge/book36.html.

5. William R. Stegner, "Diaspora," in *Dictionary of Paul and His Letters*, ed. Gerald F. Hawthorne, Ralph P. Martin, and Daniel G. Reid (Downers Grove, IL: InterVarsity, 1993), 211; Mark Reasoner, "Rome and Roman Christians," in Hawthorne, Martin, and Reid, *Dictionary of Paul and His Letters*, 851.

6. Josephus, *Antiquities of the Jews* 12.3.

Antiochus Epiphanes and the Maccabees

All this prosperity under the Seleucids disappeared around 167 BC when the Seleucid king Antiochus IV launched a vicious persecution against Jews in their land, repealing the rights his father Antiochus the Great had granted God's people. The son, Antiochus Epiphanes, tried to impose paganism on the Jewish people by banning circumcision, Sabbath-keeping, and kosher observance. He set up idols in the temple and savagely tortured faithful Jews, including the martyrs of 2 Maccabees 6–7, mentioned in Hebrews 11:35–36. Often Antiochus and his armies seemed to be on the brink of victory when God helped the Maccabee brothers and their small bands defeat their enemies. As Daniel prophesied, "Those who acted wickedly against the covenant were seduced by flattery, but those who know their God will be strong and take action" (Dan. 11:32). The Maccabees eventually drove the Greeks out of the land, purified the temple as celebrated at Hannukah each year in the Jewish calendar, and regained control of their land until 63 BC.

Messianic Expectation

By the Jewish diaspora (dispersion)—before and after the Maccabean period—throughout the Persian and then Greek and Roman empires, God spread expectation of a coming Messiah. Jews always carried with them their Scripture scrolls and therefore their rabbis' teachings that the Messiah was on his way. Because Gentiles in all these regions were fascinated by this moral and beautiful religion, many Gentiles learned of this messianic expectation. This might explain why Virgil wrote, in Eclogue 4, just before the birth of Jesus, of a child who would be divine and rule the world and bring a golden age of peace and happiness.[7]

A minority of Jews from around the diaspora went to Jerusalem for the great feasts each year. All Jewish males were commanded to go to Jerusalem for each of the three great feasts—Passover, Pentecost, and Tabernacles—but the vast majority could not afford to make this time-consuming and enormously expensive trip. This fact alone started to show Jews and some rabbis that there needed to be a new way to obey Torah commands to sacrifice, bring firstfruits, and build cities of refuge. But the Jews who could afford to go to Jerusalem in the years of Jesus's ministry brought news of the Messiah to their homes all over the empire.

7. Virgil, "The Eclogues" and "The Georgics," trans. C. Day Lewis (New York: Oxford University Press, 2009), bk. 4.

For example, it was probably diaspora Jews whom John called "certain Greeks ... who came up to worship at the feast. They came to Philip ... and asked him, saying, 'Sir, we want to see Jesus'" (John 12:20–21). In similar manner many other visiting Jews from the diaspora learned of the crucifixion. The disciples on the road to Emmaus took Jesus to be one of the visitors and asked him (Luke was chuckling as he wrote this), "Are you the only stranger in Jerusalem who does not know about the crucifixion of Jesus?" (Luke 24:18).

But the most striking sign of the power of the diaspora to spread the gospel can be seen in the story of the Christian Pentecost, where we see the homelands of thousands of diaspora Jews who had come to Jerusalem for the feast. According to Luke in Acts 2:9–11 there were "Parthians and Medes and Elamites," from what is now Iran; "residents of Mesopotamia," who might have been descendants of the ten lost tribes carried off to Assyria in the eighth century BC; "residents of Judea" distinct from the apostles and 120 disciples, most or all from Galilee; people "from Cappadocia, Pontus and Asia, Phrygia also and Pamphylia," who were probably Syrian Jews from all these provinces in what is now Turkey and included in the Roman province of Syria; and residents of "Egypt and parts of Libya that are along the Cyrene," regions of North Africa. These last were Egyptian Jews, whom Philo said numbered one million.

Then there were "the strangers from Rome." Historians estimate there were seventy thousand Jews in Rome in this period. These Jews might have brought their new faith in the risen Messiah back to Rome after Pentecost and started the church there, the same church Paul later visited and addressed in his great epistle. Finally, there were "Jews and proselytes, Cretans and Arabs." Gentile proselytes to Judaism were a sizable component of Jews in Jesus's day.[8] Judaism was immensely attractive because of its moral teaching and liturgical beauty. Gentiles who attended Jewish services often perceived that the God of Israel was vastly superior to the immoral deities of the Greco-Roman pantheon. Jesus observed that Jews had already been taking seriously their mission to be a "light to the nations" (Isa. 42:6; 49:6; 60:3): "You travel over land and sea to make one convert"

---

8. "About the time of the Hasmonean era Judaism created a proselytization ceremony that was unique in the pagan world ... that cancelled all racial distinctions and converted the foreigner as if he were born a Jew in every respect. . . . The movement for conversion was strengthened especially during the Hasmonean period, when statehood was granted the monotheistic nation and served as a powerful instrument of Jewish religious propaganda. During that era Judaism spread by means of religious conversion to all parts of the known world to which Jews came." Haim M. I. Gevaryahu, "Kaufmann, Yeḥezkel: Post-Biblical Period," in *Encyclopedia Judaica* (New York: Macmillan, 1971), 16:1350. See also Ralph Marcus, "The Sebomenoi in Josephus," *Jewish Social Studies* 14, no. 3 (1952): 247–50.

(Matt. 23:15). By worshiping the God of Israel, Jews were a light to Gentiles all over the empire, whether or not they intended to be so.

Crete and Arabia were two geographical extremities. The first represented the islands of the sea. Philo wrote that the islands of the Mediterranean—and he cited Crete especially—were "full of Jews." The Arabs were probably Nabateans from what is now southern Jordan near Petra, of *Raiders of the Lost Ark* fame. They were not from what is now Saudi Arabia, thus not the ancestors of today's Arabs.

Because of this enormous Jewish diaspora, with Jews and Gentile "God-fearers" filling synagogues all over the empire, it was no wonder that Paul and the apostles always went first to synagogues when they reached a new city. They knew they would find both Greeks and Jews already primed to hear about the Messiah.

Religions of the Far East

In the midst of all these world-shaking revolutions, more of the world's great religions arose. Buddhism, Daoism, Confucianism, and classical Greco-Roman religion grew into far-reaching religious systems that inspired millions of adherents in many of these great empires. We will look at them in chronological order and then see how they too were used by God to prepare for the messianic kingdom.

Confucius (551–489 BC) and Lao Zi (sixth century BC) emerged at the beginning of the chaotic period of the Warring States in China (771–300 BC), when the Zhou feudal system was declining and small states fought for position.

Confucius is often mistaken for teaching something like a secular humanism with no transcendent concerns. In fact, however, Master Kong, as the Chinese called him, was a religious humanist. He wrote in his *Analects* that "Heaven" appointed him to teach his doctrine, Heaven answers prayer, and Heaven both punishes evil and rewards the good.

The central thesis of Confucius's religious humanism was *jen* or benevolence. This was unselfconscious effort for the good of others, like that of the good Samaritan. It was driven by a single-minded devotion to virtue, even to the point of death. Confucius taught his disciples they should not compromise their ethics, even for one basketful of rice. This absolute commitment to the good and right was, Confucius proclaimed, the best way to have joy.

A half millennium before Jesus, Confucius taught the "Negative Golden Rule," to avoid doing what one would not want done to oneself. He enjoined humility, learning from others, and always admitting mistakes. Life, he said, should be organized around relationships, the most important being a father's love for his son and the son's reverence for his father. Rulers were to be benevolent to their subjects, and subjects ought to be loyal.

Christians would say that Confucius illustrates Paul's teaching that God's moral law is written on every human heart (Rom. 2:14–15). They would fault his restriction of love to one's family and nation, pointing to Jesus's teaching that we should love all others because they are created by the same heavenly Father. For Confucius, enemies are not to receive love but correction, whereas for Jesus, enemies are the objects of our love because this is the way God treats his enemies (Matt. 5:44–45). Confucian humanism is inspiring, but it has little to say to those who know they fail to live up to its grand ideals and who seek forgiveness and redemption.

Lao Zi (or "Old Master") reacted against Confucianism for being too conformist and moralistic. Lao Zi stressed the individual rather than society and prized freedom to live by nature. His *Dao De Jing* taught *wu-wei*—literally, "not doing," which meant returning to the roots of nature by going with the flow of things. This would free up our natural abilities when we are frustrated that things do not go our way. It refuses to retaliate against an enemy and trusts that by his vices he will destroy himself. Virtue does not come by striving but by union with nature. This seems stupid to most of the world, but reality is not what it seems; Lao Zi taught that the greatest cleverness often appears to be foolishnesss. Strength comes from weakness: water is soft and yielding but can cut through rock.

Christians agree that there is strength in what the world thinks is weakness. After all, a crucified man saved the world through what the world called a defeat. But they disagree with philosophical Daoism's sense of impersonal fate, in which the cosmos is cold and lonely and we are simply to resign ourselves to its ironic turns. The God of Israel is a Person who seeks our willing participation in his kingdom of love. Christians cannot accept Daoist confidence in the innate goodness of human nature. Nor can they follow a Way that lacks a personal Savior who gives us the strength to follow him.

Siddhartha Gautama Buddha (ca. 466–386 BC) flourished in the fourth century BC. He grew up in the lap of luxury as a prince in what is now Nepal. Disillusioned after failing to find enlightenment through Hindu teachings, he sat one night under a tree and gained the revelations that he taught for the next fifty years until he died of food poisoning. In this night, he claimed, he achieved *nirvana*, the "blowing out" of all desire, by seeing the Four Noble Truths. The first two propose that all is suffering and that the cause of suffering is desire for pleasure and recognition. These desires keep us in a cycle of reincarnation (third), and the cure for suffering is to be rid of these desires (fourth). The eradication of desire comes by a combination of belief and action, the most important of which are faith that there is nothing permanent and the practice of meditation.

The Buddha was, for all practical purposes, an atheist. There is no room for prayer or praise in his teaching, nor is there heaven or hell or final judgment. Later followers created Mahayana sometime after the first century AD (and after the introduction of Christian teaching to the Asian subcontinent) when the Buddha was raised to deity and the concept of grace was first introduced. Followers were taught that they could become Buddhas themselves and could escape reincarnation by placing their faith in one of the Buddhas.

The contrast with Christian faith is stark. The Buddha taught that there is no Creator and that we are to be lamps unto ourselves. Salvation is escape from suffering and comes by knowledge of the Buddha's teachings. For the Christian faith, on the other hand, suffering is to be embraced and conquered by becoming one with the Son who suffered. Christians agree with Buddhists when the latter teach many of the moral standards of the Ten Commandments, but the Christian tradition disagrees with the Buddhist corollary that there are no final distinctions between good and evil. The Christian God is the author of all good and opposed to all evil forever. Those distinctions between good and evil are eternal and not temporary.

For Theravadin and Zen Buddhists, there is little to no hope for life after death since nirvana is without consciousness or beings or desire. There is no continued individuality. But in the Messiah's kingdom, there is eternal life as individual selves in communion with the Triune God and all the saints forever.

Greco-Roman Religion

As we have seen, thousands of people in the Hellenistic (Greek) and Roman empires came to see the infinite superiority of the God of Israel to the gods and goddesses they had been raised with. We will not detain our story with those polytheisms that the world outside of the Far East nearly universally rejected in these centuries and beyond. But we will examine the growing monotheisms of Greece and Rome, which were largely inspired by the religious philosophies of Plato (428–347 BC) and Aristotle (384–322 BC). These two great thinkers gave Greeks and Romans reasons to reject the old polytheisms, which, by comparison, seemed contradictory and immoral. They provided ways to understand how the world of nature was possessed of beauty and order. Yet for millions, their rather distant notions of God were not enough for their religious needs. For this reason, Plato and Aristotle actually helped people move to faith in the God of Israel, particularly when this new faith was seen to be compatible with parts of what Plato and Aristotle had taught.

Plato taught that the physical universe must be the result of intelligence and goodness because it is beautifully organized and regular in its motions. Its order and stability must come from its being derived from an unchanging world of Forms graspable by the intellect. The visible world is good because it came from these Forms, which depend in turn on what is even higher, the Good. So the whole universe is directed toward good, and each part is made to perform a function that contributes to the beauty and harmony of the universe. But because the Forms use preexisting matter, which is in motion and therefore irrational (only the unchanging, according to Plato, is fully rational), the universe is also subject to disorderly elements of necessity inherent in matter. Therefore the universe is good but not perfect.

According to Plato our souls have fallen out of preexistence into this sensible world, and we must return to the supersensible world to attain our proper destiny. We have a memory of the Forms that is awakened when we see beauty because the world of Forms is beautiful. Our souls are in conflict because they are driven like a charioteer driving two horses, one with dishonorable and the other with honorable appetites. Wisdom is the practice of dying to the delights of this world and living according to the vision of the world above appearances, grasped by the mind. Knowledge is the key.

Plato is ambiguous on God. In the *Laws* he wrote that God is a self-moving World Soul who orders and inhabits the universe, cares about us and our affairs, and rewards good and evil. But in the *Timaeus* he declared that "the father and maker of all this universe is past finding out, and even if we found him, to tell of him to all men would be impossible." Matter is coeternal with God, and so God did not create the world, despite Plato's myth of a craftsman or demiurge who made the world by using the Forms as a blueprint. The demiurge used the Forms that existed as an ordered whole before he employed them.

While the Platonic God was neither a Creator nor Redeemer, Plato appealed to Christian philosophers because of his conviction that goodness is grounded in cosmic reality and that human reason can grasp something of God and his laws even if that knowledge cannot bring salvation.

Aristotle agreed with Plato that the universe had no absolute beginning. He also agreed that God is without change but rejected Plato's belief that the movement of nature was intended by an intelligent being like a demiurge. For Aristotle, there was no craftsman looking to a model of Forms and no Father who is beyond finding out. God for Aristotle was simply the object of our desire for good. Therefore, God is good and essentially thought or mind. In a famous sentence from the *Metaphysics* he wrote, "It must be of itself that the divine thought thinks (since it is the most excellent of things), and its thinking is a thinking on thinking."[9]

God's objects of thought must be limited to what is unchangeable and so himself. God is the sum total of those truths that are free from change, and it is these that he thinks. This is a fresh affirmation of Plato's stipulation that the world of sense derives from a reality outside itself.

Yet Aristotle's doctrine of the substantiality of the concrete individual was a break with Platonism. While for Plato the Forms in the heavens were more real than any individual in the world of sense, for Aristotle there are no Forms separate from individual human beings in this world.

But just as we saw for Plato, Aristotle's God is quite different from the God of Israel. The Aristotelian deity is neither creator nor providential ruler. Nor is he a personal moral agent over or in the world. Christian thinkers were nevertheless inspired by Aristotle's proposition that humans are not the measure of all things, that only God is perfectly good, and also by the Platonic and Aristotelian consensus that the human *telos* (end or goal) is God.

This is why some Christians were also inspired by a third philosophy of this period, Stoicism. Stoics like the former slave Epictetus (AD 55–ca. 135) taught that all the creation is given form by *logos*—a rational principle—which is discernible to the human mind. John the apostle took this word and claimed it is a person—the Jewish Messiah—who created the world and holds it together moment by moment. Justin Martyr (d. ca. 165) pushed this Stoic and Johannine concept further when he argued that Messiah the *Logos* was speaking through certain Greek philosophers like Socrates who had part of the *Logos*. Socrates spoke truth "in proportion to the share he had of the seminal divine *Logos*."[10] But because he "did not know the whole *Logos*, which is Christ, [he and other philosophers] often contradicted themselves."[11] Justin agreed with Paul that demons lurked behind most pagan religious ceremonies (1 Cor. 10:20–22), and he concurred that participation in part of the *Logos* was a far cry from possession of the Person of

9. Aristotle, *Metaphysics* 12.9, in Richard McKeon, ed., *Introduction to Aristotle* (New York: Modern Library, 1947), 292.
10. Justin Martyr, *Second Apology* 13, in *The Writings of Justin Martyr and Athenagoras*, ed. Marcus Dods et al. (Edinburgh: T&T Clark, 1879).
11. Justin Martyr, *Second Apology* 10, in *Writings of Justin Martyr and Athenagoras*.

the *Logos* himself. Without that person, a philosopher could never "know God, the maker of all things through Jesus the crucified."[12] So John and Paul and early Christian philosophers drew on Stoic terms and concepts but baptized them in Christian vision, which made them new and different.

China, Athens, and Jerusalem

Jews and Christians have always wondered why there are truths scattered among the deceptions in world religions. Where did these truths come from? They also have been impressed by the profound differences between the God of Israel and his kingdom on the one hand, and the religions of the ancient Near East on the other. This was true of Jewish and Christian thinkers in this period as well.

For example, Jews and early Christians were impressed by moral teachings of Buddhists, that lying and stealing and murder were condemned along with violations of marriage. But they could not accept the provisional character which Buddhists attached to these ideals when they claimed that the ethical life is merely a raft on the ocean of life that is discarded once the other shore of *nirvana* is reached. Jews and Christians insisted that good and evil are woven into the fabric of reality that persists into eternity.

Similarly, they noticed new notions of grace in Hindu *bhakti* and Pure Land Buddhism after the first century AD and the rise of Christian missions to Hindu and Buddhist lands. Yet Christians also observed that these Hindu and Buddhist concepts of grace were disconnected from the absolute holiness of the God of Israel and the infinite cost of grace—the life of the Son of God.

Christian philosophers started to notice that every concept in a world religion that seemed similar to Christian notions was nevertheless shaped by a broader narrative that was foreign to the Christian story of the God of Israel and his Messiah. For example, Buddhist Pure Land notions of grace are based on a story of Amida Buddha in which karma and liberation from reincarnation control the story, not sin and guilt and damnation. In this Buddhist story of grace, the solution to the human dilemma is not forgiveness from a holy God but release from an inevitable cycle of life, death, and rebirth.

But if the differences would prevent us from saying that these world religions teach the same things we gain from the Messiah, where did these similar teachings

---

12. Justin Martyr, *Second Apology* 13, in *Writings of Justin Martyr and Athenagoras.*

come from? Justin Martyr concluded that these pagan thinkers were learning from the Messiah in his role as *logos* or Word of the cosmos, since John's Gospel informs us that the *logos* "enlightens everyone" (John 1:9). The *logos*, Justin posited, was speaking through the philosophical religions of the ancient world such as Platonism and Aristotelianism.

This would explain their errors, as we have seen, since they did not know the whole *logos*, which is the Messiah himself. They saw the trees but not the forest. They acquired truths but out of context. They participated in only part of the *logos* rather than possessing the person of the *logos*.

Clement of Alexandria (AD 150–ca. 215) was another Christian philosopher trying to make sense of the partial truths he found in these Greek philosophies. Clement believed that these Greeks knew the accidents (qualities not essential to a thing) but only Christians knew the essence. The philosophers named God, but only Christians knew God. Or the Greek thinkers knew the true God only dimly. They had only faint knowledge of God the Creator without knowing God the Redeemer.

More recently Joseph Ratzinger (b. 1927; a.k.a. Pope Benedict) has proposed that in his mysterious providence the Triune God arranged for Greek philosophy to collide historically with the religion of the God of Israel and his Messiah. For Greek philosophy put the question of truth to its audience rather than resting content with traditional polytheisms and their fables of gods and goddesses. The Greek philosophers developed faith in a single God and criticized popular notions of the gods. This question of the true and the good is what unites the Greek and biblical worlds: they made the Mosaic/Socratic distinction between what was believed about the true and the good, on the one hand, and what they *ought* to believe about the true and the good, on the other.[13]

This collision began, Ratzinger has argued, when Jews translated the Old Testament into Greek to create the Septuagint. This started the process of intercultural encounter, with vast implications. It demonstrated the harmony between God and world, reason and mystery. The God of Jerusalem was now speaking in the words of Athens, and views of God and goodness and salvation could be compared and examined. This was the same process used in some of the Wisdom books of the Apocrypha such as Wisdom and Ecclesiasticus (Sirach), where Platonic and Stoic conceptions of morality were connected to the world created and redeemed by the God of Israel. Now Hellenists who were convinced by Plato that nature

---

13. Joseph Ratzinger, *Truth and Tolerance: Christian Belief and World Religions* (San Francisco: Ignatius, 2004), 223–27.

points to a world beyond could see higher up to a God of beauty and love in the traditions of Israel.[14]

For our purposes, the beauty of the Septuagint is that it brought an end to the Tanach (the Old Testament) being a book closed to the rest of the world because of its Hebrew language. Now Jews and Gentiles all over the Hellenistic world could understand the Bible. And since it was used in all the synagogues of the diaspora, it prepared the way for the Messiah by showing its audiences in Europe, Africa, and Asia that the Messiah had been prophesied for thousands of years. And its descriptions of the Messiah matched the identity and history of Jesus of Nazareth. Furthermore, this was the same translation used by most of the Jewish and Gentile Church for hundreds of years after the resurrection of Jesus.

Preparation for the Messiah

There were two other ways that these six centuries of revolution led to the Messiah. First, the explosion of new religions increased hunger for the true God. From Confucius, Lao Zi and the Buddha in the Far East to Plato, Aristotle, and Epictetus in the West, millions were given intimations of final truth and beauty. Untold multitudes were promised happiness without finding it. There were flashes of brilliance among these thinkers, and partial fulfillment given to many. But the oceans of blood shed by successive empires produced only limited freedom and new despotisms. The world was not becoming happier but more foolish and miserable. God was showing the world that religion and philosophy were incapable of providing happiness without the guidance of the Morning Star. The God of Israel was making foolish the wisdom of this world, until its own light was willing to serve as a handmaid to divine revelation. Then it became clear that human wisdom was vain without special revelation. When Paul was able on the Hill of Ares to use Greek learning to point to the gospel, finally the world could see that what it had worshiped as unknown was now revealed through the folly of the cross. Only that revelation could make sense of the groping (Acts 17:27) of the world's philosophers and religionists.

The second way in which these six centuries of revolution prepared the way for the Messiah was that the Pax Romana of the last revolution provided political and geographical space for the diffusion of the gospel. Just before the birth of the Messiah, the Roman Empire was at its greatest height and peace. Augustus Caesar

14. Ratzinger, *Truth and Tolerance*, 152–54.

had come to power twenty-three years before the birth of Jesus. This marked the end of the Roman commonwealth and the beginning of constitutional monarchy, which used and abused the Senate and judiciary. One could say that the power of the pagan world, "Satan's visible kingdom," was at its apogee.[15] One thousand years before, God's visible kingdom had reached its greatest height under Solomon. But now the kingdom of this world had reached its greatest success since Babel. It had achieved its most magnificent glory in terms of military, financial, and intellectual strength.

And there was peace. This peace began in 7 BC when Caesar Augustus closed the temple of Janus to signal the end of Roman conquests. It was a fitting prelude to the birth of the Prince of Peace.

Select Bibliography

Allen, Diogenes. *Philosophy for Understanding Theology*. Atlanta: John Knox Press, 1985.

Aristotle. *Metaphysics*. Translated by W. D. Ross. Available at http://classics.mit.edu/Aristotle/metaphysics.html.

Augustine. *Confessions*. Translated by Henry Chadwick. New York: Oxford University Press, 1991.

Boersma, Hans. "All One in Christ: Why Christian Platonism Is Key to the Great Tradition." *Touchstone*, January/February 2020. https://www.touchstonemag.com/archives/article.php?id=33-01-030-f.

Cleary, Thomas, trans. *Dhammapada: The Sayings of the Buddha*. New York: Bantam, 1995.

———, trans. *The Essential Dao*. San Francisco: HarperSanFrancisco, 1991.

Confucius. *The Analects*. Translated by D. C. Lau. Harmondsworth, UK: Penguin, 1979.

Edwards, Jonathan. *A History of the Work of Redemption*. Edited by John F. Wilson. Vol. 9 in *The Works of Jonathan Edwards*. New Haven: Yale University Press, 1989.

Justin Martyr. *Second Apology*. In *The Ante-Nicene Fathers*, edited by Alexander Roberts and James Donaldson, 1:188–93. 1885–87. Reprint, Peabody, MA: Hendrickson, 1994.

McClymond, Michael, and Gerald McDermott. "Providence and History." In *The Theology of Jonathan Edwards*, 224–43. New York: Oxford University Press, 2012.

McDermott, Gerald. *World Religions: An Indispensable Introduction*. Nashville: Nelson, 2011.

McDermott, Gerald, and Harold Netland. *A Trinitarian Theology of Religions: An Evangelical Proposal*. New York: Oxford University Press, 2014.

Mitchell, Donald W. *Buddhism: Introducing the Buddhist Experience*. New York: Oxford University Press, 1992.

15. Edwards, *HWR*, 279.

Plato. *The Laws.* Translated by Benjamin Jowett. Project Gutenberg. Last updated January 15, 2013. https://www.gutenberg.org/files/1750/1750-h/1750-h.htm.

———. *The Timaeus.* Translated by Benjamin Jowett. Available at http://classics.mit.edu/Plato/timaeus.html.

Ratzinger, Joseph. *Introduction to Christianity.* San Francisco: Ignatius, 2004.

———. *Truth and Tolerance: Christian Belief and World Religions.* San Francisco: Ignatius, 2004.

Virgil. *"The Eclogues" and "The Georgics."* Translated by C. Day Lewis. New York: Oxford University Press, 2009.

9

The Authority of the Tanach

Christians have a bad history with Tanach, the Old Testament. They have a sorry record of neglecting and even denigrating it. Some have wanted to eliminate it from the Bible. In this chapter we will see that the history of redemption cannot be seen without it and that for Jesus and the apostles, the Tanach was their only Bible. I will discuss Tanach's wisdom and the necessity for each part of it. Finally we will see that redemption is the central story of Tanach and that the heart of that story is the beauty of the Messiah.

The New Marcionism

Marcion of Sinope (ca. AD 85–ca. 160) was an early heretic who was excommunicated by the church at Rome in 144. Marcion had rejected the Old Testament because, he taught, it was the story of a lower creator god opposed to the God of Jesus Messiah. The teacher from Sinope reportedly was friends with the Gnostic teacher Valentinus. Marcion said the only true Bible consisted of a shortened form of the Gospel of Luke and ten Pauline epistles. The true Jesus, he believed, did not have a material body, which for him underscored why Tanach, which teaches the goodness of matter and bodies, is from an evil god. True Christianity is therefore radically different from Judaism and its Tanach.

Justin Martyr, Irenaeus, and Tertullian exposed the Gnosticism behind Marcion's rejection of Tanach and its God, and the early Church consistently taught the unity of the Old and New Testaments. But when supersessionism (the idea that the Gentile Church superseded and replaced God's covenant with the Jewish people) became institutionalized after Constantine, the perceived value of Tanach declined. If the Gentile Church had replaced Jewish Israel as God's only elect people, why, many concluded, should we pay much attention to the Hebrew Bible? Although there were plenty of medieval preachers like Thomas Aquinas and Bernard of Clairvaux whose sermons on Tanach highlighted its beauty and divinity, a Marcion-like turn was taken by some and particularly by Martin Luther in the sixteenth century. In his 1526 lectures on Jonah he declared that the plant that grew over the prophet's head was Judaism and the worm that ate it was Jesus. Jesus "abolished the Law through his Holy Spirit and liberated us from the Law and its power. Therefore Judaism withered and decayed in all the world."[1]

At the end of the eighteenth century Immanuel Kant claimed in *The Conflict of the Faculties* that Judaism "now serves no purpose and even suppresses any true religious attitude." Christianity had forsaken "the Judaism from which it sprang." As Jews realized this, he thought, they would accept the religion of Jesus, which would bring about the "euthanasia of Judaism."[2] Roughly a century later Adolf von Harnack in *What Is Christianity?* (1900) alleged that Jews thought of God as a despot and saw him only in his law, which was "a labyrinth of dark defiles." But Jesus saw God "everywhere."[3] More recently N. T. Wright has written in *The Challenge of Jesus* that the symbols of the Second Temple worldview were not bad in themselves but out of date, "to be jettisoned now that the new day had dawned."[4] (Yet Wright is to be commended for his monumental efforts showing Christians that the history of Israel is integral to the story of the gospel. But his work on Israel after the Messiah's resurrection begs for reexamination.)[5]

Marcion has been roundly condemned in the last few centuries by Christian thinkers. The full inspiration of Tanach has been affirmed by orthodox Christianity. But Marcion's conviction that the God of the New Testament has moved on from the religion of Tanach is now sounding eerily familiar. Was this the attitude of the New Testament authors, as Luther, Kant, Harnack, and Wright have alleged?

---

1. Martin Luther, *Lectures on Jonah*, in *Lectures on the Minor Prophets II*, vol. 19 of *Luther's Works*, ed. Hilton Oswald (St. Louis: Concordia, 1963), 103.

2. Immanuel Kant, *The Conflict of the Faculties*, trans. Mary J. Gregor (Lincoln: University of Nebraska Press, 1992), 95.

3. Adolf von Harnack, *What Is Christianity?*, trans. Thomas Bailey Saunders (Philadelphia: Fortress, 1957), 50–51.

4. N. T. Wright, *The Challenge of Jesus* (Downers Grove, IL: InterVarsity, 1999), 55.

5. These quotes from Luther, Kant, Harnack, and Wright are from Matthew Thiessen, "Did Jesus Plan to Start a New Religion?," in *Understanding the Jewish Roots of Christianity*, ed. Gerald McDermott (Bellingham, WA: Lexham, 2021), 18–19.

The Authority of Tanach for the New Testament Authors

The New Testament authors were Second Temple Jews. For all Jews of that period the most important symbols of their religion were the temple, Sabbath, circumcision, and kosher laws—all the things that Antiochus IV had tried to strip from Jews and their religion. After the Maccabean resistance, Jews were determined to preserve these precious symbols of faithfulness to the God of Israel. This determination was prized by Pharisees, in whose kind of Judaism Jesus and Paul were educated. Did Jesus and Paul reject these symbols and therefore the Judaism of the Second Temple?

The simple answer is no. Let's look at the temple first. In an aside that most scholars seem to have missed, Jesus affirmed that God still dwelled there (Matt. 23:21). He endorsed sacrifices and voluntary offerings there, praising the poor widow's offering in Mark 12:41–44. He assumed that his disciples would bring their gifts for sacrifice to the altar of burned offering in the inner court (Matt. 5:23) and in Luke 20 retold the parable of the vineyard from Isaiah 5 so that it was directed against its tenants (the priests) rather than the vineyard itself (the temple). He referred to the temple as "my house" in Matthew 21:13, Mark 11:17, and Luke 19:46.

Did Jesus repudiate the sanctity of the Sabbath when, for example, he defended his disciples' plucking grain on the holy day? Not at all. He affirmed its sanctity by arguing about its purpose rather than its validity, saying it was made for man and not vice versa. This is what the Pharisaic oral tradition had taught, that since the purpose of the Sabbath was life, it was permissible to "eat even unclean things" if one is famished (Mishnah Yoma 8:6). Matthew says the disciples were "craving with hunger" (Matt. 12:1). Jesus appealed to David's example—hence the Jewish Scriptures—to justify what he and the disciples did. This was a Jewish practice, to appeal to a greater principle of the Law to justify breaking a lesser commandment. Jewish tradition upheld this practice as a way of honoring the Law. Furthermore, Jesus warned his disciples to pray that their flight from tribulation would not be on the Sabbath. Why would he do that if he thought the Sabbath was no longer valid?

Circumcision has been at the center of Christian supersessionism for much of the last two millennia. It is frequently alleged that Jesus and Paul repudiated its practice as a sign of their departure from Jewish law. But then why does Luke go out of his way to show Jesus's parents presenting the baby Jesus at the temple on the eighth day after birth for circumcision (Luke 2:21)? And why does Paul say

that "the benefit of circumcision" is "much in every way" (Rom. 3:1–2)? Why did
he go to the trouble of circumcising Timothy (Acts 16:3)? Doesn't Luke answer
this question by explaining that Paul was about to take Timothy to places where
Jews would wonder why a fellow Jew remained uncircumcised (16:3)? Luke says,
"They all knew his father was a Greek," and suggests they might wonder if Timothy,
whose mother was Jewish, was renouncing his Jewishness because of paternal
influence. But did Paul do this simply to please local Jews and hide his personal
repudiation of Jewish law?

It would be difficult to think so and at the same time accept Paul's strong statements toward the end of his life in his letter to the Roman church, his most extensive reflection on Judaism: "Do we overthrow *the law* by this faith? By no means!
Quite the contrary, we uphold *the law*! . . . *The law* is holy, and *the commandment*
is holy and righteous and good. . . . God sent his own son in the likeness of sinful
flesh . . . to condemn sin in the flesh so that the requirement of *the law* might be
fulfilled in us" (Rom. 3:31; 7:12; 8:3–4). It would also be difficult to reconcile the
idea that Paul renounced Jewish law with Luke's vivid depiction in Acts of Paul
taking a Nazirite vow, which included animal sacrifices at the temple, and paying
for Nazirite vows for four others in order to prove that "you yourself [Paul] walk
by and follow the law" (Acts 18:18; 21:24).

What about kosher dietary rules? Didn't Jesus denounce these when he "declared all foods clean" (Mark 7:19)? The great Talmudic scholar Daniel Boyarin
does not think so. In *The Jewish Gospels* he argues that Jesus's declaration did not
set Jesus against kosher rules because Torah itself teaches that what goes into the
body cannot make one unclean, only what comes out of the body such as a seminal
emission.[6] Rather than attacking Torah rules on food, Jesus was defending Torah
against Pharisaic innovations. He was interpreting Torah's deeper meaning. The
Jewish scholars David Flusser and Paula Fredriksen have both concluded that Jesus
was an observant Jew, which means he did not discredit Torah teaching on kosher.[7]

The Gospels

The four Gospel authors take a similarly positive approach to the Jewish tradition.
Matthew records Jesus's promise to fulfill every "iota" (the smallest letter of the

---

6. Daniel Boyarin, *The Jewish Gospels: The Story of the Jewish Christ* (New York: New Press, 2012),
102–28.

7. David Flusser, *Jesus* (Jerusalem: Hebrew University Magnes Press, 2001); Paula Fredriksen, *When
Christians Were Jews: The First Generation* (New Haven: Yale University Press, 2018).

Greek alphabet) and "horn" (the smallest stroke of the pen in Hebrew) of the "law and the prophets" until "all is accomplished" (Matt. 5:17–18). Mark tells us that Jesus praised the poor widow's offering, told the healed leper to offer a gift for sacrifice, called the temple "my house," appealed to biblical purity laws by bidding unclean spirits to enter pigs and be drowned, and affirmed the Sabbath by debating its purpose (Mark 12:41–44; 1:44; 11:15–17; 5:1–13; 3:4).

We see signs of Luke's affirmation of Second Temple Judaism when he records that only "some" of the Pharisees opposed Jesus, other Pharisees invite him to their homes for a meal, and some Pharisees try to protect Jesus from Herod (Luke 6:2; 11:37; 14:1; 13:31). Luke never uses the word "Israel" for Gentiles or the Church.

John's Gospel is frequently misunderstood as anti-Jewish because most translations render *Ioudaioi* as "Jews" without distinguishing, as John does implicitly in his narrative, between the corrupt leaders of the temple and their allies on the one hand and Jesus's followers in Judea, Samaria, and Galilee on the other. For example, John says that many *Ioudaioi* believed in Jesus and therefore there was a division among the *Ioudaioi* over Jesus (John 11:45; 10:19–21). John uses the word "Israel" positively in his first chapter when he writes that John the Baptist revealed the Messiah to Israel and that Nathaniel was an Israelite without guile. So when John writes that Jesus told the *Ioudaioi* who sought to kill him that they were "of your father the devil," readers of most translations wrongly think Jesus is attacking all "Jews" (8:44).

Paul and Other New Testament Authors

If Jesus upheld the traditional symbols of Second Temple Judaism, Paul was no different. As we have seen in a previous chapter, he made clear that he believed in God's covenant with the Jewish people and that it was still in place despite the failure of most of his fellow Jews to accept Jesus as Messiah. They were "still beloved" because of the fathers, and God's "gifts and promises" to the Jewish people are "irrevocable" (Rom. 11:28–29).

New Testament scholar Richard Hays writes in *Echoes of Scripture in the Letters of Paul* that "Paul's readings [of Tanach] characteristically treat [it] as a living voice that speaks to the people of God. The Bible for Paul is not just a chronicle of revelation in the past; the words of Scripture sound from the page in the present moment and address the community of believers with authority. . . . Even the most mundane apodictic pronouncements in [Torah] gain unforeseen spiritual gravity when read with the ruling conviction that [Torah] must speak to us and must speak of weighty spiritual matters."[8]

Peter and John suggest the same. Peter declares that "the Spirit of the Messiah" inspired the prophets when they wrote of the sufferings and glories of the Messiah (1 Pet. 1:11). John's epistles make little direct mention of Tanach, but, as D. A. Carson puts it in the *Commentary on the New Testament Use of the Old Testament*, "Old Testament thought frequently stands behind all of the Johannine texts in some fashion or other."[9] Carson notes that John's attention is directed toward new Gnostic challenges to the theology of his gospel.[10]

According to George H. Guthrie in the just-mentioned *Commentary*, the epistle to the Hebrews contains thirty-seven quotations from Tanach, and woven throughout its pages is the Levitical logic of sacrifice and atonement.[11] The epistle of James is manifestly indebted to the wisdom books of Tanach, and the book of Revelation is packed with imagery from Tanach. According to the *Commentary*, "No other book of the New Testament is as permeated by the Old Testament as is Revelation."[12]

The Wisdom and Necessity of Each Book in Tanach

The New Testament authors implicitly knew that every part of Tanach was necessary for their "teaching, . . . correction, and training in righteousness" (2 Tim. 3:16). They also knew that each book helped make them "wise for salvation" (3:15). They saw, for example, that in Genesis (whose title is Greek, meaning "beginning") they learned of the beginnings of the cosmos, the human race, Israel, and redemption. In Exodus they saw the greatest act of divine redemption before the Messiah's cross and resurrection. Leviticus showed them God's holiness and the many dimensions of redemption that were accomplished through the perfect sacrifice of the Messiah. Numbers gave them a picture of human fickleness and God's patience as it traced Israel's wanderings in the wilderness. Deuteronomy provided for them God's deep wisdom for hundreds of situations in daily life.

---

8. Richard Hays, *Echoes of Scripture in the Letters of Paul* (New Haven: Yale University Press, 1989), 165.

9. D. A. Carson, "1–3 John," in *Commentary on the New Testament Use of the Old Testament*, ed. G. K. Beale and D. A. Carson (Grand Rapids: Baker Academic; Nottingham: Apollos, 2007), 1064.

10. Carson, "1–3 John," 1064.

11. George H. Guthrie, "Hebrews," in Beale and Carson, *Commentary on the New Testament Use of the Old Testament*, 919; cf. 919–25.

12. G. K. Beale and Sean McDonough, "Revelation," in Beale and Carson, *Commentary on the New Testament Use of the Old Testament*, 1081.

All these books of Torah came to be understood by the apostles on different levels, which the Church later taught were the literal (historical), allegorical (about the Messiah and his redemption), tropological (moral), and the anagogical (eschatological). So Paul, for example, taught that when Moses told his readers not to muzzle an ox when treading out the grain (Deut. 25:4), he also meant that preachers need to be paid for their ministerial service (1 Tim. 5:17–18; 1 Cor. 9:9–11): just as those serving in the temple partook of the meat of the sacrifices, "so too the Lord commanded that those proclaiming the gospel should be able to live by the gospel" (1 Cor. 9:14).[13] These are the literal and moral senses. Paul interpreted the redemption of the Jews from slavery in Egypt as a type of the Messiah's redemption through his passion, and the story of Adam in Genesis as pointing to the second Adam and our life with him in resurrected bodies (1 Cor. 5:7; 15:22–23). These are the allegorical and anagogical senses.

These are some of the ways in which the early Church understood Torah in typological fashion. Ever since then the Church has used typology to see the wisdom and necessity of each book in Tanach. Joshua, for example, shows us the necessity of spiritual battle to enter the kingdom and retain our place there. In Judges we see the chaos and confusion that ensue when the Church decides to do what is right in its own eyes. Ruth teaches that the borders of the kingdom of God extend beyond biological family and ethnic group. God demonstrates through the books of Samuel, Kings, and Chronicles how he redeems in the midst of apostasy and repentance, that he is a God of near-infinite mercy, and that the kingdom is not only an inward experience but also a visible society. Ezra and Nehemiah detail the battles that must be fought to return to God's rest and rebuild the Church when it has been exiled because of sin. Esther teaches that God can do the impossible in a nation if his people are prepared to give their lives. Job is a story of inexplicable suffering that can be understood only by warfare in the heavens.

The Psalms have always been the prayer book of Jewish Israel and continue to be so for Gentiles in the commonwealth of Israel. The Proverbs are shrewd rules to help God's people navigate relationships and obstacles during their pilgrimage to the heavenly Zion. Ecclesiastes is testimony to the mysteries and paradoxes of providence. The Song of Solomon is a parable of God's love affair with his people. The major and minor prophets write of God's holy love, which must often chastise his people and judge the world. They also prophesy about the coming Messiah and marvelously foresee his character and work.

13. Paul says he has not made use of this right to be paid (1 Cor. 9:12), but he affirms the right nonetheless. The exception proves the rule.

Redemption throughout Tanach

It was not only the prophets who spoke of the Messiah's redemption. As we have seen in earlier chapters, redemption is the principal theme of Tanach from the first chapter of Genesis on. So when Jesus explained to the disciples on the road to Emmaus the "things concerning himself" in "all" the Scriptures, he might have started with the "darkness over the face of the deep" and God's proclamation, "Let there be light" (Luke 24:27; Gen. 1:2–3). Perhaps Jesus then told this pair that he was the "light that shines in the darkness" that "the darkness has not overcome" (John 1:5) and that he was the Redeemer who is "the true light that enlightens everyone" and gradually drives the darkness out of every soul that receives him (1:9).

No doubt the Redeemer also talked about the Bible's first prophecy of redemption when he told the serpent that he would put enmity between him and the woman, and between the serpent's seed and the woman's seed, and that the woman's seed would crush the serpent's head whereas the serpent would strike the heel of the woman's seed (Gen. 3:14–15). In chapter 3 I discussed the ways that this foretold Satan's role in the killing of the Messiah but also Messiah's victory over the serpent, the devil, at the cross.

We can be certain that Jesus told the disciples on that Emmaus road that the exodus from Egypt was a type of his own redemption of God's people from bondage to sin, fear of death, and control by Satan. But he might have started with the Abraham story and its prophecy that blessing would come to the world through Israel, the progeny of Abraham. This, by the way, is what Jesus might have had in mind when he told the Samaritan woman that "salvation is from the Jews" (John 4:22).

God hinted, therefore, to Abraham that the Messiah would come from his loins, which meant the Messiah would be one of Abraham's descendants. So the Messiah would be a Jew, one of the chosen people. Just as Abraham and his family would bring blessing to the world, so too the Messiah and his family—the Church, which is his body along with Messianic Jews—would bring blessing to the world.

Probably the greatest son of Abraham before the Messiah was Moses. Like the Messiah, Moses was an agent of redemption as he led Israel through the wilderness, away from death and destruction at the hands of Pharaoh and his armies. Paul believed that the Messiah worked through Moses and that the Messiah actually was in the wilderness feeding Israel (1 Cor. 10:3–4). So the Messiah redeemed Israel from Egypt and throughout the forty years in the wilderness through Moses's faith and leadership.

Once Israel was in the land there was continued redemption through Joshua as he led them into battle and defeated their enemies. The Messiah through Joshua led God's people into a land of milk and honey. Gideon, another type of the Messiah, redeemed Israel from Midian with a tiny force, relying more on spiritual than earthly weapons. Samson was another redeemer for Israel, rescuing Israel from their enemy the Philistines.

Redemption from oppressive enemies was also the story of David, Israel's greatest king. Like Jesus, David was a shepherd. Like Jesus, he was hated by his brothers but defeated the enemies of God's people. Like Jesus the Redeemer, David stood between God and the people, averting punishments for sin by taking the punishment upon himself (2 Sam. 24). So David was a type of the coming Messiah in this way, besides many others.

I have already discussed the main theme of the prophets, redemption by the coming Messiah. But redemption was also a principal theme of those books of the Bible called "wisdom" literature. The Psalms are filled with prayers seeking redemption, and some such as Psalm 72 are recognized by both Jews and Christians as messianic, sketching the shape of the coming Redeemer. Proverbs outlines the choices and character of a person who knows God the Redeemer. Ecclesiastes portrays both the emptiness of life without redemption and the simple joys of the redeemed.

In short, redemption is the single most prominent theme in Tanach. Covenant is also an abiding theme from Genesis to Malachi, but covenant is simply another way of describing the relationship between God the Redeemer and his people. He has chosen unilaterally to take a people and join them to his Son the Redeemer, and he covenants to lead them by the hand on a pilgrimage to the new heavens and new earth.

The Beauty of the Messiah

In previous chapters we have touched here and there on the aesthetic dimension in God's history of redemption—the beauty of it all. Not only is the story of the holy Triune God saving sinners a beautiful story, but the Redeeming God himself (and especially his Messiah!) is the epitome of beauty.

But what is beauty?[14] For Edwards, beauty is consent to Being-in-general (his term for all of reality, which both lies in God and is separate from God). Think of

14. The following seven paragraphs are adapted from McDermott, "Drawn by God's Beauty: The Surprising Jonathan Edwards," *Beeson* (2016), 4–8. Used by permission.

this consent as each part of the creation saying "Yes" to the whole of reality. Even the inanimate creation does this. A falling rock "obeys" the law of gravity, saying "Yes." A deer running with elegance across a field is saying "Yes" to its Creator, doing what the Creator created it to do.

Edwards used another image to depict beauty. He said that it manifests the "proportion" that is a "harmony" among things that are different.[15] This harmony is a pattern that is usually pleasing to those who perceive it. By harmony he suggested not only the symmetrical harmony we would see in a French garden at Versailles but also the asymmetrical harmony we enjoy in a Japanese garden. Or even the disproportion that is part of a higher proportion or harmony—like a jazz chord that sounds dissonant when played alone but fits well within a progression of chords.

The most beautiful pattern of all and therefore the pattern of all consent and harmony is God's love among the Three Persons. By this Edwards meant each Person's loving consent to the glory and will of the other two Persons, and then to the Trinity's design for the creation. This design required infinite suffering by a human being to redeem lost humans.

Yet only a God could suffer infinitely, as Anselm once argued and Edwards echoed. And the suffering had to be by a human being because it was punishment for human sins. This is why the Mediator had to be a God-man and why this Second Person of the Trinity consented to the design.

The consent by the Messiah to the Father's plan, noted Edwards, involved astounding paradoxes. It combined divine infinity with care for finite humanity. It was a joining of infinite greatness with infinite care. Infinite justice somehow became infinite mercy. Infinite majesty displayed itself as stunning meekness. Think of it, Edwards suggested: the infinite God of the cosmos, the King of kings and Lord of lords, permitted himself to be born in a barn and to be spat on, mocked, and nailed to a cross between two thieves.

This is the epitome of beauty, and it is the beauty of the Messiah. His beauty graces the story of redemption in Tanach, for it is the story of the holy Messiah drawing an unholy people to himself and the God of Israel. For Edwards, it is beauty more than anything else that tells us who God is. In his theological classic *Religious Affections* he wrote, "God is God, and distinguished from all other beings, and exalted above [th]em, *chiefly* by his divine beauty, which is infinitely diverse from all other beauty. . . . This is the beauty of the Godhead, and the

---

15. Edwards, *Scientific and Philosophical Writings,* vol. 6 of *The Works of Jonathan Edwards,* ed. Wallace Anderson (New Haven: Yale University Press, 1980), 337–38.

divinity of the Divinity (if I may so speak), the good of the infinite Fountain of Good; without which God himself (if that were possible to be) would be an infinite evil."[16]

Because the Messiah is beauty and the story of his redemption of Israel in Tanach is a beautiful story, to live in the kingdom means to know and love his beauty. According to Edwards scholar Sang Hyun Lee, "To know and love God, therefore, is to know and love the beauty of God, and to know the ultimate nature of the world is to know and love the world as an image of God's beauty."[17]

Select Bibliography

Anselm. *Cur Deus Homo*. In *St. Anselm: Basic Writings*, translated by S. N. Deane, 2nd ed., 171–288. La Salle, IL: Open Court, 1962.

Beale, G. K., and D. A. Carson, eds. *Commentary on the New Testament Use of the Old Testament*. Grand Rapids: Baker Academic; Nottingham: Apollos, 2007.

Boyarin, Daniel. *The Jewish Gospels: The Story of the Jewish Christ*. New York: New Press, 2012.

Edwards, Jonathan. *A History of the Work of Redemption*. Edited by John F. Wilson. Vol. 9 in *The Works of Jonathan Edwards*. New Haven: Yale University Press, 1989.

————. *Religious Affections*. Edited by John E. Smith. Vol. 2 in *The Works of Jonathan Edwards*. New Haven: Yale University Press, 1959.

Flusser, David. *Jesus*. Jerusalem: Hebrew University Magnes Press, 2001.

Fredriksen, Paula. *When Christians Were Jews: The First Generation*. New Haven: Yale University Press, 2018.

Harnack, Adolf von. *What Is Christianity?* Translated by Thomas Bailey Saunders. Philadelphia: Fortress, 1957.

Hays, Richard. *Echoes of Scripture in the Letters of Paul*. New Haven: Yale University Press, 1989.

Kant, Immanuel. *The Conflict of the Faculties*. Translated by Mary J. Gregor. Lincoln: University of Nebraska Press, 1992.

Lee, Sang Hyun. "Edwards and Beauty." In *Understanding Jonathan Edwards: An Introduction to America's Theologian*, edited by Gerald McDermott, 113–24. New York: Oxford University Press, 2009.

Luther, Martin. *Lectures on Jonah*. In *Lectures on the Minor Prophets II*, vol. 19 of *Luther's Works*, edited by Hilton Oswald, 3–104. St. Louis: Concordia, 1963.

16. Edwards, *Religious Affections*, vol. 2 in *The Works of Jonathan Edwards* (New Haven: Yale University Press, 1959), 298, 274.

17. Sang Hyun Lee, "Edwards and Beauty," in *Understanding Jonathan Edwards: An Introduction to America's Theologian*, ed. Gerald McDermott (New York: Oxford University Press, 2009), 113.

McClymond, Michael, and Gerald McDermott. "Providence and History." In *The Theology of Jonathan Edwards*, 224–43. New York: Oxford University Press, 2012.

Thiessen, Matthew. "Did Jesus Plan to Start a New Religion?" In *Understanding the Jewish Roots of Christianity*, edited by Gerald McDermott, 18–32. Bellingham, WA: Lexham, 2021.

Wright, N. T. *The Challenge of Jesus.* Downers Grove, IL: InterVarsity, 1999.

Part Four

The Incarnation

10

Coming into the World

We have just finished the first main section of this book, showing that the history of redemption started just after the fall and continued until the birth of Jesus. Redemption did not wait for the *Logos* to take on flesh. Sinners started to receive freedom from the Messiah just after the fall in the garden. The whole history of the First or Old Testament was the history of redemption by the Messiah, the Second Person of the Triune God, the God of Israel. Everything in this long history of the human race from its first parents until the birth of the Second Adam was preparatory. Every bit of social and political history in these thousands of years was being used by the God of Israel to prepare the world for the birth of the Messiah.

The next chapter in the history of redemption is very short by comparison, only thirty-three years. But because these years witnessed the human life of God in the flesh, it was the most important and influential period that ever was or ever will be. Nearly all of the counsels of redemption in eternity among the three divine Persons had to do with this brief but momentous period. This was the blinding flash of light that illuminated all that had come before and everything that would follow in the next thousands of years. Everything that believers experienced from the true God was but a refraction from this explosion of light and love that was a Person.

The incarnation of God was not glorious by worldly standards. Edwards called it the time of the Messiah's humiliation. Jesus was born into near-poverty, never enjoyed earthly wealth, and ministered in a time of social and political desperation for Israel. He was ignored or persecuted by the elites of his day and died the death of a common criminal. This was the lot of the God-man who was Israel's

Messiah. But his poverty became riches for the world. His short life and death brought life to a dying world and beauty to the miserable.

Purchase of Redemption

Redemption is payment to buy something back, and in this case to buy something or someone out of slavery. These spectacular thirty-three years—the apex of all created history—were the time when the God of Israel in his three Persons made the payment to buy sinful humanity out of slavery to sin, death, and the devil. All of the millions of sacrifices before this time were anticipatory and typological, pointing forward as types to the massive antitype of the Messiah's payment. But none of these types paid one cent toward the purchase. All of the sacrifices made after these thirty-three years looked back toward this purchase. All of the acts of faith and obedience in the last two thousand years and all of the millions of sacramental re-presentations of this purchase brought the purchase into the lives of the elect. But none of these acts of allegiance and sacramental re-presentation contributed one cent toward the purchase.

The purchase began with the conception of the Messiah in the womb of the blessed Virgin Mary by the power of the Holy Spirit. The purchase was completed when the last tentacle of death slipped off the human nature of the Messiah on the morning of his resurrection. By then it was finished. So the purchase involved not only the death of the Messiah but also his life, as Paul makes clear in his Epistle to the Romans: "For if as enemies we were reconciled to God through the death of his son, much more, having been reconciled, will we be *saved by his life*" (Rom. 5:10). The entire life of Messiah, in all of its humiliation, was necessary to fulfill the Law to pay for our redemption. His death reconciled us to God by bringing us out of hell (so to speak), but his whole life of obedience to God's holy law was necessary to earn us our place in the kingdom of God for eternity, thus bringing us up to heaven (so to speak). So we are saved by works after all. Not our works, but the works of the Messiah. It was this work of the Messiah, which began in Mary's womb and was completed on Easter morning, that purchased our redemption for us. Every cent of the purchase was paid by the time of that spring morning in Jerusalem. Even if the *application* of that purchase was made to the lives of billions over the centuries through the Church's liturgy and sacraments and believers' faith, all of the actual purchase was finished by the resurrection of the Messiah.

In this chapter we will look at the Messiah becoming incarnate to give himself the capacity for this purchase, and in the next we will examine the purchase itself.

The Necessity of the Purchase

It was necessary that the Son of God take on human nature in order to make this purchase. As the divine Son he was infinitely sufficient, but without a human nature he did not have the capacity to do what was needed. Since it was humans who had broken God's law, a human needed to make the infinite tribute to God's law in recompense. As God, the Son could neither obey nor suffer. The divine nature is impassible and infinitely above all suffering. And it is impossible that God, insofar as he is God, should obey a law meant for human beings or suffer punishment meant for those humans. It was a *man* whom God warned, "You shall surely die" (Gen. 2:17). But a God-*man* could suffer and obey the Father insofar as he was man. He could be a substitute human to take the punishment meant for all other humans.

It was necessary for the divine Messiah to take created nature up into himself in order to redeem nature. But not just any nature. As Thomas Aquinas observed, the Messiah could not redeem sinful human beings by taking on angelic nature, because angelic sin was irredeemable and human sin required human payment. Edwards argued that nature must obey the law given to it, and God's law was given to humans, not angels. So the Messiah had to take on human nature in order to make the human payment of perfect obedience to God's law for human beings. And he had to live as a human being in the same world where the first human being had sinned and brought death to the race. This is why John says "the Word became flesh and dwelt *among us*" (John 1:14). He had to live as a human in the same world that humans had corrupted by their sin.

Conception

The incarnation was noteworthy in a host of ways—not least in the ways that the Messiah was conceived, was born, and had been chosen for a particular time in history. He was conceived as the son of Abraham and David, hence a member of God's chosen people and, most importantly, the scion of Israel's Davidic king, who was prophesied to be the progenitor of the Messiah. But while Jesus was descended from these world-historical Jewish figures, his conception in one sense was ordinary. He was conceived in a human womb and so was formed by Mary's human flesh and human chromosomes. But since he had no human father, his other twenty-three chromosomes came from the Holy Spirit.

This made his conception the most remarkable in human history. He was the son of a woman but not the son of any human father. He was the "seed of the woman" (Gen. 3:15) but not the seed of any man. The woman was a virgin who never had sexual relations with a man. It was a virginal conception, absolutely singular in the history of humanity. This man's generation was a miraculous work of the Holy Spirit.

Birth

At one level, the Messiah's gestation, birth, and boyhood development were entirely natural. His human nature was gradually perfected, as is that of every other child who comes out of a woman's womb. The process of birth was no different from that of every other child born of a woman. No doubt there were pain and tears.

But at another level this birth was unique, like no other birth before or since. The baby was born without the sinful nature that has come with every other child born since Cain. The Messiah had free will and was tempted as we are, but he did not have the sinful inclination of a bent will toward sin and self-obsession.

Timing

Paul says the Messiah was incarnated, born of a woman, born under the Law, in "the fullness of time" (Gal. 4:4). In God's infinite wisdom, this was the perfect time for his Son the Messiah to come into the world. All the ages preceding this had prepared for the incarnation at this precise time.

Why did God wait until after Noah's flood? Edwards suggests that the effects of sin had not accumulated enough by then, so that the Messiah's conquest of sin would not have seemed as great. Besides, human lives until then lasted most of a thousand years, which was a kind of immortality. The curse of death was not so readily seen. The admonition, "You are dust and to dust you shall return" (Gen. 3:19), would not have seemed so bad. It was necessary for the shortness of life to be lamented before the joy of Messiah's gift of never-ending life could be appreciated.

It would have been still too soon if the Messiah had come after the flood but before Moses. At that point human beings had not yet seen the full extent of pagan darkness. The human race had not so fully apostatized. Lives were shorter but not as short as after Moses.

The coming of the Messiah needed to be many ages after Moses. Only then could people see the utter futility of all the remedies tried to secure goodness and truth. Long experience trying those remedies was needed for people to see that even after many and desperate attempts to solve human dilemmas, nothing works to bring rest to the soul. These ages were needed to convince people that they needed a divine physician.

Another reason to wait a long time after the flood and Moses was to wait until the earth was more fully populated. This was needed so that when the Messiah came and his kingdom was extended, it would reach many cultures and peoples and not just a few. Then there would be more light and grace and glory to illumine the world, not to mention greater victory over the devil's kingdom.

It was also necessary for long ages of the Jewish community and religion to develop so that the Messiah's reign and sacrifice would be understood. The complex mysteries of Jewish sacrifices and worship were essential to provide Jews and, later, Christians with typological lessons—images that are far richer than rational explanations—that would illuminate the near-infinite dimensions of the Messiah's life and death and resurrected life. The tabernacle, temple, kings, and kingdoms were necessary to show the world aspects of the Messiah's kingdom that could not be seen sufficiently in the short three years of his public ministry.

Furthermore, Satan's kingdom needed to develop to its greatest extent in the four empires described in the previous chapter—Babylonian, Persian, Greek, and Roman—so that the Messiah's kingdom could be seen to transcend the greatest of these.

Even the Jewish exiles and diasporas played a necessary role. The dispersion of Jews throughout much of the world helped spread expectation of a coming Messiah and, once he came, news of his arrival.

The great development of learning during these centuries before the incarnation was also important. The Messiah's disciples, both Jewish and Gentile, soon used this learning to help develop their theology and assist their apologetic efforts to demonstrate the futility of escaping slavery to sin, death, and the devil apart from the Messiah and his kingdom in the Church.

The Greatness of the Incarnation

It is impossible to overestimate the greatness of the incarnation. The creation of the cosmos was mind-boggling, but not nearly so great as the incarnation. There was nothing greater in all of history except the death of the Messiah. Many phenomenal events have occurred since the creation, but nothing as momentous as this, God becoming man by the Son taking up into himself a human nature.

Ever since that taking up, human nature has been in the Godhead and will be forevermore.

Furthermore, because human nature is now within the very Godhead, within the inner life of the Trinity, human nature has been changed. The history of humanity has been different ever since. It is not without significance that humanity has had different ideals ever since. Human nature has continued to be sinful, and the outworking of that sinfulness has been catastrophic in horrific ways, but its ideals have been elevated. For example, because of the incarnation and the Church it caused, compassion for the suffering has become a transcultural ideal in ways that were missing from the ancient world. Human nature's vision of the good has changed for the better, even if its achievement of the good has been abysmal apart from the Messiah.

It was a great thing for God to make a creature, but a far greater thing for the Creator himself to become a creature.[1] And when the Messiah was born, he became the greatest person who was ever born or ever will be born. No study of human personality or human nature will get close to seeing clearly without examining the unique person of the Messiah become man, Jesus of Nazareth.

The Lowliness of the Incarnation

Although the incarnation was the greatest event in history before the death of the Messiah, it appeared ironically in lowly conditions. Unlike every other king who wanted to establish a kingdom, this king purposely took his place in relative poverty. Mary was poor, as indicated by the offering of doves or pigeons at her son's temple presentation (Luke 2:24). Mary did not live in abject poverty—since Joseph was a *tektōn* or stone mason and therefore was working-class or middle-class—and Joseph was born into the royal line descended from David, but Mary had to give birth in a cave and lay her baby in a feeding trough for animals. And Joseph's royal line was "fallen," as the prophet Amos had written. It needed to be "built up as in the days of old" (Amos 9:11).

The Return of the Spirit

Despite these earthly humiliations, the incarnation was marked by signs of spiritual greatness. After four hundred years during which Jews lamented the absence

---

1. Edwards, *HWR*, 299.

of revelations to prophets like Malachi by the Spirit, now the Spirit had returned. Just before the birth of the Messiah, the Spirit spoke to Zechariah, John the Baptist's father. Then the Spirit gave stunning revelations to the Virgin Mary, Joseph her husband, and Elizabeth her cousin (Luke 1:28–38; Matt. 1:20–21; 1:13–20; Luke 1:41–45). Mary was given a song by the Spirit that has become the beautiful Magnificat (Luke 1:46–55), Zechariah received a second revelation (1:63–64), the shepherds had angels appear to them and speak to them (2:8–20), Anna and Simeon received revelations about the newborn Messiah (2:36–38; 2:25–35), wise men came from the East after the Spirit had shown them a star and its meaning (Matt. 2:1–11), and Joseph was later given dreams both to warn him to flee to Egypt and to return (2:13–23).

Great Notice

It was not only human beings who received great notice of this cosmic event. Angels got word too and passed it along. They had sung at the creation, the greatest event before this, and now sang to the shepherds (Job 38:7; Luke 2:13–14). They had followed the prophecies and promises given to the prophets, had longed to see their fulfillment, and so had been waiting in expectation (1 Pet. 1:12). All along the way in the history of redemption, they had been ministers to the principal agents of redemption, such as Abraham and Jacob, and at great moments in that history such as the giving of the Law at Sinai (Acts 7:53). Now that all of these types and prophecies were being fulfilled, they were thrilled (Luke 2:10).

God's people, the Jews, were given special notice. As we have seen, Elizabeth and Mary were given appearances by angels before the birth of either John or Jesus. The baby John leapt in his mother's womb with joy when he sensed the presence of the Messiah, also in a womb, just inches away from him. Jews nearby all praised God when they heard the revelations given to Zechariah, Simeon, and Anna.

Gentiles were also given special notice of this epochal event. The wise men from the east were some of the wisest Gentiles of the ancient world. They showed that they had ears to hear signs of the most important event of their time or any time. They not only listened but acted, which is the hallmark of true wisdom. Somehow they perceived that a star, perhaps a conjunction of heavenly objects, was a sign from the true God. They not only perceived but followed that star until it led them, after an arduous journey that probably tested their resolve, to the place of the baby. They might have been instructed by the prophecy of the pagan prophet Balaam, who lived in the east and was condemned by the early Church for idolatry and immorality but nevertheless prophesied truly of the future of Judah and the Messiah. He predicted that the Redeemer would be a star coming out of Jacob—a Jew—who would exercise dominion (Num. 24:17–19). If the wise men were not instructed by Balaam, they could have gotten news of a coming Messiah from Jews in the diaspora.

Jewish Fulfillment

The wise men knew that the "king of the Jews" was about to be born (Matt. 2:2). They might have also expected that as king of the Jews he would be Jewish and conform to Jewish tradition. And that he was, as we have seen in the last chapter. For example, he did not repudiate circumcision as is often alleged. The Gospel of Luke goes out of its way to show Jesus's parents presenting baby Jesus for circumcision on the eighth day, suggesting that Mary and Joseph were observant Jews and their son the Messiah was placed within this tradition.

The temple, the center of Jewish worship in the first century, was a primary pillar in the edifice of Jewish religion when the Son of God came to this world. Contrary to allegations that Jesus traduced the sanctity of the temple, he actually regarded it with reverence, calling it "my house" and declaring that God dwelled there (Matt. 21:13; 23:21). His cleansing of the temple was an effort to wrest it from "robbers" and restore it as a "house of prayer" (21:13).

We can conclude, then, that with the incarnation of the Son of God in or near 4 BC the scepter of Judah, prophesied fifteen hundred years before the event, was returning. Jacob's blessing had predicted that the scepter would not "turn aside" from Judah until just before Judah's "seed" came and the peoples obeyed that seed (Gen. 49:10). The scepter of independent or semi-independent rule did not depart from Judah until Herod the Great died. The departure of the scepter started when the ten northern tribes revolted under Rehoboam in the tenth century BC. The scepter departed from those tribes entirely when they were conquered and exiled by the Assyrians in the eighth century. It remained with the tribes of Judah and Benjamin in the house of David until they were taken captive by Nebuchadnezzar in the sixth century. They lost it at that point but gained it back when Cyrus of Persia gave them a governor. Their scepter at this point was not an independent one, but at least they could be governed by their own laws. So Judah had the freedom to observe Jewish law under the Persians and Greeks. Then they had their own kings under the Maccabees for about a century. While they lost that independence to Rome in 63 BC, the Romans permitted them their own laws and king, Herod the

Great, who reigned about forty years while giving fealty to Rome. When he died in 4 BC, Rome gave his rule to his son Herod Archelaus, who reigned until AD 6. At that point Rome imposed direct rule. Judah lost the scepter entirely, except for the brief reign of Herod Agrippa from AD 41 to 44. There were no more "temporal kings" of Judah after this, only Roman governors.[2] Jews lost the power of life and death over their own miscreants. Thus the scepter departed from Judah "until the One came whom the peoples obeyed" (Gen. 49:10).

Now that I have discussed the significance of the incarnation and the purchase of redemption by the Messiah during this momentous time, I will turn in the next chapter to the Messiah's work—*how* he purchased that redemption.

Select Bibliography

Aquinas, Thomas. "Whether It Is Proper to Christ to Be the Mediator to God and Man." In *Summa Theologica*, translated by Fathers of the English Dominican Province, III.26.1. New York: Benziger Brothers, 1948.

Edwards, Jonathan. *A History of the Work of Redemption*. Edited by John F. Wilson. Vol. 9 in *The Works of Jonathan Edwards*. New Haven: Yale University Press, 1989.

———. *Religious Affections*. Edited by John E. Smith. Vol. 2 in *The Works of Jonathan Edwards*. New Haven: Yale University Press, 1959.

McClymond, Michael, and Gerald McDermott. "The Person and Work of Jesus Christ." In *The Theology of Jonathan Edwards*, 244–61. New York: Oxford University Press, 2012.

2. Edwards, *HWR*, 303.

11

The Messiah's Work

The Messiah redeemed the world by paying its purchase price, a life of perfect obedience to God's law that entailed abasement and affliction. This payment accomplished two things. First, he satisfied God's wrath toward sin by his humiliation and suffering. This "satisfaction" saved us from the misery of hell. Second, he won for us the joys of heaven by earning "merit." The first—satisfaction—pulled us up from our descent to hell, and the second—merit—propelled us to the heights of heaven. Jesus our Messiah by his work of redemption accomplished both. To fully understand the beauty and glory of this redemption, we must see the fullness of each but also the distinction between the two. Because they are often confused, some explanation is in order.

Satisfaction and Merit

The two words "satisfaction" and "merit" when applied to the Messiah's redemption are often used in ambiguous ways. "Satisfaction" is sometimes used for both propitiation (the suffering Jesus endured to satisfy God's wrath toward sin) *and* meritorious obedience, since both propitiation and obedience are required by God's law. "Merit" is sometimes used for both as well, since everything done by the Messiah to satisfy the Father's holy wrath is also meritorious. The confusion is compounded because the two terms, "satisfaction" and "merit," differ not by referring to different events in the life of the Messiah but by relating the same events to different divine purposes.

The two terms describe the two purposes for the one infinite price the Messiah paid for our redemption. Insofar as the Messiah's suffering paid a negative debt, it was used for satisfaction. It purchased our freedom from the obligation to suffer forever in hell. But insofar as those same experiences of the Messiah obtained a positive good, they earned for us the merit to win eternal life in heaven.

Whatever Jesus did for satisfaction, he did because of the suffering or humiliation in those deeds. By those deeds he suffered the penalty of the Law on our behalf. So when he was ignored or cursed, for example, his humiliation was the judicial fruit of our sin that he took upon himself.

But insofar as Jesus cheerfully obeyed his Father's command to minister despite these humiliations, his obedience earned merit because of the righteousness in it. His cheerful compliance fulfilled the demands of the Law before the fall—namely, obedience to God's will. Everything he did during the years of the incarnation that was a matter of obedience and virtue was part of the merit of the Messiah that purchased happiness for the elect.

Every Part of the Incarnation for Two Purposes

All that the Messiah did and experienced in his thirty-three years was for the dual purposes of both satisfaction and merit. Satisfaction was accomplished by his suffering and humiliation not only in his last sufferings in his final days but in all the humiliation he endured from the first moments of his incarnation. So, for instance, the humiliating circumstances of his birth—being born to a virgin in a cave and being laid in a feeding trough for animals—helped satisfy God's wrath toward sin. So too his growing up in a working-class family living near bare subsistence level, enduring the infirmities of sinful flesh (without a sin nature but with the decay inherited from Adam's sin) and suspicion of his conception (Matt. 1:19), and all the difficulties he endured in his last three years of public ministry.

The same for merit. This was won in *all* of his experiences and deeds, not just some of them. So every good deed for others, all his preaching and teaching—all of it achieved merit because all of it was done in obedience to the Father.

Thus, everything in his life and ministry fulfilled both purposes, satisfaction and merit. The Messiah's laying down his life for us was for satisfaction because he bore the punishment we deserved and so satisfied God's offended justice. But it was also for merit because it was an act of obedience to the Father, who *commanded* him to lay down his life for sinners. Indeed, this final passion was the *principal* part of both his satisfaction and merit.

Two more examples. His circumcision was suffering by the little baby for satisfaction (by his baby blood!), as well as obedience to his call to be a mediator as the *Jewish* Messiah. And his birth in poverty was for satisfaction because of its suffering and humiliation, as well as being for righteousness and merit because of its obedience to the Father, who had commanded it.

Merit

We have just seen that while satisfaction and merit are often confused, they are distinct and that every deed and experience of the Messiah served both of those purposes as payment for the price of redemption. Now we will look in more detail at the positive side of this purchase, the relation of the work of the Messiah to earning the merit of righteousness that earned for himself and all his Body fellowship with God and the saints forever in heaven. Seeing all this will enlarge our vision of the beauty of the Messiah and his redemption.

Obedience to All Divine Law

The first aspect of this beauty is the Messiah's cheerful obedience to all the laws that God the Father ever gave to human beings. God is a lawgiver, which means he gives commandments to his human creatures. He did this as soon as he created our first parents. Immediately after he created male and female in the image of God, he blessed them and gave them his first commandment: "Be fruitful and multiply and fill the earth and subdue it" (Gen. 1:27–28).

God gave laws to people through what has been described in chapter 4 as natural law[1]—that is, laws that are accessible to all human beings through natural reason. All cultures, for example, have known through reason and conscience that it is wrong to take the life of innocents or to break marriage vows.

God has also given "positive" commandments to certain people in unique situations. For example, God told Adam that he and his wife were not to eat of the tree of the knowledge of good and evil. God told Jonah to go to Nineveh to preach God's coming judgment.

God also gave special laws that were to be followed by Jews rather than Gentiles, such as circumcision and kosher.

---

1. See chapter 4 under "The Noahic Commandments."

In one form or another Jesus Messiah obeyed all of these different kinds of divine law. He obeyed natural law in the form of the moral law of the Ten Commandments, which has been taught by every major world religion and culture (as C. S. Lewis famously showed in his "Illustrations of the Tao" at the end of *The Abolition of Man*).[2]

Jesus Messiah also observed Jewish law. We have seen in previous chapters that while many theologians and scholars have thought that Jesus put an end to Jewish law, a closer examination of the Gospels demonstrates the opposite. He agreed with the consensus of his contemporary Jews that while Gentiles were exempt from the Jewish particularities of Mosaic law, he and his Messianic Jewish followers were called to observe them. To repeat a small part of what has been argued earlier, Jesus was circumcised, seems to have traveled to the temple three times a year as Jewish men were commanded by Torah, and fulfilled the new positive commandment to Jews to submit to John's baptism. As he said in the Sermon on the Mount, he had come not to abolish but to fulfill the Law (Matt. 5:17).

Jesus also obeyed cheerfully the mediatorial law that the Father commanded— the deeds he must do and experiences he must have as Mediator to save the world. This included the Father's commands to teach people about him (the Father), preach the gospel, work certain miracles, establish sacraments, and lay down his life. As Jesus said, he did what he saw the Father doing and spoke only the words the Father gave him (John 5:19; 12:49). None of this law involved commands to him as a man or as a Jew. They came to him because of his calling to be the Mediator between the holy God and sinful human beings. They were the chief part of the righteousness that merited heaven for himself and his followers. They were also the principal subject of the four Gospel narratives.

Perfect Obedience

Jesus's obedience was unique in three ways. First, it was perfect: perfect because he obeyed all, not just some, of God's commands—God's commands to human beings as humans, his commands to Jews, and his special commands to the Mediator. Thus Jesus obeyed every kind of law.

Jesus also obeyed every commandment of the Father to avoid sin. Jesus committed neither sins of commission nor sins of omission. His heart was always pure in his obedience, and he always aimed at the right ends in his choices. His manner of

2. C. S. Lewis, "Illustrations of the Tao," in *The Abolition of Man* (New York: Collier, 1947), 93–121.

acting was always perfectly attuned to what was proper to the situation. His degree of action was always perfect, neither too much nor too little. He was constant in all these things and always persevered to the end, no matter how difficult it came to be toward the end. For all these reasons his obedience was meritorious.

Particularly noteworthy was the Messiah's obedience during his greatest trials and temptations. He obeyed through the greatest difficulties and despite the worst of humiliation and suffering. We all know that it is one thing to obey when the commandment is easy or the circumstances are favorable. It is quite another thing when it is excruciatingly difficult to obey.

The Messiah paid the greatest honor to the Law, always treating it with the utmost respect. He showed greater love to God the Father than the angels show, even though elect angels obey with sinless perfection. As a man the Messiah did not have infinite love, but as the Son of God he did in his loving obedience, and it was because of his infinite dignity that the Messiah's infinite love was infinitely meritorious.

In All Phases of Life

The Messiah was obedient not simply in some periods such as his three years of public ministry but in every phase of life. As a child he perfectly obeyed his parents. There were no terrible twos in which he got angry at parental refusals to his toddler requests. Or boyish temper tantrums. At the age of twelve he started his mediatorial work at the temple and politely but firmly made that clear to his parents when his choice to stay behind upset his mother. But he submitted sweetly to his parents as a teenager even when he thought their requests were not always the best—and in his human nature that must have happened from time to time. As a stonemason (*tektōn*) with his father, he always gave honor to his father even if he might have seen a better way to work on a particular job.

Jesus began his public ministry at thirty, just as Kohathites started serving in the tabernacle at that age (Num. 4). This was called Jesus's "coming," which is one reason why John the Baptist asked if he was the "one to come" (Matt. 11:3). The Baptist was the voice of one crying in the wilderness, as Isaiah wrote (40:3–5). Jesus's cousin John was called by God to prepare the way of the Lord. Jesus said he was the typological Elijah who Malachi said would come before Messiah (Mal. 4:5–6). In fact, Jesus said, John was the greatest of all the prophets before the Messiah (Matt. 11:11). Edwards said the other prophets were like stars in the night that disappear just before the sun rises, just as John said he had to decrease and the Messiah increase. These words were fulfilled when John was martyred shortly after the beginning of Jesus's public ministry.

That beginning started with two dramatic events. The first was Jesus's baptism by John when the Holy Spirit appeared like a dove over the Messiah's head and the Father spoke from heaven, "This is my beloved Son in whom I am delighted" (Matt. 3:17). Then the Spirit led Jesus into the Judean wilderness down the mountain from Jerusalem, where the devil attacked him with profound temptations. Jesus emerged victorious from every one.

The Works of the Messiah

A great part of the Messiah's work was to teach and preach the words the Father gave him. He spoke from the Father's bosom, making the Father's mind and will clearer than Moses or the prophets before him. Another way of putting this is to say that he did what the rabbis said the Messiah would do. He delivered "the Messiah's Torah"—the "law of Christ" as most English translations put it (Gal. 6:2; 1 Cor. 9:21)—which would provide the inner meaning of Mosaic Torah. Both Torahs, so to speak, provided blessings and warnings. But whereas Moses delivered the words of YHWH and the rabbis spoke with the authority of others, Jesus Messiah spoke for himself, with his own authority. As he said in John, "This is my commandment" (John 15:12). This is why the synagogue in Capernaum was astonished by his authority—that he appealed to himself rather than previous rabbis (Mark 1:22).

Another part of the Messiah's work was his working of miracles. He healed thousands in mercy to the suffering but also to prove he was who he said he was. As he said to the paralytic lowered through the roof by friends, "So that you might know that the Son of Man has authority to forgive sins on the earth . . . I tell you, Get up, pick up your mat, and go home" (Mark 2:10–11). His miracles were remarkably foreseen by works and prophecies in the Old Testament—stilling the sea (Ps. 107:29), walking on the water during a storm (Job 9:8), casting out demons (Ps. 74:14), feeding crowds in the wilderness (Deut. 8:16), reading minds (Amos 4:13), raising the dead (Ps. 68:20), opening the eyes of the blind (146:8), healing the sick (103:3), and releasing those who are bound (146:7–8). All of these miracles that worked on external bodies were also images of the internal and greater work that the Messiah does in human hearts.

Just as the Messiah's teaching authority was different from that of Moses, so too was the source of his miraculous power. Moses was prevented from entering the promised land because he suggested at one point that the power was his own (Deut. 32:49–52; Num. 20). But the power for Jesus's miracles came from his own divinity. For the Messiah to deny his own power would have been a lie.

Another work of the Messiah was to call and train his apostles over the course of three years. His was a theology not of the multitudes but of the remnant. He preached to the multitudes, but most chose not to follow him when he started teaching the cost of discipleship. Most of his time was devoted to training the remnant and its leaders in the twelve. They were to become the foundation stones of his Church (Rev. 21:14).

The greatest work of the Messiah was to offer himself as a sacrifice to the Father. This was the great antitype of history, toward which pointed all the types of animal and other sacrifices and offerings made by priests and laity from the beginning of the world. As God's high priest, Jesus not only offered himself as a sacrifice to his Father but also instituted the sacrament of the Eucharist, in which members of his body could be lifted up out of linear time and enter sacramental time, where they could join the Son in that offering to the Father. It was the once-for-all offering that could be re-presented in worship through time, joining the celestial worship of the Father that is ongoing (pictured in Rev. 4–5). This was the greatest act of the Messiah's public ministry—both his institution of the sacrament at the Last Supper and his sacrifice the next day. It was the greatest act of obedience by which he purchased redemption for his body, the Church.[3]

The Messiah's Virtues

Throughout his public ministry, the Messiah's virtues shone with brilliance. But not the whole range of human virtues. For the Messiah never sinned, and some human virtues are those that belong only to sinners. Think of repentance, heartbrokenness over sin, mortification of sinful desires, and self-denial of selfish inclinations. Although Jesus in his human nature often had to deny natural human desires for pleasure and recognition, he never had to break a sinful habit or repent a sinful deed.

But Jesus displayed the full range of other human virtues. This meant all the virtues in relation to God, himself, and others. Toward God he always displayed holy fear and reverence. He resisted the sin of the fallen angels, who refused to humble themselves before human beings and the Father. The Messiah accepted the humiliation of the incarnation. Toward God, Jesus was always perfect in his

---

3. Edwards, *HWR*, 318.

love for the Father. No man ever suffered so much from love or submitted with such devotion.

Toward himself the Messiah was also virtuous. Despite being the most excellent of all people, and therefore having the most reason of anyone to be proud, he was the most humble. Even though he did miracles, his human nature did not swell with conceit. Although he knew that he was the heir of his Father's kingdom, he accepted his role of being despised and rejected.[4] He was willing to be a cursed criminal, a laughingstock, spat upon with contempt. He accepted this derision without protest.

Jesus Messiah showed the patience of Job and then some. Throughout nearly all of his passion he opened not his mouth. Like a patient lamb, he chose the contempt of the world over its praises, the Father's approval over a temporal crown.

Jesus's virtues toward other people were also exemplary. The most apparent were his meekness and love. His meekness could be seen in his calmness of spirit when he was bitterly provoked by his enemies. Even when he was abused with spite and contempt from vile men, he took it with composure. The unreasonableness of their hatred was matched only by his meekness, which actually deserved their love and honor. Yet he accepted their humiliations, which were the most undeserved that anyone ever experienced in human history. When reviled, he chose not to revile in return. Rather than being filled with a spirit of anger and revenge, Jesus prayed, "Father, forgive them, for they know not what they do" (Luke 23:34). This was unparalleled forbearance.

Jesus's love was also unparalleled. His last sufferings illustrated love more than any of his previous sufferings. They exceeded the love of any of the apostles, even that of John the great preacher of love, as an ocean exceeds a little stream.

Jesus's passion demonstrated not only his love for human beings most clearly. The furnace of his last afflictions also showed his other virtues in the brightest light: his love for the Father, desire to honor God's majesty, devotion to God's law, his obedience, humility, contempt for the world, patience, meekness, and spirit of forgiveness.[5] In these last hours the merit of the Messiah's entire life and death was most brilliantly on display.

Satisfaction

In the previous sections we have seen how all of the Messiah's life was meritorious, earning for the elect a place among the redeemed in heaven. Now we will see

4. Edwards, *HWR*, 321–22.
5. Edwards, *HWR*, 324.

how that same life in its manifold sufferings served as satisfaction of the Father's wrath toward human sin.

It was not usually easy for the Messiah to live as a man and as a Jew. But it was infinitely more difficult for him to do what was required of him as the Mediator between a holy God and sinful humanity. For example, he was born for the purpose of death. This burden was felt at his birth in his mother's suffering. There was no room at the inn, so she had to give birth in a cave with animals, without the dignity of ordinary human childbirth assisted by loved ones and common amenities. Shortly after, the baby was the object of persecution, and the family had to flee its homeland and culture. No doubt the young parents and newborn suffered much on the journey to, and exile among, a strange country and people. This was the beginning of what Simeon meant in his prophecy to Mary that a sword would "pass through your own soul" (Luke 2:35).

The Messiah's private life in Nazareth was difficult. He "led a servile, obscure life" in a humble occupation as a stonemason.[6] Earning his bread by hard labor, he suffered the curse pronounced after the fall, "By the sweat of your face you shall eat bread" (Gen. 3:19). He must have felt the humiliation of being overlooked and ignored. He was living a life of spotless purity and holiness, but in silence and without any of the glory that he deserved as the Son of God.

Yet even in his public ministry, when his glory was beginning to be seen, there was regular suffering. He had nowhere to lay his head, which probably means he was often forced to sleep in the open air and on stony ground, pinched sometimes by hunger and cold. He lived by the charity of wealthy women who accompanied his little band of disciples. Nevertheless he did not always have the wherewithal to pay the temple tax required of Jews, and so on one occasion got it out of the mouth of a fish (Matt. 17:27). He had to eat his last Passover meal not at his own house but in the borrowed room of another. His grave was not his own but another's. This was the lot of poor Jews without land.

Poverty was perhaps easier for a humble man to endure. But hatred and calumny are never easy to suffer, particularly when you know as a man that you are also the king of the cosmos. The Gospels tell us that Jesus was insulted because of his obscure home village and dubious parentage. He was condemned as a glutton, drunkard, and friend of corrupt taxmen and prostitutes; decried as a deceiver, madman, and demon possessed; denounced as a blasphemer and magician who worked by Satan's power; and excommunicated along with all who followed him.

6. Edwards, *HWR*, 325.

His enemies wished him dead and repeatedly tried to trap and kill him. More than once they took up stones to stone him; once they led him to the top of a cliff to hurl him off, but he narrowly escaped. He was hated and condemned by the leaders of the very people he came to save. As John put it, "He came to his own, and his own people did not receive him" (John 1:11).

Jesus was popular with the masses of the Jewish people during much of his public ministry, but wherever he ministered, he was also confronted by members of the Judean party led by the temple leaders in Jerusalem. These men opposed him in Capernaum—the site of his ministry headquarters—in Jericho, in his hometown of Nazareth, in Jerusalem, and even among his neighbors and relatives.

Then there were the Satanic attacks. Shortly after the beginning of his public ministry, Satan led him out into the wilderness for forty days of violent attacks, mental and physical. Jesus was alone with hunger, animals, demons, and the devil himself. While he was suffering intense weakness, the devil transported him bodily from place to place, once to the pinnacle of the temple high atop Jerusalem, and then on another occasion to the top of a very high mountain. This was the beginning of three years during which the principalities and powers inspired his human enemies to threaten and entrap him.

Last Humiliations and Sufferings

But the end of the three years was when the suffering and satisfaction were most intense. The intensity began in the garden of Gethsemane and ended only at the resurrection. Jesus's agony in the garden was so intense that it "force[d] blood through the pores of his skin," so that his whole body became spotted with blood.[7] He knew that one of his own disciples, to whom he had shown kindness and whom he had treated as family, had sold him for thirty pieces of silver. And he knew that the other disciples, once friends, would all flee and abandon him. He was led away as a criminal to be interrogated by priests and scribes who hated him. They stayed up all night just "to have the pleasure of insulting him."[8]

For hours they abused and disparaged him. These tormentors tried to get witnesses against him but found none. So they put up false witnesses. They pressed him repeatedly to confess that he was the Son of God. He would not. But when they finally forced him by swearing in the name of God, they were delighted. This

7. Edwards, HWR, 328.
8. Edwards, HWR, 328.

gave them justification, they thought, for spitting in his face, blindfolding him and punching his head, and mocking him with calls to prophesy. Then they ridiculed him for pretending to be a prophet.

On that horrible night Jesus's top disciple chose to distance himself. He claimed he would be ashamed to know him. He swore a curse on himself, insisting he did not know him. Not once but three times.

In the morning the priests and elders brought Jesus before Pilate because they had no authority to execute him. Pilate examined him and found no fault worthy of death. This infuriated the Judean leaders, so Pilate sent him to Herod, who also found Jesus innocent of a capital crime. But for sport Herod had Jesus dressed in fake royal robes and paraded through the streets of Jerusalem back to Pilate. For a second time Pilate declared him innocent and suggested he be released.

The Judean leaders with their party hacks were furious and demanded that Barabbas be released instead. So Pilate put Jesus on trial, as it were, a third time, testifying again that he found nothing wrong in this man. But for fear of these Judean leaders and what they might say to his overseers in Rome, Pilate handed the Messiah over to be crucified. Before the spikes were driven through his wrists and ankles, he endured another round of stripping and mock adornment, this time with a scarlet robe and crown of thorns.

Roman soldiers and Judean leaders bowed before him with scorn, spat on him again, and made him take a reed as a sham staff for the man they considered a fake king. They forced him to carry his cross until he collapsed under its weight. The passerby Simon of Cyrene was commandeered to shoulder it.

Crucifixion is one of the most painful forms of execution ever devised. The nails go through the ulnar nerve on the wrist, the most sensitive bundle of nerve fibers in the body, because nails in the palm would rip through the flesh under the weight of the hanging body. The word "excruciating" is appropriate because it comes from *crux*, the Latin word for cross.

The fathers tell us that even worse than the physical pain that the Messiah underwent was his mental torment, the "anguish of soul," which Isaiah described (Isa. 53:11). While the devil was tormenting him through the mockery of men, the Father abandoned him. This judicial sentence of separation removed from Jesus any source of comfort in these horrific hours. We cannot begin to imagine this infinite pain.

Finally, Jesus bowed his head and gave up his soul. "It is finished," he said. This was the most astonishing incident in the history of creation: the Son of God murdered, after being tortured in body and soul by the people he had come to save. All of this—his birth and life and ministry but especially the death that paid satisfaction—was what the angels had been longing to see for the previous millennia. This was what all the sacrifices in Jewish law and worship, and even the distorted sacrificial types in the world religions, had been pointing to since the beginning of the world.

Completion of the Purchase

Jesus Messiah continued under the power of death until the third day in its early morning hours. When Jesus's body came back to life and he stepped out of the tomb, the grand purchase of redemption was completed. Full satisfaction of the Father's wrath toward sin was made. God's justice was demonstrated. After millennia of human sin that seemed to be ignored, God showed that he hates sin and was pouring out his holy and just wrath upon it. The entire debt was being paid.

But not only satisfaction. This dreadful end was also meritorious. It won for Jesus and all his Body of followers eternal life in heaven. This was the other half of the purchase of redemption. It was fully procured. Nothing more needed to be done. Nothing after and nothing in the future. Everything had now been done by the Messiah that was needed to satisfy God's justice and win for his Body eternal life in heaven and the new earth.

The purchase price of redemption was complete. But the *application* of that price to billions of souls was not. This application would involve a different sort of affliction, the sort that Paul meant when he described his own afflictions—after the death and resurrection of the Messiah—as things that were "lacking in Messiah's afflictions . . . for the sake of his Body, which is the Church" (Col. 1:24). These were afflictions that do not help purchase redemption—for the purchase is complete and finished—but afflictions that help members of the Body *apply* their fully completed redemption to themselves and the world.

They do not help satisfy God's justice, which the Messiah's life and death satisfied in toto. Rather, they are like the persecution that came to the Messiah during his ministry and that will continue for his Body throughout history: "If they persecuted me, they will persecute you" (John 15:20). As Jesus suggested to Paul on the road to Damascus, when the Messiah's followers were persecuted after his resurrection, Jesus himself was being persecuted: "Saul, Saul, why are you persecuting *me*?" (Acts 9:4). These were the continuing "afflictions of the Messiah" (Col. 1:24) that God uses to apply the Messiah's purchase of redemption to his Body.

The purchase of redemption is an *objective* fact, completed by Jesus's resurrection. But the *subjective* appropriation of that purchase uses suffering to work its way into believers' souls. As Paul and Barnabas told their disciples, "It is necessary for us to pass through many afflictions to enter into the kingdom of God" (Acts 14:22). Somehow in God's mystery of redemption, believers must experience something of the Messiah's afflictions to receive the full benefit of his completed purchase of redemption.

Select Bibliography

Edwards, Jonathan. *A History of the Work of Redemption.* Edited by John F. Wilson. Vol. 9 in *The Works of Jonathan Edwards.* New Haven: Yale University Press, 1989.

Lewis, C. S. "Illustrations of the Tao." In *The Abolition of Man*, 93–121. New York: Collier, 1947.

McClymond, Michael, and Gerald McDermott. "Justification and Sanctification." In *The Theology of Jonathan Edwards*, 389–409. New York: Oxford University Press, 2012.

Part Five

From Christ's Resurrection to the End of the World

12

Resurrection

In the last chapter we saw that the Messiah's purchase of redemption was twofold, satisfying divine justice to save us from hell and earning merit by perfect obedience to win eternal life for his Body. Now we shall see that the last part of that purchase—the Messiah's resurrection—demonstrated all the other effects of his redemption. Before we look in detail at those effects, we shall examine briefly the centrality, plausibility, and necessity of the resurrection.

Centrality of the Resurrection

The resurrection of the Messiah was at the center of the early Church's witness. When the apostles explained the good news, the Messiah's resurrection from the dead was front and center. In his longest and most systematic epistle Paul said it was because of the resurrection that we know that Jesus is the Son of God (Rom. 1:4). When the apostles chose someone to replace Judas, they wondered who among them would join them as "a witness to his resurrection" (Acts 1:22). In Peter's Pentecost sermon the apostle told his Jerusalem audience that they crucified Jesus but "God raised him up" (2:24). Peter went on to say that David predicted the resurrection—"of that we are all witnesses"—and it was because of the resurrection that the Spirit had been poured out in front of them, causing Jews from all over the world to tell "the mighty works of God" but "each in our own tongues" (2:25–35; 2:11).

In his second speech in Jerusalem Peter focused on the resurrection again: "You killed the author of life, whom God raised from the dead, and of that we are

157

witnesses" (Acts 3:15). When Peter and John were arrested and hauled before the Sanhedrin to explain why they were "proclaiming in Jesus the resurrection from the dead" (4:2), the apostles doubled down. The lame beggar had been healed by the name of Jesus Messiah from Nazareth, "whom you crucified" and "God raised from the dead" (4:10). When the council urged them to stop preaching some time later, again the resurrection was at the heart of their proclamation: "It is necessary to obey God rather than men. The God of our fathers raised Jesus, whom you murdered after hanging him from a tree. This man, our leader and savior, God exalted to his right hand" (5:29–31).

The resurrection was the center of the message Peter preached to Cornelius and his family. "They put [Jesus] to death by hanging him from a tree, but God raised him on the third day and gave him to appear . . . to us who ate with him and drank with him after he rose from the dead" (Acts 10:39–41).

In sum, the resurrection of the Messiah was in no way superfluous to redemption or tangential to the gospel, as modern liberals from Schleiermacher to Bultmann have alleged. For the apostles from whom we get our Christian—which means messianic—faith, it was at the very center of our faith. As Paul wrote, "If Messiah has not been raised, your faith is futile and you are still in your sins" (1 Cor. 15:17).

Plausibility of the Resurrection

In the twentieth century skeptics attacked the biblical accounts of the bodily resurrection of Jesus. Their primary method was historical, arguing, as did Rudolf Bultmann, that moderns cannot believe in something that ordinary history has not attested. But more recent scholars have pointed to literary signals that support the authenticity of these accounts. N. T. Wright has led the way in his monumental *Resurrection of the Son of God*. For example, when one considers that the ancient world discounted female testimony, it is remarkable that the gospel writers acknowledge the experience of women with the risen Jesus. They even make women the first witnesses (Matt. 28:1–10; Luke 24:1–10; John 20:1–18). If the New Testament authors were making these stories up, they never would have used the testimonies of women—not unless these stories were true.[1]

The same is true of the repeated mentions of the apostles themselves being skeptical. When the two Marys and other women told the apostles of the angels at the empty tomb, "[the women's] words seemed to be nonsense; [the disciples]

---

1. N. T. Wright, *The Resurrection of the Son of God* (Minneapolis: Fortress, 2003), 607–8.

disbelieved" the women (Luke 24:11). Even after the risen Jesus showed them his pierced feet and hands, "they still disbelieved" (Luke 24:41). Thomas refused to believe even the apostles' reports (John 20:25). If the resurrection accounts were fictitious, the authors probably would have omitted anything suggesting that Jesus's own disciples had a hard time believing that he had risen bodily from the dead. The fact that more than once the evangelists point out the apostles' doubts when confronted with claims for Jesus's resurrection and then the presence of the risen Messiah himself gives us a sound basis for concluding that these stories are authentic. Only charlatans spin stories with perfect heroes. The women's testimonies and the apostles' doubts ironically make the resurrection stories all the more plausible.[2]

We also know from reliable tradition that all but John gave their lives for their testimony that they saw the risen Jesus and watched him eat. Ghosts don't eat. And liars don't go to their deaths for a lie. As Pascal wrote, "I believe only those histories whose witnesses got themselves killed."[3]

Necessity of the Resurrection

Since the Father had withdrawn from sinful humanity and refused to have direct contact with them except through his Mediator (chapter 3), it was necessary that this Mediator be alive to pass on the effects of the redemption. But if the Messiah—who was the Mediator—was dead, how could he deliver ongoing redemption to his Body? Therefore, the resurrection was necessary for his distribution of the effects of his redemption. The Messiah had to be alive to bring about all that he had died for. He had to purchase redemption as a priest, since priests offer sacrifice to procure temporary redemption from sin, and he is the Great High Priest purchasing eternal redemption. But in this case, he had to act as a king to bring about the fruit of that purchase for the lives of all his subjects.

This is what Paul meant when he wrote in Romans, "For this reason Messiah died and came back to life, so that he might be Lord of both the dead and the living" (14:9). In order for the Messiah to be the active Lord of the billions in his Body, the majority dead with eternal life and the minority living on earth, he needed to be the *risen* Lord. He could do this only if as a man he gained eternal life to share with all his brothers and sisters, for before his resurrection he had

2. Thomas Weinandy, "Jesus' Resurrection and Ascension," in *Jesus Becoming Jesus: A Theological Interpretation of the Synoptic Gospels* (Washington, DC: Catholic University of America Press, 2018), 422–24.

3. Blaise Pascal, *Pensées* (New York: Dutton, 1958), no. 592, https://www.gutenberg.org/files/18269/18269-h/18269-h.htm.

human life, which was merely mortal and temporary. But after his resurrection he had eternal life, which was immortal and which he could then share with all who rose in him. "Messiah was raised from the dead, so he dies no longer, and death no longer rules over him" (6:9). "I am he who lives, even he who was dead. But look! I am alive and will be for ages and ages" (Rev. 1:18).

The Meaning of the Resurrection

Now we will trace the different ways in which the risen Messiah brought redemption to the cosmos. These are the great effects of his purchase of redemption. Together they comprise the meaning of the resurrection of the Son of God.

The first effect or meaning was the defeat of the devil. The Messiah's resurrection from the dead showed to all the cosmos that the devil's plan to kill the Messiah forever was thwarted. On the eve of his death Jesus said, "Now shall the prince of this world be cast out" (John 12:31). The resurrection was the beginning of the overthrow of Satan's kingdom. It showed that citizens of God's kingdom no longer needed to live in fear of death, which had been among the principal chains the devil had used to keep people in fear.

Bodily Resurrection

The bodily nature of the resurrection was a powerful sign that suffering has meaning. If Jesus had saved the world apart from bodily suffering, it would have proved the Gnostics—both ancient and modern—right, that our bodies are not part of our true selves and so bodily suffering is meaningless. But Jesus as a man suffered horrendously in his body, and it was this very suffering and death that saved us from eternal death and won for us eternal life. We saw this in the last chapter, but here we will note that this is the reason why the *bodily* resurrection is so important. It shows that Jesus's very humanity saved us and that apart from that humanity there is no salvation. Every bit of *our* humanity is therefore important, including all that we suffer as men and women in human bodies.

The Gospels, especially Luke's, make vivid the bodily nature of the resurrection. The risen God-man *walked* with the two disciples on the road to Emmaus. Then he sat at table with them, blessed bread, broke it, gave it to them, and presumably ate with them (Luke 24:13–31). Then when he met with the disciples, who thought they were looking at a bodiless ghost, he told them to look at his hands and feet and to touch them: "A ghost does not have flesh and bones, as you see that I have" (24:39). To prove even further that he had a material body—albeit risen—he asked for something to eat. When they gave him broiled fish, he ate it so that they could watch (24:43).

This is another aspect of the Messiah's triumph over the devil. Satan whispers that our prosaic human lives with our real sufferings do not matter to God. That he does not care. But the fact that the Son of God took up into himself a human nature and now keeps that risen human nature and body in heaven means that *our* human nature and *our* human suffering matter. They matter in ways that other religions that do not have saviors with human flesh cannot enjoy. I use that last word deliberately. It is only when I know that my Savior also has a body and suffered in this body that I can have the joy of knowing that my sufferings are not irrelevant to God or salvation. I can also have the joy that comes from knowing that the Messiah *understands* my suffering. For he went through sufferings similar to mine. As Hebrews states, "We do not have a high priest who is unable to sympathize with our weaknesses, for he was tested in every way like us but did not sin" (Heb. 4:15).

For this reason, that Jesus was raised in a body and not just his soul—or in the minds of the disciples, as liberal theologians proposed in the twentieth century— the devil's hold by fear and despair over the hearts of billions has been broken. The bodily resurrection has shown the Messiah's members that he understands their human sufferings and that he has made those sufferings matter. The devil's kingdom has been broken, even if its final fall is yet to come.

If you remember what we saw were the purposes of redemption in chapter 1, one was to gather everything in the cosmos together. This too was effected by the resurrection. Because Messiah is the glue, as it were, that holds together everything material and spiritual in the cosmos (Col. 1:17), it was his resurrection as "the firstborn from the dead" (1:18) that makes all the creation—even those now opposed—see that he is in all things "preeminent" (1:18). By his resurrection he has demonstrated that he has done everything necessary to "reconcile to himself all things" (1:20). They will all submit to his lordship and preeminence, every knee bowed before his name, either in heaven sharing in his triumph or "under the earth" resigned to their defeat (Phil. 2:10).

Salvation and Joy

Perhaps the most direct effect of the Messiah's work of redemption is the salvation of his elect Church. We have already seen the importance of the bodily resurrection of the Messiah. Here too it is supremely significant. For it is because Messiah was resurrected in body and not just soul that the redeemed can know that they too will have resurrection bodies on the redeemed earth.

The resurrection of the Messiah also signals that the Father has vindicated the Son for his atonement of our sins, so that we now have peace with the Father. The risen Jesus shows us that the Father has made peace with us, and we need no longer fear his condemnation if we are followers of the Messiah. This is the most glorious peace possible in all the world, the peace that comes from knowing that the Father's wrath no longer remains on us and that we will be in his kingdom both now and after we die.

The Messiah's redemption was the most joyful event in all of history. In contrast, the death of the Messiah was the most shocking and most evil event in all of history. It was a day of the greatest sorrow imaginable. The Son of Man was murdered by the ones he loved and came to save. The devil himself seemed to have won the day.

But the resurrection of Messiah Jesus turned that sorrow into joy. The Church has been "given new birth into a living hope because of the resurrection of Jesus Messiah from the dead" (1 Pet. 1:3). Weeping lasted for a long night, but joy came in the morning (Ps. 30:5). This was the most joyful morning since the creation's first morning. This was the new day that YHWH had made, so we will rejoice and be glad in it (118:24).

This was the day the Church was given to mark every week until the end of the world. It was to be sanctified weekly as her "day of holy rest and joy." On this day the Church can rest and rejoice with her head.[4]

Just as Genesis 3 is the saddest chapter in all of Scripture, so the resurrection chapters in the Gospels are the Bible's most joyful.[5] They tell of the beginning of the glory of the Church's head, of the great seal that marks the beginning of the glory awaiting every member of the Messiah's Body. His resurrection is the down payment on the resurrection of all his followers.

The resurrection of Jesus began the great gospel day. This was the end of the shadows of the First Testament, full of types pointing forward. This was the beginning of the great antitype, the rising sun of righteousness with healing in his wings (Mal. 4:2). He showed on this day that he is the joyful bridegroom, the glorious conqueror commencing the glorious era that the prophets had foretold. This was the beginning of what the Church's theologians have called the eschatological

---

4. Edwards, *HWR*, 359–60.
5. Edwards, *HWR*, 360.

eighth day. It was on the eighth day of the Feast of Booths (or Tabernacles), its holy convocation day (Lev. 23:36), that Jesus proclaimed that he is the true water and light typified at that feast (John 7:37–38; 8:12). For this reason among others, the early Church taught that the resurrection marked the eighth day, the first day of the Messianic kingdom in its resurrected glory.

Glory to the Father and the Son

We saw in chapter 1 that another purpose of the history of redemption was to glorify the divine Persons. The Son gave glory to the Father by obeying his command to be a Mediator unto death, and the Son knew this pleased the Father: "Therefore my Father loves me because I am laying down my life" (John 10:17). Jesus knew his obedience would also bring the Father glory: "Father, the hour has come. Glorify your Son so that the Son might glorify you" (17:1).

Thomas Weinandy has observed that the resurrection shows us what the Father was thinking as his Son went through the agonies of his passion. "If one wishes to know the inner mind of the Father in the face of his Son's passion, death, and descent into hell, one only needs to look at the Resurrection. The Resurrection is the Father's conclusive answer to the suffering of his Son, and with it his consummate answer to all human suffering."[6]

In *Jesus the Christ* Weinandy notes that if the Father had not raised Jesus from the dead, "Jesus would rightly stand discredited and condemned as a blasphemous fraud."[7] So the resurrection was the Father's vindication of his Son's claim and suffering. In these ways it brought glory to both the Father and the Son.

Students of the Scriptures are not surprised to see that the Holy Spirit, called the "shy" member of the Trinity because his aim is to glorify the Son (John 16:14), also receives glory. Paul wrote that it was the Spirit who raised Jesus from the dead, and it will be the same Spirit who will give life to our mortal bodies after the general resurrection (Rom. 8:11). On that great day the Spirit will receive the glory he deserves.

Glory to the Saints

A final goal of the history of redemption was to glorify the saints. The resurrection accomplished much of this. Since he was the head of a Body, the members

---

6. Thomas Weinandy, "The Resurrection: The Father's Love for Jesus," in *Jesus the Christ* (N.p.: Ex Fotibus, 2017), 118.

7. Weinandy, "Resurrection: The Father's Love for Jesus," 117.

of his Body were raised with him when he was raised. As Paul put it in Romans 6:5, "If we have been united with him in a death like his, so also we will be united in a resurrection like his." We rose in him our head. Our new life in the Messiah is resurrection life itself, the firstfruits of our resurrected bodies in the world to come.

The saints get additional glory by the resurrection's proof that we have been reconciled to the Father. Before being united to the Messiah and therefore to his resurrection, we were enemies of God and alienated from the commonwealth of Israel, the source of salvation (Eph. 2:12; John 4:22). But his resurrection guaranteed that all the baptized who walk in faith are now friends of God, reconciled by the Messiah's blood. The resurrection confirms that the blood has made us friends of the Father. We now know from the empty tomb that we have the supreme glory of being friends of the true God, the God of Israel.

The resurrection of Jesus Messiah was public, within history, and in the body. This public-historical-bodily character of Jesus's raising from the dead is the guarantee of our redemption, which means the promise of our glorification. "Those whom he justified he also glorified" (Rom. 8:30).

Select Bibliography

Bultmann, Rudolf. "The New Testament and Mythology." In *Kerygma and Myth*, edited by Hans Werner Bartsch, 1–44. New York: Harper and Row, 1961.

Edwards, Jonathan. *A History of the Work of Redemption*. Edited by John F. Wilson. Vol. 9 in *The Works of Jonathan Edwards*. New Haven: Yale University Press, 1989.

McClymond, Michael, and Gerald McDermott. *The Theology of Jonathan Edwards*. New York: Oxford University Press, 2012.

Pascal, Blaise. *Pensées, and Other Writings*. Oxford: Oxford University Press, 2008.

Weinandy, Thomas. "Jesus' Resurrection and Ascension." In *Jesus Becoming Jesus: A Theological Interpretation of the Synoptic Gospels*, 412–64. Washington, DC: Catholic University of America Press, 2018.

———. "The Resurrection: The Father's Love for Jesus." In *Jesus the Christ*, 118. N.p.: Ex Fotibus, 2017.

Wright, N. T. *The Resurrection of the Son of God*. Minneapolis: Fortress, 2003.

13

The Kingdom of God

We have noted from time to time in the preceding chapters that the God of Israel is the king of the cosmos and that one of the purposes of redemption is to build the kingdom of God. The phrase is rare in the First Testament, but the concept is everywhere. The psalmist wrote, "The kingdom belongs to YHWH" (Ps. 22:28), and his royal throne is mentioned frequently. Moses's declaration that the God of Israel was telling the Egyptian king, "Let my people go," was the ultimatum of a lawful king to a usurper. The kingdom of God is at the center of both Jesus's and Paul's thinking—the subject of Jesus's forty days of postresurrection training for his apostles (Acts 1:3) and the theme of Paul's teaching in his last days at Rome (Acts 28:31)—and is mentioned more than one hundred times in that Second (New) Testament. In this chapter we will explore the meaning of this key term.

Political and Visible

Most Christians think of the kingdom of God as an invisible phenomenon, the rule of God in his followers' hearts. But for the Old Testament the concept is visible as well. For, as philosopher Michael Wyschogrod put it, the biblical covenant in which YHWH chose the people of Israel to be his own chosen people is "inherently political."[1] YHWH led his people to conquer Canaan in order to apportion to his people a land, and his covenant with them was a relationship of

1. Michael Wyschogrod, "A King in Israel," *First Things*, May 2010, https://www.firstthings.com/article /2010/05/a-king-in-israel.

mutual obligations that were not only religious but also legal and political. This was recognized in biblical and rabbinic literature, where God is called "King of All Kings" perhaps more than any other designation.

By this the Bible meant that God is king over all the rulers of the nations, but most especially Israel. There, according to Wyschogrod, he exercised his kingship through proxies—kings, prophets, and high priests. Of these three, only "king" is used for both human beings and God. This is possible because every human being is made in God's image. But even though the king's role in Israel was largely secular, the God of Israel invested Israel's kings with a special trace of his own glory, so that to see a king was to see God's proxy. For the king of Israel, particularly one in the line of David, participated in the glory of God.[2]

Davidic Kingship

But God's investment of a human king with his glory was not YHWH's original intention in the biblical story. When Israel insisted on having a king like the kings of the nations around them, God was not pleased. He told Samuel that in this desire the people of Israel were rejecting him (YHWH) as king. God's first choice was for the kingdom of God in which God was king—literally, not merely symbolically, for all decisions came from him—and used a prophet like Moses through whom to communicate. God did this while Moses was alive. He spoke with Moses "face to face," and Moses delivered his commandments and judgments to the people. Moses was not a king. Moses might have seemed to act like a sovereign, but God was the sovereign, and Moses his spokesman.

God, not the people, was sovereign over the nation of Israel. Beginning with the first king, Saul, and continuing through Israel's later kings, rulers were thought to be chosen by God, and it was only to God and his Torah that the kings were responsible. According to Wyschogrod, this is why Jewish tradition favors monarchy and why Jewish religious authorities like Maimonides have argued that the appointment of a king in the line of David is obligatory for Israel, even when in exile. Wyschogrod observes that this is why Jewish religious authorities rejected the Hasmonean line after 165 BC because it was not founded on the house of David.[3] I would add that this is also why the Davidic king was often conflated with YHWH's rule in biblical and rabbinic tradition. And why the Gospels and

2. Wyschogrod, "King in Israel."
3. Wyschogrod, "King in Israel."

Epistles put so much emphasis on Messiah Jesus being in the Davidic line as the prophesied King of Israel.

Daniel and His Influence

C. C. Caragounis writes, "No other writing of the [Old Testament] has more to say about the sovereignty of God than Daniel, where the kingdom of God is the central theme."[4] The agent for the kingdom is "one like a son of man" (Dan. 7:13) who assumes royal rule of spiritual powers at work behind earthly rulers. In intertestamental Jewish writings influenced by Daniel—the Sybilline Oracles, 1 Enoch, 1QM in the Dead Sea Scrolls, 4 Ezra—there will be a final assault on the Messiah by the ungodly, who will be defeated by the Messiah in his role as warrior. The establishment of the messianic kingdom will involve the ingathering of scattered Israelites and the restoration of Jerusalem. As in the book of Revelation, the center of the kingdom will be Jerusalem.[5]

In the New Testament

As we have seen, the kingdom of God is a central theme in the New Testament. Matthew's preferred term, "kingdom of heaven," is simply his Jewish substitution of "heaven" in an attempt to honor the second commandment by avoiding the divine name. John uses the same concept but substitutes the term "eternal life," perhaps because of his Gentile context, where life after death was usually for kings and heroes but not ordinary people. Paul teaches on the kingdom in Acts but also uses "salvation" as something of a synonym in his epistles.

Here too—in the New Testament—the concept of God's kingdom is visible and political, not merely a matter of the heart. After all, as the *Dictionary of Biblical Imagery* observes, if God is king, then Caesar is not. Neither is his client-king Herod.[6] Jesus tells Pilate that Jesus's kingdom is not of this world, and he explains that his disciples are not revolutionaries "fighting" his arrest (John 18:36). His kingdom would not come by military force. Yet it was not without its visible presence in the world. Apostles and their churches, with martyrs and bishops, could

---

4. C. C. Caragounis, "Kingdom of God/Kingdom of Heaven," in *Dictionary of Jesus and the Gospels*, ed. Joel B. Green, Scot McKnight, and I. Howard Marshall (Downers Grove, IL: InterVarsity, 1992), 418.
    5. Caragounis, "Kingdom of God/Kingdom of Heaven," 419.
    6. "Kingdom of God," in *Dictionary of Biblical Imagery*, ed. Leland Ryken, James Wilhoit, and Tremper Longman III (Downers Grove, IL: InterVarsity, 1998), 479.

be seen and heard in the world, especially when they defied political authorities with the spirit of the apostles: "We must obey God and not men!" (Acts 5:29). Paul's witness was heard at the center of the Roman Empire, and the church in Rome had outsized influence until Constantinople challenged its primacy in the fourth century. As time went on, whole civilizations were changed by the gospel message. The movement of the Spirit was invisible, but his effects on people and their institutions were visible. Not all that became visible was Spirit inspired, but there is no doubt that the Spirit revival that was early Christianity became a visible kingdom that changed the world.

The Father's or the Son's?

Whose kingdom is it? The Father's or the Son's? In the Bible it is both. Before the incarnation, it was the Father's kingdom from eternity. At the ascension the Father delegated the rule of his kingdom to the Son so that it became known as the kingdom of Jesus Messiah. But Scripture indicates that at the end of the world the Son will deliver the kingdom to the proper king of the cosmos, the Father.

In Psalm 2 YHWH declares, "I have set my king on Zion, my holy hill. . . . You are my Son. . . . I will make the nations your heritage" (Ps. 2:6–8 NRSV). The New Testament authors regarded this text as a prophecy about the Father and the Son, with the Father delegating control of the nations—God's kingdom—to the Son (Acts 13:33; Heb. 1:5; 5:5).

Daniel depicts a similar scene. "As I looked, thrones were placed, and the Ancient of Days took his seat; his clothing was white as snow. . . . I saw in the night visions, and look, with the clouds of heaven there came one like a son of man, and he came to the Ancient of Days and was presented before him. To him was given dominion and glory and a kingdom" (Dan. 7:9, 13). Once again we are told that the Father delegates to his Son the rule of the world, the kingdom of God. All ancient peoples knew that this was a king with a grand first minister to whom was given authority and power. But the King was still foremost, for it is he who *granted* dominion to "one like a son of man."

Jesus agreed that it was originally the *Father's* kingdom when he told his disciples at the last supper that he would not drink of the fruit of the vine until "I drink it new with you in the kingdom of my Father" (Matt. 26:29).

Paul wrote that at the end of the world Jesus will "deliver the kingdom to God the Father" (1 Cor. 15:24). After the Son has destroyed every rule and authority and power, subjecting all things to himself, "then the Son himself will also be subjected to him who put all things in subjection under" the Son, "so that God might be all in all" (15:28).

But then why does the New Testament also say of Jesus's kingdom "there will be no end" (Luke 1:32–33) and the "Messiah shall reign forever and ever" (Rev. 11:15)? And the Nicene Creed proclaim that his "kingdom will have no end"? Augustine believed that the Son and the Father possess the kingdom in different senses, so that at the end the Son does not hand it over in a literal sense but "brings believers to a direct contemplation of God and the Father." Edwards's view was similar.

> The church now [at the end] shall be brought nearer to God the Father. . . . And her enjoyment of him shall be more direct: Christ [the] God-man shall now no longer be instead of the Father to them, but, as I may express it, their head of their enjoyment of God, as it were, the eye to receive the rays of divine glory and love for the whole body, and the ear to hear the sweet expressions of his love, and the mouth to taste the sweetness and feed on the delights of the enjoyment of God. . . . Hereby God's communication of himself to them shall be more direct than when it was by a viceregent.[7]

Properly, then, it is the Father's kingdom. He delegated it to the Son as his mediator after the fall, as we saw in chapter 3. But after the Son has redeemed the world, the kingdom will return to the Father so that believers can enjoy him more directly, and, according to Edwards, the Son will have even more honor as the Son of God. We shall discuss this in more detail in chapter 33.

Present or Future?

During the twentieth century scholars debated whether Jesus meant the kingdom had fully arrived in his person or whether he suggested that the kingdom was still future. Most came to agree that the kingdom was both now and not-yet, with more emphasis on the not-yet. Let us examine the evidence for this in the New Testament.

There is only one saying in all the Gospels that suggests that the kingdom fully arrived with Jesus's public ministry. It is the same saying repeated in two Gospels:

---

7. Edwards, "Consummation of All Things: Christ's Delivering Up the Kingdom to the Father," Miscellany 742 in *The Miscellanies 501–832*, vol. 18 of *The Works of Jonathan Edwards* (New Haven: Yale University Press, 2000), 374.

after Jesus cast a spirit out of a deaf and dumb man, he said, "If by the Spirit of God I cast out the demons, then the kingdom of God has come upon [*ephthasen*] you" (Matt. 12:28; Luke 11:20). Scholars have recognized that there are two problems with the idea that this signaled the complete inauguration of the kingdom. First, it would obviate the significance of the cross and resurrection for the kingdom if it arrived before Jesus's passion. Second, the tense of the verb (aorist) sometimes indicates something that is certain but still in the future. So Jesus probably meant that the kingdom of God was signaling its *agent* and therefore the certainty of its coming—but not its full presence—by his exorcism. Likewise, C. C. Caragounis notes that when the Pharisees asked when the kingdom would come, Jesus said it would not come with observable signs and immediately spoke of his second coming (Luke 17:20–37). So his statement to them that "the kingdom of God is among you" (v. 21) likely meant that *in their midst* was the one who would bring it at the end of the age. The kingdom was *potentially* present, but its decisive and visible arrival still lay ahead. This was parallel to the ways that John and Paul referred to eternal life and salvation. For both of these New Testament writers, eternal life/salvation was past (in its types), present (in Jesus), and future (in full consummation).[8]

This is the only way to make sense of many other indications in the New Testament that the kingdom still lies in the future. At the Last Supper the kingdom is future: "I will not drink again of this fruit of the vine until I drink it new with you in my Father's kingdom" (Matt. 26:29; parallels in Mark 14:25; Luke 22:18). The Lord's Prayer, delivered to the world by the Gospel writers long after the ascension, petitions the Father for the kingdom to come in the future: "Thy kingdom come." Joseph of Arimathea is said by Mark to still be waiting for the kingdom after the death of Jesus (Mark 15:43). In Luke the Twelve were to "proclaim the kingdom," but the seventy-two were to announce only that the kingdom had drawn near (Luke 9:2; 10:9). John resolves this apparent contradiction with his record of Nathanael's acclamation, "Rabbi, you are the son of God, you are the King of Israel!" (John 1:49). The kingdom had been announced by the arrival of its King, but its manifest establishment still lay in the future.

What We Know

Even if we cannot know when the kingdom will come in its fullness, we can nevertheless know many of its characteristics. Biblical revelation is full of teaching about

---

8. Caragounis, "Kingdom of God/Kingdom of Heaven," 423–28.

it. We have seen in previous chapters that the Messiah has been at work since the fall to call people into it and that its rules for membership have included humility and effort to live by righteousness. The Gospels have told us more about that righteousness—that it is summed up in love for the God of Israel and love for our neighbors, even enemies. So the kingdom has an ethical character. Its members have repented of immoral behavior and seek grace to live lives that show what Jesus called "the fruits of the kingdom" (Matt. 21:43).

We also know that the kingdom comes with suffering. Paul told the disciples in Asia Minor that "through many afflictions we must enter the kingdom of God" (Acts 14:22).

Therefore, not everyone will make it. Some, perhaps many, will be shut out. Jesus said "many" are on the road to destruction, while "few" are on the way to life. "Not everyone who says to me, 'Lord, Lord,' will enter the kingdom of the heavens, but only the one who does the will of my Father who is in the heavens" (Matt. 7:13–14, 21).

But for those who realize the kingdom is the pearl of great price for which they will sell everything else, there will be a great feast, a wedding banquet full of exquisite victuals. In other words, there will be wall-to-wall joy that will continue throughout eternity.

The Restoration of Israel

When the kingdom is fully manifested, Israel will be a central part of it. Just before Jesus's ascension, the disciples asked, "Lord, will you at this time restore the kingdom to Israel?" (Acts 1:6). They seem to have had in mind from their Jewish background an earthly kingdom that was also heavenly in origin. Jesus did *not* respond, as he is often thought to have suggested, that their question was a dumb one, that they had failed to realize that his kingdom would never be visible on this earth. Instead Jesus acknowledged that he *would* inaugurate a visible kingdom for Israel—but not right then: "The Father," he said, "has fixed the time for that, and it is not for you to know that time right now" (1:7).

In *Luke's Jewish Eschatology: The National Restoration of Israel in Luke-Acts*, Isaac Oliver agrees. Luke, he argues, proposed a "bilateral eschatology" that would bring the restoration of the kingdom of Israel (Acts 1:6) along with the cosmic renewal of all things (3:21). According to Oliver, these two realizations are not mutually exclusive but complementary. To use Simeon's words in Luke's account, there would come a "salvation which [God has] prepared before the eyes of all the peoples, a light for the revelation to the nations and glory for [God's] people," Israel (Luke 2:30–32). Luke expects this corporate salvation will be made manifest in ways that affect the political, social, and economic spheres of life. So, by Oliver's lights, salvation for Luke is not just a spiritual experience that psychologically soothes the conscience of the individual, relieving it of guilt and providing reassurance of immortality. The ultimate goal of redemption is not the ascension of humans into the heavens. It concerns rather the inauguration of a kingdom that will overtake this world and be centered in Israel. God's will shall be done on earth as it is in heaven.[9]

There are indications in the book of Revelation that Oliver might be right. We are told there to expect a new earth with a new sky (Rev. 21:1), that the center of this new earth shall be the "holy city Jerusalem" (11:2, 8; 14:1; 20:9; 21:10), and that on its twelve gates shall be inscribed "the names of the twelve tribes of the sons of Israel" (21:10–12). Apparently those gates will be visible and therefore on a material earth, and they will be given Jewish names in the Jewish capital of Israel.

Some might protest that this is symbolic language in the most symbolic book of the Bible. But the same book of Revelation says that the renewed earth will have signs of *Israel* at its center, the nations will *walk* in it, and the saints will *see* the Lamb "face to face" (Rev. 21:10, 24; 22:4). There will be things to see and places to walk. It will be visible and not just invisible, Jewish and not just Gentile. It will not have boring Enlightenment-style sameness, but the beautiful divine diversity of Jews and Gentiles, Israel and the nations, men and women. All will be oriented to the Messiah, but each in ways suited to their differences. Christians who have previously thought of the kingdom as merely spiritual, internal and otherworldly, will have to rethink those assumptions, including its orientation around Israel.

Gradual Emergence

As I have suggested in this chapter, the kingdom of God is not an all-or-nothing phenomenon. Like a tree that starts with a seed that germinates and then grows gradually over decades, so the kingdom of God emerges gradually over the history of redemption. We have seen its beginning just after the fall with Adam and Eve and their family, Enoch and the nations, and then its growth through the people of Israel over the centuries. During and after the incarnation of the Messiah there

---

9. Isaac Oliver, *Luke's Jewish Eschatology: The National Restoration of Israel in Luke-Acts* (New York: Oxford University Press, 2021), esp. 1–27, 103–39.

were stages of growth. Jesus said there was an initial "coming in his kingdom" at the transfiguration (Matt. 16:28). At his ascension he was put on the throne of the cosmos at the right hand of the Father. When the pagan Roman Empire was overtaken in the fourth century by Constantine and his successors, there was a spectacular visible manifestation of God's kingdom. It was a mixture, to be sure, especially in the ways in which the new empire persecuted Jews. But it was a triumph for King Messiah in his calling to "make the nations [his] heritage" (Ps. 2:8). When the forces of Antichrist are finally defeated in the eschaton (Rev. 19:11–21), that will be by another coming of the Messiah (19:21). The final coming will be at the last judgment, where the Messiah will come to preside as Judge (Rev. 20:11–15; Matt. 25:31–46). Here the "son of Man" is also the "king," and he will say to those on his right, "Come, you who are blessed by my Father, inherit the kingdom prepared for you from the foundation of the cosmos" (Matt. 25:34).

Each of these stages in the gradual emergence of God's kingdom was an image or type of the final stage described in the parable of the sheep and the goats. Just as there will be a resurrection of the dead before this final judgment, so there were spiritual resurrections of the elect throughout the history of redemption. Just as there were dark periods of degeneracy and wickedness before each new emergence of light and redemption, there will be dark times of persecution and evil before the end of days. Each new stage in redemption is accompanied by destruction for the wicked, as for Haman and his followers in Esther, at the triumph over paganism in the fourth century, at the defeat of Antichrist, and at the final judgment. Each is attended with new advances for God's people, as in the new freedom from pagan persecution under Constantine. In each of these phases there is the end of an old heaven and earth and the birth of a new one—both temporal and eternal.

Each of these phases in the gradual emergence of God's kingdom is a step or degree in the accomplishment of the one event depicted in Daniel 7—the Ancient of Days presenting to the One like a Son of Man dominion and kingship over all peoples and nations (vv. 13–14). Sometimes the different steps are collapsed into one, as in Jesus's prophecy of the close of the age in Matthew 24. But each of these many steps pushes the kingdom a bit further. At each stage the kingdom advances, and its expansion is visible for all those with eyes to see.

Why Gradual?

But why gradual and not all at once? Why did God push along his kingdom's emergence so slowly and incrementally? We have touched on this in a previous chapter, but it is worth repeating. Only by this gradual and incremental emergence of the kingdom of God could be seen all the steps of divine wisdom. In this way God is more glorified than in a sudden explosion of light. This is the manner in which both angelic and human observers can see so much more of God's infinite sagacity. Only by seeing the long history of redemption in the emergence of the kingdom can billions of eyes perceive the divine perspicacity. The successive manifestations of irony as evil intentions are thwarted and good emerges from catastrophe to glorify God more than an instantaneous presentation. That would blind us anyway and prevent us from seeing much at all.

This gradual approach of the kingdom has the added virtue of exhibiting more gloriously Satan's defeat. By giving the dark one many ages to ply his power and trickery, God's subtle undermining of his evil ends, age after age, repeatedly displays the divine brilliance. The continual advancement of the kingdom as more and more are redeemed in culture after culture proves the gradual but eventual demise of the evil one.

Select Bibliography

Augustine. *The Trinity*. Translated by Edmund Hill. Hyde Park, NY: New City Press, 1991. See particularly 1:15.

Caragounis, C. C. "Kingdom of God/Kingdom of Heaven." In *Dictionary of Jesus and the Gospels*, edited by Joel B. Green, Scot McKnight, and I. Howard Marshall, 417–30. Downers Grove, IL: InterVarsity, 1992.

Edwards, Jonathan. "Consummation of All Things: Christ's Delivering Up the Kingdom to the Father." Miscellany 742 in *The Miscellanies 501–832*, edited by Ava Chamberlain, vol. 18 in *The Works of Jonathan Edwards*, 373–76. New Haven: Yale University Press, 2000.

———. *A History of the Work of Redemption*. Edited by John F. Wilson. Vol. 9 in *The Works of Jonathan Edwards*. New Haven: Yale University Press, 1989.

"Kingdom of God." In *Dictionary of Biblical Imagery*, edited by Leland Ryken, James Wilhoit, and Tremper Longman III, 478–81. Downers Grove, IL: InterVarsity, 1998.

McClymond, Michael, and Gerald McDermott. "The Church." In *The Theology of Jonathan Edwards*, 451–64. New York: Oxford University Press, 2012.

Oliver, Isaac. *Luke's Jewish Eschatology: The National Restoration of Israel in Luke-Acts*. New York: Oxford University Press, 2021.

Wyschogrod, Michael. "A King in Israel." *First Things*, May 2010. https://www.firstthings.com /article/2010/05/a-king-in-israel.

14

Ascension and Church

The ascension of Jesus Messiah in bodily form to heaven was a day of great joy among the saints and angels there. It was the enthronement of the Redeemer. To put the Messiah on his right hand was for God the Father to set his Son on the throne as King of the creation. God put all angels under the Son's feet, and all of heaven and earth, for the purpose of blessing the people he died for. As Paul put it, God "raised Messiah from the dead and sat him at his right hand in the heavens, far above all rule and authority and power and dominion . . . and made him head over all things for the Church, which is his Body" (Eph. 1:20–23).

Paul's words show the importance of the ascension to Messiah's work of redemption. It was the Trinity's plan to redeem the world through the Messiah and his Body, the Church, the people of God. After the fall and before the incarnation two thousand years ago, the people of God were principally the Jewish people of Israel. There were believers outside of Israel, but the source of their faith was Israel. So Edwards was right to speak of the Jewish Church in the long centuries before the Word became flesh in Jesus.

During his public ministry Jesus chose the first leaders of the messianic Church and then made clear that he would continue to dwell in and teach the world through the Church. This chapter will explain this continuation of the incarnation, as it were, through the Church—by its leaders through history, its sacraments and liturgy, the gifts of the Holy Spirit, and the inspired writings the early Church produced (the New Testament). It was the ascension of Messiah Jesus that provided the platform for the empowerment of the Church.

Beginning of the New Creation

According to Edwards, heaven was filled with greater glory and happiness at the ascension than it ever had been before. The elect angels were confirmed in grace at this point when Messiah was made their head. Until then, they were worried that they might fall and be doomed with the fallen angels. After all, God alone and not angels knows the future (Isa. 41:23), and Peter tells us that the angels were longing to look ahead to know what would happen at the incarnation (1 Pet. 1:12). But this was the time for the Father to confirm them in grace, assuring them that they would be forever removed from the danger of sinning. This brought them tremendous relief and joy.

Douglas Farrow has argued that the ascension was a homecoming for the Son, a reception in the Father's house after his harrowing rescue mission to a far land. It was not a move upward so much as to a different dimension, from the old creation to the new. It was removal to a place, but not in this world. It was the beginning of the transformation of this world, the first step in the re-creation of this world into the new heavens and the new earth.[1]

Paul writes that the Church has ascended *with* its Messiah, so that the redeemed "sit with him in the heavenlies in Messiah Jesus" (Eph. 2:6). This is why Irenaeus said that the ascension was the beginning of deification, by which believers share in Christ's glory: "Those who see God are in God and receive of his splendor" (*Against Heresies* 4.20.5). For Edwards and many of the fathers, the *bodily* ascension was just as significant as the bodily resurrection, for it is in the earthly bodies of believers that deification begins, and it will be in resurrected bodies that deification will be completed after the general resurrection on the renewed earth. John Chrysostom asked, "To what nature did God say, 'Sit on my right hand'? To that which heard, 'Dust thou art and to dust thou shalt return.'"[2] Only if Messiah brought his body to heaven can we be assured that our own bodies will be reconfigured in the new creation. The beginning of this new creation is made visible in the Eucharist, which I will discuss below.

Human minds have always had difficulty believing that God raised Jesus's body and not just his soul. Their doubts have usually come to light in their considerations of the ascension. Origen, deeply influenced by Platonic philosophy, which demeaned the body as disconnected from and essentially inferior to the soul,

---

1. Douglas Farrow, *Ascension Theology* (London: Bloomsbury T&T Clark, 2011), esp. 34–49.
2. John Chrysostom, "Sermon on the Ascension" (PG 50:441–52), quoted in Farrow, *Ascension Theology*, 40.

believed that Jesus's ascension was of his mind rather than his body.[3] Friedrich Schleiermacher, the father of liberal theology, disconnected the ascension from the person of the Messiah and agreed with Origen that the ascension was of Jesus's mind only.[4] Modern people and liberal theologians have replaced the bodily ascension with the ascension of human beings in their dogmas of human progress. They flatly reject the apostles' testimony that they witnessed Jesus rising bodily to heaven (Acts 1:9).[5]

The Ascension's Necessity

Luke suggests that the ascension was necessary for the administration of the effects of redemption. He writes in Acts that Peter proclaimed that the Messiah had to be exalted to heaven before he could pour out repentance and forgiveness to God's people in Israel and beyond: "God exalted him to his right hand as our pioneer and savior *so that* he could give repentance to Israel and forgiveness of sins" (Acts 5:31). Just as the high priest in Israel after offering sacrifice had to enter the Holy of Holies with the blood of the sacrifice in order to make his prayers effective for Israel, so too the Messiah poured out redemption for the people of God only after he was ascended to God's right hand, the antitype of the earthly sanctuary. Only from the heavenly Holy of Holies did the Messiah most effectively make intercession for "those who draw near to God" (Heb. 7:25). It is from there that he "now" pleads his sacrifice "by his own blood" (9:12, 24).

Building the Church

It is because of his bodily ascension to his place of rule at the right hand of the Father that the Messiah was given authority to build his Church. Many Christians, especially Protestants, think Jesus came merely to get souls to heaven after they die. But Jesus said he came to "build my Church" (Matt. 16:18). As we saw in the last chapter, Jesus's Church was a visible thing. One could see its apostolic leaders and their successors, who later came to be called bishops. One could see its priests and bishops and deacons on the Lord's Day as they led believers in celebration of

---

3. Origen, *On Prayer* 23, in *Origen*, trans. and intro. Rowan Greer, Classics of Western Spirituality (New York: Paulist Press, 1979), 125–28.

4. Friedrich Schleiermacher, *The Christian Faith*, ed. H. R. Mackintosh (Philadelphia: Fortress, 1976), 417–24.

5. See Farrow, *Ascension Theology*, 30–31.

the Eucharist, which they believed was their participation in Messiah's ongoing sacrificial gift to the Father of his life, death, and risen Body. They gathered together visibly for daily prayer and teaching and Eucharistic worship (Acts 2:42), both in the temple (before AD 70) and in homes. When they disciplined wayward members, they sometimes banned them from visible fellowship in the hope that they would repent and return to that visible fellowship (1 Cor. 5).

The Mystical Body of the Redeemer

But the Church is not only visible. It is also the mystical Body of the Redeemer. As the Anglican theologian Eric Mascall put it, the Church is not a voluntary association of the like-minded, but a Body of people joined in being with the ascended Messiah. The life of the Church is the life of the Trinity imparted to its members by their being joined by the Spirit to the Son. So it is not merely a society of people who believe in God but the divine Society itself that has taken up all the believers of history into union with the ascended manhood of the Messiah. It is not an organization but an organism, the living image of eternity within time. The incarnation is extended through time by the life of the Church, which makes actual for us the mystery of God in human flesh.[6]

Augustine referred to the Church as *totus Christus*, the whole Christ.[7] This phrase suggests that the Messiah is not complete without his Body. He is its head, but without all its members Christ's body is incomplete. So the "whole" Messiah is the Messiah joined to all the saints in heaven and on earth. In this sense, the Messiah lacks a certain perfection in the absence of his Body, the Church—just as a human head is incomplete without its body.

Apostles as Foundation

The apostles were the foundation of the Church. Paul wrote of "the household of God, built on the foundation of the apostles and prophets" (Eph. 2:19–20), and John of the wall of the New Jerusalem, which "has twelve foundations, and on them were twelve names of the twelve apostles of the lamb" (Rev. 21:14). What did this mean? At a minimum, that they had extraordinary power and authority

---

6. E. L. Mascall, *Christ, the Christian, and the Church* (Peabody, MA: Hendrickson, 2017; first published 1946), esp. 109–53.

7. See, e.g., Augustine, *The Epistle of St. John* 1.2, in *The Nicene and Post-Nicene Fathers*, Series 1, ed. Philip Schaff (1886–89; repr., Peabody, MA: Hendrickson, 2012), 7:461.

to transmit the teaching and power of the Messiah to his body. Through them the miraculous power of the risen Messiah confirmed the authority of their teaching. For example, when the temple leaders saw that through apostolic prayer a lame man had been healed and the apostles did not fear death, "they recognized that they had been with Jesus" (Acts 4:13). Observers took more seriously their message because of the power of Jesus that worked through them.

The apostles were responsible for the writings that became the New Testament and for the tradition that guided the interpretation of those documents. By the commandment of the Messiah, they also established the sacraments, which communicated the life and power of the Messiah to the members of his Body. For example, in the Great Commission Jesus told the apostles to baptize the nations "into the name of the Father and of the Son and of the Holy Spirit" (Matt. 28:19). Baptism was the sacrament by which believers were to be joined "to his death, buried with him by baptism into death . . . so that just as the Messiah was raised by the glory of the Father, so too [they] might walk in newness of life" (Rom. 6:3–4). In other words, baptism joins believers mystically to the Messiah, connecting at the deepest level *their* being to the being of Jesus. Jesus also gave to the apostles the sacrament of the Eucharist, by which believers share "communion in the blood of the Messiah . . . and communion in the [risen] body of the Messiah" (1 Cor. 10:16).

So the apostles were foundation stones of the Church in three ways. First, they were responsible for the writing of the New Testament both directly and indirectly. These documents became the infallible rule by which the Church interpreted both the First Testament and the Messiah's redemption. Second, for the first two centuries in which the apostolic writings were being collected, most churches were directed by the oral traditions going back to the apostles and their successors, the bishops. These oral traditions, which developed into creeds and were called the Rule of Faith, became the decisive criteria for interpreting the meaning of the apostolic writings. Early Church doctrines emerged from this symbiotic interaction between apostolic tradition and apostolic writing. Third, the apostles also gave to the churches the sacraments, which brought future generations to the ongoing life of Messiah Jesus.

Ministry

Just as the Jewish Church had a hierarchical order of ministry (chief priests, priests, Levites), the early Church soon developed its own order of ministry in bishops, priests, and deacons. During the writing of the apostolic documents (the New Testament), orders of ministry were somewhat fluid. The roles of bishops and presbyters (from the Greek word for "elders") were sometimes interchangeable. But by the second century a near-universal pattern had emerged of bishops, priests, and deacons. Ignatius of Antioch (d. ca. 117) wrote to the church at Tralles in what is now western Turkey that "without these three orders no church has any right to the name [Christian]."[8] The orders were considered three degrees in the one sacrament of what was later called Holy Order. The word "priest" was derived from the Old English for "presbyter," had the advantage of Jewish precedent, and seemed fitting for the role of presiding over worship, which for the first millennium and a half was considered a sacrifice. Just as ancient Jews never considered females for clerical roles, the early churches set aside only men for these orders (1 Tim. 2:12; 3:2; 3:12; Titus 1:6). This did not change for historic catholic, Orthodox, and Reformation Churches until the mid- and late twentieth century, when various Anglican, Old Catholic, and Lutheran churches introduced the ordination of women over protests from Catholic and Orthodox churches. (Subsequently the Vatican and Old Catholics published a dialogue in which both sides presented their viewpoints.)[9]

Sacraments

The Venerable Bede reportedly wrote somewhere that the sacraments are like the miracle-working mantle that Elijah left behind.[10] Just as that mantle was the means for Israelites to continue to see the power of YHWH, so too the sacraments were intended by Jesus Messiah for the ongoing participation of believers in his redemptive power. And, as Farrow has written, only those who "see" the bodily ascension of Jesus are ready to receive the gift of the sacraments.[11]

The Church has always taught that the greatest sacrament is the Eucharist, and it is in the Eucharistic celebration that we can see what happens in the ascension, where the cosmos is reordered to God in the Messiah. The Real Presence of the humanity of the Messiah in the Eucharist is a signal to the heavenly powers, both good and evil, that something has changed profoundly now that the ascended Messiah has shared his presence in the sacrament.

8. Ignatius of Antioch, *Epistle to the Trallians*, in *Early Christian Writings: The Apostolic Fathers*, ed. Andrew Louth (London: Penguin, 1968), 79–80.

9. *The Church and Ecclesial Communion: Report of the International Roman Catholic–Old Catholic Dialogue Commission* (Vatican: Dicastery for Promoting Christian Unity, 2009).

10. Reported by Farrow, *Ascension Theology*, 65. He cites no source, and I have not been able to find one.

11. Farrow, *Ascension Theology*, 65.

According to Joseph Ratzinger, "the substantial conversion of bread and wine" into the ascended Messiah's "Body and Blood introduces within creation the principle of radical change."[12] He compares it to nuclear fission, claiming that the ascended Messiah in the Eucharist is setting off a process that will transfigure the whole world, where eventually God will be all in all. We the members of the Messiah's Body are given a role in making the old world new, by participating in this heavenly offering and showing the world that the Messiah's Body is more than just a metaphor.

This was apparent to the early Church. Already in the first century the New Testament writers were suggesting that the Eucharist was illuminating everything about Jesus—his messianic office, miracles, death, resurrection, and ascension. The Eucharist was the vehicle of the gift of the Spirit (1 Cor. 12:13b), the means of eternal life (John 6:53–54), and the cause of the unity of the Church (1 Cor. 10:17).

Jesus said, "Do this for the *anamnēsis* of me" (Luke 22:19). *Anamnēsis* is the Greek word for the Jewish concept of the past coming into the present, as Jews believed took place every Passover. It was thought to be a lifting up out of linear time into eternity, a sacramental time in heaven, when the high priest is *"now* appearing in the presence of God on our behalf" (Heb. 9:12, 14, 24). In pre-Nicene times the Church took *anamnēsis* to be the recalling or re-presenting before God of an event in the past so that it becomes operative in its effects here and now. The Eucharist was therefore the event in which the members of the body, led by the bishop, joined their Head in his offering to the Father the sacrifice of his whole life and death. Not repetition but re-presentation, to join the celestial worship that is ongoing in heaven, pictured in Revelation 4–5.

This is why the early Church regarded the Eucharist as a sacrifice—not a new one but a participation in the ongoing sacrifice of the Son to the Father by the Spirit. The Didache (late first century) three times refers to the Eucharist as a sacrifice and quotes the same text in Malachi (1:11) that Justin Martyr (d. 165) uses in his *Dialogue with Trypho*, calling it a sacrifice. Justin uses the technical term *prospheretai* for the "sacrifices which are offered to God by us gentiles—that is, the bread of the eucharist and the cup likewise of the eucharist."[13] Soon after 200

---

12. Joseph Ratzinger (Pope Benedict XVI), *Sacramentum Caritatis* (apostolic exhortation, February 22, 2007), para. 11, Vatican website, https://www.vatican.va/content/benedict-xvi/en/apost_exhortations/documents/hf_ben-xvi_exh_20070222_sacramentum-caritatis.html.

13. Didache, in Louth, *Early Christian Writings*, 197; Justin Martyr, *Dialogue with Trypho* 116, in *The Ante-Nicene Fathers*, ed. Alexander Roberts and James Donaldson (1885–87; repr., Peabody, MA: Hendrickson, 1994), 1:257.

Tertullian is explicit that the Eucharist is a *sacrificium* and that the material of the sacrifice is the *oblationes* (offerings of bread and wine) brought by the people.[14] Cyprian (mid-third century) wrote that "the passion [of Jesus at Calvary] is the Lord's sacrifice which we offer."[15]

The other great sacrament from the Messiah was baptism, which is also a joining in the Lord's offering himself. For, as we have seen, baptism joins the baptized to the death of the Messiah so that they can also join the resurrection of the Messiah. In baptism as well as Eucharist, there is a joining—by the Spirit—of the Body of the Messiah with the Head. Since all of the life and death of the Messiah were part of his great offering and sacrifice to the Father, baptism also is a joining to the Messiah's cosmic offering.

In the last chapter we looked at the relation between the work of redemption and the kingdom of God. For the early Church the Eucharist was the principal place where redeemed humanity experienced the kingdom of God. Here they entered into the renewed world, by the *anamnēsis* of the sacrament. This was the contact of time with eternity, participation in the future kingdom, by joining his cosmic offering to the Father. The Eucharist (*Eucharist* is a transliteration of the Greek word for "thanksgiving") was the antitype of the Levitical sacrifice of thank offering, which was the only Levitical sacrifice that Jews believed would continue during the days of the Messiah (Pesachim 79a).

Early Liturgy

The sacraments were celebrated within early liturgies. The English word "liturgy" comes from a Greek word meaning "work of the people." This was the expression of what we just saw in early Christian sacraments, that the greatest sacrament was the work of the whole Body of the Messiah, clergy and laity, as they were joined to Messiah's sacrifice to the Father. Liturgy was the answer to the disciples' request, "Lord, teach us to pray." It was behind Paul's confession in Romans 8, "We do not know how to pray as we ought" (v. 26). It helps explain why God struck down Nadab and Abihu when they offered unholy fire (Lev. 10). Aaron's two sons thought they could worship in whatever manner seemed best to them rather than submitting to the precise instructions for worship from YHWH.

Christian liturgy is at least three thousand years old. It is rooted in God's instructions to Israel on how to worship him. In Exodus 19 and 24, 2 Chronicles 35, and

---

14. Tertullian, *On Prayer* 28, in *Ante-Nicene Fathers* 3:690.
15. Cyprian, *Epistle 62: To Caecilius, On the Sacrament of the Cup of the Lord*, in *Ante-Nicene Fathers* 5:363.

elsewhere, there is a repeated pattern for worship: fasting for purification, proclamation of the Word after praise and adoration and supplication, and acceptance of the Word by renewal of the covenant in sacrifice and a meal. In Second Temple Judaism at Shabbat meals and festivals we find this same pattern: a community meal with the breaking of bread and a solemn thanksgiving prayer over the "cup of blessing" in which God's great acts of redemption are recounted. This is the pattern followed by the early followers of the Messiah in their daily and weekly Eucharists.

Gifts of the Holy Spirit

We have seen that the Messiah brought the effects of his redemption to the people of God through the Church and its sacraments and liturgies. The gifts of the Holy Spirit were another means by which the Messiah ministered his life and power to his people. The principal way in which this happened was by what John the Baptist and Jesus called "the baptism in the Holy Spirit" (Luke 3:16; Acts 1:4–8). "Baptism" means "immersion," so baptism in the Holy Spirit is immersion in the Holy Spirit. While this tended to happen only to a few in the times before Jesus— for prophecy, leadership, or wisdom—in the new messianic era it was promised, as Joel prophesied (2:28–29), to all who would repent and turn to Jesus Messiah. They would be immersed in the Holy Spirit, which, since he is the Spirit of Jesus, means being immersed in the Messiah—living in the Messiah and having the Messiah live in them.

Paul says it is this that makes a person a Christian, having the Holy Spirit (Rom. 8:9). Paul also calls this the baptism in the Holy Spirit (1 Cor. 12:13), and Luke implies that this is what happened to Cornelius and his household when they first believed in Jesus as Messiah (Acts 11:15–17). The implication is that believers receive all of the Spirit when they believe, since "[God] gives the Spirit without measure" (John 3:34), and by fresh "fillings" (Eph. 5:18) of the Spirit believers appropriate more and more of the gift. Just as Joshua was told to take possession of the land he had already been given, believers are commanded to keep on being filled (present imperative) with the Spirit they already possess (5:18). Perhaps this is why the apostles are shown to have gone through at least two stages in their experience of the Spirit. They received the Spirit on the night of the resurrection (John 20:22) but did not receive the power of the baptism of the Spirit until Pentecost (Acts 2).

The early Church also spoke of the multiple "gifts" of the Spirit in Romans 12 and Ephesians 4. Every believer had the indwelling Spirit by definition, but each was given a different set of gifts, such as teaching, exhortation, generosity, helps, or mercy. But there were also extraordinary gifts of tongues, prophecy, and healing. These were given here and there and not to everyone. Paul said not all speak in tongues and not all are prophets (1 Cor. 12:29–30). After the early centuries it was thought by some that these miraculous and extraordinary gifts ceased after the age of the apostles, since, it was alleged, they were necessary only to validate the authority of the apostolic writings. But the passage most cited to support this claim in 1 Corinthians 13 ("prophecies and tongues will cease") refers to when "we will see [Jesus] face to face," which is the end of history. And the historical record of the Church over the last two thousand years is full of testimonies to miracles and extraordinary gifts.

The New Testament Canon

The last means of distributing the fruit of the Messiah's purchase of redemption was the set of apostolic writings known as the New Testament. These were interpreted by the Rule of Faith, which was made up of the three creeds (Apostles', Nicene, and Athanasian) and tradition taught by a succession of bishops whom the Church traced back to the apostles. In the first centuries the Rule was the criterion for settling disputes over the meaning of these writings. As Tertullian put it, "This rule, taught . . . by Christ, raises amongst ourselves no other questions than those which heresies introduce, and which make men heretics."[16]

In recent centuries the canon (literally, "ruler") has been questioned. Why were these books and not others chosen? The process took several hundred years. By AD 130 a nucleus of what would eventually be called the New Testament was being acknowledged, at that point consisting of the four Gospels and thirteen Pauline Letters. Hebrews and Acts were also being circulated. The other New Testament writings were received more slowly, but by 367 Athanasius declared the present New Testament as inspired Scripture in his thirty-ninth festal letter.[17]

The primary force driving the process was what Harry Gamble called the "developing pattern of the use" of Christian writings.[18] Christians asked whether a book had been used by most or all the churches from as far back as the time of the apostles. So by the time of the Council of Carthage, which in 397 endorsed

---

16. Tertullian, *The Prescription against Heretics* 13, in *Ante-Nicene Fathers* 3:249.

17. Athanasius, *Letter 39*, in *Nicene and Post-Nicene Fathers*, Series 2, 4:551–52.

18. Harry Gamble, "Canonical Formation of the New Testament," in *Dictionary of New Testament Background*, ed. Craig Evans and Stanley Porter (Downers Grove, IL: InterVarsity, 2000), 192.

the twenty-seven books of the NT, Church leaders were simply endorsing the writings that "had in the earlier period consistently claimed the attention of the Church and proven most useful in sustaining and nurturing the faith and life of Christian communities."[19] There was also what F. F. Bruce called the principle of "antiquity."[20] A document was not approved if it came after the apostolic age. This was the reason given by the orthodox churches for rejecting many of the heretics, whose writings generally came much later.

But even if a book from the first century had been read in the Church for edification, it was not received as Scripture unless it had been *treated* as Scripture during its previous readings. First Clement, for example, was read in the church at Corinth for seventy years after it was first sent there, but it was never regarded with the same reverence as the letters of Paul. When William Whiston in the eighteenth century tried to get the Apostolic Constitutions accepted as Scripture, it was not taken seriously, not only because it came from the fourth century but also because it had not been treated as Scripture before.[21]

Traditional use had to be fairly "catholic" (widespread, bordering on universal) for it to be considered authentic. It had to be found in not just a few churches but in a wide scattering of churches. Augustine said the standard was "to prefer those accepted by all catholic churches to those which some do not accept."[22]

There was also the "apostolic test."[23] There had to be some connection to the apostles, if only indirect. Mark and Luke, for example, were not among the Twelve, but Mark was thought to be Peter's translator, and Luke Paul's companion on his missionary journeys. This test was used to rule out the Shepherd of Hermas and the Didache and was an additional factor in eliminating 1 Clement from the canon.

But in some cases traditional use and attribution were not enough. Doctrinal discordance was enough to rule out documents such as the Gospel of Thomas, the Gospel of Peter, the Acts of Paul, and the Apocalypse of Peter. Eusebius of Caesarea (fourth century) rejected the gospels "of Peter, Thomas and Matthias and several others besides these, or Acts of Andrew, John and other apostles" because "nothing could be farther from apostolic usage than the type of phraseology employed, while the ideas and implications of their contents are so irreconcilable

---

19. Gamble, "Canonical Formation," 192.

20. F. F. Bruce, *The Canon of Scripture* (Downers Grove, IL: InterVarsity, 1988), 259–60.

21. Bruce, *Canon of Scripture*, 263.

22. Augustine, *On Christian Teaching* 2.8, trans. R. P. H. Green (Oxford: Oxford University Press, 2008), 35–36.

23. Bruce, *Canon of Scripture*, 256–59.

with true orthodoxy that they stand revealed as the forgeries of heretics."[24] For example, the Gospel of Peter was docetic, teaching that Jesus did not really suffer, and the Gospel of Thomas Gnostic, asserting salvation by ecstatic knowledge rather than by the life and death of the Messiah. The Apocryphon of James was another Gnostic text that suggested that the body is a prison and matter is evil.

The Apocrypha

The Apocrypha—twelve to fifteen extra books such as Sirach, Wisdom, 1–2 Maccabees, and Tobit in Anglican, Catholic, and Orthodox but not Protestant Bibles—were accepted by Jews in the diaspora but not by Jews in Israel. They were regarded as authoritative and part of Scripture by most of the fathers. For its first millennium and a half, the universal Church did not rule authoritatively on their status. Luther and Calvin rejected them because of Jewish precedent in Israel and because Catholics used them to support doctrines like purgatory that the Reformers rejected. Not to be outdone by Protestant leaders who ruled definitively on the Apocrypha, the Council of Trent (1545–63) declared that the Apocrypha are part of the Bible.

In sum, the ascension of the Messiah was a significant moment in the history of redemption. It was then that Jesus was given royal authority over the Father's kingdom, which authorized him to rule his body, the Church, in more tangible ways. The Church became the principal means to distribute the fruits of his purchase of redemption. Through the Church he gave himself to his people by its sacraments and gifts of the Spirit and kept teaching God's people through the Church's Scriptures and its traditions for interpreting the Scriptures.

In the next chapter we will explore the expansion of redemption by the Church's mission to the Gentiles.

Select Bibliography

Bruce, F. F. *The Canon of Scripture.* Downers Grove, IL: InterVarsity, 1988.
The Church and Ecclesial Communion: Report of the International Roman Catholic–Old Catholic Dialogue Commission. Vatican: Dicastery for Promoting Christian Unity, 2009.

24. Eusebius, *History of the Church from Christ to Constantine* 3.25, trans. G. A. Williamson (1965; repr., New York: Barnes & Noble, 1983), 135.

Cyprian. *Epistle 62: To Caecilius* ("On the Sacrament of the Cup of the Lord"). In *The Ante-Nicene Fathers*, edited by Alexander Roberts and James Donaldson, 5:358–64. 1885–87. Reprint, Peabody, MA: Hendrickson, 1994.

Didache. In *Early Christian Writings: The Apostolic Fathers*, edited by Andrew Louth, 185–99. London: Penguin, 1968.

Dix, Gregory. *The Shape of the Liturgy*. Westminster: Dacre Press, 1945.

Eusebius of Caesarea. *The History of the Church from Christ to Constantine*. Translated by G. A. Williamson. 1965. Reprint, New York: Barnes & Noble, 1983.

Farrow, Douglas. *Ascension Theology*. London: T&T Clark, 2011.

Ignatius of Antioch. *Epistles*. In *Early Christian Writings: The Apostolic Fathers*, edited by Andrew Louth, 53–112. London: Penguin, 1968.

Irenaeus. *Against Heresies*. In *The Ante-Nicene Fathers*, edited by Alexander Roberts and James Donaldson, 1:315–567. 1885–87. Reprint, Peabody, MA: Hendrickson, 1994.

Justin Martyr. *Dialogue with Trypho*. In *The Ante-Nicene Fathers*, edited by Alexander Roberts and James Donaldson, 1:194–270. 1885–87. Reprint, Peabody, MA: Hendrickson, 1994.

Mascall, E. L. *Christ, the Christian, and the Church*. Peabody, MA: Hendrickson, 2017. First published 1946.

Origen. *On Prayer*. In *Origen*, translated and introduced by Rowan Greer, 81–170. Classics of Western Spirituality. New York: Paulist Press, 1979.

Pelikan, Jaroslav. *Whose Bible Is It? A Short History of the Scriptures*. London: Penguin, 2005.

Ratzinger, Joseph (Pope Benedict XVI). *Sacramentum Caritatis* (apostolic exhortation, February 22, 2007). Vatican website, https://www.vatican.va/content/benedict-xvi/en/apost_exhortations/documents/hf_ben-xvi_exh_20070222_sacramentum-caritatis.html.

————. *The Spirit of the Liturgy*. San Francisco: Ignatius, 2000.

Tertullian. *On Prayer*. In *The Ante-Nicene Fathers*, edited by Alexander Roberts and James Donaldson, 3:681–91. 1885–87. Reprint, Peabody, MA: Hendrickson, 1994.

————. *The Prescription against Heretics*. In *The Ante-Nicene Fathers*, edited by Alexander Roberts and James Donaldson, 3:243–65. 1885–87. Reprint, Peabody, MA: Hendrickson, 1994.

15

Mission to Gentiles

As we saw in the last chapter, the Messiah's exaltation to the right hand of the Father gave him a cosmic platform from which to start the messianic Church, which was his primary means of grace for redeeming the world. Yet in a sense, the Church's ministry was different from that of Jesus. Jesus's public ministry was almost exclusively to Jews. He told the Twelve to "go nowhere among the Gentiles" because he had come for "the lost sheep of the house of Israel" (Matt. 10:5–6). At first he turned away the Syro-Phoenician woman, a Gentile, telling her the "children" (Jews) must be fed first (Mark 7:27). For the most part, he left the evangelization of the Gentiles to his disciples after his ascension (Matt. 28:16–20).

But after his cosmic coronation, the Messiah's Spirit led the Church to reach the Gentiles with his good news. Most Christians have been told that this was the first time that truth of the God of Israel reached Gentiles. But as we have seen in previous chapters, God reached souls after Eden and from the time of Enoch to the rise of the nations. Then after the flood, he renewed the covenant of grace though Noah and his descendants. Later, beginning with Abraham's servants, Gentiles started joining the family of Abraham. Gentiles made up thousands of the mixed multitude that came out of Egypt (Exod. 12:38), and Gentiles like Ruth and Rahab joined Israel over the centuries. "Sojourners" who did not convert to Judaism were nevertheless blessed by living among the people of Israel. All of this was to fulfill God's promise to Abraham that through him and his seed "all the families of the earth" would be blessed (Gen. 12:3).

Massive Numbers of Gentiles

But massive numbers of Gentiles coming to worship the God of Israel probably did not begin appearing until after the ascension and the rise of the messianic Church. It started with the conversion of the Roman centurion Cornelius and his household (Acts 10–11). Then after the martyrdom of Stephen the disciples were scattered and brought the good news to lands outside Judea and Galilee. As a result large numbers of Gentiles embraced the Messiah and his Father in places like Cyprus and Cyrene and Antioch (Acts 11:19–21).

Through Paul and his associates great multitudes of Gentiles were converted around the Mediterranean world, so that after a while the numbers of Gentiles exceeded those of Jews. In less than a decade after the ascension Paul was sent from Antioch to preach to Gentiles in what is now Syria and Turkey. Later missionary trips took him and his coworkers to today's Greece and Italy. By the time he got to Thessalonika in Greece, his opponents were already claiming that "these men have turned the world upside down" (Acts 17:6). There was a huge outpouring of the Spirit in Ephesus, the largest city in Asia Minor (19:1–10). Then the gospel planted roots in Rome, the chief city of the Western world.

If Gentiles were crowding the young Church, Jews were not too far behind. By about AD 57, a little more than two decades after the Messiah's resurrection, James and the elders at Jerusalem told Paul "many ten thousands [*myriades*]" of Jews (in Jerusalem) had come to faith in Jesus as Messiah (Acts 21:20). Historians have learned from Emperor Claudius's census in AD 48 that there were 7 million Jews in the empire and that about 2.3 million of those were in Israel, with two hundred thousand to four hundred thousand Jews in Alexandria, Egypt.[1] Since there was a maximum Jerusalem population of four hundred thousand, Messianic Jews were at least 5 percent of the population of Jerusalem (twenty thousand out of four hundred thousand). If that was also the percentage of Messianics among the empire's Jewish population—which is plausible though not certain—then there might have been a minimum of four hundred thousand Messianic Jews in the first century. Scholars such as David Stern think these numbers are far too small, that the number of Jewish believers was actually much larger.[2]

But the numbers of Gentiles accepting the Messiah were considerably larger, especially over the next several centuries. The apostles and their successors went

---

1. "Population," in *Encyclopedia Judaica*, ed. Cecil Roth and Geoffrey Wigoder, cited in David Stern, *Jewish New Testament Commentary* (Clarksville, MD: Jewish New Testament Publications, 1992), 300–302 (at Acts 21:20).

2. Stern, *Jewish New Testament Commentary*, 300–302.

first to synagogues (Rom. 1:16) because there they found Jews and "God-fearers," Gentiles who were already expecting a Messiah. Since they had been trained in the Old Testament by rabbis, their hearts were fertile ground for the seed of the gospel. This was the pattern in Antioch, the third-largest city in the empire. By the end of the fourth century this city in Syria boasted a half million people, and half were Christians. The Church spread to Edessa (now in southeast Turkey) and then to regions that are now Iraq, Armenia, and India. There were already established trade routes to India, and Church tradition tells us that the apostle Thomas started the Mar Thoma church there before he was martyred.

Most of the Church spread north and west, from western Asia Minor, especially the Ephesus seaport, to Italy and Spain by Paul and his company via Greece. By AD 112 the Church was so deeply planted in northwest Asia Minor (Bithynia) that the Roman governor wrote the emperor Trajan that there were many Christians of every class and profession, in both towns and villages, both sexes.

Rome had thirty thousand Christians by AD 250. Most were poorer and spoke Greek, which was at that time the language of the lower classes. Peter and Paul had died there, lending prestige to the city. In this period the gospel reached what is now France, one of whose bishops was Irenaeus in Lyon.

North Africa was thick on the ground with churches. Carthage had a large Christian community in the center of what are now Tunisia and Algeria. Every town had its bishop. Here the Church had made larger inroads among the upper classes, who spoke Latin. Cyrene, today's Libya, was heavily influenced by Christianity because, among other reasons, one of its own, Simon of Cyrene, had carried Jesus's cross (Mark 15:21). Simon's wife and son Rufus became disciples in Rome (Rom. 16:13). North Africa had been seeded with faith by the many Jews who had been in Jerusalem at that momentous Pentecost when the Spirit came down. They returned to their homes to spread their new faith (Acts 2:10). Alexandria, the second-largest city in the empire, came to have an extensive network of churches in the first few centuries. It claimed John Mark to have been its founder.

By the end of the third century some of the strongest Christian churches were in Egypt, Syria, Asia Minor, and North Africa—the region where Islam is dominant today. We will look at the rise of Islam in chapter 21.

Rapid Growth

Why did the gospel spread so quickly? Bruce Shelley argues that part of the answer was its appeal to those who were neglected by the social and political elites. The Church's second-century critic Celsus the philosopher accused it of containing "only worthless and contemptible people, idiots, slaves, poor women and children."[3] Celsus was right: the Church strove to care for the poor and despised.

Apologists had something to do with its growth. Thinkers like Aristides, Justin Martyr, Melito of Sardis, and Irenaeus showed the literary classes that the Church was more than a social welfare organization. It argued with the best Greek and Roman intellectual traditions, chewing what was good and spitting out the bones. Tertullian, for example, was the father of Latin theology and an attorney from Carthage who coined the term "Trinity." Pantaenus was a converted Stoic philosopher who trained Clement of Alexandria and may have helped evangelize India.

The Church's thinkers were of all races, but in the first centuries many of its best theologians were African—Tertullian, Cyprian, Athanasius, Clement of Alexandria, Julius Africanus, and the incomparable Augustine. As Thomas Oden has shown, this was one way that Africa shaped the Christian mind, not only then but continuing over the next two millennia.[4]

There were several other reasons, says Shelley, for the Church's explosive attraction. Its conviction that the eternal God had invaded time to save ordinary people was appealing to people who had lost hope that their lives could have meaning. The God of Israel matched the Stoics for teaching a lofty morality but added what the Stoics lacked: forgiveness and grace.[5]

Besides, this was a community that loved one another. It reached out to the poor, widows, orphans, prisoners, those condemned to mines, and victims of disaster. Christians buried the poor, even pagans. Julian the Apostate (332–63) exclaimed, "They care for our poor too!"[6]

Finally, pagans were impressed by the faith of the martyrs. Their courage and joy spoke to Roman citizens who had little of either. Hundreds of thousands in the empire's amphitheaters watched Christians die with faith. Many walked away wondering what could have produced such fortitude.

---

3. Celsus, quoted in Origen, *Against Celsus* 3.49, in *The Ante-Nicene Fathers*, ed. Alexander Roberts and James Donaldson (1885–87; repr., Peabody, MA: Hendrickson, 1994), 4:484.

4. Thomas Oden, *How Africa Shaped the Christian Mind: Rediscovering the African Seedbed of Western Christianity* (Downers Grove, IL: InterVarsity, 2007).

5. This and the next two paragraphs are based on Bruce Shelley, *Church History in Plain Language*, 2nd ed. (Dallas: Word, 1995), 34–36.

6. According to Shelley, Julian wrote, "The godless Galileans care not only for their own poor but for ours as well." Shelley, *Church History in Plain Language*, 36.

Translation

As the Messiah brought his story of redemption to Gentiles throughout history, he sometimes used their own ideas (seeded originally by his *logos*) to develop the story. In the process he redeemed not only men and women but also ideas. Let me explain.

Andrew Walls has written that Christianity is in principle the most syncretistic religion in the world.[7] By this he means that the God of Israel has chosen to unfold his truth gradually through time rather than in one blinding and all-encompassing flash of revelation and that he has used other religious and philosophical systems to help unfold and interpret his redemption. As Cardinal Newman put it so elegantly in his *Essay on the Development of Christian Doctrine,*

> As Adam gave names to the animals around him, so the Church from the first looked around the earth noting and visiting the doctrines she found. She began in Chaldea, and then sojourned among the Canaanites, and went down into Egypt, and then passed into Arabia, till she rested in her own land. Then to the merchants of Tyre, the wisdom of the East, luxury of Sheba, Babylon, the schools of Greece, sitting in the midst of the doctors, both listening and asking questions, claiming to herself what they said rightly, supplying their defects, completing their beginnings, expanding their surmises, and gradually by means of them enlarging the range and refining the sense of her own teaching. In this way she has sucked the milk of the Gentiles and sucked the breasts of kings.[8]

Evidence abounds of this larger pattern in the history of the work of redemption: God redeems not only individuals and nations but the wisdom of the nations. Christianity has often borrowed from other philosophies and baptized these borrowings into Messiah by reconfiguring them to fit the story of his redemption. In Tanach, for example, God used previously existing Mesopotamian religious rituals (sacred torches, censers, and circumcision) to teach new religious concepts to Abraham and his progeny. God also seems to have used Persian religious traditions to teach his people in Babylonian exile new understandings of cosmic warfare and life after death.

7. Andrew F. Walls, *The Missionary Movement in Christian History* (Maryknoll, NY: Orbis Books, 1996), 173.

8. John Henry Newman, *An Essay on the Development of Christian Doctrine* (Notre Dame, IN: University of Notre Dame Press, 1989), 380. With the words "sucked the milk of the Gentiles and sucked the breasts of kings" Newman alluded to the King James Version of Isa. 60:16, where God promises his people, "Thou shalt also suck the milk of the Gentiles, and shalt suck the breasts of kings: and thou shalt know that I the LORD am thy Saviour and thy Redeemer, the mighty One of Jacob."

In the New Testament we can see the influence of Hellenistic religion: the Hellenistic *theos* was often understood to be a single godhead behind many names and mythologies or an impersonal One behind all that is. New Testament authors used the word, already invested with the suggestion of the ground and force behind everything that exists, and added a new layer of meaning denoting the epitome and source of personhood. Such "translation" is always risky: while something may be gained, something may also be lost by importing foreign connotations that corrupt the original meaning. The use of the new term "Lord" for Messiah (Christ) in Antioch (Acts 11:20) by unnamed believers from Cyprus and Cyrene speaking to Greeks ran the risk of reducing Jesus to one more cult divinity alongside Lord Serapis or Lord Osiris. But because the new community was saturated in the Hebrew Scriptures, the Greco-Roman *kyrios* was reshaped into a new kind of *kyrios*, recognizably Jewish. Paul used concepts like *plēroma* (Rom. 11:25; 1 Cor. 10:26; Col. 1:19; 2:9) and *mystērion* (Rom. 11:25; 1 Cor. 2:1, 7; 4:1; Eph. 1:9; 3:3–4) from Hellenistic culture to communicate the Messiah's fullness and mystery, while at the same time guarding against Hellenistic misconceptions.

This is the principle of "translation," as Walls calls it. The Christian faith takes the word of Messiah into a new culture—which more often than not is animated by a religious vision. By using the language and concepts of the new culture, the faith is reshaped and sometimes even expanded. But the new words and ideas are also transformed by the story of redemption into which they are baptized.[9]

Redemption and Revelation

Does God's transformation of pagan concepts mean that he is giving us truth beyond what he has revealed in Messiah? No. The history of revelation *is* the history of redemption in and through Jesus Christ. So any ways in which cultures outside God's people influenced biblical revelation were always controlled by the Spirit of the Messiah. This means that the Holy Spirit subordinated and reshaped previously foreign concepts such as circumcision and lordship to fit the realities of Israel's God and redemption through Messiah. Circumcision was adapted to the redemptive purposes of the God of Israel. Jesus as Lord was radically different from the ways that Caesar was Lord.

9. The five preceding paragraphs are adapted from Gerald McDermott, "What If Paul Had Been from China? Reflections on the Possibility of Revelation in Non-Christian Religions," in *No Other Gods before Me? Evangelicals and the Challenge of World Religions*, ed. John G. Stackhouse Jr. (Grand Rapids: Baker Academic, 2001), 21–22. Used by permission.

In sum, the history of revelation is determined by the history of redemption by Jesus Messiah. This means that orthodox theology maintains a constitutive rather than representative Christology. The Messiah was the only Savior of the world, not one among many. Without Jesus, God's redemption would not be active in the world. Jesus is not a representative redeemer but the only redeemer.

If Jesus is the only way to the Father as Redeemer, his story as Son and Messiah is the only way to know the fullness of God. Orthodox theology must reject the idea that we can know anything about God *in se* (in himself) beyond or behind what has been revealed through creation, Israel, and Jesus Messiah. It is in these events and words about these events that the essence of God has been revealed. Robert Jenson and Catherine Mowry LaCugna have argued that modern quests for a god behind the God of Christian revelation suppose a transcendent being different from the God redeeming sinners through the work of the Messiah Jesus. Historic orthodoxy teaches instead that the inner being of God is revealed through his redemptive acts in history. As theologians put it, the economic (in the economy of redemption) Trinity is the immanent (in his inner being) Trinity. The fullness of knowledge of God comes through knowledge of the history of his redemption.

God's Expanding Glory

If there is no new revelation behind or beyond the Triune God, nevertheless there is new development in the history of redemption as Messiah makes himself more fully known by the progressive illumination of the Holy Spirit. What begins as an act of translation becomes a discovery of a new dimension of Jesus Messiah. The attempt to transmit faith in Messiah across linguistic and religious frontiers reveals that the Spirit of Messiah has unveiled through the centuries after the ascension more and more of the meaning and significance of the Trinity's glorious redemption. For example, the word "Trinity" and its concept were not identified explicitly in the New Testament. But the Church's theologians gradually teased them out over the Church's first three centuries amid furious debate, and in the process the Church gained new understanding of how God redeems sinners. In those centuries the fathers used words and concepts from Greek philosophy to help them articulate what it means for the trinitarian God to redeem the world. This is one example of how the Church on mission to a world of philosophy not only battled philosophy but also used parts of it to expand its own vision.

Walls suggests that this growth in knowledge of Messiah and his redemption is at the same time growth in the Triune God: "It is as though Christ himself actually grows through the work of mission—and indeed, there is more than a hint of this in one New Testament image":[10] "building up the body of the Messiah until all come to the unity of the faith and the knowledge of the Son of God, to mature manhood, to the degree of maturity of the fullness of the Messiah" (Eph. 4:12–13). In other words, as believers seek to understand Messiah and his redemption, the fullness of his glory grows.

Jonathan Edwards believed that in the history of redemption God's glory grows through the expansion of his creation and redemption. Just as Jesus increased in holiness through the course of his sufferings (God made Jesus "perfect through suffering" [Heb. 2:10]), so too God enlarges his glory and world of relationships through the progress of the work of redemption. In his *End for Which God Created the World* Edwards wrote, "God looks on the communication of himself, and the emanation of the infinite glory and good that are in himself to belong to the fullness and completeness of himself, as though he were not in his most complete and glorious state without it. Thus the church of Christ (toward whom and in whom are the emanations of his glory and communications of his fullness) is called the fullness of Christ: as though he were not in his complete state without her; as Adam was in a defective state without Eve."[11]

In one sense, God is eternally complete and perfect, fully actual and self-sufficient. Yet, at the same time, Edwards argues, God *ad extra* (God's action in creation and history) is God's external *repetition* of his own being and therefore a kind of self-enlargement, just as the beams of light from the sun are an "increase, repetition or multiplication" of its glory: God, "from his goodness, as it were enlarges himself in a more excellent and divine manner . . . by flowing forth, and expressing himself in [his creatures], and making them to partake of him, and rejoicing in himself expressed in them, and communicated to them."[12]

Sang Hyun Lee has explained that the temporal extension of God's actuality repeats in time God's internal actuality without improving it. Another way of putting this is to say that the external exercise of God's internal disposition is the temporal repetition of the divine fullness. So what happens in space and time is really and integrally related to God's own life—not by adding to God's being *ad intra* but by constituting the external extension of God's internal fullness.

10. Andrew F. Walls, *The Missionary Movement in Christian History* (Maryknoll, NY: Orbis Books, 1996), xvii.

11. Jonathan Edwards, *The End for Which God Created the World*, in *The Works of Jonathan Edwards*, ed. Paul Ramsey (New Haven: Yale University Press, 1989), 8:433, 461–62.

12. The three preceding paragraphs and the two following are also adapted from McDermott, "What If Paul Had Been from China?," 25–26. Used by permission.

"Self-enlargement" is a metaphor to represent not spatial expansion but real involvement in history through the creation of new relationships. In other words, God is a God of history, through which God truly acts and does new things. God is not timeless self-identity—as in some Platonic versions of the Christian deity— but the infinite sum and comprehension of all being and beauty for whom the incarnation was something new.

This idea of God's self-expansion in redemptive history is nothing like process theology, which sees God as an instance of the process of becoming, separate from the principle of creativity, rather than the perfect actuality upon which all being and creative process are dependent. Nor does this notion of God's extension through the work of redemption mean that God improves in character through time. It means instead that God manifests his character in and through time.

If God's glory is self-enlarging, it enlarges in part through the history of redemption, which becomes the history of revelation. Providence makes a continual progress, continually bringing forth new and different things. This is why, Edwards proposed, the Church is said by Scripture to be the completeness of Christ (Eph. 1:23), "as if Christ were not complete without the Church." The Church is the fullness of Christ and therefore adds to the completeness of Christ as the further increase of that completeness. Hence the Church, in its progressive understanding of the *meaning* of Messiah by the expansion of his work of redemption, continues to enlarge the actuality of God's self-repetition in time. God's glory is enhanced as the Church grows in her vision of his beauty. This growth in glory and vision is part and parcel of the history of redemption, especially in these centuries when witness to the Gentiles exploded.[13]

Select Bibliography

D'Costa, Gavin. *The Meeting of Religions and the Trinity.* Maryknoll, NY: Orbis Books, 2000.

Edwards, Jonathan. *The End for Which God Created the World.* In *Ethical Writings,* ed. Paul Ramsey, vol. 8 of *The Works of Jonathan Edwards,* 405–536. New Haven: Yale University Press, 1989.

Jenson, Robert. *The Triune Identity.* Philadelphia: Fortress, 1982.

LaCugna, Catherine Mowry. *God for Us: The Trinity and Christian Life.* San Francisco: Harper-SanFrancisco, 1991.

13. This paragraph adapted from McDermott, "What If Paul Had Been from China?," 27. Used by permission.

Lee, Sang Hyun. *The Philosophical Theology of Jonathan Edwards.* Rev. ed. Princeton: Princeton University Press, 1988.

McDermott, Gerald. *Can Evangelicals Learn from World Religions? Jesus, Revelation, and Religious Traditions.* Downers Grove, IL: InterVarsity, 2000.

———. "What If Paul Had Been from China? Reflections on the Possibility of Revelation in Non-Christian Religions." In *No Other Gods before Me? Evangelicals and the Challenge of World Religions,* edited by John G. Stackhouse Jr., 17–36. Grand Rapids: Baker Academic, 2001.

Newman, John Henry. *An Essay on the Development of Christian Doctrine.* Notre Dame, IN: University of Notre Dame Press, 1989.

Oden, Thomas. *How Africa Shaped the Christian Mind: Rediscovering the African Seedbed of Western Christianity.* Downers Grove, IL: InterVarsity, 2007.

Sanneh, Lamin. "Gospel and Culture: Ramifying Effects of Scriptural Translation." In *Bible Translation and the Spread of the Church: The Last 200 Years,* edited by P. C. Stine, 1–23. Leiden: Brill, 1990.

———. *Translating the Message: The Missionary Impact on Culture.* Maryknoll, NY: Orbis Books, 1989.

Shelley, Bruce. *Church History in Plain Language.* Dallas: Word, 1995.

Stern, David. *Jewish New Testament Commentary.* Clarksville, MD: Jewish New Testament Publications, 1992.

Walls, Andrew F. *The Missionary Movement in Christian History.* Maryknoll, NY: Orbis Books, 1996.

16

Persecution

Jonathan Edwards said suffering is the normal state of the Church. God's people typically suffer what the Bible calls "Zion's troubles" during the history of redemption.[1] At every point along this history *some* part of the Church is persecuted, and for most of that history the *whole* people of God is persecuted. Persecution will continue for the Church until the destruction of Antichrist, he maintained, and will yield to a general prosperity for God's people only after that point. Only then will the kingdom be given to the saints (Dan. 7:27).

For most of us this history seems forever, especially if our part of the Church is being attacked by the world. But, as Edwards reminds us, this long history is actually short compared to the eternal state of prosperity that Scripture predicts for the Body of Messiah. Then will begin the hour of relief for the woman in travail (John 16:20–21), when the woman clothed with the sun bears her child (Rev. 12:1–2) and when the martyrs under the altar see the Messiah avenge their blood (6:9–10).

In this chapter I will sketch the persecution of Messiah's Body over its first three centuries, examine its causes, look briefly at the Church's opposition to its Jewish roots, and close with a theology of the cross.

The First Century

Persecution started almost immediately after the resurrection. The apostles were hauled before the Sanhedrin and told to stop preaching the resurrected Messiah.

1. Edwards, *HWR*, 372.

Peter and John and the others said they must obey God and not human beings (Acts 5:29). They were beaten, flogged, and imprisoned. An angel let them out. Stephen was stoned, the Church was scattered, and messianic believers in Damascus were targeted for persecution. Then Jesus confronted Saul of Tarsus on the road to Damascus, and after his conversion persecution was directed at him. This was what Jesus had predicted for his followers, that they would be delivered up to tribulation and hated by all the nations for his name's sake. Some would be put to death (Matt. 24:9).

Two storms of persecution issued from Rome in the first century, one from Nero (54–68) and the other from Domitian (81–96). Nero's persecution started when he shifted the blame to the Christians for a great fire at Rome in 64. According to the Roman historian Tacitus, it was rumored that Nero started the fire to inspire his poetry. When the fire got out of hand and he noticed that it spared the Christian and Jewish areas, Nero scapegoated the Christians. They were blamed more for their "hatred of mankind" than for the fire. Romans had already suspected them because they refused to sacrifice to the Roman gods. But they also seemed antisocial: they abstained from the theater, the army, classical literature, and sports. Tacitus tells us that Nero dressed some in furs to be killed by dogs, crucified others, and set others on fire by night. It is likely that Peter and Paul were among these martyrs, Paul by beheading and Peter by crucifixion.

Domitian came to power after Titus, who had burned the temple in Jerusalem and destroyed the city following the first Jewish revolt (66–70). Domitian's aim was to restore Roman traditions, and Christians got in the way. As under Nero, the persecution was not uniformly severe throughout the empire. But there was horror enough. Clement, bishop of Rome, refers to many of the martyrs in his first epistle. This was the persecution that drove John into exile on Patmos, where he saw the visions of Revelation. Rome, for John, was the great harlot. Domitian, who wanted to be recognized as a deity, was murdered in his own palace.

Rome's Rationale

The empire had Christians in its crosshairs for a number of reasons. As we just saw, they refused to participate in social and civic activities considered normal and patriotic, like gladiatorial games in the theater, eating previously sacrificed meat at restaurants, and reverencing the Caesars as gods. Often they recognized the Roman deities as real spiritual beings—demons, in fact (1 Cor. 10:20)—but insisted that they alone knew the real Creator and Redeemer.

Because they considered idolatry the greatest sin, they avoided professions that involved it—masonry because it was used to construct pagan temples, incense-making for the same reason, teaching because it involved transmitting stories of the gods. Even working in hospitals was risky because they were dedicated to the pagan god Aesculapius, and his priests made their rounds there chanting his name.

Worshipers of the Jewish Messiah stood out because of their views of slavery, children, and sex. They rejected the practices of abortion and infanticide, common for girls and deformed babies. Sex was sacred for believers, restricted to marriage. This was in contrast to the common view of sex as an ordinary recreational activity that had no intrinsic relation to marriage. Masters regularly abused slaves, but the Church told them to treat their slaves with "good will" and warned them that their Master in heaven would hold them accountable (Eph. 6:9).

The early Church was slandered by its neighbors in the empire. It was thought to hold sexual orgies because its members were said to "love one another" and share a "holy kiss." They were accused of cannibalism because in their Eucharists, it was heard, they ate flesh and drank blood. Perhaps the most damning charge was atheism, for they rejected images of the gods of the Roman pantheon and state.

Refusal to join in emperor worship seemed seditious because this worship was believed to be the glue that held together the disparate cultures of the empire. In these early centuries citizens were often required annually to burn a pinch of incense and say, "Caesar is Lord." Christian praises in their assemblies were strikingly similar to those given to the emperor: "Worthy art thou to inherit the kingdom." For these refusals believers were considered revolutionaries.

In Revelation 13, John traced all this pressure to the devil, who wages war through the beast from the sea (imperial power) and the false prophet (imperial worship). He said believers' only defense was the blood of the Lamb and the word of their testimony (Rev. 12:11).

The Second Century

The pattern continued in the next century. In 111 Pliny the Younger, governor of Bithynia, on the north shore of modern Turkey, wrote to the emperor Trajan (98–117) that pagan temples were almost deserted. Pliny asked how he should handle the Christians, whom he had required to pray to the gods, burn incense before the emperor's image, and curse their Messiah. He executed those who did not recant. The emperor replied that Pliny should not seek out Christians but should continue to punish them if they were brought to him.

Ignatius, bishop of Antioch (Syria), was reported to authorities for refusing to honor the empire's deities. He wrote seven letters while on his way to martyrdom in Rome in the early decades of the second century. The bishop, over seventy years old, told his readers he was "God's wheat, to be ground by the teeth of beasts, so that I may be offered as pure bread of Messiah," and he urged his followers not to prevent his execution.[2] His younger friend Polycarp, who was also a bishop, was martyred in 155. When urged to recant before the crowd in a Roman amphitheater, he shouted that he would not. "For eighty-six years I have served him, and he has done me no evil. How could I curse my King who saved me?"[3]

Emperor Marcus Aurelius (161–80) presided over another round of persecution. Enlightened and refined, Aurelius proved that it was not always the worst emperors who persecuted believers in the Jewish Messiah. Because of a constant string of invasions, floods, and epidemics that many thought the gods inflicted because of Christian "impiety," Aurelius supported their persecution. This included the martyrdom of Justin Martyr in Rome, after he apparently was betrayed by another philosopher he had bested in public debate.[4]

The Third Century

Before 200 most Roman attempts to persecute were half-hearted. Because Rome's basic policy was tolerance of diverse religions as long as they paid homage to the emperor, and Jews were excepted as long as they didn't condemn Gentile idolatry, Christians were not actively pursued while they were considered a sect of Judaism. But around 200 that changed. The vast majority of believers were then Gentile, and many tried to get other Gentiles to stop worshiping the emperor.

In 202 Septimius Severus ordered that everyone in the empire had to acknowledge that the sun god reigns above all. The new wave of persecution led to the violent deaths of Irenaeus; Origen's father; and Perpetua and Felicity, two young mothers martyred in Carthage in 203. Emperor Decius (249–51) launched yet another attack on Christians. He too wanted to restore Rome's old glory and

2. Ignatius, *Epistle to the Romans* 4, in *Early Christian Writings: The Apostolic Fathers*, ed. Andrew Louth (London: Penguin, 1968), 86.
3. The Martyrdom of Polycarp, in Louth, *Early Christian Writings*, 128.
4. Henry Chadwick, *The Church in Ancient Society: From Galilee to Gregory the Great* (Oxford: Oxford University Press, 2001), 93–99.

believed, like many of his predecessors, that Christian failure to revere the gods was incurring their wrath. As Justo González has observed, this was the second third-century persecution, which, unlike the previous one, was not sporadic but systematic and universal.

According to Eusebius, the Church nevertheless prospered in the last decades of the third century. Persecution abated, respect for the new faith increased. Governors and officials tried to help Christians and treated bishops with honor. Large church buildings were erected. But in Eusebius's estimation this weakened the Church. They got too used to peace and prosperity. Bishops diminished themselves by arguing publicly with one another. Eusebius might have read Origen's (ca. 185–ca. 254) observation a century earlier that in the period between Severus and Decius churches had been packed. Christianity expanded beyond the empire to Armenia and Georgia. Whole towns in Asia Minor had adopted the faith. High Church offices attracted ambitious men.

Christians were entering the Roman army, even the officer class. Christian officers used the sign of the cross against demons when sacrifices were offered before a campaign. But tolerance was uneven. The conscript Maximilian in North Africa was executed in 295 after refusing to swear allegiance to the emperor.

The Great Persecution of Diocletian

By 303 Diocletian (284–305) had had enough. He ordered a final pogrom of the churches. Henry Chadwick reports that select churches were dismantled or destroyed. Bibles were burned. Even nobles were tortured if they refused to recant their faith. The bishop of Nicomedia, Diocletian's capital city in the east, was executed. At Antioch, one of the empire's biggest cities, horrendous tortures were inflicted on those who refused to salute the gods. Although this last great persecution was systematic, it was not enforced universally. Spain and Italy felt its full force, but Britain and Gaul saw only the demolition of some churches. In Egypt two bishops were so loved that their flocks kept them in office even after they had been forced to sacrifice to the gods. North Africa suffered mightily, however; forty-nine were executed in Carthage. The number of martyrs was not huge, but many were maimed for life after being stretched on the rack or roasted on gridirons.

The fires ended relatively soon. Diocletian got sick in 304 and shortly after handed power over to two Caesars, Galerius and Constantius Chlorus, father to Constantine.

Philosophical Enemies

Not all the Church's enemies were tyrants threatening torture and death. Pagan philosophers recognized that the Church was a movement with its own implicit philosophy that threatened theirs. So some of its best thinkers went out of their way to challenge it in writing. Celsus (flourished ca. 176) was among paganism's sharpest. An eclectic Platonist, Celsus adopted adherence to ancestral traditions as his criterion for philosophical probity. In his *Logos Alethes* (True Word) he argued that this new Jewish sect, which he thought was rebelling against its Jewish parent, was irrational to claim a crucifixion could be a victory over the devil. Its adherents proved they were aliens in the empire by their refusal to swear by the genius of the emperor.

They were also largely ignorant because of their lack of education, Celsus claimed. Most were artisans, even if some knew Plato and were intelligent. The simplicity of most Christians was what caused many good people to watch from a distance. They were intrigued by the martyrdoms, which had brought huge publicity to the new religion.

Celsus knew that Jesus was called "savior" and "God's messenger." But he thought Jesus's followers were problematic. They were divided into quarreling groups, just like the Greek philosophical schools. And it seemed too probable that Jesus was the illegitimate son of Mary. If he were truly God in the flesh, he would have appeared after his resurrection to Pilate, the soldiers, and all people everywhere. Besides, it was a priori impossible for a god to be in a human body, eat lamb, and speak with a merely human voice. His miracles might have been real but must have been performed by magic.[5]

Porphyry (ca. 234–ca. 305) the Neoplatonist reportedly was once a Christian. So he was familiar with Christian doctrine and scriptures. Like Celsus, he could not abide a faith that proclaimed only one way to the divine. And he was adamant that Christian faith did not meet his standards of what is reasonable, for its adherents did not use rational argument to ground their faith.

Against Jewish Roots

Just as the Church had philosophical enemies, its first adherents came to have theological adversaries. Soon after the first century of mostly Jewish leaders, the Church began to be dominated by Gentile leaders who forgot the Jewish origins

5. This section on Celsus draws from Chadwick, *Church in Ancient Society*, 110–13.

of their Messiah and gospel. Early Christian thinkers began to sever theology from its Jewish character. Justin Martyr (100–ca. 165) started a trend toward supersessionism that we have seen in previous chapters, a trend that developed into active persecution of Jewish followers of Jesus.

The Epistle of Barnabas (written at some point between 70 and 135) was actually the first major Christian document that concluded that Jewish sins disqualified Jews from possessing the covenant any longer. But Justin was probably the first major Church thinker to say that the Church was "true Israel." By this he meant that the Church was disconnected from Jews and biblical Israel. Since most of the Church was made up of Gentiles and a majority of Jews were rejecting Jesus, Justin said that the *Logos* in the abstract was more important than the Jewish flesh that the *Logos* took on. The Jews had their prophets, but so did the Greeks in Socrates and Plato. The Old Testament was not important because of its messianic types from the God of Israel but because it predicted the true *Logos*. So the old Israel was no longer significant. It had been superseded by the Body composed mostly of Gentiles. God must have left behind the old Israel and taken up this new Body as his New Israel.

As Oskar Skarsaune has remarked, Justin fell prey to exactly what Paul warned his Gentile readers against: "Do not boast over the branches" (Rom. 11:18). In Romans 11 Paul said the Gentiles were like "a wild olive shoot" that is grafted onto the olive tree of Israel, some of whose "natural branches" (Jews) were broken off "because of their unbelief" (vv. 20–21). He cautioned the Gentile Jesus-followers against the arrogance that forgets that "it is not you who support the root [Jewish Israel], but the root that supports you" (v. 18). Justin might not have known of Paul and his letters, so he cannot be blamed for forgetting this Pauline truth. But the pattern of arrogance can be seen in his *Dialogue with Trypho*.[6]

Irenaeus (ca. 145–202) was another Church father who betrayed these Pauline warnings. He was the Church's first great philosopher of history, who used the God of Israel's doctrine of creation to do splendid work against Gnosticism in *Against Heresies*. But he too taught that God made a new covenant with the Gentile churches that superseded his original covenant with Jewish Israel. Irenaeus wrote that God did this because the Jews were "headstrong" and their Old Testament rituals were "carnal" and "earthly." The history of Israel was a bad detour in the history of redemption, a negative rather than positive object lesson. It was necessary to prepare the human race for the Messiah, but logically it could be skipped over when

---

6. The previous two paragraphs are adapted from Gerald McDermott, *Israel Matters: Why Christians Must Think Differently about the People and the Land* (Grand Rapids: Brazos, 2017), 6–7.

telling the story of the gospel. Far better to go from Adam and the fall to Jesus as the Second Adam. The Jewish story ended with the Jews' repudiation of their own Messiah, and it was necessary that they be "disinherited from the grace of God."

Origen taught supersessionism but in a more systematic way. Influenced by the matter-demeaning Gnostics he battled, he reasoned that if Jesus's redemption was spiritual, then so were all of the Bible's promises to future Israel. They must have been about spiritual Israel, the Church, not about physical Israel with Jewish bodies. And if the Messiah had already arrived with his covenant, then God's covenant with the Jews must have ended. Although most Christians have never heard of Origen, he was hugely influential in the third and later centuries. He wrote hundreds of books that were used as textbooks for many later Christian leaders and teachers. Therefore he was indirectly responsible for centuries of later attacks on Jews by Christians who had been persuaded that God in his wrath took the covenant away from the Jews. In this way a false and unbiblical history of redemption brought untold suffering on millions of sons and daughters of Abraham.

Lest we think that all the Christian fathers were enthusiastic supersessionists in every way, it is important to note that Justin Martyr said the millennium will be centered in Jerusalem, Irenaeus taught that Israel will one day be restored, and Tertullian declared that Jews will return to the land to restore their polity. Origen had friendly personal relations with Jews, was one of the few fathers who learned Hebrew (the other was Jerome), and in his refutation of Celsus wrote that the simplest Jew understands things the Greek philosophers do not, and, unlike Plato or any other Greek philosopher, "a whole nation, dispersed throughout the entire world, obey the laws of Moses."[7] Origen did not think Israel would be restored, but he admired their law. Fourth-century historian Eusebius of Caesarea reports that third-century Egyptian bishop Nepos taught the restoration of Israel and that his writings were "most convincing" to others. The Testament of the Twelve Patriarchs is a second-century document that teaches the future restoration of the twelve tribes and reflects early Church teaching by thinkers who clearly rejected replacement theology.

Parting of the Ways

Despite supersessionist ways of rendering the history of redemption, nonmessianic Jews and Messianic Jews in the Church kept fellowship in complicated

7. Origen, *Against Celsus* 1.16, in *The Ante-Nicene Fathers*, ed. Alexander Roberts and James Donaldson (1885–87; repr., Peabody, MA: Hendrickson, 1994), 4:403.

ways until the rise of Islam in the seventh century. Isaac Oliver writes that Justin Martyr is the only Christian writer we know who exploited the second Jewish revolt (133–35) against Judaism. There was no clear and absolute "parting of the ways" between Jews and Christians in the next few centuries, for the social reality on the ground was more complicated than what the Church fathers, who wanted clear separation, would have us believe. Many Gentile believers found Jewish traditions attractive and attended local Jewish synagogues, even adopting some Jewish customs. Adam Becker and Annette Yoshiko Reed contend that Judaism and Christianity during these centuries parted and joined, and then kept parting and joining for many centuries.[8] At the beginning of the fifth century, for example, Jerome writes about "Nazoreans," Jews who believed in Jesus as Messiah and still kept Torah.

Theology of the Cross

We have seen in this book that God has led his people—whether Jews or Gentiles—along a journey that often involves suffering. Edwards said persecution is normal for the Body of Messiah. We will get to the Reformation in a few chapters, but it might be helpful in this chapter on persecution to hear from the first great Reformer, Martin Luther, on suffering and persecution. In his Heidelberg Disputation Luther distinguished between theologians of glory and theologians of the cross. The former ground their understanding of God in things that can be seen, while the latter take their knowledge of God from the Messiah's passion and cross. Only there, Luther argues, do we see the true God and our own true selves. There we see that all our works are condemned by God and that only by the work of the Messiah on the cross, in his weakness and foolishness (in the world's eyes), can we be justified before God.[9] I would add the reminder that this God is none other than the God of Israel, whose Messiah is a Jewish man. This is particularly important to remember when we're tracing the history of redemption in a Church that has killed Jews in the name of "Christ."

Alister McGrath has made the case in his *Luther's Theology of the Cross* that we can understand our own lives only if we have something like Luther's theology of the cross. The disciples must have thought after Good Friday that maybe Jesus was

---

8. Adam H. Becker and Annette Yoshiko Reed, eds., *The Ways That Never Parted: Jews and Christians in Late Antiquity and the Early Middle Ages* (Tübingen: Mohr Siebeck, 2003).

9. Martin Luther, "Disputation Held at Heidelberg," in *Luther's Works*, vol. 31, *Career of the Reformer*, ed. Harold J. Grimm and Helmut T. Lehmann (Philadelphia: Muhlenberg Press, 1957), 39–58.

not Messiah after all. The Romans seemed to have won, defeating the disciples' dreams for a new kingdom of God with Jesus at its head. But after Easter Sunday morning, seeing the resurrected Jesus, they realized that Jesus was Messiah after all.[10]

This was the significance of the cross and resurrection for the disciples, and it should be for us. The cross helps us remember that earthly defeat is part of life in the God of Israel. Suffering is normal. When it is considered in the absence of the resurrection, it can suggest that Jesus was not the Messiah and there is no redemption. But the cross is not the end of the story. The resurrection vindicates suffering and persecution for the Messiah and his Body. It shows that Christian suffering has meaning and helps us recall that evil will be punished—that despite the frequent occurrence of persecution from an unbelieving world, the Messiah's disciples will be vindicated . . . and redeemed.

Select Bibliography

Becker, Adam H., and Annette Yoshiko Reed, eds. *The Ways That Never Parted: Jews and Christians in Late Antiquity and the Early Middle Ages.* Tübingen: Mohr Siebeck, 2003.

Chadwick, Henry. *The Church in Ancient Society: From Galilee to Gregory the Great.* Oxford: Oxford University Press, 2001.

Eusebius of Caesarea. *The History of the Church from Christ to Constantine.* Translated by G. A. Williamson. 1965. Reprint, New York: Barnes & Noble, 1983.

González, Justo. *The Story of Christianity.* Vol. 1. New York: HarperCollins, 2010.

Irenaeus. *Against Heresies.* In *The Ante-Nicene Fathers,* edited by Alexander Roberts and James Donaldson, 1:359–567. 1885–87. Reprint, Grand Rapids: Eerdmans; Edinburgh: T&T Clark, 1993.

Justin Martyr. *Dialogue with Trypho.* In *The Ante-Nicene Fathers,* edited by Alexander Roberts and James Donaldson, 1:194–270. 1885–87. Reprint, Peabody, MA: Hendrickson, 1994.

———. *Second Apology.* In *The Ante-Nicene Fathers,* edited by Alexander Roberts and James Donaldson, 1:188–93. 1885–87. Reprint, Peabody, MA: Hendrickson, 1994.

Luther, Martin. "Disputation Held at Heidelberg." In *Luther's Works,* vol. 31, *Career of the Reformer,* edited by Harold J. Grimm and Helmut T. Lehmann, 39–58. Philadelphia: Muhlenberg Press, 1957.

McDermott, Gerald. "Seeds of the Word: Justin Martyr on Seeds of the Word in Other Religions." In *God's Rivals: Why Has God Allowed Different Religions? Insights from the Bible and the Early Church,* 85–97. Downers Grove, IL: IVP Academic, 2007.

10. Alister E. McGrath, *Luther's Theology of the Cross: Martin Luther's Theological Breakthrough* (Oxford: Blackwell, 1985).

McGrath, Alister. *Luther's Theology of the Cross: Martin Luther's Theological Breakthrough*. Oxford: Blackwell, 1985.

Oliver, Isaac. "The Parting of the Ways." In *Understanding the Jewish Roots of Christianity*, edited by Gerald McDermott, 104–27. Bellingham, WA: Lexham, 2021.

Origen. *Against Celsus*. In *The Ante-Nicene Fathers*, edited by Alexander Roberts and James Donaldson, 4:395–669. 1885–87. Reprint, Peabody, MA: Hendrickson, 1994.

―――. *On First Principles*. Translated by G. W. Butterworth. Gloucester, MA: Peter Smith, 1973. See particularly book 4.

Richardson, Peter. *Israel in the Apostolic Church*. Cambridge: Cambridge University Press, 1969.

Shelley, Bruce. *Church History in Plain Language*. 2nd ed. Dallas: Word, 1995.

Skarsaune, Oskar. *In the Shadow of the Temple: Jewish Influences on Early Christianity*. Downers Grove, IL: InterVarsity, 2008.

Tacitus. *The Annals: The Reigns of Tiberius, Claudius, and Nero*. Translated by J. C. Yardley. Oxford: Oxford University Press, 2008.

Testament of the Twelve Patriarchs. In *The Ante-Nicene Fathers*, edited by Alexander Roberts and James Donaldson, 8:9–38. 1885–87. Reprint, Peabody, MA: Hendrickson, 1994.

17

The Monastic Movement

Beginning in the third century and then becoming dominant in the fourth, a new model of discipleship emerged among God's people. In the first two centuries the ideal Jesus-follower was the martyr standing in the Roman amphitheater defying beasts and gladiators. But over the next two centuries the focus switched to the lonely monk in the desert fighting Satan. Why the transition?

In part it was because of the quiet times between persecutions when the Church grew lax and the ambitious fought for Church offices. Ordinary Christians wondered where they could look for leaders they could admire. The other reason was the gospel itself, which suggested that self-renunciation was an important component in the path to redemption. The New Testament referred to "widows and virgins" who renounced their desires to marry and gave themselves in chastity to the service of the Church (1 Tim. 5:1–16). Jesus called a young man to sell everything he had, spoke of men who make themselves "eunuchs for the kingdom" of God, and said one's real family was the fellowship of fellow believers (Mark 10:17–27; Matt. 19:12; Mark 3:31–35). Paul recommended that single people remain that way for the sake of undivided devotion to the Lord (1 Cor. 7:25–35).

This new model was also a reflection of the spirit of the age. Most students of the early Church contrast its ascetic ways to the self-indulgence of Christians' neighbors in the empire. Yet some of those pagan neighbors were living and urging lives of abnegation. Plato was well known for recommending in the *Republic* that his readers deny themselves food, drink, and sex, taking only what is necessary for survival. The Stoic teacher Epictetus, a former slave, called his life

209

therapy *askēsis*—the word from which we get "ascetic"—meaning the training of a soldier or athlete that restricts the life of the flesh. Even Epicurus the hedonist advised that sexual activity would impede pleasure. The Syrian prince Iamblichus idealized the Pythagorean way of abstinence from meat, wine, much sleep, and sex—the last to be indulged only for procreation. Roman-era moralists generally regarded sex as an animal drive necessary for propagation but dangerous and potentially antisocial.

Anthony

Some Egyptian Jesus-followers fled to the desert to escape persecution. There they found the first ascetics, who lived in solitude fighting their desires and Satan himself. Anthony was the most famous of these. He was orphaned about 271 when he was in his late teens. Because his parents were semiwealthy Christians, Anthony was left with a sizable estate. Shortly after their death he heard in church the story of the rich young man whom Jesus told to give to the poor everything he possessed if he wanted to have eternal life. Anthony promptly gave his inherited acres to local villagers and kept a sum to care for his sister. When he heard another text in church about Jesus saying not to be anxious about tomorrow, Anthony put his sister in a community for virgins and gave the rest of his money away. For several years he lived with an old hermit in the desert, then by himself in a derelict cemetery. When he was thirty-five he went further into the desert and settled in an abandoned fort.

Anthony's diet was salt, water, and bread, typically consumed once a day after sunset. That was when he was not fasting two to four days at a time. He slept on the ground and refused oil so that he could toughen his skin. Athanasius's *Life of Antony* recounts battles against animals (principally hyenas and snakes), demons, and the devil himself. Anthony said that he knew the demons had come close when he could smell their stench. One of his most powerful weapons was the sign of the cross, which the demons feared.

Anthony attracted many disciples, who came to live nearby. He would visit them regularly to counsel them on self-discipline, love for God, and the life of contemplation. During the final great persecution under Diocletian, Anthony visited Alexandria, hoping for martyrdom. On his second visit, years later, the illiterate but mentally sharp monk, who had memorized reams of Scripture, encouraged orthodox believers by refuting Arians in debate. In his last decades before his death at 105, Anthony was visited by thousands of people who sought his spiritual counsel and healing prayer.

Largely because of Anthony's growing renown and Athanasius's *Life*, there was a mass exodus of believers to the desert. Rumor had it—and of course this was exaggerated—that the Egyptian deserts on either side of the Nile were more crowded than the cities. These thousands of ascetics traded for food and other necessities by weaving baskets and mats. They memorized psalms and whole books of the New Testament.

Pachomius

Over time solitary monks gave way to communities of monks. The most effective organizer in the fourth century was Pachomius, a younger contemporary of Anthony. The son of pagans, he was forced into the army, where he became despondent. But he was so moved by local Christians who offered food and drink to his band of soldiers that when he was able, he quit the army and became a serious believer. Shortly after, he found an ascetic in the desert, with whom he lived for seven years.

After the visit of an angel who told him to serve others, Pachomius invited his brother to build an enclosure big enough for others. This first attempt at community failed because his recruits thought he was too demanding. In his second try Pachomius upped the ante. Now, he told the interested, they must promise absolute obedience, commit themselves to manual work, and consider no task too lowly. This worked. By the end of the fourth century, the Pachomian system was the most established network of monastic communities, and it influenced the later development of monasticism.

Each community was surrounded by a wall that kept out slave traders, who were a recurring threat to monasteries. Every monastery contained a number of houses, each of which held between twenty and forty monks. The houses had private cells for all their monks, a church meeting room for morning and evening liturgy, a refectory, a library, a kitchen, a bakery, an infirmary, and workshops. A superior general was in command of all the monks, each of whom was ranked by order of seniority in residence. Monks became full members after three years of probation. Dress was prescribed and simple. Monks slept three to a cell while sitting up. Two meals a day featured bread, fruit, vegetables, and fish. No wine or meat. There were two fast days per week.

Monks were limited in their conversation to spiritual subjects. Gossip was forbidden. Eucharist was celebrated twice a week. The communities supported themselves by making baskets and most of what they needed for daily life. When not doing manual labor, monks studied, read, and memorized Bible passages.

It seems strange to moderns, but even pagans lined up at the gates of these monasteries. There was high unemployment in this period in Egypt, when exorbitant taxes had driven people off farms and villages. And as we have seen, spiritual rigor was widely valued among pagans, and the slave trade was brisk. Not all, therefore, joined for the most spiritual reasons, but there was catechesis for new members who needed to learn the faith.

By the end of the fourth century there were large numbers of monasteries, each with two to three hundred monks. At Pachomius's death his houses held three thousand. His sister founded a nunnery under Pachomius's direction, and after his death she started more.

Kinds and Extremes

In the fourth and fifth centuries monks were known in three forms—solitaries; those loosely affiliated, like Anthony's neighbors, in a *laura*; and organized communities like those under Pachomius.

There were also extreme solitaries. The most famous was Simeon Stylites (d. 459) who lived for thirty-six years atop a pillar east of Antioch in Syria. Although his body was reputed to drip with vermin, he attracted many, even government officials, who came for counsel and healing prayer.

Other solitaries stayed in cells too small to stretch out in or lived on grass. These "athletes for God" were known for rigorous fasting from food and sleep.

Basil of Caesarea

After Pachomius the most famous organizer of monastic communities was Basil of Caesarea, one of the three Cappadocian theologians we will see again in the next chapter. Basil esteemed marriage but believed celibacy and asceticism comprised a higher way to redemption, particularly after visiting Egypt in 358 and seeing the Pachomian monasteries. His sister Macrina, a theologian in her own right, founded a convent.

Like Augustine, as we shall see, Basil started as a monk and was drawn into Church leadership and theological battle. In the intervals he retreated to the monastic life and drew up two rules for monastic community, the *Longer Rules* and the *Shorter Rules*. These show he learned from Pachomius but thought monks needed more community in order to learn how to obey the second commandment of love for neighbor. He had tested extreme austerity and found it wanting. So his communities had books read out loud during their common meals. They gave honor to agricultural and intellectual work. His monks were encouraged to confess their sins regularly to more mature brothers. The monasteries gave donations to the poor outside their walls. Basil's rules influenced Cassian's monastic rule in Gaul in the fifth century and Benedict's *Rule* in the sixth century.

Martin of Tours

Martin of Tours was a contemporary of Basil's. He was born to pagan parents who opposed his conversion to the Messiah as a teen, and they tried to discourage his faith by forcing him to join the Roman army. While serving in northern Gaul on a cold wintry night and seeing a naked, shivering beggar, Martin ripped his cape in two and gave half to the beggar. That night in a dream Jesus said to him, "What you did to the least of these my brothers you have done to me."

Two years later Martin left the army and joined the work of Hilary of Poitiers, a bishop and theologian later named a doctor (teacher) of the Church. Soon thereafter Martin became a hermit and attracted others to his hermitage. When believers in Tours sought a bishop, they compelled Martin to accept the office, even though he presented himself in rags and filth. His direct speech, refusal to judge or condemn, his insistence on living outside the city in a cell while bishop, his reputation for doing miracles while calling himself nothing more than an apprentice, and his peace and piety made a deep impression on later bishops and caused many to promote the monastic movement.

Jerome

Jerome, the Church father who gave the Church its Latin translation of the Bible (the Vulgate), was also a monk. An eloquent but vitriolic scholar and contemporary of Martin and Basil, Jerome was a solitary in Syria for three years before he became secretary to Pope Damasus and spiritual director to wealthy female converts in Rome. One of those women, Paula, traveled with Jerome to Bethlehem, where he founded a monastery and she started a convent and hospice. Among his many literary productions, Jerome translated Pachomius's rule into Latin.

Augustine

We see more of the confluence of episcopacy, theology, and monasticism in the man who was perhaps the greatest Church father and theologian, Augustine of Hippo. He was converted in part because of Athanasius's *Life of Antony* and was impressed by the monastery under his first orthodox mentor, Ambrose of Milan. When Augustine returned to North Africa, he started his own monastery with disciples in ancient Numidia, now Algeria. This first effort was oriented toward theological appropriation of pagan philosophy: its members chanted the psalms, studied other scriptures, and read Cicero and Plotinus.

After Augustine was coerced by the believers in Hippo to become their priest and was later made bishop, he founded a monastery in that city. His widow sister started a nunnery there. The rest of Augustine's ministry as a bishop was monastic in lifestyle. He was one of the many, but probably the greatest, who joined the episcopal ideal to the monastic.

John Cassian

At the end of the fourth century John Cassian took the monastic ideal to Marseilles, where he founded monasteries for men and separate ones for women. He collected the sayings of the desert fathers in Egypt and published them as *Conferences*. Although he worked mainly in France, his rule and books were favored by Greek-speaking monasteries in the East because of their criticism of Augustine's emphasis on predestination.

Cassian promoted moderation in his monasteries, focusing on the primacy of community with Eucharist at the center. He was critical of monks or communities that partook only once a year. He listed the most common temptations of the desert monks and, presumably, his own: gluttony, lust, covetousness, anger, *accidie* (boredom in prayer), vainglory, pride, and dejection or melancholy. The last of these often afflicted those who felt cut off from their families. Like all monastic communities, Cassian's forbade visits to families, even funerals.

Cassian was both pastoral and strict. He encouraged his monks not to dwell on past sins that were repented and forgiven but to avoid occasions that might tempt them afresh. He also kept watch for *sarabaites*, vagrants who wanted to mooch but would never accept authority or rule.

The following sample from an address to Cassian's monks by Abbot Moses in the first of Cassian's *Conferences* provides a glimpse into the minds of the desert fathers.

We undergo all sorts of toils not merely without weariness but actually with delight; on account of which the want of food in fasting is no trial to us, the weariness of our vigils becomes a delight; reading and constant meditation on the Scriptures does not pall upon us; and further incessant toil, and self-denial, and the privation of all things, and the horrors also of this vast desert have no terrors for us. And doubtless for this it was that you yourselves despised the love of kinsfolk, and scorned your fatherland, and the delights of this world, and passed through so many countries, in order that you might come to us, plain and simple folk as we are, living in this wretched state in the desert. . . . What is the goal and end, which incite you to endure all these things so cheerfully?

. . . [As you have told me,] we endured all this for the sake of the kingdom of heaven.[1]

Benedict

Benedict's *Rule* provided the constitution for later Western monasticism. Benedict started as a hermit in the late fifth century. Like Pachomius, he attracted others who were not ready for monastic rules. But then in 529 he founded Monte Cassino about eighty-five miles southeast of Rome, and its rule has been followed ever since by hundreds of monasteries all over the world.

Benedict was no scholar. But he had a genius for administration and profound knowledge of human nature.[2] His *Rule* is renowned for its moderation and good judgment. Food was restricted, but a daily measure of wine was given to each monk (this in an era when safe water was in short supply). Monks took vows of poverty, chastity, and obedience. Unworthy monks were sent out after a one-year probation, but all who stayed were disciplined if they broke the rules. Restraint was balanced with freedom. Whereas previous masters controlled every detail, Benedict recognized that the abbot must give freedom to address changing situations. Manual labor was balanced by religious reading, both required.

At Benedictine and other monasteries problems with chastity and poverty were few and far between. The vow to obedience was more difficult to keep, and factions were common. The story is told of an older holy hermit named Barsanuphios near Gaza who appointed his pupil Seridos to be abbot of a community where the old man was in a hidden cell never seen or heard by other monks. Seridos often

---

1. John Cassian, *Conferences* 1.2.2–3, trans. C. S. Gibson, in *The Nicene and Post-Nicene Fathers*, Series 2, ed. Philip Schaff (1886–89; repr., Peabody, MA: Hendrickson, 1994), 11:295–96, revised and edited by Kevin Knight, New Advent, https://www.newadvent.org/fathers/350801.htm.

2. Bruce Shelley, *Church History in Plain Language*, 2nd ed. (Dallas: Word, 1995), 121.

delivered judgments after, he said, he had consulted Barsanuphios. One time a faction of monks rebelled against their abbot because they had concluded that Seridos had invented this elderly monk to justify his own authority. To resolve the dispute, the monks were assembled in the refectory, where Barsanuphios suddenly appeared, washed every monk's feet, and disappeared never to be seen again.

The rhythm of Benedictine monasteries was set by seven daily offices of communal prayer, one at 2 a.m. (here is the rigor) but each one about twenty minutes (here is the moderation). All necessities of life were provided by the monks. They were the carpenters and masons and cooks, and they made their own wine. Their abbot was chosen by the community, and he consulted with the whole body before making major decisions.

Benedict's monks spent part of every day copying and reading the great literary works of antiquity. We are indebted to them for transmitting to the West the Latin Church fathers and the great works of Latin literature.[3]

Monasticism and the Way of Redemption

The monastic movement arose between the persecutions, when Church discipline seemed lax, Church offices were sometimes filled by mediocre men, and many thought the Church had declined from the high standards set by the Gospels and Epistles. The monks were an answer to the question, What does it mean to be a disciple of the Messiah? How should we follow him to be assured that we will gain the kingdom? How should we embrace the Messiah's redemption now so that we will be sure of being redeemed at the end?

It is easy to be critical of this movement. It suggested to some that our rigorous works save us, rather than the works of Jesus Messiah in his life, death, and resurrection. We are called to be a city on a hill, the salt of the earth, to let our light shine so that the world might see our good works and praise our Father in heaven (Matt. 5:13–16). But how can these things happen if we retreat from the world?

The monks believed, as did most believers in these centuries, that there were two ways to heaven, one higher and one lower. The monks were on the high road because they forsook the rewards of nuclear family. Ordinary Christians who struggled to raise families and keep them faithful were considered second-class pilgrims. This seems unfair and unbiblical, since Scripture suggests that marriage

---

3. Shelley, *Church History in Plain Language*, 122.

is the ordinary way for most, and many find that marrying and parenting can be more difficult than living in a monastery with few worries.

But in this new century when many think grace means the end of law and that striving for holiness contradicts the gospel, the monastic movement can help us better understand redemption. If we are to work out our salvation with fear and trembling (Phil. 2:12–13), and if there is holiness without which no one will see the Lord (Heb. 12:14), and if Jesus warns that only those who endure to the end will be saved (Matt. 24:13), then we must learn how to *walk* on the road to final redemption. And this walking will involve self-denial and discipline (Mark 8:34; Heb. 12:7).

If we, like many modern Jesus-followers, have a difficult time with self-denial and discipline, the monastic movement might give us some hints about how to walk on the road to final redemption.

Select Bibliography

Athanasius. *"The Life of Antony" and "The Letter to Marcellinus."* Translated by Robert Gregg. Classics of Western Spirituality. New York: Paulist Press, 1980.

Chadwick, Henry. "Monks: The Ascetic Life." In *The Church in Ancient Society: From Galilee to Gregory the Great*, 394–410. Oxford: Oxford University Press, 2001.

Fry, Timothy, ed. and trans. *The Rule of St. Benedict in English.* Collegeville, MN: Liturgical Press, 1981.

González, Justo. "The Monastic Reaction." In *The Story of Christianity*, 1:157–72. New York: HarperCollins, 2010.

John Cassian. *Conferences.* Translated by C. S. Gibson. In vol. 11 of *The Nicene and Post-Nicene Fathers*, Series 2. Edited by Philip Schaff. 1886–89. Reprint, Peabody, MA: Hendrickson, 1994. Revised and edited by Kevin Knight. New Advent. https://www.newadvent.org/fathers/350801.htm.

Latourette, Kenneth Scott. "The Rise of Monasticism." In *A History of Christianity*, 221–35. New York: Harper and Bros., 1953.

Shelley, Bruce. "Exiles from Life." In *Church History in Plain Language*, 2nd ed., 116–23. Dallas: Word, 1995.

18

Dogma and Theology in the Third and Fourth Centuries

Athanasius (ca. 296–373) was a short, swarthy Egyptian (hence the epithet "black dwarf" given him by his enemies) who was at the center of the theological debates that saved the Church from Arianism and helped establish the Trinity as the Christian vision of the true God. As a young man Athanasius went out into the desert to seek counsel from Saint Anthony, and out of this friendship over the years eventually came his biography of Anthony, which helped shape the monastic movement we saw in the last chapter.

But Athanasius became a doctor ("teacher" in Latin) of the Church because he bravely led the Church's debate in the fourth century over the relations among the three divine Persons. This was a debate about the subject of this book, the history of redemption. It started with pressing questions in the second and third centuries. How does the redemption of Jesus relate to the redemption of YHWH? How does the Son relate to the Father if both are God?

This was perplexing for those who understood the Jewish character of the faith. They wondered how their faith in the Redeemer was connected to Jewish monotheism. If YHWH is the only creator and redeemer, how can Jesus Messiah also be redeemer? And how does he relate to YHWH his Father? If deity is claimed by both, how do they share it without being two beings, which would then violate Jewish monotheism? And how does the Holy Spirit fit in? Is this an impersonal force or a divine Person? This chapter will look at how early thinkers in the Church wrestled with these questions.

Athanasius

C. S. Lewis observed that without Athanasius the new Jesus movement might have "slip[ped] back . . . into the religion of Arius—into one of those 'sensible' synthetic religions which are so strongly recommended today and which, then as now, included among their devotees many highly cultivated clergymen."[1] Athanasius's fight was long and perilous; his steadfast refusal to compromise caused him to be exiled five times. At many points along the way it seemed that all the powers of Church and world were against him. This is why his epitaph is *Athanasius contra mundum*, "Athanasius against the world."

The future bishop and theologian was five years old when Diocletian launched the empire's last ferocious persecution, and it did not stop until Athanasius was fourteen. When Athanasius was thirty he attended the Council of Nicaea (AD 325) near today's Istanbul, where he was convinced that God had come as a human being in the person of the Messiah to save his human creatures from corruption and death. The Son of God has joined our race, and like a city honored by a king's visit and thereby protected from bandits, we who have joined the Messiah are protected from attacks by the evil one. We are now free to become what God intended for us, Athanasius reasoned, to become creatures who share his own life.

Three years after Nicaea, Emperor Constantine revoked Arius's banishment, and his theology was given new life. Arius, an eloquent and educated presbyter in Alexandria, taught that Jesus was the Messiah and therefore far more than a mere man. But he was also less than fully God. By 351 a council of bishops at Sirmium (in today's Serbia) rejected the decision at Nicaea and declared for a version of Arianism. When Athanasius died in 373, his cause seemed to have been lost. It was not until eight years later at the Second Ecumenical Council, in 381, that Athanasius's orthodox Christology was affirmed once and for all.

The Incarnation Was Necessary

Athanasius's long career of fighting for the deity of the Messiah was focused on two central arguments—that the incarnation was necessary and that it actually happened. Let's look first at his contention that salvation for God's human creatures could not happen without God becoming a man. This was necessary, he insisted, because humans faced three dilemmas: (1) They had irreparably corrupted the

---

1. C. S. Lewis, preface to *On the Incarnation: De Incarnatione Verbi Dei*, by Athanasius, trans. and ed. "A Religious of C.S.M.V." (Crestwood, NY: St. Vladimir's Seminary Press, 1996), 16.

image of God originally placed in them, (2) their inner beings had become diseased, and (3) they had incurred a debt they could not repay.

Therefore, Athanasius concluded, forgiveness is not enough. Since humanity's nature had been polluted by sin, forgiveness by itself would not remove the corruption. The result is soul-sickness. We are diseased. We need a divine physician to cure us.

The key to understanding *how* God is able to accomplish all this through the incarnation of his Son the Messiah is the principle of *solidarity*. This is the idea, familiar to the ancients but foreign to the West today, that we can be joined to a person in such a way that whatever happens to that person also happens to us. So if we are joined to the Messiah, who conquered death, death's power over us has been conquered. Its power to keep us in fear and destroy us forever has been put to death. For we are joined not only to the Messiah on the cross but also to Messiah in his resurrection. The Messiah's resurrection life working within us will gradually restore our sick souls from corruption to a state of increasing un-corruption. Our sick souls will be gradually healed—if we continue in faith and the sacraments—by the Messiah's resurrection life. The result will be what Athanasius, and the Eastern churches plus Anglicans and many Catholics, call "divinization" (in Greek, *theiōsis*). This (1) restores the image of God in us and (2) heals our diseased souls. Since the God-man is infinite in his deity, (3) he can pay our infinite debt.

Athanasius argued that if Jesus were merely a creature as Arius supposed, we would not be saved. For then we would be joined in solidarity not to God but to another creature with mere creaturely nature. A creature is powerless to destroy death but instead is itself under the power of death. Another creature cannot heal sickness of souls because all creation is under a curse. And no creature can pay the infinite debt owed by humans because a creature is finite and so cannot pay an infinite debt. This is why there had to be an incarnation of God in a man for us to be saved.

The Incarnation Really Happened

The second theme in Athanasius's great work *On the Incarnation* was equally important, that the incarnation actually happened. Arius and his followers did not believe in the incarnation. The Alexandrian presbyter figured that if the Father alone is God and one, then any sharing of his nature with another person, in this case the Son, would destroy his oneness. Not only that, it would also mean two gods. Since the Father by himself has all that is necessary to be God, Arius concluded that the

Son must have been created by the will of the Father at some point in time. Hence the Son was not coeternal with the Father. God was not always a Father, and there was a time when the Son was not. Therefore the Son was a creature, the greatest and first and far greater than a mere human being, but a creature nonetheless.

Furthermore, all those familiar with Greek philosophy knew that on its terms God by definition is immutable (does not change). For change would mean change from perfection, which then becomes imperfection. Since God is perfect, he cannot be imperfect. Thus, he cannot change.

The problem for Arius and all his disciples was that the incarnation seemed to require change. God seemed to change into a man. But since God cannot change, and incarnation would require God to change, the incarnation was impossible. It never happened.

Besides, Arius reasoned, the Gospels say things about the Messiah that seem demeaning to God. As Athanasius paraphrased Arius, "How can [Messiah Jesus] be Word or God who slept as a man, and wept, and inquired [asked questions]?"[2]

How Athanasius Defeated the Arians

Athanasius's first and perhaps most important strategy to demonstrate the incarnation was to refuse to let philosophy determine the ground rules. He insisted that Arius's assumptions and terms were *philosophical* and therefore debatable and that the biblical story of salvation should determine presuppositions and establish ground rules.

Athanasius and the other supporters of Nicaea developed a distinction between *making* and *begetting*. Making produces something of a different sort from the maker, while begetting produces something of the same kind as the begetter. Bees make beehives but beget bees. Ants make anthills but beget ants. Humans make houses but beget other human beings.

The Father made the world but begets the Son from eternity. So there never was a time when the Father was not begetting the Son. And since the Father was begetting and not making, what he begat was someone of his very own identical nature and being. Hence the Son was fully divine.

This is why the Council of Nicaea said the Son was *homoousios* (of the same nature) as the Father. The Arians complained this was not a biblical word. Athanasius replied that Arians themselves used far more unbiblical words such as "ineffable"

2. Athanasius, *Apologia contra Arianos* 3.27, cited in Thomas G. Weinandy, *Athanasius: A Theological Introduction* (Aldershot, UK: Ashgate, 2007), 59.

and "ungenerate," but that the more important issue was not unbiblical *words* but unbiblical *concepts*. Sometimes, Athanasius went on, it is necessary to use an unbiblical word such as "Trinity" to teach properly and clearly a biblical concept. That is why theology is necessary and the Bible by itself is necessary but not sufficient.

Arius and his followers were adept at using Bible verses to support their position. They were masters of *sola scriptura*, Scripture alone. Athanasius and his orthodox followers had to use new words not found explicitly in the Bible such as *homoousios* and "Trinity" to defend biblical concepts. The use of biblical words by themselves was not enough to defeat heresy and teach the biblical message.

But as Thomas Weinandy has put it, "One of the most important breakthroughs and one of the most significant insights in the whole history of Christian doctrine" was Athanasius's rejection of the Greek assumption that the Father by himself has and is all that is God.[3] In place of this definition of God Athanasius reformulated the biblical portrait of God as follows: God in his inner nature is Father and always has been. Which means that since God has always been God, he has always had a Son. Therefore, the Son could not have been created at a point in time, before which he was not. No, God has always been the Father of one who has always been the Son.

Athanasius went on to respond to the other Arian philosophical challenge, that the immutable God cannot change. The Egyptian theologian replied that when the Word became flesh, God the Son remained the same in his divine nature but changed in his human nature. In his uncreated deity he was and is immutable, but in his creaturely human nature he was, like all creatures, subject to change.

The Biblical Challenge

The Arians marshaled an arsenal of biblical verses that showed Jesus's weakness, ignorance, suffering, and growth. For example, "The Lord created me at the beginning of his work" (Prov. 8:22); "God made him Lord and Messiah" (Acts 2:36); "the firstborn of many brothers" (Rom. 8:29); "The Father is greater than I" (John 14:28). Their point was to show how unlike God all these seem, at least to the Arians with their philosophical assumption that God never changes or suffers.

Athanasius replied that these texts and others like them refer to the Son not in his divinity but in his humanity. They must be interpreted in light of the big biblical story, that God took on human flesh and walked among us. So when the Bible

---

3. Weinandy, *Athanasius*, 64.

says that the Son suffered, he was suffering not in his divinity as the Word but in his humanity as a man with human flesh. As Athanasius wrote in *Apologia contra Arianos*, "God, being impassible [unaffected by the world], had taken passible flesh [flesh affected by the world]. . . . Suffering and weeping and toiling, these things which are proper to the flesh, are ascribed to him together with the body."[4]

The Arians also asked why Jesus asked where Lazarus was buried and did not know when the Last Day would come. Athanasius responded that this was to be expected given the divine plan for God to take on a fully human existence, which always involves a degree of ignorance.

Scripture and Tradition

Athanasius was a thoroughly biblical theologian who recognized that the Bible will be interpreted rightly only if it is read with help from Church tradition, which is the accumulated wisdom of the Jesus community going back to the apostles and their predecessors in Israel. It was this tradition that had been asserting long before Athanasius that Jesus Messiah was fully God and that the Holy Spirit was too, as Athanasius later argued. It took Athanasius and the Cappadocian fathers to work out the precise ways in which the divine Persons were three and one at the same time. But they were all working with previous theological and liturgical tradition that had been insisting back since the first century AD that the divine Word became flesh and dwelt among us.

The Arians refused to grant weight to tradition. They wanted to read the Bible in their own idiosyncratic ways, with an ear to elite cultural presumptions rather than the teaching of the historic Church. Athanasius recognized the critical importance of doctrine and the necessity for the biblical story to trump philosophical axioms.

Divine and Human . . . and Compromise

Athanasius showed us who the redeemer is, none other than the eternal Son of God. He also showed us that the key to interpreting the meaning of the Messiah in his incarnation is what theologians call the "communication of idioms." This is the transfer of attributes back and forth between the two natures of the Messiah, divine and human. This means that God himself (divine nature) cried as a baby in the manger and was a teenager for a few years (human nature), and that the Son

---

4. Athanasius, *Apologia contra Arianos* 3.55, 56, cited in Weinandy, *Athanasius*, 89–90.

of God (divine) did not know the date of the end (human) because he decided to set aside his omniscience at certain points during his incarnation.

Athanasius also showed us that on critical matters like redemption we should not compromise if core theology is at stake. At several points in the long debate, semi-Arians tried to get Athanasius and others by giving up the anti-Arian *homoousios* (Jesus and the Father are of the same substance/being) for the semi-Arian *homoiousios* (they are of similar substance/being). The difference between the two words—same and similar substance/being—was one letter, an iota in Greek, the key to a diphthong. Thus, Gibbon's famous remark that Christians fought each other over a single diphthong (*mo-ou* vs. *moi-ou*).

Athanasius recognized that to accept the extra letter would be taking the Greek view of lesser gods and conceding that Jesus was not equal to the Father. Athanasius suffered grievously for it, but he refused to take this middle ground. He insisted this would be a fatal compromise that would destroy the faith—and the possibility of redemption. Historians judge him to have been correct.

The Cappadocians

In the next generation, it was the work of three theologians to formulate what became Christianity's accepted understanding of the Trinity. These three have been collectively called the "Cappadocian fathers" (Basil the Great, his brother Gregory of Nyssa, and Basil's longtime friend and disciple Gregory of Nazianzus) because they were from the part of modern Turkey called Cappadocia. Like Athanasius, they discovered that holding to the truth required suffering. As we have seen, there was fierce opposition to Nicene orthodoxy for more than a half-century after the great Nicene Council of 325. In 370 the Emperor Valens, an Arian, threatened Basil with plunder, exile, torture, and death unless he changed his stance. Basil's reply was, "None of these things hurts me. I have no property, the whole world is my home, my body is already dead in Messiah, and death would be a great blessing." Things were so bad in Constantinople in 379 that mobs attacked Gregory of Nazianzus in the streets for his orthodoxy, and Arian monks broke into Gregory's chapel and profaned the altar.

Churches were corrupted by heresy and cultural compromise. Basil complained that ministers no longer dared preach what the laity had grown unaccustomed to hearing. The churches, he lamented, had cast aside the teachings of the fathers and the apostolic traditions. Their leaders, he said, were more skilled in rhetoric than theology; they taught the wisdom of this world but not the glory of the cross.

The result was disastrous for the laity: "The ears of the more simple-minded . . . have become accustomed to the heretical impiety. The nurslings of the Church are being brought up in the doctrines of ungodliness. . . . Consequently after a little time has passed, not even if all fear should be removed, would there then be hope of recalling those held by a long-standing deception back to the recognition of the truth."[5]

Because of the triumphs of heresy and its advocates' ruthless methods, the orthodox were reluctant to join battle. Gregory of Nazianzus hated conflict and was indecisive. Gregory of Nyssa was temperamentally timid. Philip Schaff writes that he was "born for study and speculation."[6] All three of the Cappadocians started their adult lives as monks who delighted in the isolation of the mystical life, removed physically and psychologically from the dangerous and depressing conflicts of the Church. As Basil put it, "[My inner] longing urges me to flight, to solitude in the mountains, to quietude of soul and body. . . . But the other, the Spirit, would lead me into the midst of life, to serve the common weal, and by furthering others to further myself, to spread light, and to present to God a people for his possession. . . . So Christ did, who, though he might have remained in his own dignity and divine glory, not only humbled himself to the form of a servant, but also, despising the shame, endured the death of the cross, that by his suffering he might blot out sin, and by his death destroy death."[7]

For the most part, the Cappadocians had to be cajoled into service. Every one of them was ordained against his will. In the days when the overwhelming acclamation of the laity was considered the voice of God, the same thing happened to Augustine as a presbyter and to Ambrose and Athanasius as bishops. After his forced ordination, Basil fled to the monastic community to avoid trouble with a bishop but then returned when persuaded by another bishop that he needed to fight Arianism. Basil then forced his bother Gregory to become bishop of the village of Nyssa because he needed his help; Gregory of Nazianzus was coerced into the presbyterate by his aged father, who was himself a presbyter and needed pastoral help. Later this same Gregory was compelled by Basil to become bishop of an obscure market town that was nevertheless important in the ecclesiastical fight against Arianism.

5. Basil, *Letter 243*, trans. Blomfield Jackson, in *The Nicene and Post-Nicene Fathers*, Series 2, ed. Philip Schaff (1886–89; repr., Peabody, MA: Hendrickson, 2012), 8:283–85, https://www.newadvent.org/fathers/3202243.htm.

6. Philip Schaff, *Nicene and Post-Nicene Christianity*, vol. 3 of *History of the Christian Church* (1910; repr., Grand Rapids: Eerdmans, 1995), 904.

7. Basil, quoted in Schaff, *History of the Christian Church*, 3:916.

It was only by the Cappadocians' willingness to suffer that orthodoxy prevailed. Basil braved threats on his life. Because of Gregory of Nyssa's orthodoxy, he was deposed and driven into exile. Gregory of Nazianzus stood firm as patriarch of the orthodox church in Constantinople in the midst of mockery and persecution. Despite his hatred of travel, he accepted Theodosius's later appointment as theological adviser that took him to Arabia and Mesopotamia. The result of their courage and eloquence was the final victory of trinitarianism in 381 at the Council of Constantinople, when Nicaea was reaffirmed and the Holy Spirit was declared to be fully divine and a Person.

Understanding the Trinity

Then as now, it was difficult to understand the Trinity. But as Augustine later observed, if we with our finite minds thought we were comprehending God, we would know we were not dealing with the infinite God. Yet if the Trinity is finally a mystery beyond human comprehension, there are nevertheless many things that God *has* revealed about it. From those revelations orthodox theologians have developed two models for helping us understand it, both of which are derived from biblical revelation.

The first model has been called the psychological model because it derives from the parts of the human personality. It was most famously developed by Augustine. It refers to the mind itself (analogous to the Father), the mind's understanding of itself (analogous to the Son or Word), and the mind's love of itself (the Holy Spirit). There is a oneness (mind) and threeness (three aspects of the mind) at the same time, starting with the one and moving to the three.

Many have pointed out that one danger with the psychological model is that it can suggest that God is one person appearing in three different modes at different times. This is the classic heresy of modalism, refuted by Jesus's baptism when three divine Persons appeared simultaneously—Jesus appearing under the sign of the Holy Spirit in the form of a dove and the Father speaking.

It is therefore helpful to balance the psychological model with the social model advanced by the Cappadocian fathers and later developed by Jonathan Edwards. This model starts with the three and moves to the one. Each of the three divine Persons has a different and distinct role. For example, in one depiction the Father is the unoriginated source of all and especially salvation, the Son is the agent of salvation, and the Spirit is the One who applies the Son and his work to the saints.

An important caveat is that the divine Persons are unlike human persons in that the former are not separate beings as human persons are. John and Mary are separate persons and beings, but the Father and Son and Spirit are one being *in* three Persons. The First Person is the Father of the Second, who is the eternal Son of the First, and the Spirit is the love between the two, who is so real that he is a distinct Person.

This social model is more characteristic of Eastern ways of thinking of God, while the psychological model is more common in Western ways of thinking of the Trinity. While the danger in the West is modalism, the risk in the East is trithe-ism, thinking that the three are three different gods rather than three persons in one divine being.

Trinity and Redemption

The theological battles of the third and fourth centuries helped believers under-stand their redemption by the God of Israel. They came to see that they were redeemed not by the Messiah alone. Or to put it more biblically, God the Father so loved the world that he gave his only Son, and he applied the Son's death and resurrection by pouring his love into believers' hearts by the Holy Spirit. Jesus ministered by the Holy Spirit's power, was enabled by the Spirit to offer himself as a sacrifice to the Father for the sake of the elect, and was raised from the dead in power according to the Spirit of holiness (John 3:16; Rom. 5:5; Acts 10:37–38; Heb. 9:14; Rom. 1:4).

In other words, the God of Israel saved his people through the Messiah and his Spirit. God is one but does his work in three divine Persons. And the greatest of God's work is redeeming sinners. God the Father initiated that work and delegated the purchase of redemption to the Son, the Spirit enabled the Son to do that work, and the Spirit joins God's people to the Messiah and his work. Redemption is by the Triune God of Israel and for his glory.

Select Bibliography

Athanasius. *On the Incarnation: De Incarnatione Verbi Dei.* Translated and edited by a religious of C.S.M.V. Crestwood, NY: St. Vladimir's Seminary Press, 1996.

Chadwick, Henry. *The Church in Ancient Society: From Galilee to Gregory the Great.* Oxford: Oxford University Press, 2001.

Kelly, J. N. D. *Early Christian Doctrines*. Rev. ed. San Francisco: HarperSanFrancisco, 1978.

Lewis, C. S. Preface to *On the Incarnation: De Incarnatione Verbi Dei*, by Athanasius, translated and edited by a religious of C.S.M.V., 11–17. Crestwood, NY: St. Vladimir's Seminary Press, 1996.

McDermott, Gerald. "Athanasius." In *The Great Theologians: A Brief Guide*, 30–47. Downers Grove, IL: IVP Academic, 2010.

Schaff, Philip, ed. *Nicene and Post-Nicene Christianity*. Vol. 3 of *History of the Christian Church*. 8 vols. 1910. Reprint, Grand Rapids: Eerdmans, 1995.

Weinandy, Thomas G. *Athanasius: A Theological Introduction*. Aldershot, UK: Ashgate, 2007.

19

Political Disintegration and Missionary Expansion

In 410 Rome was sacked by Alaric and his Goths. This was the culmination of at least a generation of barbarian advances on the Roman Empire. Thirty-two years before that, an emperor was defeated and killed at the battle of Adrianople in today's Turkey. The victors were Goths who reached Constantinople before turning west, where the empire was shaky.

The western Roman Empire had long been tottering. Until the end of the fourth century Rome's legions had kept the Germanic peoples on the other side of the Rhine and Danube Rivers. In Britain a wall separated the barbarians from the regions controlled by Roman legions.

But at the beginning of the fifth century the floodgates opened. Endless waves of German and northern tribes crossed the frontiers, wasted towns and villages, and settled in regions previously controlled by Rome. They founded their own kingdoms that were functionally independent but nominally subject to Rome. This lasted until the last emperor was deposed in 476. At that point the western empire came to an end.

From that time on, it was the Church that provided the only continuity between one civilization and the next. Eventually the barbarian invaders were converted to the trinitarian faith. But in the meantime they were Arians, and so the old theological battles of the fourth century had to be refought in the fifth century and after.

These centuries of political disintegration and Church advance illustrate a recurring theme in the history of redemption. When an old world is crumbling, people are more open to new visions of reality. When the Caesars fail, people are more willing to listen to other promises of redemption. True redemption through the God of Israel starts to make sense as false redemptions are revealed to be the illusions that they are.

Revival of the Empire in the East

While the Roman Empire was shattering in the West, it was reviving in the East. In his *First Thousand Years* Robert Wilken tells the story of Jerusalem's rise to prominence shortly after the beginning of the fourth century. At the Council of Nicaea in 325 Jerusalem was declared to be first in honor but after Caesarea in ecclesiastical importance. The bishops recognized that this was the city of David and the site of the greatest events in history—the death and resurrection of the Messiah. For the first great Church historian, Eusebius, this was the "holy place," which "from the beginning was holy" but now appeared "more holy" because here was the suffering of the Savior. Now it was "the most marvelous place in the world."[1]

By the end of the fourth century, Wilken relates, Jerusalem had become a "bustling metropolis" bursting with pilgrims and clergy, monks and nuns, a growing population, and a bishop who traced his lineage back to James the brother of Jesus and Jerusalem's first bishop. A few decades later Jerusalem was a patriarchate ranked with the greatest cities of the eastern empire—Alexandria, Antioch, and Constantine's new Eastern capital Constantinople. Its new monuments attracted pilgrims from around Europe and Asia and North Africa, and its "elaborate liturgies thrilled the faithful." By this time Jerusalem was firmly planted in the Christian imagination as a Christian (no longer Jewish) city, the city of the Christian God, and the city "of uncommon symbolic power for the Christian empire."[2]

Sanctification of Place

Wilken points out that with the rise of Jerusalem as the capital of a Christian empire—only to be enlarged in importance with the Crusades centuries later—a new understanding of place was emerging. Christians and Jews already had known that time is holy, from God's first command to keep the sabbath holy and his appointment of three annual festivals and from the beginning of Christian liturgies to mark events each year in the life of Christ and his Body such as Christmas, Lent,

---

1. Robert Louis Wilken, *The First Thousand Years: A Global History of Christianity* (New Haven: Yale University Press, 2012), 111.
2. Wilken, *First Thousand Years*, 114.

Easter, and Pentecost. But the Gallican pilgrim Egeria at the end of the fourth century wrote about the attachment pilgrims had to holy places in Jerusalem. They would stop at each place marking a site in the Gospels, say a prayer, read a biblical reading and an appropriate psalm, then say another prayer.[3]

Wilken writes of Paulinus, an Italian bishop of this period who made the pilgrimage to Jerusalem. Paulinus commented that "no other sentiment draws people to Jerusalem [like] the desire to see and touch the places where Christ was physically present" and to be able to say that they have "gone into his tabernacle and worshipped in the places where his feet stood" (Ps. 132:7).[4]

Tombs of the martyrs and saints became places of pilgrimage. There was a "new tactile piety" that preserved bones and other relics, sacred books, and liturgical items like chalices and veils. In the fourth century church buildings started to deposit relics of the martyrs in their crypts.

Was this superstition? Perhaps no more than the attachment to Paul's handkerchief and Peter's shadow, both of which communicated healing from the risen Messiah (Acts 5:15; 19:12). Besides, Jerusalem was called the "holy city" five times in the New Testament (Matt. 4:5; 27:53; Rev. 11:2; 21:2, 10), suggesting that its Jewish authors, already familiar with holy places under Moses's feet, perpetuated this sanctification of place in their writings.

The new Christian region of Jerusalem and its environs grew rapidly. Archaeological records inform us that the city's population exploded from fifteen thousand to over fifty thousand. Construction boomed. Church buildings went up at dizzying speed, attracting craftsmen and artists from around the world. More than five hundred were built in the Holy Land during this Christian era. Horticulture in and around Jerusalem blossomed with new farms and vineyards planted in uncultivated areas. Trade flourished as new cities were established. At its height in the sixth century, says Wilken, there were six cities within a few miles of each other in the Negev desert south of Jerusalem.[5]

Missionary Expansion by Eastern Churches

When Jerusalem believers thought of missions, they looked east rather than west. And it was in that direction that much of the most impressive missionary work took place in the next few centuries.

3. Wilken, *First Thousand Years*, 114–15.
4. Wilken, *First Thousand Years*, 115.
5. Wilken, *First Thousand Years*, 116.

But it is likely that faith in the Messiah had already reached India in the first century. Eusebius tells us that Thomas was chosen to bring the gospel to Parthia, which is northwest of India. Tradition has it that Thomas at first refused to head toward India because of the language barrier but then was bidden to go in a dream. By this account he baptized a king and his people but then was martyred by another king. This is plausible because ships sailed regularly between Mesopotamia and India. There is also Eusebius's account of Pantaenus, the Alexandrian teacher of Clement, who traveled to India in the late second century and found Messianic churches already established there using the gospel of Matthew in Aramaic.

The gospel was also sent east to Georgia by the end of the third century. Two bishops from Georgia attended the council at Nicaea in 325. The king of Iberia in east Georgia adopted the faith through the influence of the holy woman Nino, whose prayer had healed the queen Nana. Mirian the king was baptized in 337, with some of the princes and people following. In 609 they adopted the Christology of Chalcedon, breaking from the control of Christians in Armenia to their south.

The king of Armenia and his people were baptized in 314 in the River Euphrates by Gregory the Illuminator. Their messianic faith prized the wisdom books of the Hebrew Bible such as Psalms and Proverbs and the apocryphal books of Wisdom and Sirach. In the first few centuries of the Armenian Church many came to the Holy Land and settled in the desert south of Jerusalem, founding the monastery of Sabas, now called Mar Saba. Their bishops adopted a non-Chalcedonian Christology that held to both the divine and the human in the Messiah but without Chalcedon's formulation of it. They hold to one incarnate united divine-human nature of the Word of God, rejecting Chalcedon's two natures as suggesting Nestorianism.

Faith in the Messiah reached ancient Nubia (modern Sudan) in the sixth century through missionaries encouraged by Theodora, the wife of Byzantine emperor Justinian (527–65). But it came in the fourth century to Ethiopia, south of Sudan, through the witness of two young Syrian missionaries who were on their way to India and wound up as slaves to the king of Aksum, who listened to their stories of Jesus the Messiah.

King Ezana became the first African king to believe in Jesus the Messiah and to adopt that faith as the religion for his people. Wilken tells us that the bishop of Aksum was consecrated by Athanasius, patriarch at Alexandria in Egypt, and so it was natural for Ethiopian bishops to follow the non-Chalcedonian Christology of the Egyptians.[6]

---

6. Wilken, *First Thousand Years*, 216.

The Church in Ethiopia was deeply shaped by Jewish practices concerning ritual purity, dietary law, and circumcision on the eighth day. Their Bible includes Jewish documents from the intertestamental period such as Enoch, Jubilees, and the Ascension of Isaiah. Their New Testament includes the Shepherd of Hermas and 1–2 Clement. Ethiopia's national epic, *Kebra Nagast* (Glory of the kings), starts with the biblical story of Solomon and the queen of Sheba and goes on to explain that the queen became a Jew during her visit to Jerusalem and was impregnated by Solomon. Their son returned to Jerusalem twenty years later, learned the Law, and returned to Ethiopia with Jewish families who secreted with them the ark of the covenant. Ethiopians say it is now in the Church of Our Lady of Zion in Aksum.

The new messianic religion, thickly Jewish in flavor, sunk deep roots in Ethiopia. Wilken relates that a Catholic visiting Ethiopia in the seventeenth century was astonished by Ethiopian piety. No country is so full of churches, he said, or monasteries and clerics. The people practice regular fasting, show the deep fervor of the primitive Christians, and have "a natural disposition to goodness."

Across the Red Sea from Ethiopia is Yemen, where the messianic faith was planted in the sixth century. By that time the Church boasted a full array of bishop, presbyters, deacons, and deaconesses.

Many readers will be surprised to learn that faith in the God of Israel took root in China as early as the seventh century, according to Chinese sources. An emperor's decree records that the Persian (Christian) monk Alopen had brought Scriptures to the capital, today's Xi'an, and that those writings were "mysterious, wonderful, and calm" and told how to obtain "salvation for living beings."

Another royal decree in the eighth century referred to the messianic religion as "the Persian religion." It indicated that during this period the religion of the God of Israel and his Messiah was permitted and even supported by Chinese rulers. Later that century, in 781, a large black limestone monument was erected near Xi'an to "the luminous religion" brought by the monk Al-o-pen from Persia. It mentions twenty-seven books of scripture, baptism, worship, sabbath, rules for monks such as generosity and not holding slaves, and purification by solitude and meditation. Other documents from this period show that Chinese Christians taught reverence for ancestors, filial piety, and veneration of the emperor. Tragically, Chinese rulers launched a brutal wave of persecution in the ninth century, and by the end of the tenth century the faith was almost extinct.

But other great missionary work was bearing fruit. Much of it had been launched and supported by Timothy I (d. 823), the *catholicos* or patriarch of the

Church of the East who overlapped the eighth and ninth centuries. In his long tenure at Mosul, from his fifties into his nineties, Timothy was not only a polylingual (Syriac, Greek, Arabic, and Persian) scholar who translated treatises like Aristotle's *Topics* for the Muslim caliph; he also promoted Messianic missions to the East. For example, despite serving under Muslim rule, he was permitted to organize a mission to central Asia and another to Turks east of the Caspian Sea, where the king of the Uighurs was converted. He communicated with monks who had evangelized in China and India, and he ordained bishops for Tibet and Iranian peoples southeast of the Caspian.

The history of redemption in the first millennium, then, was a history that went as much east as it did west. The Church of the East might have been more responsible for Christianity going global than the Church of the West.

The Rise of the Papacy

As the empire in the west lost its center and devolved into semibarbarian kingdoms, the Church filled the vacuum. This was the scenario in which the bishop of Rome took on increasing significance.

As the Church grew larger in the third century, bishops met regularly. Those from larger cities exercised authority over those from smaller towns. Rome tended to have authority over all of Italy, Carthage over North Africa, Alexandria over Egypt, Antioch over Syria, and so on. General councils—meetings of all the bishops—started after Constantine came to power. Arles was first in 314, then Nicaea in 325.

In 330 Constantine established a new capital for the empire in the East where old Byzantium had stood (now Istanbul), and he named it after himself. In 381, when the new emperor Theodosius established Christianity as the mandatory religion of the empire, he called a new general council. Damasus the bishop of Rome did not attend or even send a representative. The council declared that after the bishop of Rome, the bishop of Constantinople held primacy in the East, thus demoting Antioch and Alexandria. Rome protested on behalf of these two other patriarchates.

As time went on, the bishop of Constantinople became more and more dependent on the eastern emperor, and the bishop of Rome became more and more independent of the state because of the weakness of the empire in the West. In 452, for example, Attila the Hun advanced on Rome. Bishop Leo came out to meet him, sent as an emissary of the Roman emperor. Remarkably, the Hun granted the pope's plea that the capital be spared, and the invader even withdrew from Italy, as he had promised the pope. It didn't hurt that Attila was facing epidemics and famine in his army. This negotiation, though, showed how far the bishop of Rome had come by this time, to be seen as the representative of the Western Church and even the empire.

But the idea of papal primacy grew very slowly. Leo was the first to make the biblical and theological arguments for this claim. He appealed to Jesus's words to Peter, "You are Rocky [*petros*], and on this rock [*petra*] I will build my Church.... I will give you [singular] the keys of the kingdom of heaven" (Matt. 16:18–19). Leo taught that the power of Peter lived in the office of his successors. He turned to Luke 22:32, where Jesus tells Peter, "When you have turned again, strengthen your brothers," and to John's Gospel, where Jesus three times tells Peter to tend his sheep and feed his lambs (John 21:15–19).

Jesus also urged that leadership in the Church should be based on service and warned that leaders could be led astray by Satan as Peter was. "Get behind me, Satan," Jesus snapped after Peter told him he would not go to the cross (Matt. 16:23). Centuries later Protestants pointed to Peter's threefold denial of the Lord as their evidence against his primacy, but Catholics replied that it was after Peter's repentance that Jesus told him to feed his sheep.

By Leo's time this claim gained some traction because of Rome's circumstances. It had enjoyed respect ever since Peter and Paul were martyred there, and Rome had already been the center of the empire. By the mid-third century the church in Rome had thirty thousand members with one hundred fifty presbyters and deacons.

But while the bishops of Rome since the first century had prestige, no one had asserted papal primacy until Leo. The term "pope" or "papa" was not used until the sixth century. Important bishops such as Irenaeus and Cyprian disagreed with Rome from time to time, and it is doubtful that even Leo would have asserted the sort of infallibility claimed by Pius IX and the First Vatican Council in 1870.

Yet at the Council of Chalcedon in 451 when the bishops approved the final wording that defined the relationship between Jesus's divinity and humanity, the spirit of Leo was dominant. Leo had penned a letter that insisted on the coexistence of the human and divine natures in the Messiah against Eutyches's contention for a fusion of divine and human elements in the son of God. The majority of the bishops at Chalcedon shouted, "Peter has spoken through Leo!"

Yet the council gave the bishop of Constantinople authority equal to that of the bishop of Rome. Now there were two heads of the universal Church. Several years later in 455 a new enemy, the Vandals from Scandinavia, stood on the edge of Rome poised to attack. Leo persuaded them to limit their looting to fourteen days, restrict kidnapping to a few leaders, and refrain from burning and extensive massacre.

Once more Leo had saved Rome. He took on the old emperor's title *Pontifex Maximus,* "greatest bridge-builder." But this title was not given to the bishop of Rome regularly until the fifteenth century.

Gregory the Great

The next jump in thinking about the bishop of Rome came with the election of Gregory in 590. Like many bishops before him, he fled the position before being dragged back to Rome. Because of his commitment to God and his Church, Gregory reluctantly accepted the role. Later he wrote that a spiritual leader must always maintain an inner spiritual life but not neglect Church matters.

Gregory had been mayor of Rome at one time, with responsibility for its economy. He combined executive ability with compassion for human needs. He had used his family money to found seven monasteries and distribute the rest to the poor. Later in his pre-papal life he was appointed Roman legate by Pope Pelagius II to the imperial court in Constantinople. His political training and executive ability had fitted him well for this.[7]

Soon after his election in 590 the Lombards laid siege to Rome. People thought the end of the world was at hand. Helpless citizens were mutilated, slain, and taken captive. The Church was the only institution that preserved order and civilization amid the chaos.

Gregory never stopped working despite poor health and often being confined to bed. Things were so bad that he looked forward to death. But he knew he was needed if Rome was to survive. In order to feed the population, he collected taxes. The state had collapsed, so he picked up the reins of government.

When the patriarch of Constantinople called himself a "universal bishop," Gregory protested, calling himself the "servant of the servants of God." Not only servant but in some sense head: he claimed oversight of all the Christian churches.

Gregory was a vigorous theologian. He defended orthodoxy and developed the Church's thinking about penance, saints, purgatory, and worship. Against Pelagians

7. Bruce Shelley, *Church History in Plain Language,* 2nd ed. (Dallas: Word, 1995), 165.

he taught that "Adam's fall affected all his descendants, weakening but not destroy-ing" free will. Once a person has been moved by grace to do good works, he wrote, he wins merit because the good works are the fruit of both grace and free will.[8] Augustine had previously written that even those acts of free will come by grace and therefore all merit is the merit of the Messiah because all good comes from Messiah. As he put it famously, "God rewards his own gifts."[9]

Gregory taught that sins committed after baptism must be treated with penance so that God can discipline the sinner. The greater the sin, the more one must do sacrificial deeds of penance such as fasting and prayer. He also maintained that sinners can get help from departed saints, whose prayers can be efficacious. His thinking led to the development of the doctrine of purgatory, a place where sin and guilt can be purged if sanctification is not completed on earth. This purgation is only for the saved, not a second chance for the damned.

Gregory viewed the Eucharist as a re-presentation of the sacrifice of the Mes-siah on the cross, so that it becomes freshly applicable to those present at Mass. If offered for someone in purgatory, it can help speed that person's release because it is a fresh application of the sufferings of the Messiah for that believer's sins. Gregory also fostered the development of liturgical music at worship, includ-ing plainsong that became so popular that it is commonly known as Gregorian Chant.

The Book of Pastoral Rule

Important to later Christianity was Gregory's *Book of Pastoral Rule*. The Byzantine emperor Maurice ordered this book to be translated and distributed to every bishop in his empire. Because Gregory had been a monk, in this manual for pas-tors he suggests they should teach their people ascetic (from the Greek *askēsis* or training) disciplines. Self-denial, he wrote, especially from sensual pleasures, is an essential component of discipleship, as monks had learned in the desert and monasteries for centuries by Gregory's time.

The *Pastoral Rule* is the most thorough pastors' training manual from the pa-tristic era (AD 100–600). It sets seventy-two traits in opposition. Teaching how to deal with pastoral problems, it differentiated, for example, between young and old, rich and poor, bold and modest, impatient and patient. Gregory suggests that the

8. Shelley, *Church History in Plain Language*, 169.

9. Augustine, *On Grace and Free Will* 16, in *The Nicene and Post-Nicene Fathers*, Series 1, ed. Philip Schaff (1886–89; repr., Peabody, MA: Hendrickson, 1994), 5:450.

most important task of the pastor is the care of souls, a kind of spiritual direction that he calls the "art of arts."[10] But this is an art that takes more than intellectual learning. It is dependent on the pastor's having learned ascetic discipline.

The Church in Gregory's day faced two principal problems among potential pastors. Too many wanted the position out of pride, wanting to be the top dog or center of attention. Too few contemplatives (monks in solitary or a monastery) were willing to serve a congregation, preferring a quiet monastic life to the headaches of daily congregational ministry. Gregory's response was to encourage ordination and rebuke those who were qualified but resisted. He wrote that our gifts are given by God for the purpose of serving his people. If we refuse to use our gifts for this service, we are being selfish.

Previous pastoral treatises by Ambrose and Augustine portrayed the pastor's role as threefold—teaching doctrine, administering the sacraments, and supervising charity to the needy. Gregory added a new calling, directing the spiritual growth of parishioners. The priest is to be a spiritual father.

But this is a complex business, Gregory indicated. He outlined a vast number of different spiritual states, and the good pastor must not apply a spiritual solution until he discerns the spiritual condition of his parishioner. The prescription will be different for each. For example, the poor need solace while the rich should be warned against pride. Leaders should be admonished against arrogance, and subordinates should be advised to be careful if they criticize their superiors. The impatient are not to be impetuous and the patient are to steer clear of self-pity and wrath. There are minor and grave sins, as John teaches at the end of his first epistle. So too there are lesser and greater vices. Vices of the heart are more serious than fleshly weakness.

Missionary Expansion

Gregory was responsible for a significant missionary expansion of the faith in England. He was so disgusted when he saw English boys sold into slavery at a Roman slave market that he sent the abbot (not the theologian) Augustine and forty monks to turn England back to the Christian faith. It had declined under the pressure of barbarian invasions since the faith's introduction to the island in the first two centuries. From Augustine's mission came a revival of the Church in England, and whole new tribes converted to the faith. From its Church

10. Gregory the Great, *The Book of Pastoral Rule* (Crestwood, NY: St. Vladimir's Press, 2007), 29.

eventually came the Anglo-American Protestant Christianity that was the principal missionary force in the nineteenth century to bring the faith to sub-Saharan Africa.

This was also the time of the great Irish missionaries, starting with Patrick (second half of the fifth century). We have already seen that in the late fifth century successive waves of German barbarians pillaged and destroyed most of what was then Greco-Roman civilization. Books were burned and used as furniture. Libraries were destroyed. As Thomas Cahill puts it in *How the Irish Saved Civilization*, Gothic illiterates ruled over Gothic illiterates. According to Gregory of Tours, a sixth-century bishop, not a scholar could be found in all of sixth-century Gaul who could write about what was happening.

But just before this, some of Patrick's successors like Kevin Glendalough and Columba had started to found monasteries with monks copying the classical texts of the ancient world, not only the Bible but also the great Greek and Latin works. The Irish monks became so adept at passing on and commenting on Latin culture that Cahill says the Irish "enshrined literacy as their central religious act." The result was that, as a Leyden manuscript put it, "All the learned men on this side of the sea took flight for trans-marine places like Ireland, bringing about a great increase of learning."[11]

These Irish monasteries were the world's only universities at the beginning of what have been called the Dark Ages (ca. 500–ca. 800). They hosted thousands of foreign students, who brought back learning to their homes after the end of their studies in Ireland. For over a century faith in the Messiah "survived by clinging to places like Skellig Michael, a pinnacle of rock eighteen miles from the Irish coast, rising seven hundred feet out of the sea."[12] During this time the Irish monks reconnected barbarized Europe to the traditions of Christian literacy.[13] The great monastic founder Columba (521–97) nearly single-handedly baptized and taught Scotland to read. He was also the most accomplished poet of his day and proclaimed that poetry is essential to a people, especially the Irish people. Irish monks in this tradition like Brendan the Navigator seem to have visited Iceland, Greenland, and North America.

During this period there were occasional missions to barbarians outside the borders of the old empire in the West. For example, Ulfila (little wolf) was a Goth who took up the faith in the fourth century during the Arian controversy.

---

11. Thomas Cahill, *How the Irish Saved Civilization* (New York: Doubleday, 1995), 180.
12. Kenneth Clark, quoted in Cahill, *How the Irish Saved Civilization*, 4.
13. Cahill, *How the Irish Saved Civilization*, 171.

He was ordained by an Arian bishop in Constantinople and served as bishop of the "Christians in the Gothic land" beyond the Danube River. He translated parts of the Bible into the Gothic language, notably omitting the books of Kings because he didn't want to encourage the Goths' warlike tendencies. Because of his ministry many of the Germanic tribes—Ostrogoths, Visigoths, Burgundians, and Lombards—adopted an Arian version of the faith when they came to settle in northern Italy, Spain, and Gaul.

With the western Empire in decline, the spread of the faith began to come more from baptized kings who brought it to their peoples. One of the most important was Clovis (466–511), king of a Frankish tribe. Originally an Arian, he was converted to the Nicene faith because of his Catholic wife Clotild and victory in battle after calling on the Catholic God. Gregory of Tours says Clovis was baptized into the Nicene faith in 508. It was difficult to persuade his people to give up their pagan gods, adopt Sunday as a holy day, accept new festivals such as Christmas and Easter, and adopt new marriage practices and laws. He was the first king of a Germanic tribe to convert to the Nicene faith. The Burgundians in southern Germany (516) and the Visigoths in Spain (589) would follow.

The City of God and the City of Man

With Christianity being legalized and then mandated under Theodosius (emperor 379–95), the danger grew that believers might confuse faith in the God of Israel with faith in a Christian emperor, or that a Christian ruler could think his own rule was the same as God's rule. And what if a Church leader disagreed with a Christian emperor?

The conflict between Ambrose and Theodosius brought these issues to a head. Eusebius had depicted Constantine as a priestly figure. But when in 385 the Arian boy-emperor Valentinian II through his mother Justina tried to get Ambrose, bishop of Milan, to hand over some Nicene churches, Ambrose put his foot down. In a matter of faith, he declared, it is the practice for bishops to judge Christian emperors, not vice versa.

According to Wilken, Ambrose "effectively desacralized the office of emperor by insisting that the emperor was a layman who had to reckon with an alternate authority."[14] So the establishment of Christianity in the West proceeded, Wilken adds, as much against political authority as in collusion with it.

---

14. Wilken, *First Thousand Years*, 132.

After Christians set fire to a synagogue on the Euphrates River, Theodosius, then emperor of the East, ordered the local bishop to rebuild the synagogue out of his own funds. Ambrose protested, saying the emperor had no business telling a bishop how to use Christian funds. Theodosius backed off. From our vantage point, this was morally and theologically wrong. But it agreed with ancient protocol for rival religions and again set boundaries between Church and state.

When in 388 Theodosius massacred several thousand citizens in Thessalonika after a mob had murdered a Roman commander, Ambrose compelled the emperor to do penance before he could receive the Eucharist. Ambrose effectively demonstrated that the emperor was within but not above the Church. Again, clear boundaries.

Augustine of Hippo (354–430), perhaps the greatest Western theologian the Church has seen, probed these relations between state and Church, civil and divine authority, in his monumental *City of God*. The project was triggered by pagan accusations after Rome's fall in 410 that Christian "atheism" was to blame. By this they meant that the gods withdrew their support for the Eternal City because Christians failed to worship them. Besides, Rome's fall proved the Christian god was weak since Rome had been ruled by Christians.

In this great work that was composed over thirteen years, Augustine secularized history. That is, against those who wanted to make the history of the new Rome a Christian history, with its successes regarded as rewards for its Christian leaders and citizens, Augustine said true history is not a matter of Christian empires versus secular empires, but an internal, secret history between the City of God and the City of Man. The City of God is ruled by love of God to the contempt of self, while the City of Man is ruled by love of self to the contempt of God. The one glories in God while the other glories in self. One lifts up its own head; the other lets God lift up its head.

Augustine wrote that the two cities coexist within both Christian and non-Christian empires. Rome fell because of internal moral corruption and idolatry. Bad things happen to both Christian empires and good Christians because of sin and God's secret purposes operating within both. God's judgments are always at work in earthly polities but usually cannot be discerned. Augustine quoted Paul: "His judgments are righteous and unsearchable, his ways past finding out" (Rom. 11:33). Therefore, the bishop of Hippo advised, we should hold cheap those things that come for both good and bad people, prosperity and affliction. He reminded his readers of Solomon's mandate at the end of Ecclesiastes—to fear God and keep his commandments, for that is the whole duty of man.

Killing the "Christ-Killers"

While these centuries saw great success for the history of redemption and its expansion across continents, it was also a period of great deception and tragedy. Those ostensibly devoted to the God of Israel and his Messiah started to persecute Jews, telling Jewish converts to Jesus that they could no longer lives as Jews. Many Christian leaders suggested that God hated nonmessianic Jews and had canceled his covenant with them. This thinking led to horrific campaigns against Jews in the later Middle Ages.

How could this be? We have seen the tragic history of supersessionism, the belief that God's affection for the mostly Gentile Church superseded and replaced his affection for the Jews. These Gentiles came to believe that Jews in later centuries were just like the Jewish leaders who turned Jesus over to the Romans for execution. All Jews became known as "Christ-killers." Christians came to think that the evidence for Jesus as Messiah was so clear that only obstinacy could prevent conversion. Jews deserved persecution because of their opposition to the true God.

From the time that Christianity became licit in the Roman Empire under Constantine in the fourth century and then the official religion under Theodosius, the dominant approach by the Church toward Jews was what Jules Isaac has called the *Adversus Iudaeos* ("against the Jews") tradition. The term comes from Augustine's *Tractatus adversus Judaeos* (*Treatise against the Jews*). He taught that Jews bear the curse of Cain for killing Jesus and that God's punishment has been to scatter Jews all over the world ("wandering Jews") and make them wretched. As they wander in pitiful state, they serve as "negative witnesses" to remind "all the nations" of the "prophecies which were sent before concerning Christ."

Augustine could develop his thinking in this way because of the Church fathers before him who had laid the foundations for this tradition. Justin Martyr had taught in his *Dialogue with Trypho* that the Gentile Church was the "true Israel,"[15] Irenaeus proclaimed in *Against Heresies* that God was punishing the Jews for rejecting Jesus,[16] Origen spiritualized all the promises made to earthly Israel in *On First Principles*,[17] Tertullian wrote that "Israel has been divorced" from "divine favor,"[18] John Chrysostom preached in *Discourses against the Jews*, "I hate the

---

15. Justin, *Dialogue with Trypho* 11.5.

16. Irenaeus, *Against Heresies* 4–5.

17. Origen, *On First Principles* 4: Jewish things are real only insofar as they point to the Messiah.

18. Tertullian, *An Answer to the Jews* 1, in *The Ante-Nicene Fathers*, ed. Alexander Roberts and James Donaldson (1885–87; repr., Peabody, MA: Hendrickson, 1994), 3:152.

Jews,"[19] and Ambrose proclaimed that Jesus took on a human body, "casting off the Jewish people."[20]

These Christian aspersions on Jews inspired believers to attack Jews. When European Christians traveled east through German lands for the First Crusade, they murdered thousands of Jews in the Rhineland for the crime of being Jews. The Jewish community at Mainz, one of the largest in Europe, was wiped out. For more than a century after, the preaching of every major crusade to the East produced anti-Jewish pogroms somewhere in the West.

Lessons for the History of Redemption

This chapter has provided some surprising lessons for students of the history of redemption. This era's "tactile piety," which goes back to the apostles, suggests that when the God of Israel redeems, he uses matter in an abundance of ways. Redemption that is restricted to intellectual apprehension is Gnostic, bypassing the created matter that God loves and uses to redeem.

Most of us have been led to believe that since Jesus's time Jerusalem has been controlled by Jews, Romans, or Muslims. Few are aware of the centuries when Christians controlled what Wilken has referred to as "the land called holy" or have thought about how God redeemed people in these Byzantine centuries that were filled with both perception and blindness, beauty and sin.[21] Fewer still know that most missions faced east in this era, that most of the Middle East was Christian for much of this time, and that India and China were being reached for redemption by intrepid missionaries of the Eastern churches.

God redeems in surprising ways. He used great Roman bishops like Leo and Gregory in desperate times when they served as heads of both state and Church. Even Protestants agree that in these times it was helpful to have a head bishop to whom Christians could look for leadership from distant lands. God brought redemption through the nascent papacy.

We are reminded that the history of redemption has ebbed and flowed, especially in places like England. Here the messianic faith was planted in the first or second century but suffered greatly from barbarian invasions of Germanic

19. John Chrysostom, *Homily 6: Against the Jews* 6.11, The Tertullian Project, https://www.tertullian.org/fathers/chrysostom_adversus_judaeos_06_homily6.htm.

20. Ambrose, *Concerning Widows* 3.19; 3.20, in *The Nicene and Post-Nicene Fathers*, Series 2, ed. Alexander Roberts and James Donaldson (1885–87; repr., Peabody, MA: Hendrickson, 1994), 10:394.

21. Robert L. Wilken, *The Land Called Holy: Palestine in Christian History and Thought* (New Haven: Yale University Press, 1992).

and Scandinavian tribes. God used missionaries like Augustine to bring revivals that stayed and that made deep imprints on later generations. Missionaries to and from Ireland spread the faith and preserved civilization through many dark centuries. The God of Israel presides over triumph and suffering, Church growth and decline.

Despite his ill-considered view of Jews and Judaism, Augustine's reflections on this period in the history of redemption are perhaps the most insightful. Politics is a dirty business. The Christianization of the Roman Empire meant that the religion of the God of Israel became fouled by politics. Success for God's people brought immediate perils. Caesar had persecuted them for three hundred years. When Caesar suddenly worshiped at the cross, he often subverted it and led God's people in ways that denied the cross. God's people even started killing God's people, Gentile Christians massacring Jews because they had not pierced through the veil that Paul said God had put over their eyes.

Yet just as God's people in the first century struggled with sin and heresy in Ephesus and Corinth and yet remained the body of Messiah, so too God's people in fourth-century Rome struggled to know how to relate to a Christian empire that built churches but often promoted heresy. They learned that just as redemption involves the body, even the relics of martyrs' bodies in places of worship, so too it can use the state to advance the kingdom. Yet the same state can both advance and undermine the kingdom when it is more concerned with earthly stability than transcendent ideals.

Augustine was right. The City of God is intermixed with the City of Man, with good and bad in the visible dimensions of both. The relation between the two cities in a civilization ostensibly devoted to God is a divine secret. So is the place of the City of God in a state devoted to secular aims. Redemption is often advanced in paradoxical ways, with weakness triumphing over visible power. The growth of the Church in the West as the empire collapsed is perhaps an illustration of that kingdom principle. The mushrooming of Christian Jerusalem was a signal that places in redemptive history continue to mediate saving power.

And the expansion of the Church in the East in the midst of uncomprehending regimes shows that even in earthly vessels such as despotic kingdoms the exceeding greatness of God's power can break forth. God can use places and kingdoms to advance his own.

Finally, the vessels are earthly and sinful, as is shown most egregiously in the Church's trashing of God's covenant with Israel and the Church's treatment of the chosen people. This is a good reminder that the redeemed people must always recognize that it sees through a glass darkly and should reexamine Scripture and tradition for signs that it must correct its vision.

Select Bibliography

Augustine. *The City of God*. Translated by Marcus Dods. New York: Random House, 1950.

Cahill, Thomas. *How the Irish Saved Civilization*. New York: Doubleday, 1995.

Chadwick, Henry. *The Church in Ancient Society: From Galilee to Gregory the Great*. Oxford: Oxford University Press, 2001.

González, Justo. *The Story of Christianity*. Vol. 1. New York: HarperOne, 2010.

Gregory the Great. *The Book of Pastoral Rule*. Crestwood, NY: St. Vladimir's Press, 2007.

Isaac, Jules. *The Teaching of Contempt*. New York: Holt, Rinehart, and Winston, 1965.

Jenkins, Philip. *The Lost History of Christianity: A Thousand-Year Golden Age of the Church in the Middle East, Africa, and Asia—and How It Died*. New York: HarperOne, 2008.

Latourette, Kenneth Scott. *A History of Christianity*. New York: Harper and Bros., 1953. See particularly chap. 9.

Nirenberg, David. *Anti-Judaism: The Western Tradition*. New York: Norton, 2013.

Shelley, Bruce. *Church History in Plain Language*. 2nd ed. Dallas: Word, 1995.

Wilken, Robert Louis. *The First Thousand Years: A Global History of Christianity*. New Haven: Yale University Press, 2012.

20

The Iconoclast Controversy

In 726 the Byzantine emperor Leo III banned icons and other religious images throughout the eastern empire. He claimed that an image (Greek *eikōn*, "icon") violated the second commandment ("You shall not make for yourself a carved image or any likeness of anything that is in heaven above or the earth beneath"; Deut. 5:8). By "image" was meant "any form of religious art—mosaics, frescoes, decoration of sacred vessels or garments, statues, and paintings on a board," the primary meaning of "icon" today. After the imperial edict, "mosaics were gouged from walls and icons daubed with whitewash."[1]

Leo had just returned from his second successful defense of Constantinople against Muslim armies. Muslims had taken control of much of the Middle East and North Africa, and the eastern empire was reduced to the area around Constantinople and Asia Minor (now Turkey). Some historians think Leo faced taunts from Muslims and Jews that Christians were idolaters and that he felt he needed their support for the empire. It might also have been a way for Leo, a non-Greek, to assert control over his Greek subjects, who were the most outspoken proponents of images. Leo contended that the only permissible images were the bread and wine in the sacrament.

The edict provoked a riot. An angry mob murdered the imperial official sent to replace the icon of Jesus over the bronze gate of the imperial palace in Constantinople with a cross.[2]

1. Andrew Louth, introduction to John of Damascus, *Three Treatises on the Divine Images* (Crestwood, NY: St. Vladimir's Seminary Press, 2003), 8.
2. Bruce Shelley, *Church History in Plain Language* (Dallas: Word, 1995), 148.

The riot did not deter Leo. He called a council in 730 that took further measures against icons, and he deposed a patriarch who refused to go along. Leo's son Constantine V was even more determined in his iconoclasm. Despite Pope Gregory III's council that excommunicated iconoclasts in 731, the empire's position on images stayed in place for more than a century, revoked only in 843. Yet in the first fifteen years of imperial iconoclasm a brilliant monk in the desert outside Jerusalem was writing treatises in favor of icons that have moved Christian thinking ever since.

John of Damascus

John Mansour (ca. 655–ca. 750) was born into a wealthy family in Damascus. He spent the first part of his life serving the Muslim caliph there. When he felt his service had become intolerable, John left Damascus to become a monk. Perhaps because the monastery he chose was more than a thousand miles away from the capital in Constantinople, John wrote *Three Treatises on the Divine Images*, which challenged the theology of iconoclasm (from the Greek words that mean "breaking images").

John explained that images are at the heart of the Trinity. The Son is the *eikōn* of the Father. They are also the key to God's relation to his creation, for the world is full of images of God. The sun, for example, is an image of the Son of righteousness (Mal. 4:2).[3] Similarly, the Old Testament is full of images of New Testament realities: the ark of the covenant, the jar within the ark, the mercy seat and cherubim above the ark. All of them are said by the author of Hebrews to "serve in sketch and shadow of the heavenly things" (Heb. 8:5).

God intended the earth and Jewish worship to be this way, full of images pointing to divine realities, illustrating his Word with material things. God knows our need for pictures and analogies and fills creation with them. As Jesus taught, both the birds of the air and lilies of the field teach God's care for us. The fathers, John went on, recognized that many people cannot read or don't have time and that images are commentaries on the Word.

The incarnation, John argued, is an image, the Son of the Father. Just as the

---

3. John did not make this explicit connection, but he would have affirmed it as consistent with his theology of images—that this verse at the end of the Bible suggests that the sun is an image of the Son. Significantly, even Maimonides, the greatest Jewish philosopher, taught that Mal. 4:2 is speaking of the Messiah (Mishneh Torah, https://www.chabad.org/library/article_cdo/aid/1188357/jewish/Melachim-uMilchamot-Chapter-12.htm).

Logos took on the matter of flesh, God fills the matter of the world with images of himself. Paul explained that the invisible things of God are clearly perceived through the things that have been made in creation (Rom. 1:20).

John went to the Old Testament for warrant that God was the first to make images, appearing to the patriarchs and prophets in the image of a man. "Adam saw God and heard the sound of his feet as he walked in the evening. . . . Jacob saw and wrestled with God. . . . Moses saw him as a human back, and Isaiah saw him as a man seated on a throne, and Daniel saw the likeness of a man, and as a son of man coming upon the ancient of days. No one, however, saw the nature of God [himself], but the figure and image of one who was yet to come."[4] They saw God in the image of his Son even before the later incarnation.

John drew a distinction between veneration (*proskynēsis*, literally, bowing down) given to angels and departed saints, and worship (*latreia*) owed to God alone. We may venerate or pay respect to things close to God such as holy places and martyrs, and in these cases we actually respect God because of his imprint on these places and saints. Since worship is for God alone, idolatry is giving exclusive worship to things other than God. John declared that in veneration the focus is on the Creator, not the creation: "I do not venerate matter, I venerate the fashioner of matter, who became matter for my sake and accepted to dwell in matter and through matter worked my salvation, and I will not cease reverencing matter, through which my salvation was worked."[5]

The Materiality of Redemption

John was the last of the fathers. He was declared to be a doctor of the Church by Pope Leo XIII in 1890. By this declaration the Western Church was turning again against Gnosticism, the notion that only spirit or mind matters. The Church was returning to the insistence of the apostolic fathers that redemption is not apart from matter but through matter, the material God-man and his earthly incarnation. And that in the future of redemption the earth will also be renewed and redeemed. John of Damascus showed God's people that redemption is a material thing because we human beings were redeemed by the flesh of the Messiah and will not be redeemed without our own fleshly bodies.

---

4. John of Damascus, *Three Treatises on the Divine Images* (Crestwood, NY: St. Vladimir's Seminary Press, 2003), 101–2.

5. John of Damascus, *Three Treatises*, 29.

Development of Liturgy and Sacrament

During the first seven centuries of the Jesus movement, worship was developing. Jesus said he would send his Spirit to lead his followers into all the truth, and the early Church found itself coming to a consensus by the end of this period on the basic shape of the liturgy and sacraments. As we have seen in previous chapters, the liturgy adopted the pattern of Jewish liturgical worship, both the Word-centered liturgy of the synagogue and the sacrifice-centered worship of the temple. Fairly early on the Church saw worship as centered in the sacrament but delivered by a liturgy shaped by the Word. The major sacraments came to be parts of a liturgy, especially the weekly liturgy on the Lord's Day. Even the later sacraments of marriage and Holy Order eventually included the Eucharist. So the sacraments were usually delivered by a liturgy, and the liturgy typically articulated the meaning of the sacraments.

In the first three centuries there was near-unanimous agreement that baptism brings forgiveness of sins. This is attested in the Epistle of Barnabas, Shepherd of Hermas, and the writings of Justin Martyr, Irenaeus, Clement of Alexandria, Tertullian, and Origen. Irenaeus, Tertullian, and Cyprian were convinced that baptism confers the gift of the Holy Spirit. In the fourth century Cyril of Jerusalem tells us that men and women were baptized separately because naked. They faced west to renounce Satan and then east to answer three questions about the divine Persons.

Early on there was also widespread conviction that in the Eucharist are the body and blood of the Messiah, not just his spiritual presence. In his letters to Smyrna and Ephesus Ignatius asserted this at the beginning of the second century. Justin Martyr wrote in his *First Apology* (AD 155) that the bread and wine are not "common bread or common drink" but "the flesh and blood of that incarnate Jesus." Irenaeus (d. 202) agreed but added that the bread and wine retain their earthly composition and a new reality is added to them, to make "a Eucharist composed of two things, both an earthly and a heavenly one."

It is a repeated theme in the Didache (AD 96), Justin, and Cyprian (d. 258) that the Eucharist is a sacrifice, not a new one but the one at Calvary newly available.

In the fourth century Cyril of Jerusalem's Eucharistic prayer is preceded by the kiss of peace. The prayer includes a prayer for the Holy Spirit to come down on the elements to transform them [*epiklēsis*], prayers for the world and Church and for the Eucharistic sacrifice to be a propitiation for the faithful departed. The Lord's Prayer follows. Communion begins with the words, "Holy things for holy people."

Khaled Anatolios writes that this realistic sacramental theology was part of a larger project, the participation of the human in divine life, or "deification."

"Participation in the sacraments of baptism and Eucharist was understood to be a vital and necessary means for this graced deification."[6] The fourth-century bishops, Anatolios argues, emphasized the transformation of the Eucharistic gifts as a sacrifice. But this was neither a new sacrifice nor something accomplished by the celebrant. Instead it was such a genuine recalling of the true offering by Christ that it became one with that offering. The Egyptian bishop Serapion of Thmuis (ca. 359) added that in the Eucharist the Messiah and the Spirit lead a heavenly choir of praise to the Father.

The fourth-century theologians believed that God had directed the basic development of the liturgy. So when the divinity of the Holy Spirit was questioned, Athanasius pointed to the baptismal liturgy as proof that the Spirit is equal to the Son and the Father: "Holy Baptism, in which the substance of the whole faith is lodged, is administered not in the Word, but in Father, Son, and Holy Ghost."[7]

Late in the fourth century in Antioch at John Chrysostom's church the sexes were separated on opposite sides of the nave, and the liturgical action was performed at a stone altar in the middle with a white cloth draped over the altar decorated with gold vessels and a cross.

In the early fifth century Theodore of Mopsuestia extended liturgical thinking by depicting liturgical action as recapitulating the Messiah's passion but in realistic ways. Recalling the Jewish ontology of liturgy bringing the past into the present, Theodore taught that when the deacons bring out the oblation (offering) and place it on the altar, the Messiah himself is being led out to his passion and laid on the altar, which represents his tomb. The altar linens become the linen cloths for burial.

Prosper of Aquitaine (fifth century) articulated what became widely accepted, that the liturgy determines faith—*ut legem credendi lex statuat supplicandi*—namely, the law of prayer establishes the law of belief. One might say that the Spirit, who led the Church to develop its liturgy, was thereby showing believers what to believe about their redeemer and his redemption.

Augustine

As was his wont, Augustine developed the existing sacramental practices into a sophisticated theology of sacraments. A sacrament, he proposed, is a visible word.

6. Khaled Anatolios, "Sacraments in the Fourth Century," in *The Oxford Handbook of Sacramental Theology*, ed. Hans Boersma and Matthew Levering (New York: Oxford University Press, 2015), 141.

7. Athanasius, *Four Discourses against the Arians*, in *Sacraments and Worship: The Sources of Christian Theology*, ed. Maxwell E. Johnson (Lousiville: Westminster John Knox, 2012), 45.

It joins elements of the earth to the Word of God so that sanctifying grace is released. It allows our eyes to move from the material to the immaterial but requires that our faith and not just our eyes follows the action.

Sacraments started in Israel, Augustine observed. Moses had his visible sacraments, all of which promised and pointed to the savior to come. When the Messiah finally arrived, he chose to be completed with human nature. So too he now completes himself with his Body, the Church.

In the Eucharist, he went on, the whole of the redeemed city, the New Jerusalem in its earthly stage, is offered to God as a universal sacrifice for us through the Great High Priest. In his passion he offered himself as a servant so that we might be the Body of so great a Head. Therefore, Augustine told believers about to receive the Eucharist, "Be what you can see, and receive what you are."[8]

Augustine was a realist. The sacraments confer objectively real gifts, even to the wicked. But in them these gifts do not profit. Yet the gifts remain holy within them—condemning the baptized who fail to live the faith and bringing judgment on those who do not discern the body in the Eucharist.

During the Donatist controversy after the persecutions, when compromised but repentant clerics were thought forever tainted, Augustine argued that it is the Messiah who performs the sacrament, not the priest. As long as the priest uses the Church's Spirit-inspired liturgy for the sacrament, believers can be sure they are receiving directly from their Lord the full grace of the sacrament. So Jesus is the agent of baptism and Eucharist, and the other sacraments as well.

After Augustine

In the next few centuries after Augustine, liturgical and sacramental understandings developed a bit more. Pope Leo I (served 440–61) emphasized the present reality of the Messiah in his sacraments. "What was visible in our Redeemer when on earth has become operative in sacramental signs." Believers in the Church can have even closer access to their Redeemer than those in the first century. "The Son of Man who is Son of God has in an ineffable way become more present to us in his Godhead now that he has departed from us in his humanity."[9]

Cyril of Alexandria, a contemporary of Leo, reiterated that theme. Every Eucharist, he proclaimed, is a reincarnation of the *Logos*, who is there again in his body

---

8. Augustine, *Sermon 272*, quoted in Lewis Ayres and Thomas Humphries, "Augustine and the West to AD 650," in Johnson, *Sacraments and Worship*, 160.

9. Leo I, *De Ascensione Domini II*, in Johnson, *Sacraments and Worship*, 4.

to give to the communicant. He used the well-wrought theme of 2 Peter 1:4, that believers become "partakers of the divine nature." More and more, the sacraments were seen to be activities rather than objects, events that released divine power.

Baptisms in this period were preceded by exorcism. Most baptisms were of infants, and parents and sponsors renounced the devil and his works on their behalf. They professed faith in the three divine Persons, and the priest made the sign of the cross on the infant. Baptism was indispensable for receiving communion and, like Holy Order, was thought to be unrepeatable.

A dialogue was the standard introduction to the Eucharistic prayer in most worship liturgies. "The Lord be with you," said the celebrant. "And with your spirit," the congregation replied. "Lift up your hearts." "We lift them to the Lord." "Let us give thanks to the Lord our God." "It is right and fitting so to do."

The Eucharistic prayer followed, a paean to the glory of God in creation and redemption and prayer that God would accept the sacrifice offered through Jesus Messiah. Wine was mixed with a bit of water, followed by more prayer for the Church and commemoration of faithful departed. At the end of the Eucharist the priest said in Latin, *Ite, missa est* [Go, it is sent.] Contemporaries might have thought they were being sent on mission. Aquinas later said it meant that the Messiah was sent by the Eucharistic action to the Father. In any case, the last words were collapsed into "Mass."

Protestant readers might be surprised by this, but Holy Order (the sacrament of ordination) was thought to pass through the bishops' hands an indelible sign on priests that gave them the authority to have the Messiah minister through them. Augustine said the change was irreversible, just like the indelible sign conferred at baptism (which saved the faithful and condemned the unfaithful). Leo the Great ordered that the rite of Order be restricted to the Lord's Day because, he said, that was the day of creation, Jesus's resurrection, the Great Commission, and Pentecost.

In the seventh century Isidore of Seville theorized that sacraments always take place in liturgy in order that the sacrament may be placed in a holy setting. They must be performed in the Church because the Holy Spirit dwells in the Church in a hidden way. They are mysterious because they have a secret and recondite character. Their effectiveness is neither enlarged by good ministers nor diminished by bad.

In that same century Maximus the Confessor proposed that the liturgy provides *anamnēsis* for the whole cosmos. This was why Byzantine churches came to be "miniature representations of the cosmos," with the nave signifying the earth and the dome and sanctuary heaven.[10] The Church, he believed, restores the cosmos to the unity it lost at the fall but that is regained at the incarnation and its re-presentations in the Eucharist. The bishop's entry into the Church represents the incarnation, and his entrance into the sanctuary the Messiah's ascension and second coming.

Germanus of Constantinople (eighth century) took these analogies several steps further. He linked the symbolism to ontology when he postulated that to apprehend a liturgical symbol is to participate in the reality symbolized. In this way liturgical rites become means of divinization. So the Spirit is really seen in the fire and smoke of incense. When believers see the chalice on the altar, they can see the vessel that received the mixture of blood and water from Jesus's side. The cover on the paten opens up the cloth on Jesus's head covering his face in the tomb. The priest at the altar is actually standing before the throne of God in heaven.

In the same century John of Damascus added the typological principle that he learned from Gregory of Nyssa, that just as food and drink are changed into the human body by digestion, so the bread and wine and water are "changed beyond nature through the invocation and descent of the Holy Spirit into the body and blood" of the Messiah.[11] These things must be apprehended by spiritual reason, far beyond natural reason and understanding. John rejected the idea dear to iconoclasts that the bread and wine are merely figures. No, he insisted, they are the deified body of the Lord himself. Eucharist is *metalepsis*, or participation, and *koinōnia*, or communion.

According to Andrew Louth, the iconoclast controversy of the eighth and ninth centuries (726–843) ended with renewed emphasis on the reality of the human nature of the Messiah in the Eucharist. It gave new impetus to the idea that "symbolism is multivalent, so there is no difficulty in the liturgy of the Church on earth celebrating the Paschal mystery, finding that interpreted in the Old Testament temple, and reflecting the perpetual liturgy of the heavens: indeed, bringing all these together helps to emphasize the eschatological nature of Christian worship."[12] The central act of liturgical worship, then, unites past, present, and future. It is the fulfillment of Jewish worship, allows worshipers to participate in the Messiah's passion and triumph, and begins the new heavens and earth that the Messiah will one day finalize.

---

10. Andrew Louth, "Late Patristic Developments in Sacramental Theology in the East: Fifth–Ninth Centuries," in Boersma and Levering, *Oxford Handbook of Sacramental Theology*, 175.

11. John of Damascus, *On the Orthodox Faith*, quoted in Louth, "Late Patristic Developments," 178.

12. Louth, "Late Patristic Developments," 182.

Select Bibliography

Anatolios, Khaled. "Sacraments in the Fourth Century." In *The Oxford Handbook of Sacramental Theology*, edited by Hans Boersma and Matthew Levering, 140–55. New York: Oxford University Press, 2015.

Ayres, Lewis, and Thomas Humphries. "Augustine and the West to AD 650." In *The Oxford Handbook of Sacramental Theology*, edited by Hans Boersma and Matthew Levering, 156–69. New York: Oxford University Press, 2015.

Chadwick, Henry. *The Church in Ancient Society: From Galilee to Gregory the Great.* Oxford: Oxford University Press, 2001.

Ferguson, Everett. "Sacraments in the Pre-Nicene Period." In *The Oxford Handbook of Sacramental Theology*, edited by Hans Boersma and Matthew Levering, 125–39. New York: Oxford University Press, 2015.

John of Damascus. *Three Treatises on the Divine Images.* Crestwood, NY: St. Vladimir's Seminary Press, 2003.

Johnson, Maxwell E., ed. *Sacraments and Worship: The Sources of Christian Theology.* Louisville: Westminster John Knox, 2012.

Latourette, Kenneth Scott. *A History of Christianity.* New York: Harper and Brothers, 1953. See particularly chap. 9.

Louth, Andrew. "Late Patristic Developments in Sacramental Theology in the East: Fifth–Ninth Centuries." In *The Oxford Handbook of Sacramental Theology*, edited by Hans Boersma and Matthew Levering, 170–83. New York: Oxford University Press, 2015.

21

The Rise of Islam

The seventh century brought an end to the world most Christians had known. A lightning-quick series of Arab conquests toppled both the Sasanian (Persian) and Byzantine (Christian) Empires. Never before had the political and religious structures been changed over such a vast territory in such a short time. Daniel Brown tells us of Christians such as the Armenian historian Sebeos reacting in apocalyptic tones. The new Islamic hordes were "the kingdom of Ishmael," the last of the four beasts in Daniel's prophecies. Daniel was right to predict that this Muslim beast "will eat the whole world."[1]

The Arab Conquests

It took the Arabs only thirty years to conquer all the world of the Near East. In 636 Arab armies defeated Byzantine forces at the Battle of Yarmuk near the Jordan River. This ended seven centuries of Roman rule in Syria. Shortly after, Arab Muslims captured Damascus, then Jerusalem a year later (638), and Caesarea in 640. By the next year they took over a city in Egypt that was later the site of Cairo. Alexandria fell to Islamic rule four years later (645–46).

The Arabs had already defeated the (Persian) Sasanian imperial army in 637. By 661 they ruled from the borders of central Asia to North Africa and from Yemen to northern Syria. Less than a century after that (750), Muslims had taken political control of an empire that stretched from Spain to India, and sub-Saharan

1. Daniel Brown, *A New Introduction to Islam* (Malden, MA: Blackwell, 2004), 6.

Africa in the south to central Asia in the north. Only the Franks halted the Islamic advance, in Tours in 732.

New and Old

The new Arab Muslim empire marked a realignment of religious and political power that changed the world forever. There were new ruling elites over most of the civilized world, and a new world religion had been born.

Yet not everything changed. Cities were not systematically sacked. There were few mass or forced conversions in the first generation. New churches and synagogues were still being built in the eighth century. A sign that the new rulers did not ruthlessly enforce their vision comes from archaeology: in Syria and Iraq the production of wine and slaughter of pigs were not diminished, even though both alcohol and pork were forbidden by Islamic law. The new Islamic rulers kept on minting Byzantine-style coins with the image of the emperor holding a cross and Sasanian coins in Persia that still showed Zoroastrian symbols and used Sasanian dates. So the conversion of ordinary people to the new religion did not happen overnight but took generations. Many, such as Monophysite Egyptians who resented Byzantine harassment, welcomed new rulers who permitted most of the old religious and social ways to continue. At least for a while.

Under Caliph Umar (634–44) Christians were not forced to convert, but life as *dhimmis* ("protected" non-Muslims) was demoralizing. Christians were not permitted to build or repair monasteries or church buildings. They were forbidden to practice their faith in public or proselytize—or to ride horses, carry swords, or build houses higher than those of Muslims.

Muhammad and His Beliefs

Muhammad (AD 570–632) had a troubled boyhood. Orphaned when he was six, he went to live with his grandfather, who died after two years, and finally with an uncle. It might have been these heartaches that turned the young man into a religious seeker, haunting the mountain caves above Mecca for meditation.

When Muhammad was forty, he said the angel Gabriel had started to visit him. This terrified him at first, but with reassurance from his wife Khadija and her Christian relative he came to believe that Gabriel had been sent to him by the same God who called Moses. He was to be a prophet to the Arab people. His message was that there is only one God, Allah, not 360 gods as Arabs had believed. Allah had been the name of the God for Muhammad's tribe, the Quraysh. Muhammad started to proclaim that Allah would call all human beings to judgment before him. The messages he received were dictated to him by Gabriel and then passed on to his disciples by the illiterate (according to Muslim tradition) Muhammad. These messages are said to make up the Qur'an.

The Qur'an

The Muslim holy book is about the same length as the New Testament. But unlike the latter, it contains neither histories like Acts, nor biographies like the Gospels, nor theological treatises like Romans. Instead it is a book of proclamation, that there is only one God named Allah ("the God" in Arabic). This God will judge everyone by what he or she has done with the revelation to his last prophet, Muhammad. In previous history God had sent thousands of prophets, the greatest among them Moses and Jesus. But Jews and Christians had altered the teachings of each, so God had to send the latter-day prophet from Arabia to correct Jewish and Christian distortions.[2]

Jews had taken the message of God calling every nation and changed it to focus on one people as his chosen ones. Christians were right to exalt Jesus because he was the greatest of all the prophets before Muhammad. But they had turned him into a god, which was thought to contradict Allah's monotheism. The Qur'an calls Jesus "Messiah," "word from God," "a Spirit from God," and the son of Mary who was "strengthened with the Holy Spirit." It teaches the virgin birth of Jesus and the historicity of all of Jesus's miracles in the Gospels but one, his bodily resurrection.

The Qur'an states that the Jews did not kill Jesus but that God "raised him to himself" in a way reminiscent of Elijah's translation to heaven. Because of these statements, most Muslims deny that Jesus was crucified. They also reject the idea that Jesus was God's Son, which sounds to them like a product of sexual union. This is abhorrent to Muslims, who insist on the spirituality of Allah, who infinitely transcends anything corporeal. The notion of Jesus as Savior is also repellent to Islam because it suggests spiritual irresponsibility, that we are not responsible for our own actions. Most Muslims say no human being can receive spiritual benefits

---

2. These sections on Muhammad, the Qur'an, the Five Pillars, and Sunnis and Shi'ites are adapted from Gerald McDermott, "A Thumbnail Sketch of Islam for Christians," December 3, 2014, C. S. Lewis Institute, https://www.cslewisinstitute.org/resources/a-thumbnail-sketch-of-islam-for-christians/. Used by permission of the C. S. Lewis Institute.

from another person, but mystical Muslims (Sufis) hope for intercession by the Prophet and his family to help them reach Paradise.

Muslims join Christians in expecting a second coming of the Nazarene. But Muslims think that when he returns, Jesus will tell the world it must turn to the truth of Islam.

According to the Qur'an our greatest human tendency is to turn something in creation into a god and serve it. This is idolatry. Those who don't repent and turn to Allah will wind up in hell, where they will suffer forever from boiling water, pus, and searing winds. But men who confess Allah alone and Muhammad as Prophet will enjoy Paradise with wide-eyed maidens, wine, and delicious fruits. Women will have comparable pleasures.

The Five Pillars

Entrance to Paradise is based on attempts to follow the Five Pillars. The first is the profession of faith, *shahada*. One becomes a Muslim by simply repeating in public, "There is no God but Allah, and Muhammad is his prophet." Although the Qur'an is silent on these matters, most Muslims believe Muhammad never sinned and that he performed many miracles. The latter are recorded in the many volumes of the *Hadith*, collections of sayings and deeds by the Prophet. Recent scholars are dubious of the veracity of these accounts and treat them as products of later Islamic communities. Yet these sayings and deeds are used as precedents for Islamic law, *shari'ah*.

The second pillar is prayer five times daily, *salat*. Ritual washings are to precede each prayer, and believers are to face Mecca. Most of the payers are liturgical ones of praise and adoration. On Fridays there is a prayer service at a mosque with two sermons by trained laymen. Women and men sit separately, though most women do not attend.

Almsgiving or *zakat* is the third pillar. Sunnis give 2.5 percent of their income while Shi'ites are supposed to give 20 percent. Fasting during Ramadan (*siyam*) is the fourth. Since the Islamic calendar is lunar and not solar, this month is at a different time each year. It marks the time when Muhammad received his first revelation. During this month believers are to fast from all food and liquids between first morning light and full darkness at night.

The fifth and last pillar is pilgrimage to Mecca, *hajj*. All Muslims are obligated unless they are too sick or poor, the latter disqualifying most. Mecca is believed to be the navel of the earth, the point closest to Paradise and the place where Abraham, Hagar, and Ishmael built a house of worship called the Ka'aba, which today is a giant stone cube covered by black cloth. From here, Muslims say, Muhammad made his "night journey" to Paradise after stopping off in Jerusalem. This is why they believe Jerusalem is their third-holiest site, after Mecca, where Muhammad spent the first thirteen years after receiving his revelation, and Medina, to which Muhammad then led the first Islamic community.

Sunnis and Shi'ites

Shi'ites got their name from battles over Muhammad's successor, after which they split from the majority to form their own distinct party or *shia*. They were convinced that the Prophet had chosen Ali, his cousin and son-in-law, and that future caliphs were to be from the Prophet's family. But the majority chose Abu Bakr as the new leader or *caliph*, and then later caliphs from outside the family.

The biggest event in Shia history was the martyrdom in AD 680 of Ali's son Hussein, who led an uprising against one of the "illegitimate" caliphs. Hussein has become the Shi'ite symbol of resistance to tyranny. For most of their history Shi'ites have been a small minority in the Islamic world—roughly 15 percent at present—and have felt oppressed by the 85 percent majority Sunnis.

Most Shi'ites live in Iran and Iraq. While Sunnis look for final authority to the consensus of religious scholars based on the Qur'an and Hadith, Shi'ites believe in new revelation coming through their *imams* or prayer leaders.

Do Christians and Muslims Worship the Same God?

When Muslims worship Allah, are they worshiping the God of Israel under a different name? If so, then the history of redemption took a strange turn in the seventh century. The true God was manifesting himself and his redemption through a different scripture and a new prophet, both saying things that were at variance with earlier scriptures and prophets. In 2007 Muslim scholars released "A Common Word between Us and You," which asserted that because both Islam and Christianity teach love for God and neighbor, they worship the same God. Christian scholars at the Yale Center for Faith and Culture agreed in their 2008 statement "Loving God and Neighbor Together: A Christian Response to 'A Common Word between Us and You.'"[3]

3. Both statements can be found in *A Common Word: Muslims and Christians on Loving God and Neighbor*, ed. Miroslav Volf, Ghazi bin Muhammad, and Melissa Yarrington (Grand Rapids: Eerdmans, 2010).

But the Bible and the Qur'an do not teach a similar message on love for God and neighbor. Love for God is never commanded by the Qur'an and is rarely even mentioned. The paramount commandment in the Qur'an is fear of God, not love for him. The Bible portrays God as father and shepherd and lover whom we are to love in return, but according to specialist in Islamic law Sir Norman Anderson, "In Islam, by contrast, the constant reference is to God as sovereign Lord (*Rabb*), and man as his servant or slave (*'abd*)."[4]

Love for God has been important in the Sufi mystical tradition, but many Muslim leaders have denounced Sufism as heterodox or heretical. Besides, the Sufi conception of love for God dissolves the human self in unity with the divine and dismisses the idea of God's love for us as "incompatible with the very nature of God as sublime."[5] According to both Sufi and non-Sufi Muslims, God does not have unconditional love for humans generally. He loves only Muslims who are faithful to him. In contrast, the God of the Bible pursues sinners even in their sins and offers his love to them.

If Allah does not love sinners, neither does he tell Muslims to give universal love to others. In fact he commands his followers, "Do not take as close friends other than your own people" (sura 3:118). The *Encyclopedia of the Qur'an* explains that in Islam "one can truly love only [fellow] believers, since love for unbelievers separates one from God and . . . is equivalent to lining up on the side of the enemies of God."[6] This stands in stark contrast to Jesus's command to his followers to love their enemies.

Therefore, it does not appear that Islam and Christianity share the love commands. Neither is Allah like the God of Israel, the Father of Jesus Messiah. As we saw in a previous chapter, Athanasius showed the Christian churches that the Father has always been the Father and so has always had a Son. Muslims deny this. They insist that God is transcendent, infinitely different from anything human like fatherhood. The Qur'an never calls Allah Father, and Muslims are vociferous in their refusal to consider that God could have a divine Son. This, they protest, would imply that God had sexual relations, which is abhorrent to their minds. Of course Christians deny the same but believe God is triune, three divine Persons in one divine being.

4. Norman Anderson, *God's Law and God's Love* (London: Collins, 1980), 98.

5. Murad Wilfried Hofmann, "Differences between the Muslim and Christian Concepts of Divine Love," address to 14th General Conference, Royal Aal al-Bayt Institute for Islamic Thought, September 4–7, 2007, Amman, Jordan, 5–6, https://www.kalemasawaa.com/vb//showthread.php?t=19075.

6. Denis Gril, "Love and Affection," in *Encyclopedia of the Qur'an*, ed. Jane Dammen McAuliffe (Leiden: Brill, 2003), 234–35.

Christians respond that they agree with Muslims that God is one. But for Christians God's oneness is not mathematical. It is a complex unity, a differentiated oneness. Muslims are adamant in their rejection of the Trinity and God's having a Son.

Agreement between Christians and Muslims on other attributes of God becomes problematic when examined more deeply. For example, divine omnipotence. Muslims affirm it. But they reject the Christian testimony that God's power was revealed through the weakness of the cross. Paul says, "The word of the cross is foolishness to those who are perishing, but to us who are being saved it is the power of God" (1 Cor. 1:18). Muslims concede that this shows that Allah is different from the God who permitted his Messiah to die on the cross. Allah, they say, would never send his Messiah to die such a shameful death.

Is there any way in which Christians and Muslims worship the same God? Since there is only one Creator and Redeemer, all human beings connect with the same God if they connect at all. So if Muslims somehow, despite their misapprehensions, by God's grace make some contact with God, then they find the one and only God who exists, the God of Israel whose son is Jesus Messiah. But their ideas about God are starkly different, as we have seen. They deny that God is triune and has a Son who lived on earth and died on a cross and was raised from the dead in bodily form. So if they ever connect with this God, they describe him in ways that are radically different from the true God and his Messiah. They conceive of him as someone he is not.

God as Warrior: The Crusades

One attribute of God that Muslims and most Christians affirm is God's will to sometimes send his people to war to defend themselves. For centuries, however, Christians and Muslims disagreed on the Crusades, each community believing God was against the armies of the other. Yet in the last century Christians have tended to think that God had little or nothing to do with the Crusader armies. As medieval historian Thomas Madden writes, moderns have seen the Crusades as "holy wars against Islam led by power-hungry popes and fought by religious fanatics" who were "the epitome of self-righteousness and intolerance, a black stain on the history of the Catholic Church in particular and Western civilization in general."[7]

7. Thomas F. Madden, *The Crusades Controversy: Setting the Record Straight* (North Palm Beach, FL: Beacon Publishing, 2017), 9.

Yet the Europeans, Madden observes, thought of the Crusades not as aggressive attacks on the lands of Islam but as defensive reactions to Muslim aggressions. Christians thought the Muslims were gunning for them, and they were partly right. From the time of Muhammad, the Muslim state had advanced by the sword. Arab conquerors tolerated Christians and Jews once they were subdued, but their states had to be destroyed first. And as we have seen, after Muhammad's death in 632 the states fell one after another. By the eighth century, Palestine, Syria, Egypt, and all of North Africa and Spain were defeated. In the eleventh century Seljuk Turks conquered Asia Minor, which had been increasingly Christian since the days of the apostle Paul. At the end of the first millennium the Byzantine Empire was reduced to "little more than Greece."[8] All this prompted the emperor in Constantinople to plead in desperation to Christians in Europe to help their brothers and sisters in the east. The Crusades, then, were a response to four centuries of Muslim conquests that took over two-thirds of the old Christian world.

Pope Urban called for the First Crusade at the Council of Clermont in 1095. Those who answered sacrificed much. Crusading knights were usually wealthy men who spent huge sums of money on their journey in hope of storing up treasure in heaven. They saw their participation as penitential acts of charity and love. A few got rich, but most returned with nothing. Fully half never made it home.

The Crusaders had two goals, to redeem the Christians of the East and to liberate Jerusalem and other holy places from Muslim control. Pope Innocent III, successor to Urban II, wrote his flocks, "Do you not know that many thousands of Christians are bound in slavery and imprisoned by the Muslims, tortured with innumerable torments?" According to Cambridge historian Jonathan Riley-Smith, crusading was seen as an act of sacrificial love.

Crusaders also saw themselves as pilgrims to the Holy Sepulcher in Jerusalem. They deemed the reconquest of Jerusalem as an act of restoration. It was universally seen as an act of great good, to restore to Christendom what had been taken away violently. But there were more personal spiritual reasons as well. Crusading was costly and thus penitential, an atonement for sins. Men were willing to take the risk because it was a means to save their souls, and eternal salvation was a matter of great concern.

The First Crusade (1096–99) was the only successful one. By 1098 it had restored Nicaea and Antioch, and by July 1099 Jerusalem, to Christian rule. But once the Muslims unified against the kingdom of Jerusalem, its days were numbered.

---

8. Madden, *Crusades Controversy*, 11.

The last Christian holding in the Holy Land fell in 1291. By the sixteenth century the Ottoman Turks had conquered all the Middle East, North Africa, and southeastern Europe including Greece, Bulgaria, Albania, Hungary, and other lands. Sultan Suleiman the Magnificent almost captured Vienna in 1529, stopped only by a freak storm. By this time Muslims had overrun three-fourths of the old Christian lands.

What put an end to the crusading spirit? Several things. As secular authority grew, religious unity crumbled. National churches vied with each other rather than against a common enemy. Then there was the sixteenth-century Reformation, which challenged two doctrines central to the Crusades, the secular authority of the pope and indulgences. Martin Luther condemned the Crusades as tools of a corrupt papacy. Madden observes that "an impartial observer at the time might well have concluded that Christendom was a doomed remnant of the ancient Roman Empire, destined to be supplanted by the more youthful and energetic religion and culture of Islam."[9]

That did not happen. History is full of surprises. Here is another one: the Crusades were virtually unknown in the Muslim world a century ago. The first Arabic history of the Crusades was not published until 1899, giving rise to a new (for Muslims) perception of their importance. Saladin, who dealt a decisive blow to the Second Crusade at the Battle of Hattin in 1187, which precipitated the fall of Jerusalem, had been forgotten in Muslim history because he was a Kurd, shunned by both Turks and Arabs. To add injury to insult, the Third Crusade overturned most of his conquests. It was not until 1899, when Kaiser Wilhelm II of Germany visited Saladin's tomb in Damascus and paid for a new mausoleum, that Saladin became a revered name in Islamic annals.

Madden and others have documented the cynical use of the Crusades for ideological purposes. In the 1950s colonialism was discredited in the West, and the Crusades were tarred with this brush, considered "nothing more than destructive wars of greed cynically covered in a thin veneer of pious platitudes."[10] In 1999, on the nine-hundredth anniversary of the First Crusade, Western elites and intellectuals walked in the footsteps of the Crusaders to apologize for their forebears. Middle Eastern dictators seized on this as a way to deflect criticism of their own regimes. Arab schoolchildren were taught the Crusades as clear cases of good versus evil. In historical hindsight, however, this presumed moral clarity is very recent.

9. Madden, *Crusades Controversy*, 26–27.
10. Madden, *Crusades Controversy*, 42–43.

Muhammad and Redemption

John of Damascus, who encountered Islam in its first century, saw it as a Christian heresy. How could that be? John saw that Jesus is the most developed character in the Qur'an, which is why in the Islamic tradition Jesus became the most beloved prophet before Muhammad. Muslims have criticized liberal Christians who deny the virgin birth and produce movies like *The Last Temptation of Christ*, attributing scandal to Jesus. So if Islam cannot be reconciled with Christian orthodoxy—and it cannot—Muslims nevertheless have much affection for Jesus and are disappointed that Christians think they demean Jesus.

Yet the Muslim Jesus has even less power than the Arian Jesus, whom I discussed in chapter 18. For whereas Arius believed that Jesus was a creature with messianic power to redeem, Muslims say Jesus was no more than a man blessed with power to do miracles. They deny that Jesus was a redeemer.

In that sense Muslims are right. No creature can redeem other creatures. Even if Jesus was the greatest prophet before Muhammad, the Islamic Jesus—beloved by Muslims as he is—was powerless to redeem. If Muhammad and the Islamic tradition are right, we are still in our sins. No one has conquered death for us. No one has ascended to the right hand of the Father with our human nature. There are no sacraments that convey the power of Jesus to enable us to share in the divine nature. There is no one to plead his blood for us, no one whose perfect obedience is counted as ours for our salvation (Rom. 5:10). We are of all people most to be pitied, as Paul said (1 Cor. 15:19).

But Muhammad was wrong. He was a heretic after all. The God of Israel sent his Messiah, who was the God-man. He redeemed us from our sins, declared that we can share his divine life now, and promised that believers will be raised with our bodies to enjoy the Trinity and the saints and angels forever, on the renewed earth.

Select Bibliography

Anderson, Norman. *God's Law and God's Love*. London: Collins, 1980.

Brown, Daniel. *A New Introduction to Islam*. Malden, MA: Blackwell, 2004.

Crone, Patricia. *Meccan Trade and the Rise of Islam*. Princeton: Princeton University Press, 1987.

Hofmann, Murad Wilfried. "Differences between the Muslim and Christian Concepts of Divine Love." Address to 14th General Conference, Royal Aal al-Bayt Institute for Islamic Thought, September 4–7, 2007, Amman, Jordan, 5–6, https://www.kalemasawaa.com/vb //showthread.php?t=19075.

Kaegi, Walter. *Byzantium and the Early Islamic Conquests.* Cambridge: Cambridge University Press, 1992.

Madden, Thomas F. *The Crusades Controversy: Setting the Record Straight.* North Palm Beach, FL: Beacon Publishing, 2017.

McDermott, Gerald. "Islam: The World's Most Important Religion Geopolitically." In *World Religions: An Indispensable Introduction,* 105–22. Nashville: Nelson, 2011.

McDermott, Gerald, John Cobb Jr., Francis Beckwith, and Jerry Walls. *Do Christians, Muslims, and Jews Worship the Same God? Four Views.* Grand Rapids: Zondervan Academic, 2019.

McDermott, Gerald, and Harold Netland. *A Trinitarian Theology of Religions.* New York: Oxford University Press, 2014.

Peters, F. E. *Muhammad and the Origins of Islam.* Albany: State University of New York Press, 1994.

Riley-Smith, Jonathan. *The Crusades, Christianity, and Islam.* New York: Columbia University Press, 2008.

22

The Medieval West

The golden age of the medieval West was the thirteenth century. This was the era of its greatest thinker, Thomas Aquinas (1225–74). Named after the town near where he was born (Aquino, Italy), Thomas was what we would call a beautiful mind. But he had to fight to get to that place.

When he chose to join the Dominicans after years at a Benedictine monastery where his family had placed him at age five, his brothers kidnapped him. They wanted him to remain with the Benedictines, who were more prestigious. When the brothers' arguments were to no avail, they locked him in a tower to break the young monk. When that also failed, they hired a beautiful prostitute to blacken his reputation and make him more pliable. As soon as she entered his cell, Thomas grabbed a burning stick out of the fireplace and pointed it at the woman, who screamed in fright and ran away.

Once he settled with the Dominicans, Thomas turned into a phenomenal mind with prodigious abilities. Often he would dictate to more than one scribe at a time, and on different subjects. But his legendary power of concentration could be unsociable. At a dinner with King Louis IX of France in 1269, Thomas ignored the table chatter to concentrate on how to refute the heresy of the Manichees. Suddenly he shouted, "That settles the Manichees!" He called for his secretary to take dictation, and when finished, he abruptly realized where he was. Thomas apologized profusely to the king, "I am so sorry, I thought I was at my desk."[1]

1. Brian Davies, *The Thought of Thomas Aquinas* (Oxford: Clarendon, 1993), 8.

The Dominican monk had a preternatural gift of clarity, especially when theological problems were knotty or abstruse. When Pope John XXII was asked how Thomas had reached sainthood in 1326 despite not fulfilling the standard requirement of two miracles, he said that every question Thomas answered was a miracle.

Thomas was one of the greatest minds in the history of the Church. He said he thanked God most for the gift of being able to understand everything he had ever read. But he had unworldly desires. He was known for his love for the Eucharist and a simple lifestyle, even austere. After nearly completing his *Summa Theologica* (a massive systematic presentation of Christian doctrine using Scripture, tradition, philosophy, and theology), the forty-nine-year-old fell into a trance while saying Mass. He stopped writing and spoke little, saying only that in comparison to what God had just shown him in this trance, all he had written seemed like chaff.

Thomas's writings on faith and reason, nature and grace, justification, natural law, and the sacraments set the agenda for the later Middle Ages in the West and for Roman Catholicism ever since. We will look in more detail at each of these topics later in this chapter, but let's start with how this period in the West looked at the Church and tradition. These will show us more about the ways in which redemption was understood and will perhaps add to our own conceptions of how the Messiah has been redeeming the world.

The Church as Thick and Visible Body

Someone once said the most tradition-minded centuries said the least about tradition. The same can be said about Western Christians and the Church. They could not think about God and redemption *except* by thinking about the Church. Perhaps because it was simply assumed, they spoke comparatively little about it. But the idea was everywhere as the backdrop and context in which they saw their lives—a thick conception, as moderns would say. The Church was not God for them, but it was the Church of God. It was the House of God, the pillar and foundation of the truth (1 Tim. 3:15). Even if they could not quote Tertullian, they agreed with him that it was the Body of the Three Persons, the only hall where the Father celebrates the wedding of his Son. It was the Mother that brought them into the spiritual world.

Here, it was near-universally believed, God makes himself visible. Not only when the priest elevates the host at Mass but throughout the week and year through daily masses or prayers, in rituals in the parish church that take every person through life, from cradle to grave, beginning with baptism, through confirmation, marriage, the churching of women after childbirth, to last rites and burial. At church Christians heard about what they believed were the most important things in life—the Ten Commandments, the Seven Works of Mercy, the Seven Virtues, the Seven Deadly Sins, and the Seven Sacraments.

The medieval man and woman in the West believed that on Sunday the redemption of the world was reenacted through the mystery of the Mass. When they looked at that elevated host, they were looking at the body of the Redeemer, and somehow they were participating in Calvary for the sake of their own sins and those of their loved ones. The medieval Mass started with confession of sin led by the priest; an opening collect or prayer; readings from an epistle and Gospel; recitation of the Creed; an offering of bread and wine, which they believed was joined with the Messiah's offering of himself to the Father; the Lord's Prayer; communion; and blessing and dismissal. Although most medievals did not take communion more than once or twice a year, in English parishes Christians would take turns baking a loaf of bread for the offering, and after the blessing it would be cut up for distribution to the congregation. As Roy Strong has put it, the Mass and all the other services throughout the year were "the people's theater." Church was where they got to see the drama of redemption played out in myriad acts throughout the year and their lives.

Medievals knew the Church was more than what happened at their parish. They knew it was a gigantic organism that included all the angels, all the cosmos, and the living and the dead. It had three parts: the Church Militant, here on earth; the Church Suffering, composed of those in purgatory completing their sanctification; and the Church Triumphant, those in heaven awaiting the Messiah's second coming. They knew implicitly that the Church transcended time. As Aquinas wrote, the Messiah was the head of those who preceded him in time. These were the Old Testament saints and some outside Israel like Job who looked forward to him and therefore were part of his Body, the Church.

Yet medieval believers also knew that the Church was still full of spots and wrinkles. It could be a testing ground or even stone of stumbling in times of multiple popes, heresies, and divisions. Theologians and preachers often likened the Church to a moon with its waxing and waning, sometimes reflecting the light of the sun (Son) and sometimes obscured in darkness. Some quoted Augustine, whose thought dominated their period, that the Church was pure and shining because the Messiah illuminates her, but ugly and sinful in herself. Yet she can become beautiful once again, Augustine continued, when she confesses her sins and weeps penitent tears.

Tradition as the Bible's Talmud

Jews say their final authority is not the Old Testament but the rabbinic commentary on that revelation, which is the Talmud. God speaks to Jews as they ponder the rabbis' musings, which teach them how to interpret the Bible. They learn how to understand the Hebrew Bible in a Jewish way by studying the great Jewish thinkers who gave their minds and lives to God's Word, arguing with each other and learning from each other, all in the pursuit of God's ways for their days.

Most Christians throughout the ages, including the apostles and their successors, have taken tradition in a similar way. The apostles were Jews who learned from oral tradition about Tanach. Of course they had the revelation of the Messiah already come, and this revelation transformed their perceptions of everything they had learned about God's Word from their rabbinic teachers. But the early teachers of the Jesus movement learned primarily not from the emerging texts of the New Testament alone but what the bishops had taught in a continuing tradition from the apostles, *using* the New Testament writings as their basis. They learned, for example, in the first few centuries that the way to understand the New Testament's referrals to God as both one and three was through what the bishops called the Trinity. They also learned what that word meant. They dared not teach their own idiosyncratic conceptions but were warned by the fathers to "hand down" faithfully what the accumulated wisdom of the Church had delivered, as Paul himself had taught (1 Cor. 11:23; 15:3; 2 Thess. 2:15). The Latin word for "hand down" was *trado*, and from this the word "tradition" is derived.

But during the medieval period in the West, the way Church theologians and leaders used tradition changed in a subtle but significant way. Heiko Oberman famously described the transition as moving from Tradition I to Tradition II. Until Basil the Great (329–79) and Augustine (354–430), Tradition I was the only game in town. Theologians and Church leaders saw Scripture and tradition as coinherent. The Church through its bishops, it was believed, taught the proper way to interpret the Bible, claiming that the apostles passed down this *kerygma* or gospel message to their successors. It followed that if this was from the apostles, it must be right, since they had been responsible for the New Testament. Tradition was living since it was passed down by living people in oral teaching and was the real meaning of the written books. There was no daylight between the two. Both issued vertically from the same source, the Word of God in revelation by the work of the Holy Spirit.

One caveat, however. This coinherence took place only within the Church. Once people opined on the meaning of the Bible outside the churches of the apostolic succession, they were certain to teach wrongly. Only within orthodox churches could revelatory truth through and about the written scriptures be assured. In this period before Basil and Augustine, the word *traditio* included two concepts—the vertical *traditio dei* coming directly from God to the writers of Scripture and the ongoing Church interpreters in the apostolic succession, and the horizontal Church tradition by itself that developed over the course of the centuries but was considered valid only if it could be proved by written Scripture. The two, the vertical and horizontal, were considered not finally distinct but a mutually reinforcing twofold cord. The Church's teaching could be corrected by Scripture when it strayed, but Scripture alone was considered strange if not seen through the prism of the tradition of Church teaching. Most of the latter was summarized by the early creeds.

Tradition II

In 374 Basil the Great took a new turn in his treatise *On the Holy Spirit.* He urged Christians to pay equal respect and obedience to both written and unwritten Church traditions. Canon lawyers started to take from this a new theory of two sources. No longer were Scripture and Church tradition mutually reinforcing elements of one message. Now they were essentially disconnected.

Augustine reinforced this fifty years later but left in place the earlier Tradition I. So his legacy to the Middle Ages was a tension between the two. On the one hand, he taught a coinherence of Scripture and tradition (Tradition I). But on the other hand, he spoke of an authoritative oral tradition outside of Scripture (Tradition II). He cited Gospel passages telling us that the Spirit would guide the Church "into all the truth" after Jesus left. Augustine said these would be things not addressed in Scripture such as the baptism of heretics. Did it really work if they proved to teach against the received tradition? Abelard pointed to later Church teaching about Mary, Bonaventura cited the *filioque* clause, and Thomas the form of the sacrament of confirmation. All were admitted to be unaddressed by Scripture but believed to have been taught by the Holy Spirit through the Church.

Jan Hus (ca. 1372–1415) and John Wycliffe (ca. 1331–84) both opposed teachings of Rome and have been championed as proto-Protestants. They did indeed oppose Tradition II, which they thought responsible for false—because unbiblical—teachings such as transubstantiation. Wycliffe accepted a trans-formation of the elements but not the disappearance of the substance of the elements. Yet Hus and Wycliffe did not endorse *sola scriptura*. They held to Tradition I, in which tradition is necessary to properly interpret the Bible, but in cases where the Church must decide dubious matters Scripture should be the final arbiter. The two greatest nominalists, however—Duns Scotus and William of Occam—taught a plump version of Tradition II.[2] They asserted that there was an unwritten oral tradition coming through the episcopal succession and that there might be new revelation coming to the bishops. They thought that Scripture without these new teachings would become, as Oberman puts it, "fossilized," but that Scripture alone without tradition's help would lead to "arbitrary fantasies."[3]

Faith and Reason

Let us return to Aquinas. Most of his thinking was accepted by the Western Church and became dominant until the Reformation and beyond. Among his most important was the way he distinguished faith and reason. In short, he argued that reason alone can tell us much about God, such as that he exists and is perfect and good, but we must accept by faith the truths that lead to salvation such as redemption by the God-man on the cross. These truths are taught not by reason but by the Church. Thomas went to Scripture to teach this distinction. Paul, he pointed out, told the church at Rome that "what can be *known* about God is plain to them, because God has *shown* it to them. For his invisible attributes, namely, his eternal power and divine nature, have been *clearly perceived*, ever since the creation of the world, in the things that have been made. So they are without excuse. For although they *knew* God, they did not honor him as God or give thanks to him" (Rom. 1:19–21 ESV). Thomas again quoted Paul to say that the preaching of the cross proclaimed by the apostles is foolishness to the world, so worldly reason will never accept it (1 Cor. 1:18–31).

Thomas's Five Ways or proofs of God's existence are often ridiculed for supposedly claiming to be able to convince anyone, even skeptics. But Thomas's *Summa Theologica* was written as a seminary textbook to train ordinands and clergy. The

---

2. Nominalism, from the Latin *nomen* or name, is the tradition that believes all universals such as "man" or "humanity" are only names, and that the only realities are individuals. So there is no common human nature, for example, linking all human beings.

3. Heiko Oberman, *The Harvest of Medieval Theology* (Durham, NC: Labyrinth, 1983), 393.

Five Ways were intended to confirm the faith of believers, not convince village atheists. Thomas knew that prejudice often prevents reason from listening to God's voice speaking through his creation.

The Dominican theologian is famous for baptizing Aristotle. Thomas took the Greek philosopher's best arguments and pressed them into service of the gospel, while rejecting those that were impediments. For example, he used Aristotle's theories of causes and perfection in his Five Ways to argue that there must be something that causes change or motion in things without itself being changed or moved by anything. Since there are varying degrees of perfection, there must be a source of perfection. The movement toward goals by unintelligent things like animals and planets suggests they are governed by an intelligence that has set their goals.

Nature and Grace

Jews and Christians had wondered for millennia (already in Thomas's day!) where nature stops and grace starts. What is preprogrammed by God into the creation as opposed to special new divine work that depends on God's will and our will? Thomas is well known for his dictum that "grace perfects nature." This means that nature, which is God's creation and tool, is directed by God to higher work— namely, our holiness—when God decides to do a special work in us through the means of grace such as sacraments. God can also speak to us in a special way through the liturgy or Scripture or another believer. These three are means of grace that go beyond nature—for example, our creation in God's image—to move us closer to the image of the Son of God so that we can "participate in the divine nature" (2 Pet. 1:4).

Grace has different meaning for Protestants and Catholics. Protestants think of it more as God's attitude of favor toward those who trust in his Son. Catholics usually think of grace as a special work of God within us changing us from the inside. Paul suggests the latter in Romans 5:5: "Hope does not put us to shame, because God's love has been *poured into our hearts* through the Holy Spirit who has been given to us." Thomas leans toward this meaning of grace when he distinguishes it from nature. Grace for him is God's perfecting of what he created. This idea of perfecting reflects Thomas's notion, influenced by Aristotle, that everything in the cosmos has been given by God an inner *telos* or goal toward which it moves. If God does a special new work for believers to assist that movement, it is grace.

Justification

Like Athanasius and Augustine, Thomas saw justification (our acceptance by God into the realm of salvation) as something that is an inner work of grace. It is also for Thomas a legal declaration by God that we are covered with the righteousness of the Messiah. Luther thought that Thomas's focus on an inner grace suggested that we are saved by what is in us and therefore our own works. But Thomas taught clearly that whatever happens within us when we are justified is only because of the work of the Messiah, both in his life and death and resurrection and by the Spirit working within us. Luther was bothered by Thomas's frequent use of the word "merit" in his discussions of justification, but Thomas said it was the Messiah's merit given to us.

Thomas was impressed by the emphasis in the teaching of Jesus and the apostles that we must persevere in the faith in order to have final justification. Therefore, he believed, as did Luther, that we can be justified at one point in life—say, after baptism—but then lose our justification if we do not persevere. The soul with rocky soil receives the gospel with joy and endures for a while but falls away when persecution or tribulation comes.

Protestants, following Luther, have tended to dismiss Thomas on justification as teaching works righteousness, the idea that our works will save us. In fact Thomas taught the priority of grace before justification and the necessity of grace to persevere to the end. All this, he wrote, is by the work of the Messiah to assist our will to keep on cooperating with his.

Natural Law

One of Aquinas's most important achievements was to systematize a "natural law" tradition going back to Aristotle, Cicero, and Augustine. This was the idea that unaided reason can teach us moral absolutes that are good for all times and places. But these absolutes, he taught, are general principles and not specific rules. Every society in history will need to tailor the general principles to what it judges to be for the common good. For example, the first principle of natural law is "that good is to be sought and done, evil to be avoided."[4] Life is not meaningless, in other words. The fabric of the cosmos is stitched with moral guidelines. Society should seek those guidelines and apply them to its members.

4. Aquinas, *Summa Theologica* I-II.94.2, trans. Fathers of the English Dominican Province (New York: Benziger Bros., 1948).

It is good to preserve life, according to a second guideline. A third is that men and women should learn what they can about the meaning of life (for Thomas this is God). Procreation and the education of the young are good things. People should shun ignorance, not offend needlessly, and pursue civility with others. These are general moral rules that reason can discern.

A notable corollary is that when civil law corresponds to natural law, it is just and "participates" in God's "eternal law."[5] If civil law violates natural law, it might be the duty of a Jesus-follower to practice civil disobedience. This was Martin Luther King's conclusion in his discussion of natural law in his epochal "Letter from Birmingham Jail." It shows the relevance of Thomas's thinking to our own redemption, which is a life of pilgrimage on our way to the New Jerusalem.

Sacraments

In previous chapters we traced the development of sacramental theory among the fathers of the Church, especially Augustine. Thomas added more, and in ways that have remained with the Western Church ever since. For instance, Thomas accepted Augustine's explanation that "the visible sacrament is the sacred sign of the invisible" work of the Redeemer. Aquinas added several notions that help us see how the Messiah *applies* his redemption to us.[6]

First, he taught, the sacraments enable us to become the Messiah's "contemporaries." Often Jesus-followers lament that they did not get to see and hear Jesus on earth; some think their faith would be stronger if they could have lived in first-century Israel. But Thomas asserts that in the sacraments the real God-man Jesus, the same one who walked the dusty trails of Galilee, comes to us with his words and physical touch. He comes through time to be *our* contemporary. He is ours and we are his. When we are touched by water or wine or bread or oil in the sacraments, we are touched by the body of Jesus himself.

Second, Thomas explained that sacraments are fitting for us because we are sensory creatures, and they bring Messiah to our senses. This is the first and most natural way for us to know anything and, therefore, the perfect way to grow in knowledge of Jesus. By the "sensory" dimension of sacraments in which the full humanity (not just the divinity) of Jesus comes to us, the newness of life that Jesus won for us through his redemptive work is given to us and intensified. In this way

5. Aquinas, *Summa Theologica* I-II.91.2; I-II.93.3.
6. This section is based on Aquinas, *Summa Theologica* III.60–73.

the sacraments make faith and doctrine real and existential. They are the means by which faith, hope, and love are perfected within us.

Third, Thomas suggested that because most knowledge comes from external things or people outside us, the sacraments are more reliable as external actions impinging on us than internal impressions are, since we can mistake our own desires for internal impressions from the Holy Spirit.

Fourth, according to Aquinas, the sacraments are reenactments of Jesus's life, death, and resurrection applied to us. In baptism, we are joined to his death. In the Eucharist we consume his resurrected body. In the sacrament of penance (private confession) we hear Jesus say to us what he said to the apostles, "Your sins are forgiven."

Fifth, Thomas emphasized that the sacraments are not only *signs* of Jesus's redemption but actions that *cause* Jesus's redemption to be applied to us anew. The sacrament of Holy Order causes an indelible sign to be placed on the priest's soul. The sacrament of matrimony confers a special grace on a man and woman in their becoming one flesh. The *epiklēsis* prayed by the priest at the Eucharist brings the Holy Spirit to transform the elements on the altar.

Rome versus Jerusalem

Thomas Aquinas is the most emblematic thinker of the medieval Church in the West. His thinking helped guide the ways that the Western Church became formed, and much of it remains among Roman Catholics and those in other liturgical/sacramental churches.

Unfortunately the medieval Church in the West continued the hostile approaches to Jews that we have seen in earlier periods of Church history. In the otherwise spectacular Notre Dame cathedral in Paris (built between 1163 and 1345) there is a prominent statue of a woman titled "Synagoga" whose head is encircled by a sinister serpent indicating, in Eugene Korn's words, "a not-so-subtle transition from the falsehood of Judaism to the wickedness of Jews." In other medieval Church depictions, Jews are "portrayed as genetically determined, weak-willed, filthy swine who were the antithesis of Christian virtue and integrity."[7] In Wittenberg, Germany, where Luther started his reforming career, a relief on the church wall shows Jews sucking a pig's teats and a rabbi staring into the pig's anus.

---

7. Eugene Korn, "From Constantine to the Holocaust," in *Understanding the Jewish Roots of Christianity*, ed. Gerald McDermott (Bellingham, WA: Lexham, 2021), 133.

At the end of the twelfth and beginning of the thirteenth centuries, Pope Innocent III ruled that Jews must wear distinctive badges so that Christians could identify them and stay away. In the late fifteenth century, the Spanish Church oversaw the killing of one hundred thousand Jews, forcibly converting another hundred thousand, and exiling a further one hundred thousand. From the twelfth century on and into the modern period, Jews were accused of blood libels (sacrificing Christian children for their blood to make unleavened bread) which precipitated massacres and pogroms. Generally Jews were seen as money-grubbers who preyed on innocent Christian neighbors. In Shakespeare's *Merchant of Venice*, Shylock the Jew, who seems more interested in money than virtue, illustrates this late medieval prejudice against Jews. (Yet more careful readers noticed that Shakespeare subtly criticized this anti-Semitism. In a famous speech in act 3, Shylock protests against the prejudice that Christians show toward Jews merely because they are Jews and says he will "execute villainy" against his Christian debtor because Christians have taught him villainy by their own villainy toward Jews.)

So while Jesus-followers grew in their understanding of redemption during this period in the West, they were diminished in their souls to the extent that they misunderstood and persecuted Jesus's relatives.

Redemption and the Medieval West

The Messiah continued to redeem souls throughout the West during the Middle Ages. We could say that their understanding of, and to some degree their experience of, the Messiah and his redemption were deepened. They saw that the Messiah came to start a Church and to redeem through its ministrations. Its depiction of redemption in worship, sacraments, Word, and culture permeated life, with meaning given to every last detail for those who wanted to look. There was no clear line separating the secular and sacred. The Church had ways of speaking and ministering to every dimension of reality. That made sense to average Jesus-followers, who knew that the Messiah intended to be Lord of all. Just as they knew that the Messiah walked the earth in visible form, the Church made the Messiah visible in a myriad of ways. This ought to be, theologians reasoned, since redemption is of our bodies and not just minds, and Jesus surely meant to have redemptive impact on society.

Medieval Christians believed that God had revealed himself primarily through the Church as it preached and homilized on the written Word. But they also believed that their bishops and priests had received revelation from the apostles about what that Word meant and therefore how to explain it. Until later in this period the Word and its interpretation were considered to be one and the same. But after a while these two elements, Scripture and tradition, which had been in tension in Augustine's thought, broke apart into two competing authorities. That break contributed to new understandings of redemption in the Reformation.

But in the meantime Aquinas's vision helped most medieval believers process redemption. He helped them see that God redeemed by using special revelation to supplement natural revelation, faith to complete knowledge of the Creator with knowledge of the Redeemer. His thinking showed them how to see grace as perfecting nature. Redemption was not a once-for-all event to be accepted intellectually with no more attention needed, but a journey along a long pilgrimage. Successful completion of redemption would come from the Church and its sacraments and liturgy, so that the Word might fully form faith, hope, and love. This was the fullness of redemption.

Millions were redeemed, profiting from the sights and sounds and tastes of the medieval Church. But it was far from perfect. Its continued tragic treatment of Jews was a telltale sign.

Select Bibliography

Chesterton, G. K. *Saint Thomas Aquinas: The Dumb Ox.* New York: Image Books, 1974.

Congar, Yves. *True and False Reform in the Church.* Translated by Paul Philibert. Collegeville, MN: Liturgical Press, 2011.

Davies, Brian. *The Thought of Thomas Aquinas.* Oxford: Oxford University Press, 1993.

King, Martin Luther, Jr. "Letter from Birmingham Jail." Martin Luther King, Jr. Research and Education Institute. https://kinginstitute.stanford.edu/sites/mlk/files/letterfrombirmingham_wwcw_0.pdf.

Korn, Eugene. "From Constantine to the Holocaust." In *Understanding the Jewish Roots of Christianity,* edited by Gerald McDermott, 128–47. Bellingham, WA: Lexham, 2021.

Lubac, Henri de. *The Splendor of the Church.* Translated by Michael Mason. San Francisco: Ignatius, 1999. First published 1956 by Sheed & Ward (New York).

McDermott, Timothy. *Aquinas: Selected Philosophical Writings.* New York: Oxford University Press, 1993.

Oberman, Heiko. *The Harvest of Medieval Theology.* Durham, NC: Labyrinth, 1983.

Strong, Roy. *A Little History of the English Country Church.* London: Jonathan Cape, 2007.

Thomas Aquinas. *On the Truth of the Catholic Faith: Summa contra Gentiles.* Translated by Anton Pegis. New York: Image Books, 1955.

———. *Summa Theologica.* 5 vols. Translated by Fathers of the English Dominican Province. New York: Benziger Bros., 1948.

23

Messiah outside the West

In chapter 19 we looked at how the gospel spread to the East in the first millennium, and in the last chapter I discussed the history of redemption in the medieval West. But what about those areas of the world not typically known for Christianity such as India, China, and Africa in the first millennium? In this chapter we shall see that the gospel has been in India for two thousand years, was brought to China in the seventh century, and was spread through much of Africa in the first few centuries after the incarnation of the Messiah.

Thomas Christians in India

About AD 200 a Christian in Edessa wrote the Acts of Thomas, purportedly telling the story of Thomas's mission to India.

> [Shortly after the ascension of Jesus] we the apostles were all in Jerusalem ... and we portioned out the regions of the world, in order that each one of us might go into the region that fell to him. ... By lot, then, India fell to Judas Thomas, also called Didymus. And he did not wish to go, saying he was not able to go on account of the weakness of the flesh; and how can I, being a Hebrew man, go among the Indians to proclaim the truth?[1]

1. Acts of Thomas, in *The Ante-Nicene Fathers*, ed. Alexander Roberts and James Donaldson (1885–87; repr., Peabody, MA: Hendrickson, 1994), 8:535.

While he was speaking, the narrator went on, Jesus appeared to him in the night and told him not to be afraid, for "my grace shall be with you." Thomas protested again, telling Jesus he would go anywhere but India.

As the angry Thomas was muttering, a merchant from India happened by, looking for a carpenter to take back to India to build a palace for his master, King Gundaphoros. Jesus spotted the merchant, named Abbanes, at the market about noon and asked him if he wanted to buy a carpenter. Yes, he replied, no doubt shocked that Jesus would know the reason for his mission to Israel.

The Messiah told Abbanes he had a slave carpenter, "and I want to sell him." Jesus pointed to Thomas on the other side of the market and said Thomas would cost thirty pounds of silver.

After Abbanes paid Jesus the silver and brought Thomas on board a ship bound for India, the merchant asked Thomas what kind of work he did. "I work in wood making ploughs, yokes, balances, boats, oars, masts. I also work in stone, making slabs, temples, and royal palaces."

Abbanes was delighted. "We need a carpenter like you."

According to this account, Thomas was given a large sum of money once he got to this region of India. He was told to use it to build a big, beautiful palace for King Gundaphoros. Thomas proceeded to give it all away to the poor while preaching the gospel, healing the sick, and driving out demons.

When some time later he was called by the king to show him the palace, Thomas replied that the king would be able to see the palace only after he died. This infuriated Gundaphoros, who ordered Thomas to be shackled in prison.

But that night the king's brother died and appeared to the king in a vision, telling him that he had seen the palace Thomas had built in heaven. The king promptly believed in Thomas's gospel and God and was baptized.

Thomas then went to other regions of India preaching an ascetical gospel that made many converts. One was a queen who angered her husband the king when she refused him the marriage bed. This time Thomas was killed, pierced by swords thrown by the king's soldiers.

Historian Samuel Moffett tells us that "one of the oldest and strongest traditions in Church history is that Thomas the apostle carried the gospel to India not long after the resurrection and ascension of Jesus Christ."[2] Yet for centuries historians doubted this story from the Acts of Thomas because, among other things, there was no historical record of a King Gundaphoros. But then in 1834 in the Kabul

---

2. Samuel Hugh Moffett, *A History of Christianity in Asia*, vol. 1, *Beginnings to 1500* (New York: Harper-Collins, 1992), 25.

Valley of Afghanistan an explorer found coins with a name in Greek and old Indian script: Gundaphar. Other coins were found from Bactria (northwest of India) to Punjab (north India) with the same name on them, Gundaphar. Near the end of the nineteenth century a stone tablet discovered near Peshawar contained six lines in the Indo-Bactrian language naming Gundaphar and dating him in the first century AD, making him a contemporary of Thomas. Historians have determined that Gundaphar was "the most powerful king to rule the Indian north between the end of the Maurya empire and the rise of a Kushan dynasty in the Punjab about AD 70."[3] The beginning of his reign in AD 19 has been called one of the few fixed dates in this period. Moffett says he was perhaps even more powerful than his contemporaries in the Persian Empire.

There is additional evidence for the basic outline of this Thomas account. Our histories contain abundant testimony to maritime travel between the ancient Near East and India—far more than skeptics have thought possible. Strabo, the Greek historian and geographer, wrote that on a visit to Egypt about the time of Jesus he found 120 ships sailing for India from the Egyptian head of the Red Sea. It is likely that there was more direct communication between India and the West in the first two centuries AD than in any of the later centuries until the fifteenth-century voyage of Vasco da Gama. Travel to India no doubt exploded after it was discovered about AD 40 that monsoon winds blow toward India across the Arabian Sea in the summer and blow back toward the Red Sea in the winter. We have records of ships on that route in that century of up to seven sails and carrying 200–300 tons.

Perhaps about AD 50 one of these ships was carrying a Jewish carpenter to India. We also know that carpenters were in demand in the East. For example, Greek carpenters were brought in that period to build a palace for a king in Tamil in southern India.

Besides these historical clues, there are abundant statements among the Church fathers that Thomas was an apostle to India. The churches of India have been claiming this for two millennia. In Syrian accounts Thomas's martyrdom is attributed to the jealousy of Brahmin priests rather than celibacy. A group of Brahmins is said to have ordered Thomas to worship the goddess Kali in her sacred grove. Thomas refused by making the sign of the cross, which caused the grove to burst into flames and the royal soldiers to spear him.

As Moffett observes, these two accounts are not mutually exclusive. After preaching in the north, Thomas appears to have gone to southwest and southeast India until he was put to death perhaps near Madras.

3. Moffett, *History of Christianity in Asia*, 1:30.

There is also evidence for a second major missionary effort in this early period. About one 120 years after the traditional date for Thomas's martyrdom (72), the church of Alexandria claims it sent its most famous scholar, Pantaenus, to India. Jerome wrote in the fifth century that Pantaenus was sent "to preach Christ to the Brahmans and philosophers there."[4] Origen and Clement of Alexandria, disciples of Pantaenus, both wrote of gymnosophists (the ancient Greek word for "naked philosophers" in India, who regarded clothing as detrimental to purity of thought), and Clement distinguished between Sarmanae and Brahmans, two distinct kinds of Indian religious groups. Jerome said Pantaenus preached "to the Brahmans."

So already before the end of the second century, Moffett concludes, "the Christian church had been planted halfway across Asia in India, first by the apostle Thomas . . . and then strengthened by the visit of the theologian Pantaenus from Egypt."[5]

Nestorians in China

In 1623 workers in Xi'an, capital of the ancient T'ang dynasty, uncovered a stone monument more than 9 feet high and 3.3 feet wide of black limestone. It was inscribed with Chinese characters beneath a design with a cross at the top rising from a lotus blossom. The title under the cross was "A Monument Commemorating the Propagation of the Ta-ch'in [Syrian] Luminous Religion in China."

This monument was erected in AD 781 to celebrate the Christian religion that was propagated by a Nestorian missionary in the Chinese capital in 635, 136 years before. For historical context, Moffett reminds us that this was roughly the same time that Aidan went to England as a missionary from Iona, and a half century before Willibrod brought the gospel to Frisian tribes in northern Europe. It was a century and a half before Charlemagne converted the Saxons.[6]

Before proceeding, I need to explain that Nestorians (who prefer to be called "Christians of the East" or the "East Syrian Church") have been wrongly accused of holding to two persons in the God-man because of Nestorius's use of *prosōpon* rather than *hypostasis* for the Messiah's person. Nestorius did not take seriously enough the ancient tradition of *communicatio idiomatum*, from Origen and Athanasius, according to which whatever is said of one nature, divine or human, is said

4. By "Brahmans" Pantaenus and other fathers probably meant those of the Brahmin caste, the highest and priestly cast in India.

5. Moffett, *History of Christianity in Asia*, 1:39.

6. Moffett, *History of Christianity in Asia*, 1:288–89.

of one and the same person. Hence Nestorius should not have balked at saying that Mary was the "Mother of God" because he himself had said that "there are not two Gods or two Sons" but "the person [*prosōpon*] is one." So later Nestorians believed in the unity of the person with two natures but refused the judgment of the Council of Ephesus, which excommunicated Nestorius but which was convoked without fifty Antiochian bishops who would have sided with Nestorius.

This East Syrian mission was not the first presence of Christians in China. East Syrians might have come with the first Persian embassy in the fifth century (many Persian merchants were Nestorian Christians), and East Syrian missionaries had been working successfully in Bactria (now Tajikistan and Uzbekistan) for one hundred years before this. At the end of the sixth century Turkish prisoners of war captured in China and sent to Constantinople had crosses tattooed on their foreheads to ward off pestilence, according to Christians among them.

But this monument was set up in the golden age of Chinese history—during the T'ang dynasty (618–907), its most illustrious—and along the Old Silk Road. It was the first recorded notice, as far as we know, of the entrance of missionary faith to the Chinese Empire.

The monument speaks of "a highly virtuous man named Alopen" who "decided to carry the true Sutras [scriptures] with him" and have them translated in the imperial library. The Chinese emperor "investigated the Way . . . [and] was deeply convinced of its correctness and truth." So he "gave special orders for its propagation."[7]

The monument goes on to commend "Bishop Alopen's teaching" as "mysteriously spiritual and of silent operation." Its "most essential points . . . cover all that is most essential in life." Its principles are "so simple" and "helpful to all creatures and beneficial to all men. So let it have free course throughout the Empire."[8]

The emperor T'ai-tsung wanted a revival of learning, so he set up a library with two hundred thousand volumes. Alopen was received as a special guest to this library, where he was ordered to begin translating his scriptures (the Bible). Under this religiously tolerant emperor the Church began to grow. In 638 the first Christian church building was erected at the capital, Chang'an, the largest city in the world at that time. By that time there were twenty-one monks in China, probably all Persian. Alopen was elevated to the rank of archbishop, ten more churches were built, and monasteries were established.

But the fortunes of the Church changed when T'ai-tsung died in 649 and his son's second wife, Wu Hou, "the wicked witch of traditional Chinese history,"

7. Moffett, *History of Christianity in Asia*, 1:291.
8. Moffett, *History of Christianity in Asia*, 1:292–93.

started to pressure her husband to make Buddhism the favored religion of the empire. Wu was then hailed as the incarnation of the Chinese people's messiah, Maitreya Buddha, and soon mobs attacked the churches and monasteries in the capital.

More trouble came after Arab armies defeated Chinese armies at Talas in 751, marking the end of Chinese control over central Asia. Soon this area was converted to Islam. But there were hopeful signs nonetheless. New missionaries from Persia arrived by sea in 744 with a bishop named Chi-ho. Until 781 when the monument was raised, the community of Christians grew in strength. Christianity was becoming the religion of many of the emperor's Uighur allies. We know of Issu, an East Syrian priest who was also a high-ranking general in the Chinese army, a career not uncommon for Buddhist and Christian priests. Issu's son Ching-ching (or Adam) was the missionary-scholar who probably composed the inscription on the monument and translated large parts of the Bible into Chinese. He is likely the author of the Chinese translation from Syriac of the *Gloria in Excelsis Deo*, which is still sung in Syriac by East Syrian Christians. Moffett adds that Protestants did not have this hymn of praise until seven centuries later, during the Reformation.

Intriguingly, historians know that Adam had contacts with two famous men in the history of Japanese Buddhism—Kukai, who founded the Shingon sect of Tantric Buddhism, and Saicho, who started the Tendai or Lotus school out of which emerged Pure Land, Zen, and Nichiren Buddhism. Several of these schools, especially Pure Land, show the influence of Christian theology in teachings like salvation by grace through faith. Adam's contacts with these Chinese thinkers suggest the possible sources for these Christian-influenced Buddhist sects.

Between 781 and 980 the Christian faith appears to have disappeared from China, if one looks at historical records. Some historians have speculated that it was the heterodoxy of Nestorianism that was responsible. They have pointed to the Buddhist and Taoist language in the monument inscriptions, which suggests syncretism. But the discovery in the 1890s of nine Christian manuscripts demonstrates that the theology of the East Syrians (Nestorians) was more orthodox than the monument itself led some to believe. Skeptics had charged that Nestorian Christianity weakened the deity of the Messiah by focusing too much on his humanity and that it divided the deity from the humanity, thus producing two persons rather than the one person of orthodoxy. But in these documents there are none of the worst Nestorian diatribes that suggest unorthodoxy such as those against Mary as the mother of God or God-bearer. There is an ambiguous phrase that could be translated "divided by person" or "divided by nature," but in Chinese the distinction between "person" and "nature" is virtually impossible to translate.

In the earliest manuscript, probably written by Alopen, we can see all the orthodox essentials. Yesu (the Chinese transcription for Jesus) "gave up his body . . . to be sacrificed for the sake of all mankind." The text affirms original sin, substitutionary atonement, the virgin birth and the cross, the Ten Commandments and repentance, eternal punishment for unbelief, salvation by faith and not works, condemnation of idols and love for enemies, subjection to governmental authorities and care for the poor. Alopen's "Discourse on Almsgiving" has a lengthy condensation of the Sermon on the Mount and vivid accounts of the crucifixion and resurrection.

The use of Buddhist and Confucianist imagery to describe these Christian beliefs has led critics to dismiss these documents as syncretistic. But it is difficult to distinguish this debate from the nineteenth-century dispute over the hellenization of the gospel. The upshot of the latter was the realization that the fact that the fathers used Hellenistic terms to describe biblical concepts did not mean that the gospel itself had been subordinated to Hellenistic narratives of actualization. Just as then, so too in this period in China Alopen and his allies used cultural language to relate Christian concepts.

Then why did the Chinese Church collapse at the end of this period? The answer seems to be not persecution or theological compromise or even foreignness, as Moffett notes, but dependence on a political system. Christians relied too much on this one friendly dynasty. When it fell, all was lost. The Church had not sufficiently distanced itself from its political patrons. Moffett writes, "Thus the first wave of the Christian advance in China came in with one wave of the political tide and was washed out by the next."[9]

How Africa Shaped Theology and the Church

Many believers imagine that the gospel came to Africa only in the nineteenth century with European missionaries. But the fact of the matter is, as we have seen in previous chapters, that Africa north of the Sahara and all the way to the southernmost origins of the Nile was evangelized and settled by Christians since the first-century Pentecost. What is perhaps more interesting for our purposes is to learn of the enormous impact of African Christianity on the history of redemption. It turns out that Christian thinking over the last two thousand years has been shaped deeply

9. Moffett, *History of Christianity in Asia*, 1:314.

by the African Messianic ("Christian") imagination seen in Africa's literature, philosophy, physics, and psychological analysis. Let us explore this phenomenon.

Thomas C. Oden estimates that early African Christianity settled on four million square miles—across Egypt, Sudan, Ethiopia, Eritrea, Libya, Tunisia, Algeria, Morocco, and regions further south.[10] Messianic or Christian history, Oden reminds us, was determined by Africa in ways we need to recall—by the Jews in African Egypt, Joseph's long sojourn in African Egypt, Moses's ministry in African Egypt and Sinai, the holy family (Joseph, Mary, and Jesus) in African Egypt, the early African martyrs Mark and Perpetua, and the great African doctors of the faith Athanasius and Augustine.[11]

At its zenith Alexandria was larger than Rome or Antioch. It played a larger role in the world of ideas, literature, and learning. For centuries it was one of the three leading cities of the ancient world. The Church of Alexandria was founded by Mark the apostle. The capital of African Christianity, it enjoyed 660 years of growth before the Arab conquests. The gospel headed here immediately after Pentecost, turned south to Ethiopia with the Ethiopian eunuch, and spread like a prairie fire across North Africa in the 40s, 50s, and 60s.

Africa was the epicenter of martyrdom. The apostle Mark bore witness by his death in Alexandria in the first century, the seven men and five women of the North African town of Scilli died bravely for their faith toward the end of the second century, and in the third century we have the fiery witness of the noblewoman Perpetua and the slave woman Felicitas, along with bishop Cyprian in Carthage. Not to mention thousands more.

We have studied Antony and his monastic system in chapter 17 but perhaps not recognized the African origins of this movement that spread to Spain, Gaul, Sardinia, Sicily, and Italy when Christians were forced to flee North Africa during the Vandal and Arab invasions. This was the crisis that resulted in Antony, Pachomius, and Macarius of Africa establishing patterns that were replicated in Provence, the Po Valley, Ireland, and many other regions of Europe.

If African monasticism shaped European piety, it also played a principal role in determining future Church dogma. For example, says Oden, "the great Cappadocian writers, upon whom so much depended in post-Constantinian Christianity, could not have done their work without the scriptural expositors of the Nile."[12]

---

10. Thomas C. Oden, *How Africa Shaped the Christian Mind: Rediscovering the African Seedbed of Western Christianity* (Downers Grove, IL: InterVarsity, 2007), 13.

11. Oden, *How Africa Shaped the Christian Mind*, 14.

12. Oden, *How Africa Shaped the Christian Mind*, 47.

Before them was the great Athanasius, who crucially defended classical Christology against Arian readings of John. The Arian controversy itself was "thoroughly African in character, language, and spirit."[13]

It was not only the great Nicene but other councils that demonstrated African patterns for ecumenical decision-making. A century before Nicaea, African churches in Carthage, Alexandria, Hippo, and Milevis resolved controversies by mutual consent and a conciliar process. Arianism, Sabellianism (modalism), Gnosticism, and Pelagianism were debated and decided in Africa before they were debated elsewhere.[14]

Partly because of rhetorical and dialectical skills honed by the Africans Tyconius and Augustine, Africa had an outsized influence on the rise of the first universities. The earliest medieval universities followed "methods of text examination, curricular patterns and philosophical imperatives" refined by Africans as early as Pantaenus and Clement of Alexandria in the second century.[15] The academic community in Constantinople was patterned after academic communities and libraries in Cyrene, Alexandria, Carthage (in Tunisia), and Hippo (in Algeria).

Oden argues that "Christian scholarship was born in the leading academic center of the ancient world, Alexandria," and that Christian exegesis first matured in Africa.[16] The Cappadocians introduced Origen's basic teaching and forms of exegesis to Europe and Asia in the *Philocalia* (ca. 360). Even the early Bibles, both the Septuagint and old Latin Bibles (before Jerome's Vulgate), were out of Africa.

African Roots of Christian Theology

What is redemption? How does the God of Israel redeem? These are theological questions, the classical answers to which were principally developed by Africans. Two of the greatest were Origen (ca. 185–ca. 254) and Augustine (354–430). Origen grew up in Alexandria to become the greatest biblical interpreter of early Christianity. Augustine's mother was a Berber; he was raised in a Numidian town with people from different races.

Later Christian thinkers sought out and imitated the theological prowess of great African intellects like Origen and Augustine, Lactantius (end of the third century), Tertullian (155–222), and Pachomius (292–348). These African minds

---

13. Oden, *How Africa Shaped the Christian Mind*, 48.
14. Oden, *How Africa Shaped the Christian Mind*, 50.
15. Oden, *How Africa Shaped the Christian Mind*, 44.
16. Oden, *How Africa Shaped the Christian Mind*, 44.

had figured out how to best read the Law and the Prophets (although, as we have seen, some missed the continuing significance of God's covenant with the people and land of Israel), how to think philosophically, and how to teach the ecumenical rule of triune faith in a cohesive manner.

Oden adds that Christian ideas of universal history came far more from Africa than Europe. The best-known early Christian historian was Eusebius of Caesarea, whose *Church History* (completed 325) was dependent on Africans Minucius Felix, Arnobius, Lactantius, Tertullian, and Origen. But the granddaddy of all universal histories was the inimitable *City of God* (completed 426) by the African Augustine.

Even Neoplatonism, which has had great influence on Christian theology through Augustine and others, was African in origin. Some of its most influential expositors such as Philo, Ammonias Saccas, and Plotinus were Africans.

In sum, the transmission of important ideas about the God of Israel and his redemption was not from north to south, as the Enlightenment often taught, but from south to north. "Western penitential practice was profoundly shaped by Optatus of Milevis," argues Oden.[17] Thinking about justification was influenced by the work of Marius Victorinus and Augustine, apologetics by deliberations of Minucius Felix, universal history by Lactantius, apocalyptic interpretation by Primasius, civil disobedience by Athanasius, ecclesiology by Cyprian, theological method by Tertullian, eschatological courage by Africa's martyrs like Perpetua and Felicitas, and practically every major topic in redemption by Augustine.

In short, according to Oden, "During the formation of early ecumenical Christianity, Africa was more like a creative intellectual dynamo than a submissive sycophant."[18]

The History of Redemption outside the West

We can learn two things about the history of redemption from this little review of redemption outside the West in the first millennium. First, the God of Israel moves his people to bring his gospel to lands far beyond Israel. He sent one of the original twelve to India, the massive subcontinent of Asia, to seed messianic communities that have continued for two millennia. He moved his people to bring the Word to China several centuries later, and a liturgical and sacramental Church not long after

---

17. Oden, *How Africa Shaped the Christian Mind*, 59.
18. Oden, *How Africa Shaped the Christian Mind*, 61.

that. His principal missionaries were Persians, believers from a land not typically associated with the Jewish Messiah. Africa has had the gospel for two millennia and was the home of the faith's best theologians—in fact, the ones who laid the doctrinal foundations for orthodox Messianic communities ever since. In sum, the God of Israel has redeemed far-flung tribes in ways we could never imagine.

Second, redemption has been an Asian and African story for longer than it has been a European one. The faith started in the Near Eastern part of Asia, established its theological roots in Africa, and spread east and south to central Asia and Africa at the same time that it was just beginning to reach the savage barbarians of Europe. The history of redemption has featured Europe and the Americas in the last two centuries. But for most of its long history it has centered far from those shores in the larger continents of Asia and Africa. The God of Israel has been a relative latecomer to the white tribes of the West.

Select Bibliography

Acts of Thomas. In *The Ante-Nicene Fathers*, edited by Alexander Roberts and James Donaldson, 8:535–49. 1885–87. Reprint, Peabody, MA: Hendrickson, 1994.

Moffett, Samuel Hugh. *A History of Christianity in Asia*. Vol. 1, *Beginnings to 1500*. New York: HarperCollins, 1992.

Oden, Thomas C. *How Africa Shaped the Christian Mind: Rediscovering the African Seedbed of Western Christianity*. Downers Grove, IL: InterVarsity, 2007.

24

Reformation and Counter-Reformation

This book is about how the Messiah has accomplished redemption through the course of human history. We have seen that the Messiah is the agent of redemption, at the behest of the Father, who is the God of Israel, and that the Father also uses the Spirit in the process. As Irenaeus put it, the Son and the Spirit are the two hands of God to redeem sinners.

In the sixteenth century the *process* of redemption came under intense scrutiny. An Augustinian friar named Martin Luther (1483–1546) started to charge that late medieval theologians had gotten the process wrong. The result was that human beings were exalted and God was diminished. Too much had been made of what a human being does in the process, and too little of what God does. In fact, he alleged, it seemed that people were redeeming themselves and God was merely the spectator in the end. That was awfully close to pagan ideas of redemption. The Church in the West divided over the protests that Luther started, with Protestants separated from Catholics to this day. In this chapter we will look at these new ideas and focus on what Luther and other Protestants focused on: justification, or the means by which a holy God accepts sinners into his holy kingdom.

Late Medieval Theologians

Luther called justification "the summary of all Christian doctrine."[1] For, he reasoned, if we get this wrong, then everything that follows is also wrong. Conversely,

---

1. The original statement is in Latin in his Galatians commentary: "Siquidem amisso articulo iustificationis amissa est simul tota doctrina Christiana." Martin Luther, *In epistolam S. Pauli ad Galatas*

if justification was conceived rightly, then the rest of theology stood a better chance of being biblical and orthodox. Much of what Luther thought went wrong can be traced back to theories of divinization articulated by Athanasius and Augustine. Divinization was the notion that in redemption men and women are gradually filled with God's own life, following the fathers' favorite verse, "Precious and great promises were given to us, so that through them you might become partakers of the divine nature" (2 Pet. 1:4).[2]

As this doctrine developed in the Middle Ages, particularly in the fourteenth and fifteenth centuries, the implication emerged that we are accepted by God only after we have become righteous by the infusion of God's holy nature. The problem for conscientious souls like Luther was their recognition of their deep sinfulness. What, he asked, if I don't sense this divine nature in me but self-seeking and sensuality instead? Does that mean I am damned and was never accepted or justified by God?

A second problem developed from the teaching of the Fourth Lateran Council (1215) that no sin will be forgiven by God unless it is confessed to a priest. Luther sometimes panicked that in his self-protective selfishness he had overlooked a mortal (leading to spiritual death) sin. After all, the Bible teaches that our own hearts are deceptive (Jer. 17:9). How can we be sure that we have known all our sins?

A third problem was raised by the fifteenth-century teaching of the German theologian Gabriel Biel, that God gives grace only to those who try their best. Again Luther worried. What if my self-deceptive mind convinces me I am doing my best when I really am not? How can I know?

Breakthrough

Luther's solution came from studying Paul's letters and biography. He came to see that Paul had his own breakthrough when he was trying to kill followers of the Jewish Messiah. Active rebellion, not trying his hardest to follow the Messiah, preceded Paul's conversion! Then he read Paul's words in Romans 5:6 that the Messiah died for the *ungodly*, not the godly. Luther concluded that God is not seeking religious and moral perfection before he bestows grace on a wandering

---

Commentarius [1531] 1535 (WA 40/1:48). WA refers to the German edition of Luther's works: *D. Martin Luthers Werke*, 58 vols. (Weimar: Bohlau, 1833–).

2. This and the next section are indebted to Alister E. McGrath, *Luther's Theology of the Cross: Martin Luther's Theological Breakthrough* (Oxford: Blackwell, 1985).

soul. Instead, he joins sinners to the Messiah even while they are fighting him! They are saved not because they are good but despite their being bad. The key to salvation is not moral goodness but believing in the work of the Messiah to save those who are ignoring or fighting him. Sinners must believe in the Messiah's works rather than their own.

Luther moved the discussion from the language of medicine to the language of the law court. Grace in justification was not a substance infused into a sick soul, as Athanasius and Augustine had suggested, but absolution pronounced by a judge to a guilty prisoner declaring him to be free of accusation. The judge *imputes* innocence to the prisoner because his guilt and penalty were taken by someone else. God accepts the righteousness of the Messiah, which Luther said is "alien" to our nature, and imputes it to us, making it ours. Our sins are not so much removed as no longer counting against us. This is what Luther called the "happy exchange." We exchange our sins and condemnation for the Messiah's righteousness and eternal life.

Inner versus Outer

For Augustine and his medieval disciples, in contrast, in justification we are *made* righteous on the inside. For Luther, however, the essential thing in justification is that God *declares* us righteous because of the righteousness of the Messiah, which is outside of us.

Catholics and Protestants talked past each other in the sixteenth century because they defined "justification" differently. Catholics used the word for both initial acceptance and the lifelong process of sanctification, but Protestants restricted the word to initial acceptance only. This is the principal reason why Protestants rejected inner change for justification of sinners and why Catholics thought Protestants were ignoring the need for inner renewal. Although Luther always accepted the need for sanctification and, like Catholics, sometimes merged the two terms into one, for the most part he restricted justification to initial acceptance by God and barred inner renewal from that. So he insisted that justification is not based on our inner healing from sinfulness but on what the Messiah accomplished on the cross and in his resurrection. Therefore, sinners seeking God must look not inside themselves but outside themselves, to the Messiah's work.

In the last century the debate over justification has centered on the difference between infusion and imputation. Protestant theologians have argued that justification is only about imputation, while Catholics, continuing to collapse sanctification into justification, have insisted that justification must also involve infusion. Protestants often point to Luther to seal their interpretation. But recently Finnish Lutheran scholars, working through previously underexamined Luther manuscripts, have shown that while Luther taught imputation, he did not neglect infusion. In his 1535 *Lectures on Galatians* the reformer wrote, "Where the confidence of the heart is present . . . there Christ is present. . . . This is the actual formal righteousness on account of which a man is justified."[3] Imputation for Luther, Tuomo Mannermaa argues, was not a legal fiction about a person who is no different after faith. Faith brings union with the Messiah, and God's love is then "poured into our hearts by the Holy Spirit" (Rom. 5:5). On this basis, says Mannermaa of Luther's view, the legal verdict of justification is pronounced.

Therefore, the difference between Augustine and Luther is not as sharp as Protestants have alleged. Luther did indeed emphasize the legal over the medicinal, and he insisted that sinners are justified even while they are fighting the Messiah as Paul did. But Luther would never agree with later Lutherans who have rejected the theory of infusion from any part of justification or rejected the need for sanctification to complete justification.

Calvin on Justification

John Calvin (1509–64) was a second-generation Protestant reformer who agreed with Luther on justification. He reaffirmed that God saves sinners, not good people, that God takes the initiative in salvation, that our good works do not save us but that the works of the Messiah do. He added two new emphases that propelled his followers on a different trajectory from Luther's. Unlike Luther, Calvin stressed predestination (Luther believed in predestination but chose not to talk about it much). For Calvin this doctrine is about God's priority, that we do not make the first move in our pilgrimage to God's kingdom, but that God always does, and that for the elect, which Calvin showed is a biblical concept in both Testaments, God chose them from before the creation. Yet Calvin also warned that it is better to think of predestination retrospectively than prospectively. That is, it is better to look back on one's journey to God and Church and realize that God started us on the journey and was guiding us every step of the way. It is dangerous, on the other hand, to speculate on *why* God chose us and not the neighbors

---

3. Luther, *Lectures on Galatians*, quoted in Tuomo Mannermaa, *Christ Present in Faith: Luther's View of Justification* (Minneapolis: Fortress, 2005), 27.

who seem hell-bent. Calvin also taught that we can know that we are among the elect if we see spiritual growth in our lives and if we accept orthodox doctrine and continue in the Church and her sacraments.

Calvin's second difference from Luther was his focus on sanctification. Since the word comes from the Latin *sanctus* (holy), it is a lifelong pursuit of holiness. It is always mixed with sin and never pure, he warned. It means we should regularly repent and die to our own desires. It involves cultivating our hearts with love and reverence for God, which flow from seeing his goodness to us: "I call piety that love conjoined with reverence for God which the knowledge of his benefits induces."[4]

For Calvin, then, justification is a gift of God to sinners that starts them on a long road to increasing holiness.

Anglicans

The renewed Church of England in the sixteenth century became best known for King Henry VIII's break from Rome and his six wives. The new Church was less well-known for its view of justification. Its early creed known as the Thirty-Nine Articles, codified in 1571, took what came to be seen as a Protestant position on justification, emphasizing the merit of the Messiah over human merit. It stated that we are accounted righteous only by the "merit of Christ" and not by our own works (art. 11) and that works before justification do not please God but in fact are sinful because they suggest refusal to accept the Messiah's righteousness (art. 13). Works before justification do not "deserve" what medieval theologians called a "grace of congruity," which would put God in the debt of human beings so that he is bound to confer salvation. Yet the Articles also contained catholic notes. Good works, they assert, are necessary to make true faith known (art. 12), and predestination for the elect is claimed without Calvin's predestination of the damned (art. 17).

Richard Hooker (1554–1600), the premier Anglican theologian of the English Reformation, is similarly balanced between Geneva and Rome. This can be seen in his famous 1586 sermon on justification in London. First he rejected the idea, held by both Puritans and Catholics in his day, that one can be saved only by holding to all their distinctive doctrines. The essential thing is holding on to Jesus Messiah as Lord and Savior. One can hold false doctrine, either Roman or Puritan, and still be saved as long as one retains that essential.

---

4. John Calvin, *Institutes of the Christian Religion*, ed. John T. McNeill, trans. Ford Lewis Battles, 2 vols., Library of Christian Classics 20–21 (Philadelphia: Westminster, 1960), 1.2.1 (p. 1:41).

Hooker is well known for his subtlety, and on justification he is no less subtle by distinguishing three different kinds of righteousness—the glorifying righteousness of human beings in the world to come, which is perfect; justifying righteousness, which is perfect but not inherent; and sanctifying righteousness, which is inherent but not perfect.

Hooker struck Protestant notes by restating that we cannot be justified by inherent righteousness, for justifying righteousness is from the Messiah, not ourselves. God puts away our sins by not imputing them to us. He accepts us as perfectly righteous because of the Messiah's righteousness and treats us as if we have fulfilled all that is commanded by the law. Hooker cited 2 Corinthians 5:21, "He [God] has made him to be sin who knew no sin, so that we might become the righteousness of God in him."

Hooker said that Rome perverted the truth of the Messiah by teaching justification by inherent righteousness. Hooker never denied inherent sanctification but denied that this is the righteousness of justification, which comes, he preached, from the faith of Abraham and is the righteousness that comes "not through the law but through the righteousness of faith" (Rom. 4:13).

Yet while striking distinctly Lutheran and therefore Protestant chords, Hooker also sounded catholic chimes. He proclaimed that Catholics can be saved since their teaching grasps the essential of the Messiah's work for our salvation. Salvation, he warned, is more complex than Puritans and Lutherans would concede. For salvation is not by Christ alone apart from our justifying faith. Nor is it by Christ alone apart from our works for sanctification. The implication of the latter was that baptism and later professions of faith do not guarantee salvation if there is backsliding that is never repented—that is, no further sanctification. Neither does Christ alone save from faith alone apart from works, as James teaches (James 2:24).

So for Hooker salvation is a complex affair. Involved in the process or journey are calling, justifying, sanctifying, and glorifying. In each of these steps along the way Messiah works alone, but not *without* these steps and components. None other than the great theologian of salvation, Paul the apostle, taught this same complexity of process (Rom. 8:30; 1 Cor. 1:30).

Anabaptists

Anabaptists got their name from their Catholic and Lutheran enemies, who mocked them for their re(ana)baptizing. For Lutherans and Catholics and Calvinists, infant baptism was good for life. The Anabaptists said baptism is a profession of faith, which infants cannot make, so all those baptized as babies must be rebaptized once they come to intelligent faith.

On justification, Anabaptists sounded almost Catholic in their emphasis on human works. This came from the Anabaptist fixation on discipleship as the center of the Christian life. Relationship with Jesus Messiah "must go beyond inner experience and acceptance of [orthodox] doctrines. It must involve a daily walk" and transformed lifestyle.[5]

Menno Simons (1496–1561), the greatest Anabaptist theologian, did not like Luther's doctrine of justification by faith alone because it seemed to downplay works. Simons denounced Luther's dismissal of the book of James as an "epistle of straw." "What bold folly! If the doctrine is straw, then the chosen apostle, the faithful servant and apostle of Christ who wrote and taught it, must also have been a strawy man; that is as clear as the noonday sun. For the doctrine shows the character of the man."[6]

On the other hand, Menno was impressed by Luther's stress on the cross, that we are saved by what the Messiah did there. He also liked Calvin's doctrine of sanctification and its corollary that a true believer will grow in grace, persevering until the end of life. But whereas Luther and Calvin stressed the objective side of salvation—that we are saved by what the Messiah did and not what we do and that a different kind of outward life results from the new birth—Menno emphasized the interior process of salvation. He particularly stressed the necessity of the experience of the new birth as the prerequisite to water baptism.

For Menno and Anabaptists, then, justification was not for babies (although they believed God would take babies to heaven if they died). It was the beginning by faith of a life of discipleship marked by good works. Without those good works there was no justification.

The Council of Trent

Cardinal Pole of England opened the first session of the Council of Trent (1545–63) with the declaration that God sent the Protestants and Turks as punishment for Catholic sins. "We left the well of living waters," he confessed, "wishing to heal these ills [of church division] by our own power or prudence." Pole said that Catholic leaders like himself should be like Christ, "who took upon himself all the sins of all"

5. Bruce Shelley, *Church History in Plain Language* (Dallas: Word, 1995), 253.
6. Menno Simons, *The Complete Writings of Menno Simons*, ed. John Wenger (Scottdale, PA: Herald, 1956), 333–34, quoted in Timothy George, *Theology of the Reformers*, 2nd ed.(Nashville: Broadman, 2013), 284.

because "we the shepherds . . . of these evils are in great part the cause." It was "our ambition, our avarice, our cupidity" that caused shepherds to be "driven from their churches, and the churches starved of the Word of God." Unless the Spirit comes to condemn "us before ourselves, we cannot profess that he has yet come to us."[7]

The session on justification published its decrees near the beginning of the council (1547), suggesting their importance. Many of the declarations show that the delegates were listening to Protestant criticisms. For example, the bishops declared that "faith is the beginning of human salvation, the foundation and root of all justification," because neither faith nor works "merit the grace of justification." Like Protestants, they asserted that neither nature nor law can liberate us through free will alone. Human beings freely assent and cooperate with that grace, but "man himself . . . does absolutely nothing while receiving . . . the illumination of the Holy Ghost." The bishops' confession of human inability sounded like something from Luther or Calvin: Man is not able "by his own free will and without the grace of God to move himself to justice [the Vulgate's *iustitia*, translation of the Greek *dikaiosynē* or righteousness] in His sight."[8]

The council's description of the event of justification rang the chimes of Protestant themes of Christ-centeredness and grace.

[Adults] are disposed to that justice when, aroused and aided by divine grace, receiving *faith by hearing*, they are moved freely toward God, believing to be true what has been divinely revealed and promised, especially that the sinner is justified by God *by his grace, through the redemption that is in Christ Jesus*; and when, understanding themselves to be sinners, they, by turning themselves from the fear of divine justice, by which they are salutarily aroused, to consider the mercy of God, are raised to hope, trusting that God will be propitious to them for Christ's sake; and they begin to love him as the fountain of all justice, and on that account are moved against sin by a certain hatred and detestation, that is, by that repentance that must be performed before baptism; finally, when they resolve to receive baptism, to begin a new life and to keep the commandments of God.[9]

The bishops added that sinners must have faith "in his blood for our sins" and that this faith requires a new birth: "If [human beings] were not born again in

---

7. Hans Hillerbrand, ed., *The Reformation: A Narrative History Related by Contemporary Observers and Participants* (Grand Rapids: Baker, 1987), 462, 463, 464, 465.

8. "Sixth Session: Justification," in *Canons and Decrees of the Council of Trent*, trans. H. J. Schroeder (Rockford, IL: Tan Books, 1978; first published in 1941), 35, 32.

9. "Sixth Session: Justification," 32.

Christ, they would never be justified, since in that new birth there is bestowed upon them, through the merit of His passion, the grace by which they are made just." All of this happens by God's initiative, not ours: "The beginning of that justification must proceed from the predisposing grace of God through Jesus Christ, that is, from His vocation [calling], whereby, without any merits on their part, they are called."[10]

Causes of Justification

Like Hooker, the fathers at Trent saw justification as a complex entity whose causes were many. Using Aristotelian models of causation, they wrote that the final causes of justification are the glory of God and Christ and eternal life. Its efficient cause is the merciful God, who washes and sanctifies by grace; its meritorious cause, our Lord Jesus Christ, who merited justification by his passion on the cross and made satisfaction for us to God the Father; its instrumental cause, baptism; and its formal cause, God's justice, which renews the spirit of our minds.

Like Luther, the Tridentine fathers stated that in justification we are not only imputed by God to be just but we also receive justice (again, their word for righteousness) within us. They quoted the same Pauline verse that Luther did (Rom. 5:5) about God's love being poured by the Holy Spirit into the hearts of those who are justified. Therefore, they argued, faith, hope, and charity are infused at the same time into the hearts of the justified. Faith alone, they added, does not unite us to the Messiah without hope and charity. For faith without works is dead (James 2:17, 20), and Jesus said that to enter life we must keep the commandments (Matt. 19:17).

Rejection of Protestant Justification

The fathers rejected Protestant assurance of salvation and knowledge of one's predestination. They denied that the ordinary Christian can have such certainty about one's salvation and warned that it is dangerous to presume that one will persevere to the end. It is true, they wrote, that he who began a good work will perfect it, working in us to desire and accomplish his work (Phil. 1:6; 2:13). But Scripture also admonishes those who think they stand to take heed lest they fall (1 Cor. 10:12) and to work out their salvation with fear and trembling (Phil. 2:12).

Departing from Calvin (though not Luther), they taught that one can have justification and then lose it by mortal sin. But one can be justified again, they hastened

10. "Sixth Session: Justification," 31.

to add, through the sacrament of penance and the merits of the Messiah. In fact, according to Trent, a person can increase in justification. They said this because, as we have already seen, they saw justification as including both regeneration and sanctification. This was actually a Protestant truism that one increases in sanctification. But because Protestants usually failed to understand what Catholics meant by the word "justification" and thought of it as simply legal acquittal pronounced by God, it made no sense to them to increase in it. How could one grow in acquittal? They missed the fact that they actually agreed with Catholics on growth in sanctification.

Catholics were guilty of their own misunderstandings, thinking that Protestants were not dedicated to obedience because of their belief in justification by faith alone. By the (unbiblical) phrase "by faith alone," they meant that works do not help us gain acquittal; only our faith in the Messiah's works does that. The Anglican condemnation of all works prior to justification did not help. But the bishops at Trent did not pay enough attention to this distinction and therefore doubled down on the need for obedience to God's commandments. As if Protestants were suggesting antinomianism, Trent warned that no one "should consider himself exempt from observance of the commandments."[11]

Nor, they intoned, should any Christian say that obedience to the commandments is impossible. Scripture teaches that God's commandments are not burdensome (1 John 5:3), and Jesus said his yoke is sweet and his burden light (Matt. 11:30). Hence he expects us to obey him: "If anyone loves me, he will keep my word" (John 14:23). No one should flatter himself with faith alone if he is not suffering with the Messiah, for Paul warned that we are heirs of Christ provided that we suffer with him (Rom. 8:17). Trent implicitly criticized Calvin by adding that it is wrong to say that the just person sins in every good work.

So Trent emphasized what its fathers thought the Protestants were neglecting, the necessity of good works. The bishops also corrected what they deemed was an unbiblical denunciation of rewards. Eternal life is promised in Scripture, they insisted, as a reward for good works and merit. Not that merit is ours alone, for merit is infused into us through the merit of the Messiah. It is only by infused strength from Christ that the justified do good works. Far be it from a Christian to trust or glorify himself and not the Lord. But Paul teaches in Romans that God will render to every person according to their works (2:6).

The decree on justification closed with anathemas. They were divided between what we might say reinforced Protestant assertions about justification and those

---

11. "Sixth Session: Justification," 36.

that strengthened Catholic reminders. Among the Protestant themes were anathemas against those saying persons can be justified before God by their own works or natural power or against the teaching of the Law without divine grace. Another was against those who say that forgiveness comes only by believing "with certainty and without any hesitation arising from his own weakness," missing the human imperfection in all faith.[12]

On the Catholic side was an anathema against those saying that a person's will in no way cooperates with the grace of justification or that the human will is merely passive in justification. Another was against those who say that before justification human free will is lost or destroyed, and there was one against those who say justification is only by imputation and not also infusion of grace and love. Other anathemas condemned the notions that the Ten Commandments are not for Christians, that eternal life does not have the condition of keeping the commandments, or that the Messiah was not also a legislator whom we are to obey.[13]

Redemption and Justification

We might be justified in thinking that God permitted the division of the Western Church in the sixteenth century for one reason if not others, to correct previous false doctrines and clarify right thinking about redemption by the Messiah. The false doctrine was that our own good works save us and that Jesus merely ratifies our good decisions or that redemption is a human work that the Messiah simply illustrated. Or that although the Messiah died for our sins, the justified are those who try hard enough to follow him, so that it is our efforts that persuade God to save us. No, the Reformation and Counter-Reformation agreed that even our best efforts to please God are useless to save us, and only the Holy Spirit can open our eyes to start our journey out of bondage to sin and toward freedom in the Messiah. This agreement was highlighted by Lutheran and Catholic theologians in their groundbreaking *Joint Declaration on the Doctrine of Justification* in 1999[14] and in an earlier statement (1997) on justification ("The Gift of Salvation") by the group called Evangelicals and Catholics Together.[15]

12. "Sixth Session: Justification," 42, 44.

13. "Sixth Session: Justification," 42, 43, 44.

14. *Joint Declaration on the Doctrine of Justification* (1999), Lutheran World Federation, https://www.lutheranworld.org/what-we-do/unity-church/joint-declaration-doctrine-justification-jddj#.

15. Evangelicals and Catholics Together, "The Gift of Salvation," *First Things* 79 (January 1998): 20–23, https://www.leaderu.com/ftissues/ft9801/articles/gift.html.

The sixteenth-century division and debate help us to see that distinctions are necessary. Redemption by the Messiah, while simple in the sense that Messiah does the work, is not simplistic in the sense that its depth can be rendered by one phrase. "By Christ alone," for example, misses the necessity for faith that works by love (Gal. 5:6) and the need for the human will to "work out [our] own salvation with fear and trembling" while recognizing that it is "God at work within you both to will and to work for his good pleasure" (Phil. 2:12–13).

The distinctions between imputation and infusion are not only theological markers, sadly, between some kinds of Protestants and Catholics, but also help-ful reminders of the legal work that Messiah did outside of us and the curative work he does inside of us. The distinction between justification and sanctification refreshes our knowledge of the difference between the beginning of redemption in a person's life and the completion of that work through the rest of their life. The biblical term "predestination" reminds us that God planned the redemption of his elect before the foundation of the world. And reflections by Anglicans like Hooker reassure us that at the end of the day and our lives, it is not correct theology but the Messiah in his love that saves us. We don't have to have assurance of salvation or precise theological knowledge to be redeemed with certainty and precision by Jesus our Messiah.

Select Bibliography

George, Timothy. *Theology of the Reformers.* 2nd ed. Nashville: Broadman, 2013.

Hillerbrand, Hans, ed. *The Reformation: A Narrative History Related by Contemporary Observers and Participants.* Grand Rapids: Baker, 1987.

Mannermaa, Tuomo. *Christ Present in Faith: Luther's View of Justification.* Minneapolis: Fortress, 2005.

McGrath, Alister E. *Luther's Theology of the Cross: Martin Luther's Theological Breakthrough.* Oxford: Blackwell, 1985.

Oberman, Heiko. *Luther: Man between God and the Devil.* New Haven: Yale University Press, 1989.

"Sixth Session: Justification." In *Canons and Decrees of the Council of Trent,* translated by H. J. Schroeder, 29–46. Rockford, IL: Tan Books, 1978. First published in 1941.

25

The Western Church
since the Enlightenment

Since the Enlightenment of the eighteenth century, Christians have been confronted with a number of pressing issues that have forced them to rethink redemption and its history. In this chapter we will examine what are perhaps the five most pressing—the rise of revivalism in the eighteenth-century awakenings; liberalism rooted in appeals to human experience; Darwinism in the nineteenth century, which called into question the biblical story of creation; religious pluralism, which seemed (to some) to challenge the uniqueness of the Messiah; and the notion of development of doctrine.

The Eighteenth-Century Awakenings: Revivals and the History of Redemption

In 1734 in the western Massachusetts city of Northampton teenagers and twenty-somethings started getting serious about God. Before this point they had been like most young people in the modern era, showing more interest in parties and the opposite sex than religion. Their preacher, Jonathan Edwards (1703–58), wrote that the town generally was characterized by "licentiousness . . . and lewd practices." But suddenly, he wrote, "the Spirit of God began extraordinarily to set in," and people began to think earnestly about "the eternal world."[1]

---

1. Jonathan Edwards, *A Faithful Narrative*, in *The Great Awakening*, vol. 4 of *The Works of Jonathan Edwards* (New Haven: Yale University Press, 1972), 146, 149.

Changes came over young and old alike. "There was scarcely a single person, old or young, left unconcerned; the work of conversion was carried on in an astonishing manner; souls did, as it were, come by flocks to Jesus Christ."[2] This was the Little Awakening of 1734–35, which swept up and down the Connecticut River valley.

The Great Awakening of 1741–42 spread far wider, from Maine in the north to Georgia in the south. Its principal revivalist was George Whitefield (1714–70), whom Harry Stout has called America's first celebrity. Benjamin Franklin was one of his biggest fans, marveling at how Whitefield's audiences hung on to every word and often wept, even though, as Franklin put it, Whitefield called them "half beasts and half devils."[3] People said Whitefield, trained for the London stage by famed actor David Garrick, could bring a grown man to tears by saying the word "Mesopotamia." Because of that training, Whitefield was able to address crowds of ten thousand and twenty thousand with no sound system and have them guffawing one moment and weeping the next.

One of the other great preachers of the Awakening was Edwards himself. He never finished his sermon "Sinners in the Hands of an Angry God" at Enfield, Connecticut, on July 8, 1741, because people were crying out in fear that the earth would open and swallow them up. This was the match that set on fire dry timber of spiritual hunger up and down the Eastern Seaboard. Historians agree that the American Revolution might never have occurred without the Awakening. Before this revival people thought of themselves as Virginians and New Yorkers and Massachusettsites, but after the Awakening they called themselves Americans. For vast numbers in each colony had a common experience of the new birth. This gave the colonials a unity they had previously lacked.

As I wrote in the first chapter of this book, Edwards believed that revivals are the key to the history of redemption. Religious awakenings and reformations have been the engine that drives history, and especially the history of redemption. Edwards saw this in Israel's history, where covenant renewals under leaders like Moses, Joshua, David, Hezekiah, and Josiah were religious revivals that led to the expansion of redemption. Other revivals that changed the course of history, according to Edwards, were the rise of the early Church under Jesus and the apostles, the continuing revival of this Jesus movement that eventually overthrew

---

2. Edwards, *A Faithful Narrative*, 150.

3. *Benjamin Franklin's Autobiography: An Authoritative Text*, ed. J. A. Leo Lemay and P. M. Zall (New York: Norton, 1986), selection reprinted by National Humanities Center in 2009: http://national humanitiescenter.org/pds/becomingamer/ideas/text2/franklinwhitefield.pdf.

the pagan Roman Empire, and the development of the Church after Constantine, which set up the nations of early modern Europe. Edwards believed that the Reformation was another revival that, as we saw in the last chapter, helped sharpen understandings of how redemption is effected. Then there was the Great Awakening, which led to the rise of the American nation, and the Civil War, which historians say would not have occurred without the Second Great Awakening, which precipitated the abolitionist movement.

But Edwards emphasized that the line of progress through revivals is neither straight nor pleasant. His *History of the Work of Redemption* begins with the theme of suffering, the idea that, as he puts it later in the work, "every true Christian has the spirit of a martyr."[4] The story of redemption always involves the conflict between good and evil, strife between the righteous and the wicked. But this history of redemption is less the triumph of Jesus-believers over their enemies than the triumph of God himself.

Interestingly, for Edwards the Antichrist is an apostate rather than a pagan. He is someone with experience in the community of faith. His rise at the end of history is preceded by many "types" of the Antichrist, little antichrists who imitate his patterns of pride and persecution. Because of the many antichrists in the history of redemption, the pattern of development of the history of redemption is complex and convoluted. It is cyclical and meandering at the same time, like the movement of a corkscrew, which turns round and round but progressively pushes forward.

Edwards noted that the Church has often seemed to be approaching the brink of ruin, when all seemed lost with hope gone. But the darkest hour, he reminded his readers, comes just before the dawn. God has a habit of bringing glory out of the destruction of excellence. And despite the seeming recurrence of tragedy and deliverance, there is movement forward. Each successive era is closer to the glorious consummation than the ones that came before.

Edwards compared the history of redemption to a huge river with innumerable branches, each with "diverse and contrary courses" eventually discharging themselves at the mouth of the river into the same ocean. The different streams look like "jumble and confusion" to us because we cannot see from one branch to another. Neither can we see the whole system of the river at once, so as to see how all are "united as one." The courses of the different streams seem "very crooked." If we look from a distance, it seems there are "innumerable obstacles

---

4. Edwards, *HWR*, 454.

and impediments." Yet they all unite at last. Their "partial discords" finally emerge into "universal concords."[5]

Michael McClymond has written that for Edwards the history of redemption shows no straightforward, linear advance but a tortuous and obscure path of gains and losses. It is full of afflictions and deliverances, promised yet deferred fulfillments. Yet it is intelligible nonetheless. Edwards disagreed with Gibbon and Voltaire, who both were agnostic on history's ultimate outcome. The American theologian was convinced we can know from Scripture history's outcome. It is like a mystery novel in which the conclusion explains everything that precedes. We know from the Bible that the Messiah will conquer his opposition at the end of history, and he will rule with his saints.[6]

Liberalism and Human Experience

During the debates over the revivals in the eighteenth century, the role of human experience in redemption came to the fore. Liberal critics like Charles Chauncy (1705–87) denounced the revivals as the excrescence of human passion, while revivalists like James Davenport (1716–57) reveled in their intense emotions and denounced the intellect as a source of delusion. In the nineteenth century the Romantic movement proclaimed that the root of authentic religion was in the emotions. The father of liberal theology, Friedrich Schleiermacher (1768–1834), deeply influenced by this movement, held that the essence of religion was *Gefühl*, a feeling of absolute dependence. Edwards's profound writings on religious affections addressed all the issues in these debates over the role of human experience in true religion.

Edwards charged, first, that both critics and proponents of the Awakening misunderstood the role of the intellect in true religion. He rejected all dichotomies that set the mind against the heart, and he proposed that religion is centered in the *affections* instead. The affections, he argued, are something like what previous generations called the *soul*, where the unity of a person is found in their inclinations or loves, which drive the thoughts of the mind, the feelings of the emotions, and the choices of the will. While "Old Lights" opposing the Awakening claimed to favor reason against emotions, "New Lights" favoring the revivals tended to criticize reason while promoting emotions. Edwards argued that both sides missed

5. Michael McClymond and Gerald McDermott, *The Theology of Jonathan Edwards* (New York: Oxford University Press, 2012), 240–41.

6. McClymond and McDermott, *Theology of Jonathan Edwards*, 233–43.

the harmony in biblical psychology, which unites every person in his basic loves, which determine the mind, will, and feelings.

Emotions, then, are only one dimension of religious experience and therefore redemption. Sometimes the redeemed must choose *against* their feelings, as when Jesus chose to go to the cross *despite* his feelings. Emotions that overwhelm our judgment such as a fit of rage are opposed to true religious experience in the redeemed.

The problem with many interpretations of redemption is that they isolate the emotions or the will and posit the center of the person there. In contrast, Edwards kept insisting that the human person is a unity centered in the affections. He rejected the threefold division of the person into mind, will, and emotions, which went back to Plato and became popular in later faculty psychology. He also rejected a hard dichotomy between the will and affections, where theorists pit the will against the affections, with the will as final arbiter. This is incoherent, said Edwards, because the will cannot determine itself apart from the mind and its loves. If it could, there would have to be a second will telling the first what to do. On the contrary, every choice of the will is informed by the mind and comes out of the basic loves of the soul.

The unity of persons is found in their affections, their most basic love for God or self. Edwards was like Augustine, who divided the City of God from the City of Man on the same basis, love—love for God at the expense of self in the City of God and love for self at the expense of God in the City of Man. One's strongest loves, for Augustine, are the "gravity" that points the self either up toward God or down to the world. Love for self and world is the counterfeit love that for Edwards is at the heart of all false religion.

Edwards and Schleiermacher on Experience

Liberal religion in the eighteenth century was systematized by Friedrich Schleiermacher. For Schleiermacher, the father of liberal theology, religious experience is the source of redemption. But is this true redemption? It will help to compare Edwards and Schleiermacher on this question. They were agreed that the human person is unified by affections, basic loves. They also agreed that the essence of religion is not in the will (ethics) or the intellect (doctrine). Neither accepted religious experience at face value; each believed experience must be evaluated critically.

The similarities stop there. Whereas Schleiermacher focused on religious experience in general, Edwards restricted his scrutiny to experience involving claims

about the Messiah and his redemption. The German theologian limited himself
to the anthropological horizon, convinced that we cannot know God objectively.
All we know, he asserted, is God's relation to us through our feeling of absolute
dependence. Edwards, on the other hand, proclaimed that we can have objective
knowledge of God through Scripture.

For Schleiermacher, Scripture consists of human reflection on religious
experience. Since our experience tells us nothing about the Trinity or virgin
birth or second coming, and only dimly about miracles, he left little to no
room in his systematics for the first three and only tentatively for the last.
Theology for Schleiermacher is a reflection on religious experience, not on
the words of Scripture.

Edwards did not ignore religious experience. In fact he published numerous
accounts by believers of their conversions. He was more critical of experience
than Schleiermacher and did more public analysis of concrete experiences than
the German thinker. This is why the Schleiermacher scholar Richard R. Niebuhr
has observed that Schleiermacher "falls below the standard set by Jonathan Edwards in his sensitivity and perspicacity in the realm of the Christian and religious
affections."[7]

The two differed on anthropology and epistemology. For Schleiermacher there
is only one kind of human being, and everyone in this species has an inbuilt
God-consciousness. But for Edwards there are two kinds, and they are radically
distinct—the regenerate, who have gone through a miraculous new birth after
being dead in their sins, and the unregenerate, who have never seen the beauty of
God in the Messiah because they have not experienced the new birth.

The same goes for epistemology, how we know what is true. For Schleiermacher
there is only one way, an inborn God-consciousness, which teaches all human beings their dependence on the universe if they reflect on that natural consciousness.
But for Edwards there are two ways of knowing, one for those who have only this
consciousness and another for those who receive the miraculous gift of spiritual
vision, which enables them to see the beauty of Jesus.

Modern Science and Creation

If the eighteenth century opened the question of experience in redemption, the
nineteenth century saw new questions about the relation of science to redemption.

7. Richard R. Niebuhr, *Schleiermacher on Christ and Religion* (New York: Scribner, 1964), 17.

Charles Darwin's (1809–82) theory of natural selection made many wonder if God was necessary to creation, which led to follow-up questions about redemption. If the world came about on its own, then could human beings be redeemed on their own by their own efforts?[8]

Some answers started to appear in the twentieth century as scientists explored one of the biggest mysteries in biology specifically and science generally—how life arose in the first place. Evolutionist Richard Dawkins admitted in 2008 that "no one knows" the answer to this question.[9] In *Signature in the Cell*, Stephen C. Meyer writes, "Leading scientists—Francis Crick, Fred Hoyle, Paul Davies, Freeman Dyson, Eugene Wigner, Klaus Dose, Robert Shapiro, Dean Kenyon, Leslie Orgel, Gerald Joyce, Hubert Yockey, even Stanley Miller—[have] all expressed skepticism either about the merits of leading theories, the relevance of prebiotic experiments, or both." One of the popular theories was based on prebiotic simulation experiments in which scientists such as Stanley Miller tried to simulate the production of amino acids and other building blocks for life on the early earth. But in every case "undesirable by-products [reacted] with desirable building blocks to form inert compounds, such as a tar called melanoidin"—without the intervention of the scientist. Whatever success these experiments had always relied on manipulating "chemical conditions both before and after performing 'simulation' experiments." No life arose without the activity of a conscious, deliberate mind from the outside.[10]

Evolutionary algorithms supposedly showed "the creative power of mutation and selection . . . to generate functional information" for early cells. But to the extent that any algorithm modeled a realistically biological process, it depended on an information-rich instruction set provided by computer programmers. In other words, in no case did an experiment or computer model successfully show the possibility of life coming from random mutations and natural selection alone.[11]

Alister McGrath, who holds a PhD in molecular biology from Oxford University, argues that RNA and DNA are such complex structures that the probability of

---

8. This section on science and creation above is adapted from a few pages in the chapter on science, Gerald McDermott, "Science: The Wonder of the Universe," chap. 4 in *Everyday Glory: The Revelation of God in All of Reality* (Grand Rapids: Baker Academic, 2018). Used by permission of Baker Publishing Group.

9. Richard Dawkins, interview by Ben Stein, in *Expelled: No Intelligence Allowed*, documentary film, directed by Nathan Frankowski, Premise Media Corporation, 2008

10. Stephen C. Meyer, *Signature in the Cell: DNA and the Evidence for Intelligent Design* (New York: HarperOne, 2009), 334–35.

11. Meyer, *Signature in the Cell*, 335–37.

their arising spontaneously is "widely conceded to be vanishingly small." McGrath recalls Hoyle's warning: "The chance that higher life forms might have emerged in this way is comparable with the chance that a tornado sweeping through a junk-yard might assemble a Boeing 747 from the materials therein." McGrath thinks Hoyle overstates his case a bit, neglecting "the apparent capacity for self-organization within the biochemical world." Yet he also shows that there is a massive gap between the origin of carbon, nitrogen, and oxygen in stellar cores and the origins of life itself. Therefore, he concludes that the origins of life "are unquestionably anthropic." They require the fundamental constants of nature to have been fine-tuned in ways that suggest an intelligent designer. In and of itself the Big Bang was not capable of producing the basic building blocks—carbon, nitrogen, and oxygen. The formation of stars needed the gravitational constant, and the weak nuclear force could not have been different by one one-hundredth, or life would never have been possible.[12]

Physicist Stephen Barr argues that natural selection is insufficient to explain life because it requires life for it to be able to operate. In other words, it requires self-reproducing organisms that are able to pass on their traits genetically. How can it produce the first life if it needs life to operate? Another problem is that even the first "primitive" life form was enormously complicated. It appears to have had an elaborate structure involving dozens of different proteins, a genetic code containing at least 250 genes, and many tens of thousands of bits of information. "For chemicals to combine in random ways in a 'primordial soup' to produce a strand of DNA or RNA containing such a huge amount of genetic information would be as hard as for a monkey to accidentally type an epic poem." Barr raises the possibility of an infinite number of planets making theoretically *possible* a monkey typing *Hamlet*, but then suggests this might be simply a way for skeptical scientists to avoid allowing the Divine Foot in the door.[13]

Barr concedes that there is evidence that natural selection has taken place. What he doubts is that natural selection is sufficient to drive the whole process of evolution. Take the Cambrian Explosion, he argues, a mere five-million-year period during which evolutionary changes took place one hundred times faster than any evolutionary scientists dreamed possible. It was not only the *time* that appears implausible but the *complexity* produced. The information required to

---

12. Alister McGrath, *A Fine-Tuned Universe: The Quest for God in Science and Theology*, The 2009 Gifford Lectures (Louisville: Westminster John Knox, 2009), 131, 134, 142.

13. Stephen M. Barr, *Modern Physics and Ancient Faith* (Notre Dame, IN: University of Notre Dame Press, 2003), 74–75.

put together a bacterium would fill the *Encyclopedia Britannica.* The human brain contains 100 million neurons, each of which is connected to as many as a thousand other neurons. It dwarfs in sophistication any computer we know. Yet this brain—think of that of Mozart, Shakespeare, Einstein—is said to have evolved from an ape's in five million years. Based on what evolutionary scientists have told us, this is impossible. The complexity that had to be produced in this short period of time is nearly unimaginable. To conceive of this vast complexity, Barr draws a comparison. Humans are capable of building a jumbo jet, he says, but nothing "as sophisticated as a housefly or a mosquito."

The bottom line is that when we look *down* at the tiniest parts of the living cell— the microcosm in contrast to the macrocosm of the universe—we find the same mysteries cosmologists find when looking *up.* It seems highly unlikely that either could have arisen by chance. Both seem to have required massive fine-tuning, and the cell's enormously complex information processing seems suspiciously preprogrammed. Both, that is, show the glory of God in his creation. Glory in the heavens above and glory in the cells below.

The implication for our study of the history of redemption is that, first, creation is important because it is the creation that is redeemed. Yet the self-creation of the universe is impossible. Physicists agree that a Big Bang started it all. But what led to the Big Bang? Where did the matter come from that exploded? These answers are no more clear than answers to the origins of life. Not all scientists agree that natural selection has occurred in the ways that Neo-Darwinists claim. Even those like Barr who acknowledge that it has occurred fail to see how it can explain the origins of life. We are left with two conclusions: first, that there is the same mystery we have found at important junctures in redemption history, and second, that we can certainly say that science can never provide certainty about the most basic questions of life.

Religious Pluralism and the Uniqueness of the Messiah

European exploration of Africa and Asia in the fifteenth and sixteenth centuries caused Jesus-followers to ask if he was just another religious founder who taught fear of God and love for fellow human beings. Was redemption by the Messiah simply another way of redemption alongside that of the Buddha or Confucius?

Gotthold Lessing (1729–81) knew of these European discoveries and was struck by the reports of Chinese who seemed virtuous without hearing the gospel. His conclusion was that "accidental truths of history can never become the proof of necessary truths of reason."[14] His conclusion illustrates the Enlightenment's conviction that ultimate meaning could be found only through general truths accessible to all times and all places. Since the gospel had not been made known in such a universal way, its particular assertions could not be taken seriously.

The problem with Lessing's rule was that Jesus was one of these accidents of history not in the sense that his appearance was unintended by God but in the sense that news of the incarnation was not known to every human being in history. Another problem was that no doctrine of any world religion fulfills Lessing's criterion. Take the notion that there is a god who controls the world. The Buddha did not teach that, and many Buddhists today are monists who reject the idea of a personal god who runs the cosmos. The same can be said for Hindu disciples of Advaita Vedanta, the most respected Hindu philosophical tradition, and for philosophical Daoists. If there is no single religious doctrine that all the world religions agree on, then for Lessing and the Enlightenment there is no necessary truth of reason that tells us about true religion. We are finally left agnostic and ignorant, without a clue to the meaning of reality.

Is it a problem that Jesus is a historical particularity, a man shaped by first-century Jewish culture? Not at all. Part of the beauty of the gospel is that Jesus was like us. Each one of us was shaped by a particular culture. But his obedience and sufferings were *for us*, who are from every culture and time. Each of us was limited by our time and place, and the Messiah, though he had all knowledge available to him, chose to live much of his life with limited knowledge like the rest of us. Because he shared our limitations, we can know that he understands us and that his sufferings were like ours. This is a redemption that not only liberates but comforts.

In the twentieth century John Hick's *God Has Many Names* (1980) made an argument similar to Lessing's. But rather than focusing on necessary truths of reason that cannot be found in any historical particularities, Hick argued that there is an essential sameness in every world religion. After he had visited mosques, synagogues, and temples, it seemed "evident to [him] that essentially the same kind of thing is taking place in them as in a Christian church—namely, human beings opening their minds to a higher divine Reality, known as personal and good and as demanding righteousness and love between man and man."[15]

The problem again is that there are major world religions that do *not* conceive of ultimate reality as personal. We have already mentioned the Buddha's original

14. Gotthold Ephraim Lessing, "The Proof of the Spirit and of Power," in *Lessing's Theological Writings*, ed. Henry Chadwick (London: Adam and Charles Black, 1956), 53.
15. John Hick, *God Has Many Names* (Philadelphia: Westminster, 1980), 17–18.

teaching, the Hindu philosophy of Advaita Vedanta, and philosophical Daoism of the *Dao De Jing*.

Pluralists like Lessing and Hick have said that Jesus-followers are arrogant to insist on our name for God when the name of any god reflects only local traditions. We must be tolerant of other religions and not think ours is better, because there is no one way to God.

This position is actually less than tolerant, because every religion teaches that it is the best way to God or whatever is ultimate. Gavin D'Costa has shown that even the Dalai Lama, who is famous for saying that no one should change her religion, tells insiders that the *best* way to spiritual ultimacy is by Tibetan Buddhism and that the best of the best ways is his *dge-lugs-pa* school of Tibetan Buddhism. Pluralists would say this *must* be wrong because no human conception of ultimacy can possibly be final. In effect, then, pluralists declare all the major religions arrogant because they all teach that only their way is right for reaching the highest level of reality. Is that not arrogant?

We see, then, that the world religions do not teach all the same thing. Let's say a bit more about the uniqueness of the Messiah and his redemption. No other religious founder claimed to be God in the flesh (even Hindus concede their avatars only appeared to be human). Whereas the Buddha confessed that he was no more than a man and said that we must be lamps unto ourselves, Jesus said that to see him was to see God and that he is the light of the world.

The Church's central claim, that the crucified Messiah rose from the dead, is unparalleled in the world religions. Although this cannot be proven to a skeptic with a closed mind, we have the testimonies of his followers that they thrust their fingers into the holes in the body of the risen Messiah and ate with him a breakfast of fish and bread. Neither ghosts nor hallucinations eat a fish sandwich.

No other religious founder came even close to promising salvation from sin, death, and the devil by a crucified Messiah who draws believers up into the life of a triune community of love. Nor does any other religious founder give Jesus's unique answers to the problem of pain. The Buddha taught his followers to escape suffering, whereas Jesus showed the way to conquer suffering by embracing it. This is why Buddhists look to a smiling Buddha seated on a lotus blossom while Jesus-followers worship a suffering Messiah nailed to a cross.

The redemption that the Messiah brought is unparalleled. While the world is smaller today because of technology that makes knowledge of other religions more available, we can easily see that nowhere else is there anything like Jesus's redemption. No other religion comes even close.

Looking Back: The Development of Doctrine

Another outcome of the modern era on believers' thinking about redemption was the idea of development of doctrine. This was most famously addressed by the Anglican theologian John Henry Newman in his *Essay on the Development of Christian Doctrine* (1845). He argued that the Holy Spirit directed the Christian community over the centuries in their understanding of the blinding revelations that came through Israel and the apostles. For example, as we have noted in previous chapters, the word "Trinity" is nowhere in the New Testament. Neither is the concept that has become accepted by nearly all churches across the world—one divine being in three divine Persons. It took the Church three hundred years of conflict and argument to finally agree on both the word and the concept. Newman concluded the Holy Spirit was guiding the Church through these first three centuries to understand the Godhead and that Jesus promised this before he ascended to the Father: "When the Spirit of truth comes, he will guide you into all the truth" (John 16:13).

All of the later doctrines proclaimed by universal councils such as Nicaea and Chalcedon go back to the Scriptures and early tradition. If they are not there explicitly, they are there in germ form according to Newman, and it sometimes takes centuries to tease them out in ways that help Christians respond to alien cultures.

The gist of Newman's proposal is that the principle of "antecedent probability" suggests that God would watch over his own work and direct and ratify those developments which faithfully explicate what he had revealed. Thus the Church, like its Lord, "increased in wisdom" (Luke 2:52). Like the human mind, which "cannot reflect upon [a great idea] except piecemeal," the Church must develop a great idea given in biblical revelation by a series of tests and conflicts.

Whatever the risk of corruption from intercourse with the world around, such a risk must be encountered if a great idea is duly to be understood, and much more if it is to be fully exhibited. It is elicited and expanded by trial, and battles into perfection and supremacy. . . . In time it enters upon strange territory; points of controversy alter their bearing; parties rise and fall around it; dangers and hopes appear in new relations; and old principles reappear under new forms. *It changes with them in order to remain the same. In a higher world it is otherwise, but here below to live is to change, and to be perfect is to have changed often.*[16]

16. John Henry Newman, *An Essay on the Development of Christian Doctrine*, ed. Ian Ker (Notre Dame, IN: University of Notre Dame Press, 1989), 100 (emphasis added). The previous paragraph is taken from Gerald McDermott, *The Great Theologians: A Brief Guide* (Downers Grove, IL: IVP Academic,

Newman saw the principle of development in the Scriptures. For example, YHWH told Abraham that he and his progeny would be a blessing to the nations, but the reality of this could be seen only later in Torah and the Historical Books, and then expanded even more in the Prophets. This is the principle, Newman explains, that God works out gradually what he has determined absolutely.

In the New Testament Newman pointed to Jesus's statement that he did not come to abolish the Law or the Prophets but to fulfill them (Matt. 5:17). This is another pattern in God's development of doctrine, that he does not reverse but perfects what has come before. Jesus's perfection of the Law is a development of the Law to its fuller meaning.

Newman believed that development of doctrine follows from the principle of the incarnation, which is the very heart of the good news. Just as the Word became flesh, the words of God become flesh in developed ideas as Church history progressed. For example, original sin is not taught in those words but has been adopted by the Western churches explicitly and, one might say, by the Eastern churches implicitly in their teaching that goodwill is inadequate and only grace will move us toward salvation. The Reformation and Counter-Reformation gave us new understandings of how we are saved in their debates over justification, the period of Protestant orthodoxy showed us in a new way what it means for the Bible to be inspired, and the last two centuries have shown Christians in fresh ways what it means to be the Church.

New Revelation?

Because Newman had been an evangelical in his youth, he pointed to evangelical beliefs that had come from development of doctrine. None was stated explicitly in the Bible, and each had to be developed from implications rather than explicit texts: the right to bear arms, the duty of public worship, the substitution of the first for the seventh day as Sabbath, infant baptism, and the Protestant idea of *sola scriptura* (using the Bible alone as authority for faith and practice). Newman was opposed to *sola scriptura* but wanted to show evangelicals that even their theological method was inferred from rather than taught explicitly by the Bible.

Was Newman teaching new revelation? No, he replied to critics, these were implications and developments of the revelation given to Israel and the Church.

2010), 158; several sentences below on "the principle of the incarnation" are from McDermott, *Great Theologians*, 160.

God is infinite and has infinite aspects, so we should not be surprised that it takes millennia to unpack them. The revelation of the infinite God "cannot, as it were, be mapped, or its contents catalogued; but after all our diligence, to the end of our lives and to the end of the Church, it must be an unexplored and unsubdued land, with heights and valleys, forests and streams, on the right and left of our path and close about us, full of concealed wonders and choice treasures."

Another objection was that Newman was uncritical, simply accepting every new development that comes along. Some ask today whether he would accept gay marriage as a faithful development of the original revelation of Israel and the apostles on love and marriage. The answer to this question would involve the use of Newman's sophisticated set of seven "notes" of faithful development—it must correspond to its rudiments, show a continuity of principle, assimilate and absorb, be a logical result of original teaching, be seen in earlier anticipations, conserve orthodox teaching from the past, and show energy and permanence.

In short, a faithful development is one that shows continuity with the original revelation. It develops rather than destroys that original revelation. In the case of gay marriage, it would not be difficult to see its contradiction to what Moses, Jesus, and Paul wrote about the union of a man and woman for procreation, illustrating the joining together of fundamental difference, the holy Messiah with his sinful body. In gay marriage there is no possibility of procreation and there is no fundamental difference. It is a sterile joining of sameness.

What are the implications of development of doctrine for the history of redemption? Among other things, it means that we should not expect the Messiah's community to rely on biblical prooftexts alone. If the Spirit was leading the Messiah's body over the last millennia, we would expect doctrines that are developments not found word-for-word in the Scriptures but consistent with those Scriptures. If a new proposed doctrine is inconsistent with major teaching of the Scriptures and the fathers, we should be wary.

Select Bibliography

Barr, Stephen M. *Modern Physics and Ancient Faith*. Notre Dame, IN: University of Notre Dame Press, 2003.

Dawkins, Richard. Interview by Ben Stein. In *Expelled: No Intelligence Allowed*. Documentary film. Directed by Nathan Frankowski. Premise Media Corporation, 2008.

D'Costa, Gavin. *The Meeting of Religions and the Trinity*. Maryknoll, NY: Orbis Books, 2000.

Hick, John. *God Has Many Names.* Philadelphia: Westminster, 1980.

Lessing, Gotthold Ephraim. "The Proof of the Spirit and of Power." In *Lessing's Theological Writings,* edited by Henry Chadwick, 51–56. London: Adam and Charles Black, 1956.

McClymond, Michael, and Gerald McDermott. "The Affections and the Human Person." In *The Theology of Jonathan Edwards,* 311–20. New York: Oxford University Press, 2012.

———. "Providence and History." In *The Theology of Jonathan Edwards,* 224–43. New York: Oxford University Press, 2012.

McDermott, Gerald. "Science: The Wonder of the Universe." Chap. 4 in *Everyday Glory: The Revelation of God in All of Reality.* Grand Rapids: Baker Academic, 2018.

———. *World Religions: An Indispensable Introduction.* Nashville: Nelson, 2011.

McDermott, Gerald, and Harold Netland. *A Trinitarian Theology of Religions: An Evangelical Proposal.* New York: Oxford University Press, 2014.

McGrath, Alister E. *A Fine-Tuned Universe: The Quest for God in Theology and Science.* Louisville: Westminster John Knox, 2009.

Meyer, Stephen C. *Signature in the Cell: DNA and the Evidence for Intelligent Design.* New York: HarperOne, 2009.

Newman, John Henry. *Essay on the Development of Christian Doctrine.* Notre Dame, IN: University of Notre Dame Press, 1989. First published 1845.

Niebuhr, Richard R. *Schleiermacher on Christ and Religion.* New York: Scribner, 1964.

Schleiermacher, Friedrich. *The Christian Faith.* Edited by H. R. Mackintosh. Philadelphia: Fortress, 1976.

Stout, Harry S. *Divine Dramatist: George Whitefield and the Rise of Modern Evangelicalism.* Grand Rapids: Eerdmans, 1991.

26

The Oxford Movement

In the nineteenth century in England a movement arose that has had continuing influence on Protestants and Catholics. It has also changed the views of many Jesus-followers concerning the redemption won by the Jewish Messiah. As a result of this movement both Protestants and Catholics have come to place more emphasis on the Church's role in redemption, especially its liturgy and sacraments. In this chapter we will look briefly at its history, dominant themes, and the ways these themes might help us understand the history of redemption.

A Brief History

The Reform Act of 1832 opened a new era in English history by admitting to the House of Commons Protestant dissenters (who did not accept the Church of England and its Prayer Book) and Irish Roman Catholics. Conservatives within the Church of England realized that sixteenth-century Anglican theologian Richard Hooker's vision of Parliament as England's (Anglican) people of God no longer worked. Then when Parliament reduced the number of Irish bishops by ten and diverted the moneys that would have come to them, Anglican priest and Oxford professor John Keble (1792–1866) was enraged. What now appeared to be a secular state was exercising authority over God's Church. In 1833 Keble preached a sermon in Oxford titled "National Apostasy" that started a movement called by the name of the university where most of its leaders studied and taught. Richard Hurrell Froude (1803–36) was an Oxford poet, Edward Bouverie

Pusey (1800–1882) was the Regius Professor of Poetry, and John Henry Newman (1801–90) was a fellow of Oriel College at Oxford and became the movement's early leader and then most famous thinker.

These Oxford men had been growing in their distaste for the liberal theology represented by the Noetics at Oxford's Oriel College, a famous group of intellectuals led by Richard Whately whose 1822 book promoted the value of healthy agnosticism. Whately argued that Scripture says nothing about how Jesus's disciples should be organized. Renn Hampden, Oxford's Regius Professor of Divinity, claimed that ethics is more important than dogma and that the purpose of revealed facts is to stimulate innate moral instincts. Oriel fellow Thomas Arnold proclaimed that the officers of a Christian state should see themselves as Christian ministers with authority to preach and administer the sacraments. To the leaders of the Oxford Movement, these liberals misrepresented God, the Church, and redemption.

Beginning in 1833 Newman and his band published a series of essays called Tracts for the Times, intended to rally both clergy and laity. The first three tracts, all by Newman, were on the apostolic succession (direct lineage for bishops from the apostles), the Church, and the liturgy. In 1834 there were thirty more, with the most important on the Church of England as the *via media* or middle way between Protestantism on the left and Rome on the right.

At the same time that these early tracts were gaining wide readership, Newman's Sunday afternoon sermons at St. Mary's in Oxford were attracting big crowds. They were so popular that Oxford colleges changed their dinner hour to keep students away from what was called "Newmania." These *Parochial and Plain Sermons*, later published in many editions, suggested "in the austere beauty of their prose that the messenger had received his message of the supreme importance of personal holiness from another world."[1]

Momentum for the movement kept building until tract 90 provoked sharp hostility. Written by Newman and titled *Remarks on Certain Passages in the 39 Articles*, it maintained that the Articles don't condemn worship practices widely known to be Catholic, only "Romish" excesses concerning purgatory, adoration of the sacrament, images, and relics. To many Anglicans, however, Newman now appeared to be anti-Protestant. Since England had feared Catholicism since its Reformation, when Cranmer and other reformers were burned at the stake by

---

1. Sheridan Gilley, "Keble, Froude, Newman, and Pusey," in *The Oxford Handbook of the Oxford Movement*, ed. Stewart J. Brown, Peter B. Nockles, and James Pereiro (Oxford: Oxford University Press, 2017), 99.

(Catholic) Queen Mary, and the 1605 Gunpowder Plot was believed to be a Catholic plan to assassinate the English king, many Anglicans now came to see the movement as Catholic rather than Protestant and therefore un-English. Pusey was suspended from preaching at Oxford for two years after saying that it was consistent with the Church of England to hold the Eucharist as a "commemorative sacrifice."[2] Newman took less of a public role and gathered a small community in semimonastic life outside Oxford. Several years later, in 1845, Newman was admitted to the Roman Catholic communion. After this point the movement reorganized around Pusey, the saintly scholar who wrote prolifically and continued to lead the "catholic" way that was neither Roman nor Calvinist.

Dominant Themes

The suppression of the Irish bishoprics set Keble on a new exploration of the meaning of "the Church." He and the other movement leaders started with this theme of the Church as a God-given supernatural society that is fundamentally independent of the state and governed by its own leaders, the bishops, who are successors to the apostles. Its clergy were threefold—bishops, priests, and deacons—and their most important task was the celebration of the Eucharistic sacrifice. Pusey's tract 81 was a three-hundred-page collection of extracts from sixty-five sources in the early fathers all the way up to the nineteenth century arguing that the Eucharist is a sacrifice which re-presents the Messiah's sacrifice to the Father.

This was an example of the movement's *high sacramental theology*. If the Eucharist was participation in the ongoing presentation of the sacrificed Lamb to the Father pictured in Revelation 4 and 5, necessary for holiness in believers, baptism was a new creation, the beginning of Christian life. Here, as H. E. Manning put it, "the gift of life [received in baptism] is not a power, a principle, but a very and true Person dwelling in us."[3] Newman argued that this is why the typical Protestant doctrine of justification is faulty. The primary instrument of justification is not faith alone but baptism. Baptism creates faith to be what it is, so faith is secondary to the sacraments. Justification is received by faith, which comes through baptism and brings God's inward presence, which must be nurtured by obedience.

2. J. R. H. Moorman, *A History of the Church of England*, 3rd ed. (Harrisburg, PA: Morehouse Publishing, 1980), 346.
3. H. E. Manning, *Sermons* (1851), 1:166–67, quoted in Aidan Nichols, O.P., *The Panther and the Hind: A Theological History of Anglicanism* (Edinburgh: T&T Clark, 1993), 125.

This nurture fosters *theōsis* or *divinization*, another major theme of the movement. Newman read the Greek fathers in the original language and learned from
them that following the Messiah in the life of the Church enabled participation
in the divine nature through sacraments and obedience. They put greater stress
on *the mystery of the incarnation* than the atonement per se, a Christ-centeredness
that stressed the gradually growing oneness of the believer with the Messiah in
mystical union. As the humanity of the Messiah participates in the divinity of
the Son of God, so too his disciples participate in his divinity, gradually growing
in holiness. This is why the movement was known for its strong devotion to the
person of Jesus, illustrated by the poems of Christina Rossetti, some put to music
like the classic hymn "In the Bleak Midwinter."

Rossetti's poems illustrate the theme of *mystery*, which the Oxford thinkers set
over against what they considered Roman oversystematization. Newman complained that "Rome would classify and number all things. She would settle every
sort of question, as if resolved to detect and compass by human reason what runs
out into the next world or is lost in this" (*The Via Media of the Anglican Church*).
In contrast, Pusey wrote in his *Lectures on Types and Prophecies*, "Greatness and
indistinctness commerce together."[4]

This is why, Newman wrote in *The Arians of the Fourth Century*, the early Church
practiced the *disciplina arcana* or what he and his followers called the principle of
reserve. The early Church, at least in the East, refused to teach all doctrine immediately to everyone. In fact they deliberately withheld talking about their greatest
mysteries to seekers, holding them in *reserve* for several years while seekers became proselytes enrolled in catechesis. The greatest mysteries were reserved until
baptism following (sometimes) three years of spiritual training. While previous
Anglican theologians had focused primarily on the Western fathers, where there
was less emphasis on reserve, Newman read deeply in the Eastern fathers, where
this principle was paramount.

The principle of reserve issued from the movement's conviction of the *personal
character of religious knowledge*, as Sheridan Gilley has termed it.[5] True knowledge
of the divine proceeds not intellectually in the strict sense but person to person,
from God to the believer and from one believer to another. Newman's motto was
"Heart speaks to heart."[6] In contrast to William Paley's use of evidences from
nature to prove divine design, the Oxford theologian subordinated reason and

4. Newman and Pusey are here quoted from Nichols, *The Panther and the Hind*, 122.
5. Gilley, "Keble, Froude, Newman, and Pusey," 99.
6. Gilley, "Keble, Froude, Newman, and Pusey," 99.

proof in religion to conscience, which imprints on the hearts of believers the moral law and images of God as ruler and judge. James Pereiro says Newman was influenced by the Cambridge Platonists, who insisted that reason has a subjective dimension, especially in the case of religious knowledge.

Pereiro shows that Keble reversed the Enlightenment view that intellectual education would lead to moral rectitude. The Oxford Movement leader denied that the search for truth, especially in religion and ethics, can be separated from the pursuit of goodness. Moral uprightness, he averred, is the fundamental condition for clear intellectual perception and therefore should be an aim of education at all levels. Keble quoted Jesus: "A good will to do His Will shall know of the doctrine if it is from God" (John 7:17).[7]

The tractarians were agreed that the Enlightenment was wrong to presume that the intellect apart from the moral will could know truth. They insisted on the determining influence of the will on the intellectual process in general and religious thought in particular. They believed that Vincent of Lérins's rule (the catholic faith has been believed everywhere at all times by all) was not, as Pereiro puts it for Froude, "of a precise mathematical nature" but moral. Therefore, determining what was the general view of the fathers for Newman and others "required a judgment based on probabilities, in which only the right *ethos* could serve as a sure guide."[8] Moral truth cannot be apprehended unless it is practiced. Obedience opens the door of understanding. The more conscientiously one follows the Messiah, the deeper and more stable the apprehension of truth.

Keble was most responsible for introducing the concept of *ethos*. By this he meant the spirit and atmosphere of a time and place. Froude and Newman developed the concept to suggest a body of oft-hidden intellectual, moral, and spiritual assumptions on which a set of beliefs is held, which count for more than explicit reasoning and argument. In other words, what is often more important than right doctrine is the right spirit of believing. The first might hide a stubborn will, while the second is the doorway to growth and holiness.

This *emphasis on holiness* is another mark of the movement. Holiness rather than peace is the goal of the believer's pilgrimage. The movement's William Ward wrote that only a Church having holiness in itself and in the lives of its saints can teach with an authority more than human. The tractarians pointed to holy saints all along its eighteen hundred years of Anglican history from Alban and Anselm

7. Quoted in James Pereiro, "The Oxford Movement's Theory of Religious Knowledge," in Brown, Nockles, and Pereiro, *Oxford Handbook*, 187.

8. Pereiro, "The Oxford Movement's Theory of Religious Knowledge," 195.

through Thomas Becket and Margery Kempe to its own leaders like Keble and Pusey.

These, then, are the themes that for the tractarians signaled the movement as *catholic but not Roman*. They argued that they held to the faith of the universal Church of Jesus-believers, especially in the first millennium. Pusey argued that Roman Catholics brought changes to that faith with transubstantiation and juridical purgatory. Others venerated Mary but objected to later Roman doctrines of her immaculate conception. The Anglican Newman was disturbed by the emerging Roman doctrine of papal infallibility. Saint Peter, he wrote, was not infallible at Antioch when Saint Paul disagreed with him, nor was Liberius, the bishop of Rome, when he excommunicated Athanasius.

But if the tractarians pushed back against Roman claims, they also resisted assertions that the *via media* was essentially Reformed or Protestant. As Aidan Nichols has observed, Newman faulted Luther and the Reformed on the principle of private judgment, charging that this was a cancerous growth at the heart of all Protestantism. Keble accused Protestants of a rationalist spirit that leads to false religion. Instead of private judgment—every Protestant deciding for himself what the Bible means based on *sola scriptura*—the Tractarians, argues Timothy Larsen, upheld the collective witness of the early Church fathers as the authoritative interpreter of the Scriptures. This might be why Brian Cummings writes that when the preface to the 1662 Prayer Book says, "It hath been the wisdom of the Church of England . . . to keep the mean between the two extremes," it meant the "'middle way' between the Catholic and Reformed traditions."[9]

The Oxford Movement and Redemption

The leaders of the Oxford Movement warned English Jesus-followers against subtle errors in thinking about the ways that the Messiah redeems souls. Their insistence on redemption through the Church was an admonition to reject the idea that all that matters is my personal relationship with Jesus. They remind us that the Messiah ministers through his whole Body, and we are courting eternal danger to think that we can follow Jesus without the encouragement and discipline of his Body. They suggest that we court Gnosticism if we think that redemption is all about what we believe in our heads rather than the matter of the sacraments

---

9. Brian Cummings, ed., *The Book of Common Prayer: The Texts of 1549, 1559, and 1662* (Oxford: Oxford University Press, 2011), 748.

and the bodies of other believers and their ministers. They warn us against a subtle Pelagianism in which we try hard to follow Jesus without realizing that the Messiah wants us to yield to his work of divinization within us. And we risk deception if we imagine that all that matters is an emotional experience years ago when what the Messiah wants of us is a long pilgrimage of self-denial and sacrifice, powered by grace at every step.

The Oxford Movement is an apt correction to Western Christian conceptions of worship. Its thinkers captured the early Church's Jewish recognition that the essence of worship is sacrifice and that the meaning of human worship is to join the ongoing sacrifice of the Son to the Father by the Spirit. This means that when we participate in the Eucharist, we find the Messiah in his offering, which is the liturgy and sacraments of the Church. They are the Messiah at work.

Finally, the tractarians should encourage us to reject intellectualized visions of redemption, where salvation is thought to depend upon cerebral grasp of propositions. We need Newman and Pusey and Keble to alert us to the biblical suggestions that the will is the key to the mind, that heart speaks to heart, and that spiritual growth depends less on theological understanding than the mystery of moral willingness.

Select Bibliography

Brown, Stewart J., Peter B. Nockles, and James Pereiro, eds. *The Oxford Handbook of the Oxford Movement*. Oxford: Oxford University Press, 2017.

Cummings, Brian, ed. *The Book of Common Prayer: The Texts of 1549, 1559, and 1662*. Oxford: Oxford University Press, 2011.

Gilley, Sheridan. "Keble, Froude, Newman, and Pusey." In Brown, Nockles, and Pereiro, *Oxford Handbook*, 97–110.

Larsen, Timothy. "Scripture and Biblical Interpretation." In Brown, Nockles, and Pereiro, *Oxford Handbook*, 231–43.

Moorman, J. R. H. "The Oxford Movement and After." In *A History of the Church of England*, 3rd ed., 338–61. Harrisburg, PA: Morehouse Publishing, 1980.

Nichols, Aidan, O.P. "The Oxford Movement and Its Aftermath." In *The Panther and the Hind: A Theological History of Anglicanism*, 114–29. Edinburgh: T&T Clark, 1993.

Pereiro, James. "The Oxford Movement's Theory of Religious Knowledge." In Brown, Nockles, and Pereiro, *Oxford Handbook*, 185–99.

27

The Explosion
of Pentecostalism

On April 14, 1906, an African American Holiness preacher named William J. Seymour, the son of former slaves in Louisiana, started leading a prayer meeting in Los Angeles in a dirt-floor, broken-down black church that was being used as a barn. Days before this, one person in the prayer group had started speaking in tongues, an ecstatic prayer language like that of the early Christians in Acts of the Apostles. Soon hundreds were crowding into this church on Azusa Street in Los Angeles, in an industrial zone with skid-row flavor. Word spread like wildfire—of the restoration of the early Church with healings and tongues and prophecy. Soon there were three services every day, morning till night, for three and a half years. At the peak of this revival, eight hundred crowded inside on Sunday mornings, five hundred outside. Rich and poor, educated and uneducated, people of every color came to see. Most were transformed. Within two years this Azusa Street revival had spread to twenty-five nations. In hindsight, it was the single most influential Christian revival to take place anywhere in the world in the twentieth century.

We will look a bit more closely at this Pentecostal revival, its worldwide spread, and the character of the movement that emerged. I will ask what made Pentecostalism attractive to (eventually) hundreds of millions, and then I will suggest what this tells us about the Holy Spirit and the history of redemption.

Azusa Street

The genesis of this Pentecostalism lay in the 1890s, when Charles Parham, a Wesleyan Holiness preacher in Kansas, started a Bible school in Topeka where he taught his students that at the turn of the new century would come a worldwide revival that would bring the second coming of the Messiah. Parham's prophecy seemed to be fulfilled when on January 1, 1900, his student Agnes Ozman started speaking in tongues. Parham soon developed the doctrine that the gift of tongues is *the* sign of the baptism in the Holy Spirit.

When Parham took this teaching to Houston, he forced new student William Seymour to sit outside the classroom and listen through the open door because he was black. Seymour took this doctrine to a black Holiness congregation in Los Angeles but soon found himself locked out of that church because they thought he was implying that their holiness was insufficient. Seymour gathered sympathetic listeners to the front porch of a home nearby. When the crowd made the porch collapse, Seymour and his disciples found the Stevens African Methodist Episcopal Church on Azusa Street. It was in disrepair and used for storage, but because of the industrial neighborhood they knew their noise at all hours would not bother the neighbors.

For the first three and a half years of this revival, it seemed heavenly. No one was rejected because of skin color, dress, or lack of education. Whites submitted to a black leader who was humble but firm. Thirty Native Americans were welcomed from a nearby mission. Early advocates wrote, "The color line was washed away in the Blood" of Jesus.

There were earthly scenes reminiscent of the early Church. According to the Azusa Street newsletter *The Apostolic Faith*, the blind received their sight, a fifteen-year-old girl came back to life with a vision of heaven after her doctor had given her up for dead, people were so overcome by the Spirit that they shook involuntarily with "the jerks," there were visions of hell with demons and human beings in flames, and healings abounded. Piles of discarded crutches, canes, braces, and other medical paraphernalia rose from the floor.

News reports brought not only thousands of inquirers but also police. Some were arrested for disturbing the peace when they tried to bear witness in the streets. *The Apostolic Faith* reported, "We praised the Lord and the marshal and his deputies put their hands over our mouths and choked us quite severely without avail. One brother was handcuffed." The court and jury "were moved to tears" by testimony at the trial, and the case was dropped after the jury disagreed with one another.[1]

---

1. David Dorries, "Azusa Street Revival," in *Encyclopedia of Religious Revivals in America*, ed. Michael McClymond, 2 vols. (Westport, CT: Greenwood Press, 2007), 1:37–42.

When Seymour decided to marry an African American woman instead of Clara Lum, a white woman who edited *The Apostolic Faith* and might have had romantic aspirations for Seymour, Lum absconded with the mailing list. Parham had also denounced the revival with racial slurs because of its interracial harmony. Soon the leadership fell out on racial lines, and the revival fires were extinguished. By 1916 there were three hostile sections in American Pentecostalism, largely determined by race.

Worldwide Spread

As we have seen, pilgrims from Azusa Street took their faith to other parts of the world almost immediately, and Azusa-like revivals started spreading in other parts of the world. But there were nearly simultaneous Pentecostal outpourings far from the United States that appear to have been unconnected to Azusa Street: in Wales (1904–5), in the Khassia Hills in North India (1905); at Pandita Ramabai's mission in Mukti, India (1905–6); at the Hebden mission in Toronto (1906); in Pyongyang during a Korean Pentecost (1907); and in Valparaiso, Chile, among Methodists (1909). Because of what seems to have been the independence of at least the Indian and Toronto revivals, historian Adam Stewart thinks the origins of modern Pentecostalism were multiple and not singular.

Whether the last century's Pentecostal movement arose in one or several places in the same decade, there is little doubt that, as Allan Anderson estimates, Pentecostal churches are the fastest-growing Christian groups in the world today. By some calculations, there were 600 million Pentecostals in 2015, and there might be 800 million by 2025. Even if those numbers are inflated, Pentecostals are nevertheless estimated to be 25 percent of all Christians in the world. Eighty percent of that (roughly) half-billion are in Africa, Asia, and Latin America. In some countries (Brazil, Guatemala, Kenya, South Africa, and the Philippines) Pentecostals make up one-third of the population.

Let's look a bit more closely at the three biggest continents. In Asia, the majority of evangelicals are Pentecostal. The Han Chinese independent churches in China are Pentecostal and are estimated to include 80 million worshipers. The largest Chinese church is the China True Jesus Church, which holds a Oneness view of the Godhead (rejecting the Trinity) and regards worship on the Saturday Sabbath as necessary for salvation. The Philippines boasts the largest group of Roman Catholic "charismatics" (Pentecostals) in the Roman communion, seven million. Yonggi Cho was an Assembly of God (largest Pentecostal denomination) pastor (1936–2021) who founded the Full Gospel Church in Seoul, South Korea, which claimed in 2020 to have 800,000 people, the largest congregation in the world.

In Africa, the vast majority of independent churches are Pentecostal, with a total of 426 million members. Zambia has had two Pentecostal presidents. The German Pentecostal evangelist Reinhard Bonnke has held enormous crusades in Africa, reaching more people than Billy Graham. In 2000 it was reported that Bonnke's Pentecostal rally in Lagos, Nigeria, brought 1.6 million to attend one meeting.

Latin America has more Pentecostals than any single continent. According to Pew Research, 28 percent of the continent's population in 2005 was Pentecostal. Brazil is the biggest Pentecostal nation, with the largest number of Pentecostals in the world, 25 million in 2010 and no doubt considerably more by 2020.[2]

Even largely secular Europe has seen impressive growth among Pentecostals. Ukraine has the highest number of Pentecostals in all of Europe, 780,000 before the 2022–23 war with Russia. Its biggest church, the Embassy of the Blessed Kingdom of God in Kiev, with 20,000 members, was pastored before the war by a Pentecostal pastor from Nigeria. Romania has 300,000 Pentecostals, half of whom are Roma (gypsies).

In North America growth continued after the splits among the early Pentecostals. The biggest black denomination in the United States is Pentecostal, the Church of God in Christ. Pentecostals who infiltrated mainline denominations dropped the insistence on tongues as the only evidence of Spirit baptism and became known as "charismatics," from the Greek word for "gift," *charisma*. The Catholic charismatic movement started in 1967 at Duquesne University and the University of Michigan and has since spread to one hundred nations, with more than 100 million Catholic charismatics. The Lutherans, Methodists, Baptists, and Mennonites have also had charismatic renewal movements, all of which refuse revivalist methods of the early Pentecostal movement and consider other signs besides tongues to be valid evidence of the baptism in the Holy Spirit.

2. Pew Research Center, "Spirit and Power—A 10-Country Survey of Pentecostals," October 5, 2006, https://www.pewresearch.org/religion/2006/10/05/spirit-and-power/; Pew Research Center, "Overview: Pentecostalism in Latin America," October 5, 2006, https://www.pewresearch.org/religion/2006/10/05/overview-pentecostalism-in-latin-america/; David Masci, "Why Has Pentecostalism Grown So Dramatically in Latin America?," Pew Research Center, November 14, 2014, https://www.pewresearch.org/short-reads/2014/11/14/why-has-pentecostalism-grown-so-dramatically-in-latin-america/. See also Todd Johnson, "Counting Pentecostals Worldwide," *Pneuma* (January 2014), 265–88.

The Character of the Movement

Perhaps the most striking feature of the early years of the modern Pentecostal movement was its interracial character. In a stunning departure from that era's Jim Crow segregation, different races mixed freely under the leadership of a black man. This was no doubt made easier by Seymour's humility. Never an overbearing leader, David Dorries notes, Seymour supervised "without dominating or controlling the proceedings." He "provided firm and decisive leadership when necessary, but his general approach during the revival was to allow the Holy Spirit to move freely."[3]

This racial comity so upset Seymour's mentor, Parham, that the latter declared publicly that God was "sick at his stomach" over this racial harmony. Parham was later charged in a San Antonio court with committing sodomy with a young male hymn singer. The charge was never proven, but Parham's reputation never recovered. Despite Parham's diminished influence, racism continued to cause divisions, which might be why Seymour decreed that future heads of the Azusa Street mission would be persons of color.

Parham had taught, and Seymour repeated, the doctrine that the gift of tongues was the only valid sign of Spirit baptism, a subsequent experience after the new birth. But over time this doctrine was dropped by many Pentecostals. Seymour was one of the first to change, eventually teaching that love was the supreme evidence of Spirit baptism and that tongues apart from love were insufficient. Pentecostals in Chile fairly early on also decided that gifts other than tongues could be valid signs of Spirit baptism. Most charismatics reject the Parham doctrine, and many classical Pentecostal groups do as well.

Allan Anderson has observed that Pentecostals over the last century can be found in three varieties—classical Pentecostals, stemming from the early revivals like Azusa Street; charismatics in older churches; and "autochthonous prophetic churches in the Majority World and the Charismatic independent churches." What unites them all, he writes, is an emphasis on "the Word and Spirit at play," where "everyone has a contribution to make to the service, much like the creative combination of spontaneity and order in a jazz performance." All acknowledge the "immediate presence of God in the service," all expect miraculous intervention by gifts of the Holy Spirit, most encourage congregational participation in worship and prayer, many dance and sing, most have some sort of altar call, and almost all call out "Amen!" or "Hallelujah!"[4]

3. Dorries, "Azusa Street Revival," 39.
4. Allan H. Anderson, introduction to *An Introduction to Pentecostalism: Global Charismatic Christianity*, ed. Allan H. Anderson, 2nd ed. (Cambridge: Cambridge University Press, 2014), 5, 2.

One of the recent revivals coming out of classical Pentecostalism featured the theology of Israel and might account, in part at least, for the prevalence of post-supersessionism (rejecting the idea that the Gentile Church has superseseded or replaced Jewish Israel in God's affections) in the charismatic-flavored churches of the Global South. The Brownsville Revival, also known as the Pensacola (FL) Out-pouring, erupted on Father's Day 1995 and lasted until 2000. Margaret Poloma reports that unlike the Toronto Blessing (1994–2005), with its more casual char-ismatic emphasis on a "loving God (or Father) playing with his children," the Pensacola revival "attracted those who preferred a more traditional Pentecostal style" with hellfire preaching, altar calls, and testimonies filled with moaning and weeping. In November 1999 one of its four principal leaders, Messianic Jewish scholar Michael Brown, addressed one of the revival's semiannual pastors' con-ferences (which typically attracted 1,500 leaders) on the topic "Israel Shall Be Saved!" The response was electric.

Brown explained that the Church is indebted to Israel for its Scriptures, the Messiah, and the apostles. The Church must repent of its arrogant replacement theology, anti-Semitic practices, and contradictory theology: "If the Church has replaced Israel, then God is a liar, and He might just replace the Church! (Jer. 30:11; 31:35–37; 33:19–26)." We have the sure promises of God, he continued, that "Israel has not stumbled beyond the point of recovery" (Rom. 11:11). The salvation of Israel will usher in the Messiah's return to earth (Matt. 23:39).[5]

Appeal

How can we explain this recent explosion of churches from nowhere to becom-ing the fourth-largest group of Christians in the world? At the sociological level, we can say that Pentecostalism has become the preference of poor people. It has been said that in Latin America liberation theology opted for the poor, but the poor opted for Pentecostalism. Worldwide, the poor find in its churches hope for healing, connection with God, and promises of prosperity.

But Allan Anderson finds five other reasons for the attraction to Pentecostal-ism.[6] First, "infectious enthusiasm." There is joy in most Pentecostal gatherings,

---

5. Michael L. Brown, "Israel Shall Be Saved!," address to pastor's conference, November 10, 1999, notes shared by Brown with the author, August 8, 2022.

6. Allan H. Anderson, "Pentecostal and Charismatic Christianity," in *The Wiley Blackwell Companion to World Christianity*, ed. Lamin Sanneh and Michael J. McClymond (West Sussex, UK: John Wiley and Sons, 2016), 661–62.

and joy attracts. People often feel fear and despair, but seeing joy from the apparent presence of the Spirit causes many to want that experience.

Second, "positive attitude to mission." Part of the DNA of Pentecostalism is the imperative to share their gospel. This evangelistic drive causes Pentecostals to cross boundaries—both geographical and ecclesial—to share their joy and Spirit. It is no wonder it has migrated so quickly around the world.

Third, "leadership based on calling." For Pentecostals there is less separation between clergy and laity, for the call of the Holy Spirit does not depend on education or social status. The shepherds smell like the sheep. More important are spiritual gifts and the ability to preach effectively.

Fourth, "salvation in the here and now." Perhaps most attractive to the world's poor is the Pentecostal conviction that God wants to break into our mundane world of problems with solutions. He wants to save us not only from sin, death, and the devil but also from evil spirits, sickness, and poverty. The emphasis on prosperity in many Pentecostal churches has drawn much criticism, but it has also encouraged millions to escape addictions and provide for their families.

Fifth, "the Church as community." In a world of loneliness and exclusion, Pentecostal and charismatic communities offer a haven of love and friendship. For multiple millions, these churches provide a new family for those escaping broken homes and fractured relationships. The new community gives members a new identity, which is especially attractive to those who have hated or not known who they are.

Who Is the Holy Spirit?

The Pentecostal explosion of the twentieth century brought to the fore a new question for many Jesus-followers: Who is the Holy Spirit? He has traditionally been regarded as the shy member of the Trinity because of Jesus's teaching that the Spirit does "not speak on his own authority" but "will glorify me, for he will take what is mine and declare it to you" (John 16:13–14 ESV). But Pentecostalism has helped restore what was latent in the tradition, that the Spirit is a divine Person rather than a force. He is a fully equal member of the Trinity, radiating power and love.

Hundreds of millions of Pentecostals have found the Spirit to be a source of joy who cares about their daily struggles. He cares about their health and can heal uncurable afflictions. He knows the despair of poverty and can help his people find relief. He knows the spiritual darkness that afflicts billions and has the power to drive out demons. He tells the lonely and disgraced that they are important to him and that he will give them spiritual gifts if they receive the baptism in the Holy Spirit. He can give them gifts of tongues, prophecy, and discernment of spirits. Most important, he will go with them into every situation of everyday life, so that there is no profane place in the world that the Spirit cannot invade and redeem. These are some of the ways that millions have found the Holy Spirit to be God in Person who brings them redemption in personal ways.

The Spirit in the History of Redemption

In our study of the history of redemption, we have focused largely on the Father and the Son. It can be easy to forget the shy member of the Trinity and not realize that every act of God in the history of redemption involves all three Persons. God is one being in three Persons, and each of the three acts in every movement of redemption. The Spirit was hovering over the face of the waters (Gen. 1:3) at the creation and was resting on the Messiah at every step of the way as he redeemed men and women after the fall. For, as Isaiah prophesied, the Spirit of YHWH rested on the Messiah through all his history of redemption, "the Spirit of wisdom and understanding, the Spirit of counsel and might, the Spirit of knowledge and fear of YHWH" (Isa. 11:2). It has taken the Pentecostal movement to reacquaint many Jesus-followers with this Third Person in the Godhead. It reminds us that the Father sends the Son to redeem sinners *by* the Holy Spirit.

We might also recall Edwards's thesis that the history of redemption is driven by the history of revival. The Pentecostal movement is certainly a revival, or series of revivals, and they too have propelled redemption. Through these revivals the Messiah has become known to hundreds of millions. With that number of people involved, it is not surprising that the history of nations has been affected, just as in past millennia. We can see this impact in three nations most influenced by Pentecostals—Brazil, Guatemala, and Zambia. Both Zambia and Guatemala have had two Pentecostal presidents. Zambia recently declared itself a Christian nation, but without legal discrimination against Islam or other non-Christian religions. Brazil has the largest number of Pentecostals in all of Latin America, as we have seen. It illustrates the futility of identifying Pentecostalism with a political orientation, for while president Jair Bolsonaro (2019–22) was Pentecostal and conservative, president Luiz Inácio Lula da Silva (2003–10, 2023–) is a left-leaning politician who contributed to Brazil's largest Pentecostal church and was supported by millions of Pentecostals. The *favelas* of Brazil are enormous slums where it is said only two things are known to function—organized crime and Pentecostal churches.

If nothing else, we can learn something important about the history of redemption from these political realities: God redeems in the darkest places in shocking ways. He did that in a cave two thousand years ago, and he is still redeeming through the Messiah in favelas in Brazil. The light shines in the darkness, and the darkness has not overcome it.

Select Bibliography

Anderson, Allan H. Introduction to *An Introduction to Pentecostalism: Global Charismatic Christianity*, edited by Allan H. Anderson, 2nd ed., 1–16. Cambridge: Cambridge University Press, 2014.

———. "Pentecostal and Charismatic Christianity." in *The Wiley Blackwell Companion to World Christianity*, edited by Lamin Sanneh and Michael J. McClymond, 653–63. West Sussex, UK: John Wiley and Sons, 2016.

Dorries, David. "Azusa Street Revival." In McClymond, *Encyclopedia of Religious Revivals*, 1:37–42.

McClymond, Michael, ed. *Encyclopedia of Religious Revivals in America*. 2 vols. Westport, CT: Greenwood Press, 2007.

Poloma, Margaret. "Pensacola (Brownsville) Revival." In McClymond, *Encyclopedia of Religious Revivals*, 1:320–23.

Robeck, Cecil M., Jr. "The Origins of Modern Pentecostalism: Some Historiographical Issues." In *Cambridge Companion to Pentecostalism*, edited by Cecil M. Robeck and Amos Yong. New York: Cambridge University Press, 2014.

Stewart, Adam. "From Monogenesis to Polygenesis in Pentecostal Origins: A Survey of the Evidence from the Azusa Street, Hebden, and Mukti Missions." *PentecoStudies* 13, no. 2 (2014): 151–72.

Synan, Vincent. "Pentecostal Revivals." In McClymond, *Encyclopedia of Religious Revivals*, 1:320–23.

28

World Wars and Holocaust: The Problem of Evil

The twentieth century was the bloodiest century in history. More human beings were killed in war and more killed by atheist regimes than in all the previous religious wars put together. Perhaps the most shocking killings were of the innocent: the tens of millions killed because of their faith or nationality and the six million Jews murdered because they were Jews. This chapter will review these crimes and ask what all people of faith ask: How can radical evil be explained in the face of an all-good and all-powerful God of Israel? More pointedly for this book, How can we believe in redemption when the Messiah has permitted such evil?

World Wars

The statistics from the two world wars boggle the mind. In World War I nine million were killed in combat while more than five million civilians died from bombs, hunger, and disease. Millions more died from the Armenian genocide at the hands of the Ottoman Empire, 7–12 million died during the Russian Civil War, and between 60,000 and 200,000 Jewish civilians were killed during Russian pogroms during the Russian Empire, mostly in the Pale of Settlement in present-day Ukraine.

The totals from World War II were even worse: 16 million military dead, 45 million civilian deaths. Then there were deaths from ideology before and after

World War II. According to *The Black Book of Communism*, more than 100 million perished at the hands of communists—65 million in the People's Republic of China, 20 million in the Soviet Union, and another 9 million combined in Cambodia, Vietnam, North Korea, Ethiopia, Afghanistan, Eastern Europe, and Latin America.

Holocaust

As disturbing as the numbers of people killed was the nature of the cruelty of the Holocaust. The biggest killing center of European Jewry was Auschwitz, a death camp in Poland that murdered two million—two thousand every twelve hours. Jews who were not immediately sent to the gas chambers were condemned to work as slaves in inhuman conditions. Paul Johnson reports that they were roused for work at 3 a.m., ordered to move at a trot even when carrying heavy materials, and were given no rest periods. Anyone leaving his ten-meter-square zone was shot. There were floggings each day, several hangings every week. Average weight loss was seven pounds a week. Workers burned up their own bodies and died of exhaustion.

Millions of Germans knew something horrible was being done to the Jews. Almost a million Germans worked in the SS alone, and the SS were directly responsible for rounding up and killing Jews. According to Johnson, "Countless Germans heard and saw the endless trains rattling through the night, and knew their significance, as one recorded remark suggests, 'Those damned Jews—they won't even let one sleep at night.'"[1]

Lest we think Hitler and the SS were the principal anti-Semites in Germany, Johnson argues that "race paranoia was deeply rooted in German culture and had been fostered by generations of German intellectuals." It antedated and dwarfed Hitler. "In a sense, then, it was the German people who willed the end; Hitler who willed the means."[2]

But historians don't let the Allies off the hook. Britain permitted only seventy-five thousand Jews fleeing Hitler over five years to enter Palestine, for fear of the Arabs who had the oil Britain needed for her war machine and empire. Roosevelt spoke with "sympathy for the Jews but did nothing practical to help them get into America," even after news of genocide had reached the World Jewish Congress in August 1942. In April 1943 an Anglo-American meeting of officials in Bermuda

1. Paul Johnson, *Modern Times: The World from the Twenties to the Nineties*, rev. ed. (New York: Harper-Perennial, 1992), 419.
2. Johnson, *Modern Times*, 420.

decided "that neither nation would do anything to help the Jews," and neither would criticize the other for its apathy. Johnson calls it "a mutual anti-conscience pact." Only Churchill supported action for the Jews at any cost. But the prime minister was overruled by his colleagues, led by Anthony Eden, whose secretary noted, "He loves Arabs and hates Jews."[3]

Moral Relativism?

In a century when moral relativism seemed the dominant moral rule, some charge that the British and Americans were guilty of excusing their own moral sins against their enemies, the Germans and the Japanese. When in the first two years of the war England was on the defensive against nightly German bombing raids, Churchill initiated mass bombing of German cities in retaliation. Since it was long before the Allies had the means to launch invasions of North Africa or Nazi-occupied France, it was the only offensive weapon then available to the British. The raids culminated in the fire-bombing of Hamburg on the night of July 27–28, 1943. Royal Air Force bombers created temperatures of 800–1000 degrees centigrade, which sent firestorm winds of colossal force, killing 40,000 civilians. The destruction of Dresden on the night of February 13–14, 1945, was even more horrific. American and British bombers dropped 650,000 incendiaries on the city, killing 35,000 men, women, and children.[4] One month later, on March 9–10, 1945, the Americans firebombed Tokyo, killing 83,000 and injuring 102,000 people.

Then in August 1945 American bombers dropped atomic bombs on Hiroshima and Nagasaki (home for 12,000 Christians), killing 45,000 the same day in the first city and 40,000 in the second. Perhaps another 120,000 died later from aftereffects.

Were the Americans breaking moral law to drop the atomic bombs? President Truman and the Allied commanders estimated that without those bombs an invasion of Japan would have been necessary, and it would have cost a million Allied casualties along with Japanese deaths ranging from ten to twenty million.

Whatever the verdict on Hiroshima and Nagasaki, the greatest mass murderer was not Hitler or even Stalin, who is believed responsible for 30–40 million

---

3. Johnson, *Modern Times*, 420–21.

4. According to Richard Evans, casualty figures have varied mainly due to false information spread by Nazi German and Soviet propaganda. Some figures from historians include 18,000+ (but less than 25,000) from Antony Beevor in *The Second World War*, 20,000 from Anthony Roberts in *The Storm of War*, 25,000 from Ian Kershaw in *The End*, 25,000–30,000 from Michael Burleigh in *Moral Combat*, 35,000 from Richard J. Evans in *The Third Reich at War*; see Evans, *The Third Reich at War, 1939–1945* (London: Allen Lane, 2008), Kindle loc. 13049.

"unnatural deaths," including four million Ukrainians in a famine he created in 1932–33 (the *Holodomor* or "starvation killing"). Valerie Strauss and Daniel Southerl wrote in the *Washington Post* that internal evidence from China suggests that Mao Tse-tung surpasses Hitler and Stalin in the devilish category of mass murder. "One government document that has been internally circulated and seen by a former Communist Party official now at Princeton University says that 80 million died unnatural deaths—most of them in the famine following the Great Leap Forward. This figure comes from the Tigaisuo, or the System Reform Institute, which was led by Zhao Ziyang, the deposed Communist Party chief, in the 1980s to study how to reform Chinese society."[5]

Augustine on Radical Evil

The numbers were smaller, but Augustine of Hippo lived through a period that saw its own radical evil. When Visigoths sacked Rome in 410 and then invaded North Africa, where Augustine was bishop, there was plenty of cruelty. Christian men were tortured and put to death "in a hideous variety of cruel ways," their bodies often left unburied; wives and "unmarried maidens" were raped; and many Christians were led away into slavery. In his monumental *City of God*, the eminent Church father lamented "all the slaughter, plundering, burning and misery."[6]

Years before he wrote *The City of God,* the North African theologian had concluded, after wrestling with the Manichean dualist and material philosophy of evil, that evil is not a thing or even power but the absence of good.[7] It is produced by the abuse of freedom when the will, both angelic and human, defects from God and corrupts itself.[8] We humans are caught up in evil because we are intimately related to Adam, whose sin has infected us all.[9] This infection is "original sin," an inherited proclivity in every human to self-will and self-obsession. God is all-powerful and permits evil because he uses it for his mysterious purposes.[10]

Augustine responded to the North African horrors in ways that might shock us moderns. Of those who were tortured in order to discover their possessions, he said the torture "possibly taught them that they should set their affections" on

---

5. Valerie Strauss and Daniel Southerl, "How Many Died? New Evidence Suggests Far Higher Numbers for the Victims of Mao Zedong's Era," *Washington Post,* July 17, 1994.

6. Augustine, *The City of God,* trans. Marcus Dods (New York: Modern Library, 1950), 16, 9, 21.

7. See Augustine, *Confessions* 7.1, 3–5, 12.

8. Augustine, *City of God* 11.17.

9. Augustine, *City of God* 14.1.

10. Augustine, *City of God* 11.18, 22.

eternal life, a "possession they could not lose." Of those who were put to death in cruel ways he asked, "Of what consequence is it what kind of death puts an end to life, since he who has died once is not forced to go through the same ordeal a second time?" If one has lived a good life pleasing to God, then "that death is not judged an evil." It becomes evil only if followed by eternal "retribution."[11]

Augustine comforted women who lived through the shame of rape and wondered if they had any fault in it. The bishop wrote that no, as long as their will remained "firm and unshaken" during their violation, "nothing that another person does with the body, or upon the body, is any fault of the person who suffers it." But he knew, probably from extensive pastoral experience, that women still felt shame and wondered if others believed the atrocity was "committed with some assent of the will." He reassured them that "shame invades even a thoroughly pure spirit from which modesty has not departed." Of those who committed suicide "to avoid such disgrace, who that has any human feeling would refuse to forgive them?" This he said despite long sections in this same first book of *The City of God* condemning suicide as a serious sin that in some cases brings spiritual death.[12]

But why, some asked, did God permit these atrocities? Augustine's first and last answers appealed to the "deep providence of the Creator and Governor of the world." He quoted Paul's words in Romans: "Unsearchable are his judgments, and his ways past finding out" (11:33 KJV). He said that faithful women must not complain "that permission was given to the barbarians so grossly to outrage them; nor must they allow themselves to believe that God overlooked their character when he permitted acts which no one with impunity commits." God permits these things only by his "secret judgment," but reserves these "wicked desires" to the "public and final judgment." Yet it is possible, wrote the bishop of souls, that some "Christian women had some lurking infirmity which might have betrayed them into a proud and contemptuous bearing, had they not been subjected" to these atrocities, "lest prosperity should corrupt their modesty" later and destroy their souls.[13]

Where Was God?

Augustine came back to the question of whether God had abandoned his Church in these black days of murder and atrocity. Where was he when his people were crying out for rescue? Augustine's answer was that God was everywhere but usu-

11. Augustine, *City of God* 1.11.
12. Augustine, *City of God* 1.16; on suicide, 1.19–27.
13. Augustine, *City of God* 1.28.

ally unperceived. God allows suffering as a test to prove our perfections or to correct our imperfections.

Job is the classic example of God's testing a man. Satan had insisted that Job was righteous only because God bribed him: "Have you not put a hedge around him and his house and all that he has? . . . Lay your hand on all that he has, and he will surely curse you to your face" (Job 1:10–11). After Job then lost his wealth, children, and health, he spent many of the remaining chapters arguing bitterly with God, protesting his innocence, and even cursing the day he was born. But he never cursed God.

After the Holocaust many Jews asked why God sent them this horrific test. Messianic Jews Jonathan Williams and Bruce Kleinberg point to the cross. "One cannot equate the cross where Yeshua suffered for our sins with the death camps like Auschwitz. Yet the Messiah, destined to die and fulfill the prophecy of Isaiah chapter 53, understood the anguish of human suffering at a level very few of us, other than Holocaust victims, could imagine. His suffering does not make the Holocaust more palatable, but it helps us to see that God might understand our anguish a little more than we thought."[14]

C. S. Lewis asked why God tests us if he already knows what is in our hearts. After his wife's death, he speculated in *A Grief Observed* that God may test our faith for our sake, not his. He suspected that he needed to see the flaws in his faith. "[God] always knew that my temple [of faith] was a house of cards. His only way of making me realize the fact was to knock it down."[15]

In answering the question of whether God was absent, Augustine concluded with reminders of God's secret working. "Our God is everywhere present, wholly everywhere; not confined to any place. He can be present unperceived, and be absent without moving; when he exposes us to adversities, it is either to prove our perfections or correct our imperfections; and in return for our patient endurance of the sufferings of time, he reserves for us an everlasting reward."[16]

The Two Cities

Augustine set the problem of evil in the context of his philosophy of history. *The City of God* helped its readers understand evil by secularizing history. Against

---

14. Jonathan Williams and Bruce Kleinberg, "Why Did God Allow the Holocaust?," *Chosen People Ministries*, accessed October 16, 2023, https://www.chosenpeople.com/god-allow-the-holocaust/.

15. C. S. Lewis, *A Grief Observed* (New York: Seabury, 1961), 42.

16. Augustine, *City of God* 1.29.

those who wanted to make the history of the new Rome a Christian history, with its successes regarded as rewards for its Christian leaders and citizens, Augustine said true history is not a matter of Christian empires versus secular empires, but an internal, secret history between the City of God and the City of Man. The two cities coexist within both Christian and non-Christian empires. Rome fell because of internal moral corruption and idolatry. Bad things happen to both Christian empires and good Christians because of God's secret purposes operating within both.

Augustine's composite portrait of human nature is of a good thing gone bad. The good God had made humanity good, but by its own perverse choices it has become corrupted. Since self-obsession and lust and pride are so deeply rooted in human nature, salvation cannot come from anything within us. It must come from Someone *beyond* us.

Because of our pride it is nearly impossible to recognize this until we feel pain. As Lewis explained in *The Problem of Pain*, the experience of evil has a way of showing us that something is wrong. Pain is "God's megaphone."[17] If our life is threatened, everything that seemed so important (money, status, house, car, prestige) suddenly seems trivial. Pain shatters the illusion that all is well; it punctures the myth that what we have is enough. It also takes out of our hands what was keeping us from accepting what God wants to give us. People who never had time for religion might be moved for the first time to seek God.

Augustine wrote that God uses the same suffering in different ways for different people. For the wicked, it might be punishment and perhaps a goad to repentance, just as the flood was a punishment for the wickedness of Noah's generation and as Israel's exiles were divine discipline for her idolatries. He cautioned believers, however, against assuming that all evil is punishment from God. People believed that about the man born blind in John 9, but Jesus admonished them that the man's blindness was sent for the glory of God, and he rebuked the disciples who thought the Galileans executed by Pilate and the eighteen Jews killed by the fall of the Tower of Siloam were worse sinners than those who did not suffer such deaths (Luke 13:1–5).

As we saw above, Augustine wrote that evil comes to believers to "correct their imperfections." God wants to make his people more and more holy, taking what was created in his image and changing it into his likeness. Good parents know this intuitively when raising their children. They would rather see their kids suffer than remain spoiled and immature. Lewis wrote that an artist will take

17. C. S. Lewis, *The Problem of Pain* (New York: Macmillan, 1962), 81.

endless trouble over a masterpiece and inflict endless trouble on a canvas or piece of marble, with chipping and scraping, as if the work were alive and conscious. So too a lover hurts with his beloved but rather than alleviate the suffering will permit it if he knows it will make her a better person. Each believer is a child of the heavenly Father, a work of art on the divine easel, the beloved of the divine lover. Augustine would say that we must let God be God and allow him to be repelled by the stains in our character and apply to us the suffering needed to erase those stains.

Power to the Good and the Wicked

Augustine also wondered why God, who gives power as he pleases, gives it to both good and wicked people. We who live after the twentieth century ask the same, after the horrors perpetrated by wicked people in that century. Augustine proposed one reason, that if God gave power only to good people, then his saints might grow to like the kingdoms of this world too much and fail to yearn for the City of God.

There are other reasons, he wrote, but God keeps them hidden. For most of us most of the time, and especially after the unprecedented evils of the world wars, Holocaust, the Gulag, and the killing fields of Pol Pot, we are left with mystery. We simply do not know, and God gives us little more than faint clues.

Augustine said this should not be surprising. For if we could understand God and his ways, it would not be the Triune God we were understanding. It would be a figment of our imagination that we had cut down to our size. The true God is infinite and we are finite, so we should expect that we will not understand him and his ways.

Job discovered this at the end of his ordeal. He never did get an answer to the "Why me?" question. We the readers are given the answer at the beginning—a cosmic contest between God and Satan—but Job was never told. Yet after he got a fleeting glimpse of God's creative power and beauty, he threw himself on the ground and repented. He exclaimed, "I spoke of things I did not understand, things too wonderful for me to know. . . . I heard of you with the hearing of my ears, but now I see you with my eyes. Therefore I abhor myself and repent in dust and ashes" (Job 42:3–6). Job now knew that his demands to understand the evil that had befallen him were foolish. He was content to know that God permitted it.

This was something like Paul's realization after his thorn in the flesh. It was probably a disease, because of the Greek word he uses for "flesh," and we know it brought him scorn. Three times he asked God to remove it. He received no answer the first two times, but after the third request, the Messiah spoke. "My grace is enough for you, for my power is made perfect through weakness" (2 Cor. 12:9).

Evil in the History of Redemption

Apparently Paul's strength was preventing him from experiencing the fullness of the Messiah's power. The same, no doubt, can be said of us when evil comes our way. The experience is painful, but our helplessness and weakness in the face of it have a way of opening us up, in ways impossible while we are strong, to the deep and invisible power of the Messiah. That doesn't mean we will know why evil has been permitted to come our way, but it does help us realize something about evil in the history of redemption—that for those who accept it, it somehow opens the door to a new dimension of redemption.

We know that the Messiah's redemption protects us from the final evil of God's wrath and eternal separation from his love. But we also know that the path toward that final redemption often wends its ways through dark days of evil, sometimes horrific evil. In those days we might feel tremendous pain and confusion. Much of the pain is from not knowing why God has permitted this suffering to come our way. We have to say that about the Holocaust: no one seems able to do more than scratch the surface of this monumental mystery, which now is part of what Paul calls the "mystery" of Israel (Rom. 11:25).

Yet we can say two things. First, we can remind ourselves of what Augustine taught in *The City of God*, that when God's ways are mysterious in permitting radical evil, we can nevertheless know that his reasons are always just and wise.

And second, we can affirm that the cross and resurrection of the Messiah are clues to that justice and wisdom. Somehow God uses even radical evil to bring final redemption, just as he used the greatest evil in human history—the murder of the Son of God—to bring redemption to the cosmos.

Select Bibliography

Augustine. *The City of God*. Translated by Marcus Dods. New York: Modern Library, 1950.

———. *Confessions*. Translated by Henry Chadwick. Oxford: Oxford University Press, 1991.

Brown, Peter. *Augustine of Hippo*. Berkeley: University of California Press, 1969.

Fintel, William A., and Gerald R. McDermott. *Cancer: A Medical and Spiritual Guide for Patients and Their Families.* Grand Rapids: Baker Books, 2004.

Johnson, Paul. *Modern Times: The World from the Twenties to the Nineties.* Rev. ed. New York: HarperPerennial, 1992.

Lewis, C. S. *A Grief Observed.* New York: Seabury, 1961.

———. *The Problem of Pain.* New York: Macmillan, 1962.

Panné, Jean-Louis, et al. *The Black Book of Communism: Crimes, Terror, Repression.* Cambridge, MA: Harvard University Press, 1999.

Strauss, Valerie, and Daniel Southerl. "How Many Died? New Evidence Suggests Far Higher Numbers for the Victims of Mao Zedong's Era." *Washington Post*, July 17, 1994.

29

The Church's New Center of Gravity in Asia and Africa

World Christianity historian Todd M. Johnson reports that in 1910 the majority of Christians worldwide lived in the global North, "with only small representations in Oceania, Africa, and Asia." Sixty-six percent of all Christians lived in Europe, and only 2 percent in Africa. By 2010 the proportions were reversed: Europe had only 25 percent of the world's Christians, and the global North merely 40 percent, while 67 percent of all Christians were in the global South and 22 percent in Africa. Asia had 15.4 percent of the world's believers in the Jewish Messiah.[1]

This will mean changes in the way believers think about the Messiah and his redemption. Already we have seen sharp distinctives arising in Asian and African Christianity. Most notable perhaps have been its independence from Enlightenment presumptions and the continuity believers in these continents have seen between their Christian faith and earlier primal religions. These might mean increasingly important changes in the way we understand the history of redemption. We will explore these global South distinctives and then discuss their impact on a theology of redemption.

---

1. Todd M. Johnson, "The 100-Year Shift of Christianity to the South," Gordon-Conwell Theological Seminary, October 9, 2019, https://www.gordonconwell.edu/blog/the-100-year-shift-of-christianity-to-the-south/.

Primal Religions

Both Simon Chan of Singapore and Kwame Bediako (1945–2008) of Ghana have observed that Christian theology and primal or folk religions often bear striking theological similarities. Primal religions are typically holistic, seeing the physical and spiritual worlds as interpenetrating rather than rigidly separated as Enlightenment-influenced thinkers tend to conceive of them. Transcendence in everyday life is expected. Primal religions stress the community rather than the individual in isolation. They recognize unseen spirits in the nonhuman world, believe in the ontological significance of names, hold initiation rites that join the individual to the community, and see marriage as the joining of families and not simply individuals. Perhaps even more importantly, for primal religion death is not extinction but entrance into another mode of existence. Asian primal religion has a penchant for myths and stories, painting and poetry, the concrete and imaginative. In all of these features, there is remarkable theological similarity to early messianic religion, that of Jesus and the apostles.

Chan notes that the contiguity between primal religions and Christianity was recognized by many Church fathers such as Justin Martyr, Irenaeus, Clement of Alexandria, and Origen. It was called the *vestigia Dei* (footprints of God) or *prisca theologia* (ancient theology). The latter is the term for an ancient Jewish and Christian belief that God had sprinkled seeds of his truth among the pagans. He permitted fallen angels, who had once known much of the truth, to start false religions so as to direct worship to themselves under the guise of the true God. In order to gain credibility they mixed the false with the true and, in the process, distributed seeds of true religion among the folk and primal religions of the world.

Chan and Bediako both think this theological similarity between the primal religions and Christianity is why the latter has spread so quickly in the global South. As Chan puts it in *Grassroots Asian Theology*, "Whether the knowledge of a supreme being in many ancient cultures owes its origin to some primeval revelation or traces of ancient people's memory of a prelapsarian state, the fact of the matter is that it is often a point of contact between primal religious societies and the gospel. It constitutes a de facto *praeparatio evangelica*. It prepares the way for the gospel and accounts for its ready reception in these societies."[2]

Bediako believed that because of this principle of God coming to primal peoples through something like what the *prisca theologia* depicts, the God of Israel

---

2. Simon Chan, *Grassroots Asian Theology: Thinking the Faith from the Ground Up* (Downers Grove, IL: IVP Academic, 2014), 62.

preceded the missionaries by millennia. Bediako's colleague Lamin Sanneh, from The Gambia, added that the central categories for biblical religion were already there in primal religion—God the Creator, Messiah, creation, history—so that Christianity had been "adequately anticipated." This imbued African cultures, Sanneh wrote, "with eternal significance and endowed African languages with a transcendent range."[3] Bediako was convinced that in contrast to the evangelization of Europe, where the gods came out of a polytheistic matrix without a high creator god, "in Africa, the God whose name had been hallowed in indigenous languages in the pre-Christian tradition was found to be the God of the Bible, in a way that neither Zeus, nor Jupiter, nor Odin could be."[4]

John Mbiti of Kenya agreed. "God the Father of our Lord Jesus Christ is the same God who has been known and worshipped in various ways within the religious life of African peoples" and who therefore "was not a stranger in Africa prior to the coming of missionaries."[5]

The Communion of the Saints

One of the most salient characteristics of primal religion is the importance of the community over the individual, so that one is defined not simply by membership in the community but by an ontological bond. One's being is shared with the being of the community through an initiation ceremony at which a libation is poured and the names of both living and dead are recited. At that point the "living dead" (as the Africans call them) become present, and the new member shares a soul bond with those who have passed on to the netherworld as well as those still in the flesh. The many Asian rites for the veneration of ancestors are similar. The dead are never simply dead but live on in another realm.[6]

This is why Asian and African believers take more seriously than those in the West the communion of the saints. They resonate with the traditional doctrine that Christians on earth are in communion with the saints in heaven—all those who are one with the God of Israel and his Messiah and ever have been down

---

3. Lamin Sanneh, "The Missionary Inheritance," in *Christianity: A World Faith*, ed. Robin Keely (Tring: Lion, 1985), 303–11, quoted in Kwame Bediako, "Five Theses on the Significance of Modern African Christianity: A Manifesto," in *Landmark Essays in Mission and World Christianity*, ed. Robert Gallagher and Paul Hertig (Maryknoll, NY: Orbis Books, 2009), 99.

4. Bediako, "Five Theses," 100.

5. John Mbiti, quoted in John Kinney, "The Theology of John Mbiti: His Sources, Norms, and Methods," *International Bulletin of Missionary Research* 3, no. 2 (1979): 68, cited by Bediako, "Five Theses," 108.

6. Chan, *Grassroots Asian Theology*, 72.

through the ages. This is why Watchman Nee (1903–72), the great Chinese church planter and martyr, said that "the material" of the Church is the Messiah, and the Church is the corporate Messiah, "the Christ in all the Christians around the world *throughout all the centuries* put together."[7]

So believers in Africa see the solidarity of the family extending beyond the grave, as their ancestors venerated their ancestors. William Wadé Harris (1865–1929), whom Bediako called "the first distinctive African Christian prophet of modern times," "did not think in terms of what Moses did or Jesus did in the Bible, but of how his new ancestors, Moses, Elijah, and supremely Jesus Christ, interacted with him."[8] Harris, along with hundreds of millions of Asian and African believers today, did not think of the biblical saints as those who did things in ancient times so much as his ancestors with whom he was now in communion.

This conviction of communal and family solidarity affects the global South's view of God, sin, salvation, and the Christian life. Sin, as Chan puts it, is not against an impersonal law but against a community, breaking its harmony. The Trinity is an ordered family under the loving leadership of the Father, whose three Persons agreed to enlarge the family by including human beings and angels. Jesus is the greatest ancestor. Salvation is not just personal acquittal but corporate justification. It is the restoration of one's standing in the family of God. Christian life is essentially communal. Participation in the common life of the family of God—the Church—by baptism and Eucharist means sharing in the being of God, which is shared ontologically with every member. The good news of the gospel is being invited to join this family from every people, tribe, tongue, and nation (Rev. 7:9).

Because of this global South vision of family extended through time, believers in Africa and Asia are particularly sensitive to the question of the salvation of their ancestors who never heard the gospel of the Messiah. Because of the ontological (at the level of deepest being) sharing in baptism and Eucharist, which we have seen in previous chapters and which global South believers appreciate, some of the indigenous Asian churches have created elaborate liturgies for evangelizing and communing with their ancestors. Chan notes that the historic doctrine of the intermediate period after death and before the final judgment suggests that the soul is not in its final condition until that judgment. He and many others before him have noted that Paul implies the significance of the intermediate period when

---

7. Watchman Nee, *The Glorious Church* (Anaheim, CA: Living Stream Ministry, 1993), 29, quoted in Chan, *Grassroots Asian Theology*, 181–82 (emphasis added).

8. Kwame Bediako, "Scripture as the Interpreter of Culture and Tradition," in *Africa Bible Commentary*, ed. Tokunboh Adeyemo (Nairobi: WordAlive; Grand Rapids: Zondervan, 2006), 4.

he prays for Onesiphorus, who is already dead, asking that the Lord "grant him to find mercy on that Day," the day of judgment (2 Tim. 1:18). On this and other grounds Asian churches stress the need for personal reception of the Messiah by their ancestors. This sets their practice apart from Mormon proxy baptisms for the dead, where there is near-universal salvation. Indigenous Japanese churches recognized that just as many reject Jesus in this life, many rejected God's calling to them in the past. Chan concludes, "Given the broad consensus in the doctrine of the communion of saints and its ramifications with regard to those who have not heard the gospel or are in need of further growth in communion, the ritual practices of the [Japanese indigenous churches] relating to deceased ancestors may not appear so far-fetched after all. It could, in fact, contribute toward a fuller understanding of the communion of saints."[9]

Subordination Is Not Subordinationism

The global South Church's conviction that family is the most basic ontological structure goes, as it were, both up and down. As Chan expresses it, the Trinity is the divine family. Its hierarchical order, shaped as a divine monarchy, shows that subordination need not be oppressive. There is love and mutuality among the three Persons, subordination without subordinationism. It is because of this divine order in the godhead that Asian and African theologians can think of hierarchical orders without the necessity of domination. They speak of conversion as transforming family relationships from domination to respect and reciprocity. Chan cites a line from a house church hymn, "Old Granny believes in the Lord, her temper is much improved." Relationships between husbands and wives are analogous to order in the Trinity, where the Son and Spirit submit joyfully to the Father. It is in her subordinate position that the wife stands as a type of the Church in its submission to her Lord. "One has good reason," Chan observes, "to question whether egalitarianism is the scriptural trajectory in light of the overwhelming testimony of the Christian tradition, both Catholic and Orthodox, of the hierarchical nature of trinitarian and human relations."[10] (Not all African theologians agree with Chan, for recently several African churches have introduced women's ordination even up to the level of bishop.)

Hierarchy in the Church is another implication of the family of the Trinity. Just as the Godhead is a monarchy characterized by love and service, so too there is

9. Chan, *Grassroots Asian Theology*, 197.
10. Chan, *Grassroots Asian Theology*, 76.

no reason to think of hierarchical orders in the clergy as necessarily oppressive or to think that egalitarian democracy is the rule for the Church. African and Asian believers see ordered hierarchy in the family and the Church as a typological reflection of order in the Trinity. Chan notes that the hierarchical view of the Trinity is more universal than the egalitarian model. African theologians tend to agree. Nigerian theologian Yusufu Turaki, for example, writes in the *Africa Bible Commentary* at Ephesians 5:22–33, "The biblical model for marriage presented here applies to marriages across all cultures and ages, including African marriages. A wife is told to submit to her husband because of her reverence for Christ (5:22). Her submission signals her acceptance of God's institutional order in the family and the church. God has made the husband the head of a family, just as Jesus Christ is the Head of the church."[11]

Honor and Shame

The global South reads Scripture differently, seeing emphases that had been invisible to global North theologians for centuries. Bruce Nicholls, for example, has discovered that Scripture puts more emphasis on the honor-shame matrix than the pattern of guilt and forgiveness. The Bible, he notes, addresses honor and shame more than twice as often as guilt and forgiveness.[12] It speaks from the matrix of honor and shame 345 times (300 in the Old Testament and 45 in the New), while the guilt/forgiveness pattern arises 155 times (145 times in the Old and 10 times in the New). That is a ratio of 69 to 31: when treating God's redemption from sin, Scripture puts it in a shame/honor matrix 69 percent of the time and in a guilt/forgiveness framework 31 percent of the time. For an example of the first, Psalm 22's description of the Messiah's agonies is in terms of honor and shame: the Messiah is scorned by men and despised by the people, all who see him mock him, and people stare at him and gloat over him (Ps. 22:6–7, 17). The psalmist worships YHWH for putting Israel's enemies to "everlasting shame" (78:66). Paul says God chooses the foolish things of the world to shame the wise, the weak things of the world to shame the strong (1 Cor. 1:27). The cross was considered foolish and weak because of all the ways it dishonored the victim. It stripped the victim naked, scourging was often public as for Jesus, carrying the cross naked through the streets was another public humiliation, and the Romans made sure to

---

11. Yusufu Turaki, "Ephesians," in Adeyemo, *Africa Bible Commentary*, 1436.
12. Bruce Nicholls, "The Role of Shame and Guilt in a Theology of Cross-Cultural Mission," *Evangelical Review of Theology* 25, no. 3 (July 2001): 235.

put the crosses in public places. As Timothy Tennent writes, "Everything is done to maximize the shame."[13] The New Testament bears plentiful witness to this. As Hebrews puts it, Jesus "endured the cross, scorning its shame" (Heb. 12:2).

Because Jesus was publicly shamed on the cross, Paul tells the Colossians that in his own public shame Jesus made a public spectacle of the devil, shaming the powers and authorities by his triumph there (Col. 2:15). He told the Philippians that this triumph was rewarded with honor: Jesus was given a name of honor above every other (2:9).

This is why the global South resonates more with Anselm's atonement theory than most global North theologians do.[14] Anselm stresses the ways in which the atonement addressed the honor due the Father, for sin as he conceived it was principally failure to give God the honor due him. The death of the sinless God-man accumulated value infinitely adequate to satisfy the wounding of the divine honor. For Anselm and his culture, like that of the global South, sin is a loss of honor—which is why sinners fall short of the *glory* of God. Sin brings shame to God's name and his family, the Church. Tennent observes that Anselm does not ignore the forensic nature of the atonement but grounds it in the deeper biblical matrix of honor and shame: "Anselm does rely heavily on the concept of objective, judicial guilt, but roots it in relational, not merely legalistic, soil by demonstrating that objective sinful acts that render us guilty arise first and foremost out of a personal rejection of God whereby we have refused to give him the honor that is due him."[15]

The global South tends to follow this Anselmian approach. Justification for these believers is a forensic act that removes legal guilt but even more a divine action that removes the sinner's shame and confers a new status of honor. Asian and African theologians tend to consider atonement theologies since the Reformation as excessively juridical, their focus on guilt and acquittal out of *balance* with the greater biblical concentration on shame and dishonor.

This affects global South conceptions of worship. It is less a personal experience and more a public way of bringing honor to God. Worship is to give the God of Israel the glory and honor due him. It should suggest a holy presence that elicits reverence and awe, fear and trembling. And just as the devil's defeat at the cross was a public spectacle, so too proper worship must be a public ritual that gives honor to the true God.

13. Timothy C. Tennent, *Theology in the Context of World Christianity: How the Global Church Is Influencing the Way We Think about and Discuss Theology* (Grand Rapids: Zondervan, 2007), 90.

14. Chan, *Grassroots Asian Theology*, 44, 83.

15. Tennent, *Theology in the Context of World Christianity*, 100.

Chan suggests that the Enlightenment is the philosophical root of modernity's characteristic sin, the elevation of individual rights at the expense of divine prerogatives: "Sin disorders the filial relationship with God and fraternal relationship with other humans, turning family members into discrete individuals fighting for individual 'rights' and 'equality' and bringing *dishonor* to God and *shame* to the sinner."[16]

Priestly Mediation

In Asian and African churches, pastors are regarded in priestly ways. Chan reports that in India's Nagaland ministers often complain that they are stretched thin because their parishioners will not settle for lay leaders to dedicate homes, children, or even hunting weapons. Despite Protestant emphasis on the priesthood of all believers, even Protestant Asians and Africans see a special mediatorial role for ordained pastors. Ironically, this is akin to the role that Orthodox and Catholic churches accord to their own priests, who are said to share in the Messiah's priesthood. Just as ancient Israel had levels of priesthood—Israel as a nation of priests, men called to be priests, chief priests, and a high priest—so too older churches have bishops, priests, and deacons who are believed to *mediate* the Messiah's own priesthood among God's people. Even if Protestants in Asia and Africa don't have a sacerdotal view of the ministry, they nevertheless share in their understanding of clergy as mediators of God's gifts and graces. Their pastors serve as *de facto* priestly mediators.

Global South theologians point to Paul's ministry for precedent. Paul described his own work as priestly: "It was given to me by God to be a priestly servant of the Messiah Jesus on behalf of the Gentiles, serving as a priest for the good news of God so that the offering of the Gentiles might be acceptable, sanctified by the Holy Spirit" (Rom. 15:15b–16). Paul apparently saw his missionary activity as a priestly work of offering people up to God as acceptable sacrifices. Significant numbers of global South believers, even Protestants, see their pastors in ways ancient Jews saw their priests, as sharing in the priesthood of the whole nation but also serving as special mediators of God's life and truth to his people.

Intermediate Powers

Most Christians in the global North think of a simple monotheism in which there is one God, the physical cosmos, and nothing else "between" except for

16. Chan, *Grassroots Asian Theology*, 203 (emphasis added).

angels, who have no daily impact on their lives. But for believers in the ancient world, both Jews and Jesus-followers, the cosmos was chock-full of beings both benevolent and malign. God mysteriously permitted Satan to remain as "god of this world," and Satan controlled whole armies of wicked angels and their foot soldiers, called demons. The generals of these armies were Paul's principalities and powers, which sometimes controlled whole nations, as demonstrated in the tenth chapter of Daniel.

Christians in the global South share this worldview. The primal religions that still permeate much of Africa and Asia instill fear, which is the general atmosphere in these societies. Fear of witchcraft, fear of accusations of witchcraft, fear of spirits and angry ancestors who have not been properly appeased, fear of fate, fear of death. It is because of these threatening spiritual powers that the *Christus Victor* model of the atonement, where the Messiah conquers Satan and the powers at the cross, is the most dominant model of the atonement in these societies. Hebrews 2:14–15 resonates powerfully: through death the Messiah destroyed the one who has the power of death—that is, the devil—and delivered all those who through fear of death were subject to lifelong bondage.

Traditional Africans and Asians did not believe in a dramatic opposition between good and evil, nor did they hold to a devil as the personal principle of evil. But the coming of the God of Israel to Asian and African self-consciousness has brought a new dualism. According to missiologist Andrew Walls, the "old divinities" were transposed from amoral powers that controlled fate to demons that are "the embodiment of opposition to the God of church and Bible."[17] Accounts of early conversion movements "frequently centre on power encounters between the evangelist (in the stories, almost always African, hardly ever a Western missionary) or some seminal local Christian figure on the one hand, and the local ruling spiritual power (represented often by a shrine, cult, society or guild) on the other."[18]

Because African and Asian believers see this world as the frontier of human and spiritual activity, with good and evil powers at war for human souls, the Messiah's position at the right hand of the Father in ascension victory is a powerful antidote to fear. His triumph has brought freedom from fatalism and fear of spirits and has launched healing from sickness and demonic oppression. In India, believers include the caste system in the powers that the Messiah conquered in his victory—if not fully in history, at least legally and spiritually. Furthermore,

17. Andrew F. Walls, *The Cross-Cultural Process in Christian History* (Maryknoll, NY: Orbis Books, 2002), 124.

18. Walls, *Cross-Cultural Process in Christian History*, 125.

Christian theology in these lands is equipped to deal with the poisoned social relations that follow from traditional witchcraft and its accusations. The message of forgiveness and reconciliation, along with freedom from fear, brings healing to broken and frightened souls.

All of this means that in the global South Messiah Jesus takes on a visage different from what the North has seen since the Enlightenment. For grassroots Pentecostals in Asia, he is not the liberator from sociopolitical oppression as in liberation theology, but the Messiah with a fivefold gospel: savior, sanctifier, baptizer, healer, and coming King. According to Bediako, the three primary christological categories for African Christians are Christ as healer, Christ as master of initiation, and Christ as ancestor.[19] While in the global North the Messiah is often reduced to a distant figure who procured forgiveness thousands of years ago, in Africa and Asia he is one's contemporary who has brought believers into the divine family, where they find honor, healing, and daily connection with biblical ancestors.

Continuous Redemption, Contested Pluralism, and a Different Bible

There are other lessons from believers in the global South. The first is their recognition that in the Bible redemption is not only past but present and future. The Scriptures speak of our having been saved, our being saved, and our future salvation. Believers in the South notice the emphasis in Hebrews on faith as faithfulness and perseverance. They stress faith as a personal relationship with Jesus, but just as importantly they recognize the corporate and continuous nature of redemption, less salvation as a crisis experience in one's past and more the need to continue on the narrow way despite obstacles. As Chan writes, conversion is not merely "some kind of grand rescue operation associated with certain types of evangelical preaching; rather, salvation is part of a larger process of being united with God and being transformed by that union to become Godlike."[20] Sanctification is just as important as justification. Deification or participating in the divine nature (2 Pet. 1:4) comes from the pursuit of holiness, and without holiness no one will see the Lord (Heb. 12:14).

Another lesson that global South churches can teach the North is that contested pluralism is the normal state in the history of societies with a Christian presence. Bediako says African Christianity can help Northern believers to see

19. Bediako, "Five Theses," 104.
20. Chan, *Grassroots Asian Theology*, 123.

that the recession of faith in the West and its need to be reevangelized are nothing new. The rise of the New Age can be likened to primal religions in the South. The experience of religious and cultural pluralism is normal in Africa, and the churches there can show how claims to the lordship of the Jewish Messiah need not be silenced amid competing claims to lordship. Secularity therefore should not be accepted as necessary to modernity.

The churches of the South also demonstrate a new, or perhaps the ancient, way of understanding the Scriptures. A hint can be seen in Paul's reference to "our fathers" in his letter to Gentiles in Corinth. Israel's history became their adoptive history. African believers have always had a strong sense of this, according to Bediako. The Bible was not something merely to be believed in; its history was to be shared. Its characters were typically seen by Africans as both their contemporaries and ancestors. Scripture is a story in which they participate. This is why, Bediako argues, "the people in the Bible will not be made perfect without us (Heb. 11:40), nor we without them."[21] This is why the Gentiles in Paul's churches saw the Hebrew Bible as their book, explaining not only Israel's history but their own as well. Africans have always seen their capacity to suffer as not unlike the suffering of the ancient people of Israel. Culturally, Africans have felt a deeper connection to ancient Israel than have people in the North. This is why Nigerian Anglican bishop Samuel Crowther (ca. 1809–91) argued 150 years ago that after the Gospels and Psalms, the holiness code of the book of Leviticus needed to be translated into African languages. It is why Leviticus remains one of Africa's favorite books.

Freedom from Enlightenment Categories

In a telling statement, Andrew Walls has concluded that "the real strength of Christianity in Africa may prove to be its capacity for independence of Enlightenment categories."[22] This is true of most Asian Christians as well. It has been this freedom that has enabled global South believers to retrieve the biblical vision in ways that have eluded global North theologians since the Enlightenment. Christian intellectuals since the seventeenth century, captured by Enlightenment prejudices, have tended to see the Church as a voluntary association of the like-minded rather than the earthly branch of a divine society linked organically through space and time. They have regarded the gospel as a set of principles rather than the good news of

21. Bediako, "Scripture as the Interpreter of Culture and Tradition," 4.
22. Walls, Cross-Cultural Process in Christian History, 122.

a divine family reaching down to embrace sinners. Modern Christian theologians have considered the world to be the primary locus of the Spirit's work instead of the Church as the principal embodiment of what the Holy Spirit is doing on earth. Sin for Enlightenment-inspired Christians is social injustice, and spirituality is therefore sociopolitical liberation. But for most global South believers sin is breaking God's commandments, which dishonors the divine family headed by the trinitarian God and violates the harmony of the Body of the Messiah. For believers attuned more to modern European thought than biblical vision, nature and spirit are fundamentally different realms experienced with conviction only after death. But for the majority of believers in the global South, it is characteristic of the Spirit to relate to matter in the here and now. Thus, it is no stretch for Asian and African worshipers to conceive that bread and wine can be transfigured into the body and blood of the Messiah through the priestly ministry of their pastors. Or that water can be used by God to translate a human being from the domain of darkness to the kingdom of God's Son. They know their everyday worlds are pierced regularly by divine light and heavenly power.

The Future of the History of Redemption

The God of Israel has always held special attraction for the poor, weak, and despised of this world. But there is little doubt that the future of world Christianity—the Church beyond Euro-America that Walls and Sanneh have highlighted in recent decades—will be among the relatively poor and absolute poor in the global South. Their experience of redemption will shape the theology and practice of believers in the God of Israel and his Messiah Jesus for decades, perhaps centuries, to come—if the Lord tarries. That means that more and more believers will see God having prepared for the gospel in primal religions and that communion of the saints means participation in the Church triumphant as well as the Church militant. They will understand that God does not define equality the way that the world does, that an ordered and hierarchical Church and family need not entail oppression. They will recognize that redemption is from shame and not just guilt and that it is elevation to honor and not simply forgiveness. It is membership in a new family that has been connected to the divine family of the Trinity. It will perceive that leadership in the Church is priestly mediation of the Messiah's own being and gifts and that the atonement was a victory over the powers that keep men and women in fear and bondage. It will know that faith cannot be separated from faithfulness until the end, that contested pluralism is the norm in history, and that the Bible is a story in which we are invited to participate. These are some of the gifts of the global South churches to our experience of the history of redemption.

Select Bibliography

Bediako, Kwame. "Five Theses on the Significance of Modern African Christianity: A Manifesto." In *Landmark Essays in Mission and World Christianity*, edited by Robert Gallagher and Paul Hertig, 95–115. Maryknoll, NY: Orbis Books, 2009.

———. "Scripture as the Interpreter of Culture and Tradition." In *Africa Bible Commentary*, edited by Tokunboh Adeyemo, 3–4. Nairobi: WordAlive; Grand Rapids: Zondervan, 2006.

Chan, Simon. *Grassroots Asian Theology: Thinking the Faith from the Ground Up.* Downers Grove, IL: IVP Academic, 2014.

Johnson, Todd M. "The 100-Year Shift of Christianity to the South." Gordon-Conwell Theological Seminary, October 9, 2019. https://www.gordonconwell.edu/blog/the-100-year -shift-of-christianity-to-the-south/.

McDermott, Gerald. *God's Rivals: Why Has God Allowed Different Religions? Insights from the Bible and the Early Church.* Downers Grove, IL: IVP Academic, 2007.

———. "What If Paul Had Been from China? Reflections on the Possibility of Revelation in Non-Christian Religions." In *No Other Gods before Me? Evangelicals and the Challenge of World Religions*, edited by John G. Stackhouse Jr., 17–35. Grand Rapids: Baker Academic, 2001.

Nicholls, Bruce. "The Role of Shame and Guilt in a Theology of Cross-Cultural Mission." *Evangelical Review of Theology* 25, no. 3 (July 2001): 231–41.

Sanneh, Lamin. *Translating the Message: The Missionary Impact on Culture.* Maryknoll, NY: Orbis Books, 1989.

Tennent, Timothy C. *Theology in the Context of World Christianity: How the Global Church Is Influencing the Way We Think about and Discuss Theology.* Grand Rapids: Zondervan, 2007.

Walls, Andrew F. *The Cross-Cultural Process in Christian History.* Maryknoll, NY: Orbis Books, 2002.

Watchman Nee. *The Glorious Church.* Anaheim, CA: Living Stream Ministry, 1993.

30

Israel Returned, Renewed, and Restored

As Ari Shavit wrote, the twentieth century was "the most dramatic century in the dramatic history of the Jewish people."[1] After one in every three Jews in the world was murdered in the Holocaust, just three years later the state of Israel was established. That remarkable sequence has led some to see a connection between the resurrection of the Messiah on the third day and the resurrection of his flesh-and-blood people in the state of Israel three years after the murder of a great part of their body. It was another remarkable sequence twenty years later that in the same decade saw both the reunification of Jerusalem after two thousand years and the birth of a new movement of Messianic Judaism. Many have since observed that this movement is a necessary link between the two expressions of the Messiah's body—his Gentile followers in the Church and his Jewish followers in the remnant of Israel who walk in his Jewish ways. This chapter will explore the striking phenomena of the last two centuries—the return of Jews to the land in unprecedented numbers and the rise of Messianic Judaism—and ask how Zion relates to the Gentile Church and the redemption of the world.

New Developments after the Reformation

For most of Christian history after the fourth century, Jews who came to receive Jesus as their Messiah were forced to renounce their Jewish identity and stop

1. Ari Shavit, "In Israel, a Dream Made Real," *Wall Street Journal*, November 29, 2013.

practicing Mosaic law. Converts such as Rabbi Solomon Halevi in the fifteenth century, who became the bishop of Burgos in 1414, did what all learned Jewish converts were expected to do: denounce rabbinic writings as blasphemous. But then, as we saw in previous chapters, there were remarkable new developments. Puritans in the sixteenth century and Pietists in the seventeenth century began to recognize that Jesus appealed frequently to Torah and that the rest of the Old Testament prophesied that the Jews would return to the land one day. Puritan scholars in the seventeenth century were obsessed with eschatology (theology of the end), plotting when the return would take place and how it would connect to "all Israel" accepting their Messiah. Yet some influential Christian writers such as Henry Finch (d. 1625) and Increase Mather (d. 1723) wrote that Jewish return to the land would come first and conversion only later. Suddenly, as it were, significant Christian leaders were reevaluating the supersessionism that had been enforced since the fourth century.

In the nineteenth century Christian scholars in Europe such as Franz Delitzsch and Hermann Strack presented Judaism as a less developed form of Christianity. John Nelson Darby (1800–1882), an Anglican priest, developed a philosophy of history called dispensationalism. This schema had the Jewish people at its center and claimed that true Gentile believers would be raptured off the planet while the Jews who remained as the 144,000 would be the Messiah's emissaries on the earth. The spread of dispensationalism created a newly positive attitude toward Jews among conservative Protestants. These popular movements of Puritans, Pietists, and dispensationalists stimulated efforts to convert Jews through institutions such as the *Institutum Judaicum* at the (Pietist) University of Halle in 1728 and the London Society for Promoting Christianity amongst the Jews in 1809.

All of this stimulated the Hebrew Christian movement of the nineteenth century. At first this was a nationalist and not religious movement. The Beney Abraham (1813) and the Hebrew Christian Prayer Union (1882) were Jewish Jesus-believers seeking to remain within the Jewish people, unlike Jewish converts of most of the previous fourteen hundred years who turned away from the Jewish people. These Hebrew Christians supported Zionism (the effort to establish a Jewish homeland) but proclaimed their freedom from Mosaic law.

Yet then Joseph Rabinowitz (1837–99), a Jewish intellectual from Bessarabia, traveled to Palestine in 1882 to see whether Jewish settlement in the land might free his people from centuries of persecution. While standing on the Mount of Olives looking at the holy city, Rabinowitz was suddenly convinced that Jesus was the Messiah, who alone could save Israel. He proceeded to establish in Kishinev (in what is now Moldova) an autonomous Jewish assembly called Israelites of the New Covenant in the 1880s. He and his fellow Jewish disciples of Yeshua tried to live within the confines of the Jewish people and took up Torah practice such as circumcision, Sabbath, Passover, and other Jewish holidays. Sadly, the Russian government never gave them permission to form a congregation, but news of this distinctly Jewish assembly within the greater Body of the Messiah spread to other Jewish disciples of Jesus.

One was Paul Levertoff (1878–1954), a Russian Hasidic Jew who immigrated to England, where he became an Anglican priest. Levertoff thought that the mystical Hasidic world was the most congenial environment for a new community of Torah-practicing believers in Yeshua. He was uncomfortable with traditional Christian missions to Jews, which presumed Jesus had started a new religion alien to rabbinic Judaism. Instead, he favored theological conversation and practical cooperation with Jews.

Another Jewish thinker influenced by Rabinowitz was Lev Gillet (1893–1980), a Russian Orthodox priest from France who argued in his *Communion in the Messiah* that the rabbinic tradition is of value and needs only to be complemented by messianic perspectives. Gillet saw in Jewish suffering of the last two millennia the travails of Isaiah's Suffering Servant, which might lead to the consummation of history. He argued that when Jews orient themselves toward the kingdom of God, they are unwittingly acting "for and in the Messiah." A community of Jews so oriented would form a true Christian and a true Israelite commune in the same Messiah, albeit partially and only implicitly, but one day totally and explicitly. Although he thought the word "conversion" wrongly suggests that Jews abandon Judaism when coming to Yeshua, nevertheless he called for two conversions. Israel must convert so that it can partner with the Church, and the Church must convert so that it can rejoin Israel. Because of its overwhelming numerical and political strength, the Church's conversion is more critical. Without it, Christians will miss much of who the Messiah is and the fullness of the redemption he offers. For to the degree that the Church is ignorant of Judaism, it is ignorant of the Messiah.

The 1960s

In his *Postmissionary Messianic Judaism*, Mark Kinzer explains that three phenomena of the 1960s brought new changes to the fledgling Jewish Messianic movement.[2] One of the religious versions of the counterculture of that decade was the Jesus movement, which crested in 1971 when "the Jesus Revolution" was featured on an April cover of *Time* magazine. Many new disciples were Jewish, some of whom founded Jews for Jesus. This creative and sometimes-abrasive approach to the Jewish people was an outgrowth of evangelical Protestantism that saw Torah practice as optional for Messianic Jews and often sent converted Jews to evangelical congregations.

A second phenomenon of the 1960s that influenced Jewish believers was the new pluralistic ideal that prized different ethnic identities over the American "melting pot," which would submerge ethnicity in "American" identity. African Americans promoted "black power," some Hispanics wanted to be known as "Chicanos," and American Indians took up the "Native American" moniker. To be "Jewish" was another identity to be valued, at least before old prejudices returned and especially if it meant a way to distinguish themselves from a nominally Christian American culture.

The third 1960s-era event was the Six-Day War in 1967, which reunified Jerusalem. This gave Jews around the world a sense of pride and strengthened the conviction of dispensationalists that Israel is at the center of history.

All of these dynamics in the 1960s and early 1970s contributed to the emergence and growth of Messianic Judaism. Kinzer reports that the movement was characterized by charismatic praise, Israeli dance, fragments of Jewish liturgy, Saturday worship, the advocacy by some of biblical dietary laws, and traditional head coverings and prayer shawls. Although there were these Jewish distinctives, most took their theology from American evangelicalism, which regarded their Jewish ancestors over the previous two millennia as alienated from salvation because the vast majority did not have explicit faith in Yeshua.

There was comparable movement within Roman Catholicism. In 1979 the Association of Hebrew Catholics was founded by Father Elias Friedman (1916–99), a South African Jew who had joined a Catholic monastery in Haifa in 1954. Friedman was a Zionist who saw Jewish resistance to Yeshua-faith as part of a divine plan that will be reversed only at the end of history, when the Jewish people collectively will accept their Messiah. He spoke of traditional Christian missions to Jews, which failed to recognize the divine origins of Jews' "partial hardening" (Rom. 11:25), as blinded and fanatical. Unlike some later Messianic Jewish groups, this association of Catholic Jews was opposed to Torah practice and saw little value in rabbinic Judaism.

---

2. Mark S. Kinzer, *Postmissionary Messianic Judaism: Redefining Christian Engagement with the Jewish People* (Grand Rapids: Brazos, 2005), 286–88.

Zion and the Church

The return of Jews in large numbers to the land over the last two centuries, the establishment of the state of Israel in 1948, and the rise of Messianic Judaism with a character not seen since the early Church—all of these developments have led to fresh examination of the relation of Zion to the Church. Where does the (largely) Gentile Church stand vis à vis Israel? Is one part of the other? Where does non-Messianic Israel fit in?

Since the Holocaust and especially in the last five decades scholars have kept returning to Romans, Paul's most mature statement on the Church and Israel, to answer these questions. William S. Campbell has been among the most acute students of this letter, the closest thing we have to a systematic theology from Paul. Campbell argues that the church at Rome was mostly Gentile and inherited from the Roman *imperium* prejudice against conquered Judea and its people.[3] Even though some of its Gentile members were mentored by Jesus-believing Jews and took up Jewish practices while remaining Gentile, most of the Gentile membership, because of this prejudice, despised both Jesus-believing Jews and the Jewish practices of some of their fellow Gentiles. Paul reminds the Gentile believers that they were grafted into the olive tree of Israel *among* other branches and not "in their place" (Rom. 11:17) as the RSV wrongly translates. Gentiles are warned not to be presumptuous, for they and Jewish believers have common roots and are on the same tree. The old tree was not cut down and replaced.

Paul acknowledges that while tens of thousands of Jews have accepted their Messiah (see Acts 21:20 and its *myriades*, plural for *myriad* or ten thousand), most have not. The burden of Romans 9–11 is to explore this "mystery" (Rom. 11:25). As Campbell puts it, Paul's response is that Israel has stumbled and been hardened, but these are only temporary states and not final destiny. Israel failed to obtain what she sought because of her ignorance (10:2) and was destined for rejection of Jesus by God himself (11:25, 28–32). But Israel is also destined for restoration, when "all Israel will be saved" (11:26), when the remnant of Jewish Jesus-believers will be reunited with the rest of Israel. This will come, as Craig Keener has observed, only after all the Gentiles have had their opportunity to accept the Jewish Messiah (11:28–32). The restoration of Israel will bless the whole world (11:12, 15). This will not mean the salvation of every last Jew in history, for "not

---

3. William S. Campbell, "The Relationship between Israel and the Church," in *Introduction to Messianic Judaism: Its Ecclesial Context and Biblical Foundations*, ed. David Randolph and Joel Willitts (Grand Rapids: Zondervan, 2013), 196–205.

all who come from Israel are of Israel" (9:6). But in that restoration God will move on all the tribes for a wholesale embrace of Yeshua as Messiah.

One Body of Messiah in Two Expressions

In the meantime, before the final restoration of Israel, what is the relation between the (mostly) Gentile Church and the Jewish remnant? And what about the rest of Jewish Israel? We can infer from Romans and other Pauline letters such as Ephesians that the Body of Messiah comes in two expressions. One is the Gentile Christian Church, which is "the assembly of the faithful from the nations who are joined to Israel" through the Jewish Messiah. The other is the assembly of Jewish believers in Yeshua. "Together [they] constitute the one Body of Messiah, a community of Jews and Gentiles who in their . . . distinction and mutual blessing anticipate the shalom" of the renewed earth to come.[4]

Campbell argues that this is what Paul means in Ephesians 2: the Gentiles are "no longer strangers and sojourners, alienated from the commonwealth of Israel, but fellow citizens with *the separated ones* [the literal meaning of *tōn hagiōn*, probably referring to Jewish Yeshua believers] and members of the household of God" (Eph. 2:19–20). According to Campbell, Paul here makes clear that Gentile believers do not become Israelites per se but associate members of the commonwealth of Israel. Particularity, not universality or sameness, is the mark of Paul's ecclesiology. Just as men and women retain their different sexes after becoming one in marriage, so Jews and Gentiles remain as Jews and Gentiles after sharing in the commonwealth of Israel because of their oneness with the Jewish Messiah. This divine diversity, Campbell insists, is not a vestige of remaining sinfulness but an original divine intent. God always intended to have Gentiles join Israel without becoming Jewish, just as he always intended marital unity with distinctions to mirror the Messiah's unity with the Church without collapsing distinctions between a holy Messiah and his unholy Church.

Campbell notes that the supposition that all distinctions are eliminated in redemption not only ignores the male-female differentiated unity in marriage but reflects Enlightenment "imperialism," which obliterates the past for the sake of uniformity. This seeks unity through sameness, destroying difference. Instead, redemption by the Messiah transforms without demolishing distinctions.

4. Union of Messianic Jewish Congregations, "Defining Messianic Judaism," (2005), quoted in Daniel C. Juster, "Messianic Jews and the Gentile Christian World," in Rudolph and Willitts, *Introduction to Messianic Judaism*, 136.

Distinctions are retained but relativized. The ingrafted branches don't become natural branches, but they are on the same tree. The circumcised never become uncircumcised but "circumcision and uncircumcision are nothing" (1 Cor. 7:19) when it comes to redemption in the new creation. Men and women retain their distinctions, and Gentiles and Jews retain *their* distinctions, but all are redeemed by union with the Jewish Messiah.

For Paul, new creation communities are places where ethnic distinctions are recognized but not permitted to become means of discrimination. This is why he tells the members of the Roman church to "accept one another" in chapters 14 and 15. Those who regard Jewish practices as unimportant should not look down on those who consider them worthwhile, and vice versa. There is universalism in redemption by the Messiah, but it is a universalism with particularities that persist. Campbell maintains that at the end of days when God establishes his kingdom on the renewed earth, two groups together will constitute his people—Israel redeemed from exile and Gentiles redeemed from idolatry.

Messianic Judaism is the crucial connection—Dan Juster calls it the "organic bridge"—between today's Gentile Church and the wider Jewish community.[5] Catholic priest Peter Hocken (1932–2017), scholar and participant in Messianic-Catholic dialogues, was convinced that the Gentile Church cannot deal with Israel adequately until it confronts Messianic Judaism. The first significant church division, he argued, came from the fourth-century rejection of the legitimacy of the early Messianic Jewish community, a rejection that established the roots of anti-Semitism in the Church. The modern Messianic Jewish community provides the churches with the opportunity to change this tragic history, but only by rejecting replacement theology and focusing on the mystery of ingrafting.

But if today's Messianic Judaism is critical to Gentile churches, it also serves the wider Jewish community by constituting, as Kinzer puts it, its eschatological firstfruits, sanctifying the whole (Rom. 11:16) and revealing the ultimate meaning of Jewish identity and destiny. Part of that meaning can already be seen. Irving Greenberg points out that when Christianity forgot its Jewish roots, it skewed toward a metaphysical dualism that radically separated matter from spirit, thus minimizing the religious significance of the body and those parts of God's law that concern our life in the material world. Thus, it is no surprise that Gnosticism has been a recurring heresy in a Church that is cut off from its Jewish character.

5. Juster, "Messianic Jews and the Gentile Christian World," 137.

Zionism and the Jewish State

No doubt one reason that Jews have regarded matter more highly than Christians is that they prize the land of Israel. This is no wonder since God's gift of the land to Abraham and his descendants (Gen. 12:1–9) is repeated explicitly or implicitly one thousand times in the Hebrew Bible.[6] And for the last fifteen hundred years Jews have prayed from the Amidah three times a day that the temple would be rebuilt on the land. The Jewish prayer book is full of prayers that yearn for the land of Zion. Therefore, it is a myth that Zionism—the notion that Jews deserve a homeland like every other people and in their ancient land—is a modern, nationalist invention of the nineteenth century. More than six centuries before Theodore Herzl, the father of modern Jewish Zionism, French Talmudic scholars immigrated to Palestine in the thirteenth century to settle. This ambition to reclaim the ancient Jewish home was renewed by the settlement of Hasidic communities on the land in the eighteenth century. When large numbers of Jews came to the land at the end of the nineteenth and beginning of the twentieth centuries, there were both secular and religious Jews in the migrations. The latter were moved by Talmudic passages like the following: "Dwelling in the land is equal to all the commandments in the Torah" (Midrash Sifre Re'eh 80).

It is also true that Christian Zionism played a role in Jewish Zionism and the eventual establishment of the state of Israel. The work of Henry Grattan Guinness is a case in point. At the end of the nineteenth century he lived in Paris, where Colonel Dreyfus was his neighbor; the vicious anti-Semitism that led to Dreyfus's false conviction in 1894 convinced Herzl that Jews needed a Jewish state. Fascinated by astronomy and its connections to the 1,260 days predicted by Daniel, Guinness argued in Dreyfus's books *The Approaching End of the Age* (1878) and *Light for the Last Days* (1887) that two key dates for the restoration of the Jewish homeland would be 1917 and 1948. Guinness died in 1910, but before he died, Arthur Balfour, then a member of Parliament, wrote that he had read his books and "studied them closely." In 1917 Balfour was Britain's foreign secretary and penned the "Balfour Declaration" that committed Britain to support for "a national home for the Jewish people."

In June 1917 General Sir Beauvoir de Lisle told Field Marshal Sir Edmund Allenby that he would surely be in Jerusalem by the end of 1917 because of what he had read in Guinness's *Light for the Last Days*. He added that Allenby should not

---

6. This section is drawn from Gerald McDermott, *Israel Matters: Why Christians Must Think Differently about the People and the Land* (Grand Rapids: Brazos, 2017), 49, 139–40. Used by permission of Baker Publishing Group.

"ride in state, for that is reserved in future for One higher than you." On December 11, 1917, Allenby got off his horse at Jaffa Gate and walked into the Old City with a humility "that was rare for him." Though Guinness was dead by this time, he had rightly predicted two dates that were crucial for the future state of Israel.[7]

While the return of Jews from all over the world in the last two hundred years was unprecedented and seems to have been a fulfillment of biblical prophecy, the establishment of a Jewish state is a bit different. The Zionist movements, both secular and religious, were, as Kinzer remarks, integral but imperfect expressions of God's plan in human history.[8] They were necessary for the rebirth of Jewish life in the land, which is a divine work with profound eschatological implications. The state, on the other hand, serves the Jewish people and nation but is not identical to them. It is a necessary instrument rather than an ultimate end. Every state protects a people gathered on a land, and the last century proved that the Jewish people need governmental protection more than any other. But the present Jewish state might not be the last one, is imperfect like any other state, and therefore is not beyond criticism. Christians and Jews can regard its establishment as something of a miracle and in fact portentous when considering its birth three years after the end of the Holocaust, even hinting at a connection between Jesus's death and resurrection. But it is still a human and imperfect state and, like every other state, needs to be called to account when it strays from natural law and the biblical covenant to which it is remotely dedicated. We cannot know the present state's connection to Israel's restoration at the eschaton, but we can be fairly confident that the existence of a Jewish state is at least a step on the road—short or long—to that restoration. Right now it is necessary as a protection for the covenanted people.

Israel's Restoration

Jean Cardinal Daniélou once remarked that biblical prophecy "is the announcement of the fact that, at the end of time, God will accomplish works still greater than in the past."[9] Jews have rightly complained that Christian emphasis on the finished work of the Messiah is problematic because it subordinates the future

---

7. These two paragraphs come from information conveyed to me by Henry Grattan Guinness's great-grandson, Os Guinness, on December 31, 2022.

8. Mark Kinzer, *Jerusalem Crucified, Jerusalem Risen: The Resurrected Messiah, the Jewish People, and the Land of Promise* (Eugene, OR: Wipf & Stock, 2018), 254.

9. John Cardinal Daniélou, "The Sacraments and the History of Salvation," *Letter and Spirit* 2 (2006): 211.

to the past. They have also pointed out that the Church has tended to spiritualize and individualize the eschaton so that it becomes indistinguishable from the lot of the soul after death. The result has been a diminution of true hope, which for Jews (as it ought to be for Christians!) is far more exciting—to be resurrected with a community and inhabit a new creation. But Christians have too often downgraded the spectacular hope that we find in the New Testament Church, suppressing the faith of more biblically informed theologians like Daniélou.

Perhaps Paul is the best example of New Testament hope for stupendous events in the future. Paul was looking forward to the restoration of the twelve tribes of Israel when he told Agrippa that he was on trial for hope in the promise God made to "our fathers, to which *our twelve tribes* hope to attain, as they unfailingly worship night and day" (Acts 26:6–7). He told the Jewish elders in Rome, "It is because of the hope of Israel that I am wearing this chain" (28:20).

What was this hope? Most scholars agree that Ezekiel's vision of the dry bones coming to life in chapter 37 was a prophecy that Israel as a people would be resurrected as a people in the land to honor YHWH. This vision came to Ezekiel just after God told him in the preceding chapter (36) that one day he would "sprinkle clean water" on Israel, cleanse them from all their uncleanness, and give them a new spirit and new heart. Both the dry bones prophecy and this one about a new heart link this resurrection and renewal to Israel's return from the nations back to the land (36:24; 37:12, 14, 21). The spiritual renewal comes *after* the return to the land.

Peter also spoke of a future restoration of Israel. In his second speech in Jerusalem after the Pentecost miracle, he spoke of a future *apokatastasis* or restoration that was still to come (Acts 3:21). Remember, this was after Jesus's resurrection, by which time, according to many Christian theologians and Bible scholars, *everything* was completed. But Peter would have disagreed, for he said a future restoration was still to come. He uses the same Greek word that's used in the Septuagint— the early Church's principal text for the Bible—for the future return of Jews from all the nations back to the land. At some time after that, Peter was saying, there would be restoration.

Luke has Peter use the same Greek root Jesus used when he prophesied just before his ascension that one day he would restore (*apokathistaneis*) the kingdom to Israel (Acts 1:6). This Greek word was a technical term for the restoration of the Davidic kingdom in its ancestral capital. It was often used in the Jewish literature of the period (in the Septuagint at Hosea 11:11; Jer. 16:15; 24:6, and in Josephus's *Antiquities* 11.2, 63) for Israel's future restoration.

The hope of Israel, then, is not the resurrection of Jesus but the restoration of Israel that Jesus's resurrection anticipated. Jesus suggests that his second coming will inaugurate it, for he prophesies that when he returns, the Jewish people of Jerusalem will have had their eyes opened to welcome him (Luke 13:35). Some scholars say that he will *wait* until Jerusalem turns to him, so that it will be the conversion of Israel to her Messiah that will catalyze his return. Whether his return is conditional on Israel's welcome or causes that welcome, it is clear that the prophets, Paul, Peter, and Jesus all looked to a future restoration of Israel with all twelve tribes and the kingdom of God centered in Jerusalem. This will be a time, Jesus said, when the world will be "reborn" (*palingenesia*) and his apostles will rule the twelve tribes (Matt. 19:28).

Jesus also suggested a sequence of events before the eschaton. He told his disciples in Jerusalem that the lead-up to his second coming ("when they see the Son of Man coming in a cloud") and Israel's restoration ("your redemption") would be the end of "the times of the Gentiles" (Luke 21:27, 28, 24). When would that be? When Jerusalem was no longer "trampled underfoot" or controlled by Gentiles (21:24). Since Jerusalem was reunited after the Six-Day War in 1967 and Gentiles abandoned control after two thousand years, some think that the times of the Gentiles are coming to a close. Others say that might be so, but they caution that the transition from the times of the Gentiles to Israel's restoration in the eschaton could be an extended process rather than a singular event. It could be a sequence that culminates in corporate Jerusalem welcoming her Messiah but a sequence that began long before.

The Grand Story

The restoration of Israel is exciting because it is biblical, and the true biblical story is far more interesting than narratives of Christian theology that flatten out its eschatology. Yet even this attention to Israel's end and its role in the world's redemption misses a bit of the grander story to which it contributes.

As Kinzer has depicted it, what I have just been narrating is the beautiful end to a story that God started at the creation.[10] The world was created good but not holy. Because of Adam's sin, to which we have contributed by our own sins, the world is now wounded and needs healing. It is broken and needing wholeness. The covenant with the patriarchs and its embodiment at Sinai initiated the move

10. Mark Kinzer, *Israel's Messiah and the People of God: A Vision for Messianic Jewish Covenant Fidelity*, ed. Jennifer Rosner (Eugene, OR: Wipf & Stock, 2011), 122–25.

from the sixth day, as it were, to the seventh day, from the profane to the holy, from imperfection to wholeness.

In this covenant God pitched his tent within the people Israel. Her sacrifices enabled Israel to assume her role as the world's priest, offering herself to God in worship for the sustenance and redemption of the world. Amid her successes Israel also failed—a microcosm of the failures of the nations—but her Messiah summed up all that Israel was intended to be. He embodied Israel and was the perfect Israelite. He was the perfect temple, priest, and sacrifice. His resurrection from the dead was as Israel's perfect martyr whose blood was shed both to atone for sins and to prepare the way for the world to come. In his resurrection and gift of the Spirit, and in the founding of the twofold Body of the Messiah, which extends Israel's heritage among the nations, the new world was realized proleptically—that is, in advance. The harmony and mutual blessings of this twofold body, the Church and Messianic Judaism, anticipate the shalom of the new world to come. The body's sacraments, especially baptism and Eucharist, convey the beauty and harmony of the world to come in the here and now. They too are proleptic, just as *kashrut* (separating pure from impure food) and Sabbath are foretastes of the world to come.

For millennia, readers of the New Testament have puzzled over the eschatological discourses of Mark 13 and Matthew 24, which seem to conflate predictions of the destruction of Jerusalem in AD 70 with prophecies about the end of the world. Now we are beginning to see that this is another example of how God speaks typologically throughout the history of redemption to point to future events in that history. There was a real presence of the final judgment in the judgment of Jerusalem in 70. Israel's history has always been full of types that point to antitypes in the history of the nations. God called Israel to link earth to heaven, to serve as a microcosm of the universe, and to anticipate a future in which the whole creation will become God's temple with Jerusalem as its Holy of Holies.

Select Bibliography

Ariel, Yaakov. *Evangelizing the Chosen People.* Chapel Hill: University of North Carolina Press, 2000.

Campbell, William S. *Paul and the Creation of Christian Identity.* London: T&T Clark, 2008.

———. "The Relationship between Israel and the Church." In Rudolph and Willitts, Introduction to Messianic Judaism, 196–205.

Daniélou, John Cardinal. "The Sacraments and the History of Salvation." *Letter and Spirit* 2 (2006): 203–15.

Gillet, Lev. *Communion in the Messiah: Studies in the Relationship between Judaism and Christianity.* Eugene, OR: Wipf & Stock, 1999.

Greenberg, Irving. *For the Sake of Heaven and Earth: The New Encounter between Judaism and Christianity.* Philadelphia: Jewish Publication Society, 2004.

Hafemann, Scott J. "The Redemption of Israel for the Sake of the Gentiles." In Rudolph and Willitts, *Introduction to Messianic Judaism,* 206–13.

Hocken, Peter. "The Messianic Jewish Movement: New Current and Old Reality." In *The Challenges of the Pentecostal, Charismatic and Messianic Jewish Movements: The Tensions of the Spirit,* 97–116. Burlington, VT: Ashgate, 2009.

Juster, Daniel C. "Messianic Jews and the Gentile Christian World." In Rudolph and Willitts, *Introduction to Messianic Judaism,* 136–44.

Keener, Craig. "Interdependence and Mutual Blessing in the Church." In Rudolph and Willitts, *Introduction to Messianic Judaism,* 187–95.

Kinzer, Mark. *Israel's Messiah and the People of God: A Vision for Messianic Jewish Covenant Fidelity.* Edited by Jennifer Rosner. Eugene, OR: Wipf & Stock, 2011.

———. *Jerusalem Crucified, Jerusalem Risen: The Resurrected Messiah, the Jewish People, and the Land of Promise.* Eugene, OR: Wipf & Stock, 2018.

———. *Postmissionary Messianic Judaism: Redefining Christian Engagement with the Jewish People.* Grand Rapids: Brazos, 2005.

Rudolph, David, and Joel Willitts, eds. *Introduction to Messianic Judaism: Its Ecclesial Context and Biblical Foundations.* Grand Rapids: Zondervan, 2013.

Shavit, Ari. "In Israel, a Dream Made Real." *Wall Street Journal,* November 29, 2013.

———. *My Promised Land: The Triumph and Tragedy of Israel.* New York: Spiegel and Grau, 2013.

Willitts, Joel. "The Bride of Messiah and the Israel-ness of the New Heavens and New Earth." In Rudolph and Willitts, *Introduction to Messianic Judaism,* 245–54.

Part Six

The Eschaton

31

The Messiah's Return and Final Judgment

The history of redemption will come near to a close with the second coming of the Messiah and his presiding over the final judgment of every human being who has ever lived. These are momentous events that Scripture and tradition have revealed with surprising detail. We will explore some of the most common questions about them such as the time and signs of the *parousia* (Greek for "coming") and the process of the final judgment. At the end of the chapter we will reflect on the age-old question of the millennium.

The Manner of the Return

Scripture emphasizes the certainty and suddenness of the return of the Messiah to earth. Jesus said he would come on the clouds and with great power and glory (Mark 13:26) and that his return would be like the approach of a thief in the night when everything seems safe and normal (Matt. 24:36–51). Peter predicted that there would be scoffers in all ages doubting the return (2 Pet. 3:1–10), and liberals such as Social Gospeler Walter Rauschenbusch and New Testament scholar Shailer Mathews said it would be only figurative and not bodily. But Jesus said his return would be visible ("They will *see* the Son of Man coming in clouds"; Mark 13:26) and bodily ("This Jesus . . . will come in the same way you saw him go up into heaven"; Acts 1:11).

People will respond with joy and terror. Those who have been walking with him will be overjoyed that finally their persecution will be over, but those refusing the call of God on their lives will tremble with terror, hiding in caves and rocks in the mountains (Rev. 6:15–17).

One Return

Dispensationalists think there will be two returns, one "for" his saints in a *rapture*, where the Messiah will remain in the upper air and take all true believers off the face of the earth (they cite 1 Thess. 4:15–16) before a great tribulation, and then another "with" his saints seven years later, after the tribulation. But in 2 Thessalonians 2:1–12 there is only one coming or *parousia* to gather together his saints, and it is *after* the tribulation with its apostasy and "man of lawlessness," who proclaims himself to be god (vv. 1, 3–8). Jesus suggests the same in Matthew 24, where the elect are "gathered" *after* "the tribulation of those days" (vv. 29–31). There, too, there is only one second coming of the Son of Man.

Soon Is Not Imminent

Many scholars have claimed that Jesus and the apostles were wrong to think that the second coming would be imminent, in their own generation. But there is exegetical evidence that this claim misses the subtleties of the text. When Jesus was nearing Jerusalem and his passion and some were thinking the kingdom of God was to appear immediately, he told them the parable of the ten minas to suggest that there would be time to invest before his coming (Luke 19:11–27). And as we have seen, he also stated at several points in his earthly ministry that certain things had to happen first, such as the completion of the times of the Gentiles.

How then can we understand the occasional predictions of the Gospels that Jesus would come soon and prayers in the New Testament that he come quickly? First, not all comings were the second coming. Before his transfiguration he told his apostles that some would not taste death before they would see him coming in his kingdom (Matt. 16:28). By that he meant the manifestation of his kingdom glory on the mount with Moses and Elijah. So that was a coming that *was* imminent, but it was not the second coming, which was *not* imminent.

Second, the Greek word used three times by Jesus for "soon" in Revelation 22 is *tachy*, which often means "suddenly" or "unexpectedly." So Jesus advises us in the last chapter of the New Testament most likely *not* that his coming will be after a short period of time but that it will be sudden and unexpected.

Third, Newman observed that Jesus's association of "soon" with "like a thief" shows that his meaning was not about chronological time but apocalyptic surprise. Newman added that the kingdom is full of apparent contradictions, and the contrast between coming soon and waiting for millennia is one of many. The lines of God's providence and history will meet at last even though now they seem parallel. People in sleep or drowning or euphoria can think years are passing. They suddenly become other people, nature or grace dispensing with time.[1]

Other contradictions related to the second coming, Newman continued, include that between our praying for his coming and working out our salvation to make our election sure. Or knowing that his eyes are too pure to behold sin yet being confident that he is all-merciful and desires my salvation because he died for me. It is like the mingled feelings of a son who obtains forgiveness from his father. The resolution of the contradiction between his father's wrath and the son's hope for forgiveness lies in the latter's conviction that mercy triumphs over judgment.[2]

Signs

I just mentioned Jesus's prediction that the fullness of the times of the Gentiles needed to play out before his return. Scripture points to other signs before the end. Since Paul says that Israel's conversion will mean life from the dead for the Gentiles, it seems that Israel's national turning will take place before a worldwide Gentile revival and that both will precede the Messiah's return. Perhaps that is what Haggai meant by the Messiah becoming the desire of the nations (2:7) and what Isaiah meant by his prophecy of the earth being full of the knowledge of YHWH, as the waters cover the sea (11:9).

Jesus said there would be false messiahs, world wars, earthquakes, and famines (Mark 13). He and Paul said there would be a great apostasy and persecution of the Church before the end, which will culminate in the rise of the Antichrist or man of lawlessness (2 Thess. 2). So if there will be a massive worldwide revival among Jews and Gentiles before the beginning of the eschaton—the "prosperity of the Church" that Edwards and the Puritans predicted—it will also be a time of great persecution of the Church. We saw this strange mixture during the horrific

---

1. John Henry Newman, "Shrinking from Christ's Coming," in *Parochial and Plain Sermons* (San Francisco: Ignatius, 1997), 988–95.

2. Newman, "Shrinking from Christ's Coming," 988–95.

Cultural Revolution in China (1966–76), when millions were massacred and millions came to Christian faith, and it seems we will see the same pattern of blood and glory worldwide near the end.

One further sign before the end, predicted by Jesus, will be the worldwide proclamation of the gospel (Mark 13:10). This appears to be implied by the fullness of the times of the Gentiles. Apparently there will be a convergence of all these events—conversion of Israel, worldwide evangelization, Gentile revival, and severe persecution of the Messiah's twofold body led by the forces of Antichrist. Darrell Johnson argues that Revelation portrays Satan imprisoned in the pit but manipulating society through the two beasts, a political power from the sea and a religious power from the earth.

Some would argue that in the 2020s we were already seeing all of these events in play. Others insist that the fullness of revival and persecution, particularly the conversion of Israel, is yet to come. And so the signs of the second coming have not yet been completed.

Until Then

Scripture indicates that while we are watching the signs and praying for the Lord to return, our primary responsibility is to be watchful. We are never to presume that we are ready but always to guard against complacency, lest we become like the foolish virgins, who were unprepared for the bridegroom's coming. Jesus hints that it is easy to become complacent because just before he comes it will be like the days of Noah—normality in eating and drinking, marrying and giving in marriage, buying and selling (Luke 17:26–37). Joseph Ratzinger adds that in the Eucharistic liturgy we have a warning against complacency. For it is a *parousia* in our midst, the coming of our Lord now to anticipate his second coming. Each Eucharist is a "tensed yearning" of the already and not yet, when we enjoy his coming now but are exhorted to guard our lives faithfully for his final coming.[3]

Judgment and Glory

Edwards believed that the final judgment would be the Church's greatest glory. For most of her suffering state she received *grace* to endure persecution, but now

---

3. Joseph Ratzinger, *Eschatology: Death and Eternal Life*, 2nd ed. (Washington, DC: Catholic University of America Press, 1988), 203.

she will receive *glory* as her reward and crown. All the graces and glorious things in the past were types and shadows of the glory to come, to be bestowed at the final judgment. When the Messiah comes to rescue Israel and the Church as their enemies surround Jerusalem, the Messiah's armies of angels shall appear in the skies and terrify God's enemies. The suffering saints will be immediately relieved. They will see that the redemption that had been promised for millennia has finally arrived in its final stage. They will not only overflow with joy but will also be covered with shining glory in the events to follow.[4]

Images of the Judgment

We are not given a precise timetable of events connected with the final judgment, but Scripture is full of images that leave a lasting impression. As the *Dictionary of Biblical Imagery* unpacks them, a first image is *separation*.[5] History will be shown to have been bipolar, divided between the City of God and the City of Man, to use Augustine's categories. Just as the flood separated the few righteous from the millions of wicked, just as the ten plagues in Egypt separated God's people from those who cast their lot with Israel's enemy Pharaoh, and just as the twelve spies were separated into the ten fearful and the two hopeful, so too Jesus told parables about a winnowing fork that separates the wheat from the chaff and a harvest separating the righteous from the wicked. C. S. Lewis offered that each group gets what it wants. In his *Great Divorce* Lewis has George McDonald (a universalist in his writings) say from heaven that there are those who "say to God, 'Thy will be done,' and those to whom God says, in the end, 'Thy will be done.'"[6] Those who hate admitting sin and see no need for holiness get a kingdom with an abundance of one and nothing of the other. Those who repent of their sin and plead for holiness get a Savior who frees and fills them. Seventeenth-century Anglican divine Jeremy Taylor wrote that God "threatened horrible things to us if we would not be happy."[7]

Another image is of judgment as a *casting away from God's presence*. Just as Adam and Eve were cast out of Eden in judgment, and Israel was twice exiled

---

4. Edwards, *HWR*, 502–6.

5. "Judgment," in *Dictionary of Biblical Imagery*, ed. Leland Ryken, James C. Wilhoit, and Tremper Longman III (Downers Grove, IL: InterVarsity, 1998), 470–74.

6. C. S. Lewis, *The Great Divorce* (New York: Macmillan, 1946), 72.

7. Jeremy Taylor, "Christ's Advent to Judgment," http://www.authorama.com/worlds-great-sermons-3.html, quoted in "Judgment," in *Dictionary of Biblical Imagery*, 473.

in judgment, the final judgment will be punishment as destruction "away from the presence [literally, "face"] of the Lord and away from his powerful glory" (2 Thess. 1:9).

A third image is judgment as *exposé*. The shroud of anonymity will be stripped away as each individual stands naked before the Judge of the universe. The righteousness of the suffering saints will be manifested. Edwards noted that "their inherent holiness" will "be made manifest, and all their good works be brought to light," especially the righteous deeds they performed in secret. They will finally be heard before the cosmic judge, particularly those who were ignored by unjust judges. The saints "shall declare their cause and rise up in judgment against their persecutors," declaring the cruelties inflicted on them.[8] All secret wickedness perpetrated over the ages shall be brought to light. Things spoken in the dark and in the closet will be exposed to the light and proclaimed before all the angels and humans who ever existed.

Then there is the image of *shock*. Many of those who were first on earth will be last in the kingdom, and they will be astonished to discover this at the judgment. Some who said, "Lord, Lord," to the Messiah in the Church will be devastated to hear the Messiah tell them, "Get away from me. I never knew you" (Matt. 7:23). Jesus said the same to the foolish virgins who cried expectantly, "Lord, lord, open to us." Surely they were shocked when he replied, "I do not know you" (Matt. 25:11–12).

Finally there is the image of *wrath in war*. The Bible often depicts God as a bloodstained warrior (Deut. 32:40–42; Isa. 13:4; 34:5–6; 63:1–16) who uses wine to cause madness and death. In the poetic and prophetic books this wine of wrath is given to both Israel and her enemies (Job 21:20; Ps. 75:8; Jer. 25:15–29; Ezek. 23:31–34). Jesus drank freely of this cup of wrath for the sake of his Body (Matt. 26:42), and unbelievers will be forced to drink this at the final judgment (Rev. 14:9–10).

The Judges

Who will judge? Scripture indicates that God will be both prosecutor and judge of the wicked. But since the Son was the redeemer and revealer of the Father, and all sin is therefore against his work and Body, the Father has delegated to him the execution of judgment (John 5:22).

---

8. Edwards, *HWR*, 503.

According to Paul, the saints will somehow judge with the Messiah (1 Cor. 6:3). Edwards remarked that when the devil told Adam and Eve they would be as gods, little did he realize they would join the Son of God in judging him. Louis Berkhof wrote that the saints will condemn the world by their faith as Jesus said the Ninevites will condemn the unbelieving generation of his day (Matt. 12:41). Ratzinger notes Jesus's testimony that for many, their response to his words will be enough to condemn or acquit them on the last day (John 12:48).

The Judged

According to Edwards, the devil will be judged first of all. He who judged the Church will now be judged by the Church and her Lord. He will see the consequences of the death of the Messiah that he procured and will tremble even in his pride and stubbornness. All the devil's demonic helpers shall join him in horror as the Messiah and his body appear in glory to expose and condemn them. All of the Messiah's other enemies—especially those who mocked and spat on him and all in his Body—will face their accusers with quaking limbs and chattering teeth. Their knees will knock one against the other. Think of Pharaoh, Antiochus Epiphanes, Julian the Apostate, all the rulers who have tortured and murdered believers down through the centuries, Gog and Magog, the communists who ordered the torture and killing of one hundred million innocents, Hitler and his Nazis who massacred six million Jews and several million others.

They will be judged, as Ratzinger has written, not just for one moment of time but for all the pathways of their lives that reveal their fundamental orientation.[9] The sum total of an individual's decisions will indicate that person's basic stance toward Truth, which is a Trinity of Persons.

Degrees of Judgment

Just as there are degrees of sin (Jesus told Pilate that he who handed him over was guilty of a *greater* sin [John 19:11]), so there are degrees of reward and punishment. Jesus told the parable of the talents with differing rewards in the midst of a discourse about his return and final judgment, just before the parable of the sheep and the goats (Matt. 24:36–25:46). He said that Sodom will receive a more tolerable judgment than Capernaum for refusing his teaching (11:23–24). Paul

9. Ratzinger, *Eschatology*, 209.

told the Romans in his great letter on justification by grace through faith that God will judge the secrets of men by Jesus Messiah, each one "according to his works" (Rom. 2:6, 16). As we saw in a previous chapter, Scripture teaches justification by faith ("allegiance" is a better translation) but judgment by works (that reveal that allegiance).

When Jesus was telling his disciples to prepare for the coming of the Son of Man, he told a parable about disobedient servants. Those who knew the master's will would get a severe beating, but those who did not know would receive a light beating. The lesson was that reward and punishment will be graded, based on what each person has been given: more will be demanded of those to whom more was given (Luke 12:35–48).

Sequence

Jesus said no one knows the day or hour when the Son of Man will return and judge the world. But we can know something of the sequence of events from indications in written revelation. The sequence will start when the Messiah returns. The whole world will see him. The wicked will shriek and cry with terror. The Church of God will lift its head and know that its redemption has drawn near. Believers will see infinite love in their Redeemer's face. They will burst with joy over the knowledge that they will be eternally free from harassment by wicked people and devils.

The dead shall then be raised, graves opened, and all the inhabitants who have ever lived on the earth will appear: Adam and Eve, Seth and Abel and Methuselah and all the saints who were their contemporaries, Noah, Abraham, Isaac, Jacob, the prophets, and all the holy martyrs down through history. They will join all the saints in Jewish and Church history until the end of the world. Apart from the saints, but visible to all, will be the wicked from all of history—the heretics and skeptics and persecutors. The Bible says the wicked will be on the left hand of the Messiah and the righteous on his right.

Edwards stipulated that at this point the body of everyone will be changed. The wicked will be fitted so that they can endure eternal torment without dissolution. The saints' bodies will be transformed to be like the Messiah's glorious body. These resurrection bodies will be incapable of pain or sorrow but will be adorned with beauty and glory and incorruption.

After the judgment that lays bare what every human being has done for good or evil—believers' sins revealed as forgiven, unbelievers' sins exposed as damning—

comes the sentencing. The Messiah will say to those on his right, "Come, those of you blessed by my Father, inherit the kingdom prepared for you from the foundation of the world." The Messiah will pronounce these words with infinite love and a sweet voice, causing every heart on his right to swell with joy. This sentence of justification will be especially sweet for those who had been condemned in this world. The honor given to believers will be delicious for those who have been despised and shamed in this world: they will have crowns put on their heads. They shall shine forth like the sun with Jesus Messiah in glory, in the sight of all their enemies (Matt. 13:43; Dan. 12:3).

Then the Messiah's enemies will receive their sentence of condemnation. "Depart from me, you cursed ones, into everlasting fire prepared for the devil and his angels" (Matt. 25:41). No doubt these words will strike horror in the hearts of all on the Messiah's left. There will be horrified looks, moaning, and gnashing of teeth.

At some point after the wicked have been sentenced and cast into the everlasting fire, the Messiah will bring his Church, his bride, to his Father's house for the marriage supper of the Lamb. Whether this is literal or figurative, it means perfect redemption. The Body of the Messiah, both Jewish and Gentile, will be cleansed by the blood of the Lamb and enjoy perfect holiness.

Purgatory?

Most of the Church since its earliest centuries has believed that for most believers a cleansing process or period is needed to complete the gradual sanctification that was started before death. Protestants believe this cleansing process takes place instantaneously at death, while Catholics have believed from early centuries that it extends beyond death. Eastern Orthodox believe in cleansing after death and in prayers for the dead but reject Catholic specifics about temporal punishment in a place called purgatory.

Because the vast majority of Christians and even some Jews have held to some kind of postmortem cleansing, I will sketch briefly an outline of the issues that touch on our history of redemption. First, Scripture suggests that forgiveness of sin does not preclude punishment for that sin. In 2 Samuel, David still had to be punished by God after being forgiven for his adultery and murder. Aquinas observed that in Mark 8 the blind man was healed in stages rather than all at once. Thomas reasoned that even after the guilt of mortal (deadly; 1 John 5:16–17) sin is forgiven, the remnants of a sinful disposition remain that must be chastised and reformed.

Second, Scripture is adamant about the necessity of holiness for redemption. Hebrews tells us that "without [holiness] no one will see the Lord" (Heb. 12:14). Peter warns us that we must be holy in all our conduct because it is written, "You shall be holy, for I am holy" (1 Pet. 1:15–16). The psalmist informs us that no one can enter the presence of God without clean hands and a pure heart (Ps. 24:3–4). John the seer proclaims that nothing unclean shall enter the holy city of the New Jerusalem, and only those who have washed their robes will have a right to the tree of life (Rev. 21:27; 22:14).

Third, there are subtle indications in the Bible of the need to pray for the dead. In the Apocrypha, accepted as canonical by most of the fathers, Judas Maccabeus is commended for praying for dead soldiers who need to be loosed from their sins of wearing pagan amulets on their bodies (2 Macc. 12:39–45). The assumption seems to have been that they were on their way to being with God forever because they had made a fundamental decision for Truth by dying for the people of the God of Israel, but that they had to be purged of the sinful tendencies that compromised them.

Paul prays in 2 Timothy for Onesiphorus, although even Protestant scholars like Gordon Fee agree that Paul knew he was dead.[10] Paul appears to be praying for Onesiphorus during the intermediate period between death and the Messiah's return that "the Lord would grant to him to find mercy from the Lord on that day" (2 Tim. 1:18). Perhaps this is why Paul prays for the Philippians that he who began a good work in them will complete it not before their deaths but "at the day of Jesus Messiah," suggesting an intermediate period in which something would be perfected in them (Phil. 1:6). It might also be why Jesus warned disciples to reconcile with their adversaries lest they be thrown into "prison" (*phylakē*), which they would not get out of until they had "paid the last penny" (Matt. 5:25–26). This Greek word for "prison" was a term for Hades that suggested to both Tertullian and Cyprian, as Ratzinger reports, a place for purification after death. This was especially pertinent for the "weak, average Christians who did not find the strength to accept martyrdom in times of persecution" and thus publicly denied the Messiah but later asked for reconciliation with the Church.[11]

Some of the fathers pointed to 1 Corinthians 3, where Paul speaks of one's work being burned up, with the result that the builder "will suffer loss, though he himself is saved, but only as through fire" (v. 15). Because of this and other passages John Chrysostom asked, "If Job's sons were purified by their father's sacrifice,

10. Gordon Fee, *1 and 2 Timothy, Titus* (Peabody, MA: Hendrickson, 1988), 236.
11. Ratzinger, *Eschatology*, 223.

why should we doubt that our prayers for the dead are of no help?"[12] Gregory the Great reasoned that when Jesus said the blasphemy against the Holy Spirit cannot be forgiven in this age or the one to come, he must have meant that some sins *can* be forgiven not only in this age but also in the one to come (see Matt. 12:32).[13]

Not Satisfaction but Sanctification

Both Aquinas and Ratzinger have taught that the Messiah's passion made satisfaction sufficient for all sins. So if there is suffering in purgatory by the saints, it does not contribute to the Messiah's atonement or satisfaction. Rather, its purpose is to complete sanctification, the increase of holiness necessary to see God. Ratzinger helpfully adds that "purgatory is not . . . some kind of supra-worldly concentration camp where man is forced to undergo punishment in . . . arbitrary fashion." Instead "it is the inwardly necessary process of transformation" that enables a person to be capable of full redemption by the Messiah and unity with the whole communion of saints. "It does not replace grace by works, but allows [grace] to achieve its full victory precisely as grace." We need to be transformed, and an encounter with the Lord is "the fire that burns away our dross to become vessels of eternal joy." Its root is the christological grace of "penance, the idea of the constant readiness for reform which marks the forgiven sinner."[14]

Evangelical theologian John Stackhouse questions the Protestant view of instant purification at death. This "express executive elevator" suggests that those who work hard on holiness in this life are wasting their efforts.[15] For it will be done painlessly for them at death. If God can reprogram them instantly, why doesn't he do it at their conversion? And if there are no shortcuts to holiness in this life, why should we expect shortcuts in the next? And what about hardened sinners who repent on their deathbed? Will they be given the same holiness accorded to lifelong saints who, like Jesus, "learned obedience through suffering"?

If the vast majority of the Church has been right to pray for the dead—not to get the damned out of hell but to help the forgiven make their way toward the holiness necessary for seeing our Lord—it does not mean we know clearly the nature

---

12. John Chrysostom, *Homily 41*, in *The Nicene and Post-Nicene Fathers*, Series 1, ed. Philip Schaff (1886–89; repr., Peabody, MA: Hendrickson, 1994), 12:254.

13. Gregory the Great, *Dialogues* 4.39, https://www.tertullian.org/fathers/gregory_04_dialogues_book4.htm#C39.

14. Ratzinger, *Eschatology*, 230–31.

15. John Stackhouse, "The Hard Work of Holiness: Protestants and Purgatory," *Christian Century*, June 3, 2014, 26–29.

of the suffering that a purgatory might entail. Perhaps, as Ratzinger proposes, the Messiah himself is "the judging fire which transforms us and conforms us to his own glorified body." In this case, "the purification does not happen through some *thing* but through the transforming presence of the Lord himself, whose burning flame" melts what is hard in our hearts and pours into it a softening that makes it fit for the living organism of his body.[16]

When does this take place? Most believers have concluded that it does not come instantaneously at death but in the period between death and the day of the Lord. Most of us know there is plenty that needs to be burned off from us before we have the holiness without which no one will see the Lord. We may not know precisely when or how it will take place, but we can be sure that it will be before we are able to enjoy the messianic banquet. That is, before final redemption.

Preparation

Whether the completion of sanctification occurs at death or after death, Scripture is clear that "without holiness no one will see the Lord." And all believers—Catholic, Protestant, Orthodox, and Pentecostal—acknowledge the teaching of Scripture and tradition that the coming judgment calls for preparation. We are to live in righteousness. As Paul puts it, we should walk in a manner worthy of the calling to which we have been called (Eph. 4:1). This is a believing response to the call of the Father on our lives, made through his Son and Spirit. Our creation, the history of Israel, and the testimonies of Jesus and the apostles—all of these urge us to prepare for the final judgment. Noah prepared by obedience (Gen. 6:13–22). The Israelites in Egypt prepared by obeying YHWH's instructions through Moses and were spared God's wrath on Pharaoh and his land (Exod. 12:1–28). Paul tells us to prepare by living lives of self-control, faith, hope, and love (1 Thess. 5:1–11). In a word, we are to be watchful.

A Millennium?

In the second and third centuries of the Church, and then again in the last few centuries, many believers have been convinced that at some time before the Messiah's return there will be a thousand-year reign of the saints on earth when evil shall be banished. Based on six verses in Revelation 20 (vv. 2–7), some theologians have

16. Ratzinger, *Eschatology*, 229.

held that during this time at the end of history the devil will be shut up in hell and the Church will no longer suffer. Kings and queens shall be nursing fathers and mothers (cf. Isa. 49:23 KJV), the kingdom shall be in the hands of the saints, all nations will coexist in sweet harmony, Church government will be well ordered, and there will be great temporal prosperity. Every person will sit under their own vine and fig tree (2 Kings 18:31; Isa. 36:16); it will be a time of great joy. But just at the end of this millennium there will be a great apostasy. As Edwards, one of the greatest promoters of a literal millennium of this type, put it, the enemies of the Messiah will be as numerous as the sands of the sea, the devils shall come out of the pit, and the Church shall be threatened with extinction again. Only the Messiah's appearance in flaming fire will save his body from elimination.

Pre-Nicene fathers of the Church held to something like this view. Justin Martyr wrote of peace and plenty in a restored Jerusalem; Irenaeus warned believers against taking allegorically the biblical promises of a restored Jerusalem; Hippolytus wrote similarly. In the third century Nepos, a bishop in Egypt, predicted a literal millennium. Even in the fourth century, after Constantine and Nicaea, the apologist Lactantius and the African bishop Quintus Julius Hilarianus expressed confident hope for a literal millennium. The fifth century saw another revival of millennial expectation in apocryphal writings like the Vision of Paul.

But starting with Augustine at the end of the fourth and beginning of the fifth centuries, the Church rejected the intrahistorical fulfillment of complete redemption that a literal millennium represents. Augustine and his theological successors recognized that most Old Testament prophecies end with the vision of a golden age that appears to be a new creation, replete with earthly peace and prosperity, a divine monarchy centered on the throne of David, a utopian age of moral and spiritual perfection. But they also recognized that, apart from the six verses in Revelation 20, the Bible never clearly separates end-time restoration from the apocalyptic return of the Messiah. Never do biblical authors sharply distinguish the Church's suffering from its missionary spread as long as it remains within history before the Messiah's return.

The passage at the beginning of Revelation 20 is a case in point. Darrell Johnson points out that just before the six millennial verses is a scene in which the kings of the earth assemble to make war against Jesus, and just after the six verses Satan is released to gather the nations for war. Johnson argues that all of these passages describe the same battle, with the reign of the saints taking place in the midst of the war.[17]

---

17. Darrell W. Johnson, *Discipleship on the Edge: An Expository Journey through the Book of Revelation* (Vancouver: Regent College Publishing, 2004), 340–41.

How can that be? The key is to realize that John relates the order of his visions, which is not the same as the order of events. He tells us what he sees next, not what happens next. The book of Revelation does not proceed in chronological order, which is similar to John's Gospel—widely regarded as depicting theological rather than chronological order (narrating, for example, the expulsion of the money-changers from the temple at the beginning rather than the end of Jesus's earthly ministry).

Another key is to see that the dragon is thrown down when the child is born in Revelation 12. This means that the beginning of the incarnation marks the beginning of Satan's binding, just as in Mark's Gospel the beginning of the *euangelion* comes after Jesus conquers the devil in the desert. The devil is alive but not well for Mark and John. He has been in the abyss since Jesus was born and particularly since the cross and resurrection of Jesus. But like a mafioso who runs an evil empire from prison, so too the devil works through two beasts, the political power from the sea and the religious power from the earth.

This fits with Paul's theology. Paul argues that the powers of evil were crippled but not killed at the cross and that in the meantime those who are one with the Messiah are already reigning in the heavenly places. The Messiah is there at the right hand of the Father in those same heavenly places, and we are in him (Eph. 2:5–6). Thus, all things are ours. All this in the midst of persecution.

For Johnson, one thousand years is not a statistic but a symbol (not surprising in the most symbolic book of the Bible).[18] It represents a long time of saints reigning in Christ before his return, which is to be preceded by a furious attack on the Church by the devil and his minions.

This is consistent with the picture we have of Jesus's eschatology in Luke and Acts. As Isaac Oliver describes it, neither the restoration of Israel nor the renewal of creation will occur before Jesus's *parousia* (coming).[19] It is not wrong to call it millennial, for it is collective and terrestrial, as opposed to individual and celestial. It will be an eschatological age of earthly peace and abundance, clearly portrayed by Jesus as taking place here on earth. So Justin Martyr and Irenaeus were correct to say that there will be a millennial existence in a renewed Jerusalem. But modern postmillennialists are wrong to think this would come before the *parousia* of the Messiah or that, until his return in glory with armies of angels, there ever would be a time in history when the Church would not be persecuted in the midst of revival.

---

18. Johnson, *Discipleship on the Edge*, 337.
19. Isaac Oliver, *Luke's Jewish Eschatology* (New York: Oxford University Press, 2021).

But after that return there will be no more persecution, and the suffering Church of the God of Israel will enjoy eternity in the new heavens and new earth. What will that be like?

Select Bibliography

Berkhof, Louis. *Systematic Theology.* Grand Rapids: Eerdmans, 1941.

Ferguson, Everett, ed. *Encyclopedia of Early Christianity.* New York: Garland, 1990.

Johnson, Darrell W. *Discipleship on the Edge: An Expository Journey through the Book of Revelation.* Vancouver: Regent College Publishing, 2004.

Lewis, C. S. *The Great Divorce.* New York: Macmillan, 1946.

Newman, John Henry. "Shrinking from Christ's Coming." In *Parochial and Plain Sermons,* 988–95. San Francisco: Ignatius, 1997.

Oliver, Isaac. *Luke's Jewish Eschatology.* New York: Oxford University Press, 2021.

Ratzinger, Joseph. *Eschatology: Death and Eternal Life.* 2nd ed. Washington, DC: Catholic University of America Press, 1988.

Ryken, Leland, James C. Wilhoit, and Tremper Longman III, eds. *Dictionary of Biblical Imagery.* Downers Grove, IL: InterVarsity, 1998.

Stackhouse, John. "The Hard Work of Holiness: Protestants and Purgatory." *Christian Century,* June 3, 2014.

32

The New Heavens and the New Earth

Throughout this book I have been referring to the new heavens and new earth as the renewed world that is the future of what Jews and Christians have called "heaven" for millennia. It will be the end—both purpose and conclusion—of the work of redemption. But many questions remain. Does it have any relation to purgatory, if there is one? Does it have a place? What will our bodies be like? What is the beatific vision? What else will we see and do there? Is it true that there will be levels, greater and lesser degrees of joy there? Will our friends and family be there? What about our pets and other animals? We will explore these questions and others with the help of the five greatest writers on heaven—Augustine, Thomas Aquinas, Jonathan Edwards, C. S. Lewis, and Peter Kreeft.

The Beginning of Heaven

We saw in the last chapter that most Christians and some Jews have believed in a cleansing of some sort after death before heaven. Most have known intuitively or from Scripture that "without holiness no one will see the Lord" and that this will not be achieved instantly at death. Protestants have objected that Jesus told the good thief that he would see him that day in Paradise and that death is represented in Scripture as a triumph. And wouldn't purgatory detract from the finished work of the Messiah on the cross?

386

Christians like C. S. Lewis have replied that purgatory is for sanctification, not satisfaction for sin, so that it does not negate the finished work of the cross. Sins were paid for there, but some still need to be surgically removed from us sinners. In *Letters to Malcolm* he wrote, "Our souls *demand* Purgatory, don't they?"[1] We don't want to go to see the king with bad breath and smelly clothes and are willing for pain if it means we can be cleaned up first. Even Jonathan Edwards, a Protestant who rejected the idea of purgatory, nevertheless preached that "if men would go to heaven, they must first be made fit for it."[2] Holiness, he wrote, is "absolutely necessary" to escape hell. Peter Kreeft argues that something like purgatory is the beginning of heaven. There (or then) we will see all the harm we have done by our sins with a sensitized and mature conscience. It is a suffering more intense and useful than fire or physical pain, but it will know at the same time God's compassion.[3] We will forgive ourselves because we will know that God forgives us. And we will see not only the hellish effects of our sins but also their heavenly effects, the ways that God used even them for the good. For this and other reasons Catherine of Genoa wrote that purgatory, the entrance to heaven, will be joyful, not gloomy. Its pains will be more desirable than the most ecstatic pleasures on earth. Perhaps part of the pleasure will come from knowing that the pains help give us the thickening, as Kreeft puts it, that we need to endure and enjoy the divine substance that is fire. "Our God is a devouring fire" (Heb. 12:29).

Geography

Jonathan Edwards believed that heaven will be a material, new earth at the top of the universe, beyond, as we would say, what astronauts or space probes could reach. This, he thought, is the third heaven where Paul said he was lifted (2 Cor. 12:2). It will be new as in newly glorified or refurbished after the existing earth has been burned up and made the new hell for the devil and the damned.[4] For Peter predicted that "the heavens and earth that now exist are being kept for fire reserved for the day of judgment and destruction of the wicked" (2 Pet. 3:7).

1. C. S. Lewis, *Letters to Malcolm: Chiefly on Prayer* (New York: Harcourt Brace Jovanovich, 1964), 61.

2. Jonathan Edwards, sermon on Colossians 1:12, *Works of Jonathan Edwards Online*, vol. 67, http://edwards.yale.edu.

3. Peter Kreeft, *Everything You Ever Wanted to Know about Heaven . . . but Never Dreamed of Asking* (San Francisco: Ignatius, 1990), 69.

4. Edwards, *HWR*, 506–9.

It seems, however, that there is a problem with this interpretation. The repeated biblical references to the new heavens (literally, skies) and new earth as *renewed* and having their center in Jerusalem, plus the fact that this is the only passage in Scripture that speaks of fire destroying the earth, suggest that Aquinas was closer to the biblical vision—that the renewal or restoration of this world will be *prepared for* by a purifying fire. Peter might even have been saying that the earth has been preserved by God *until* the fires of hell are unleashed on Satan and the damned. The rest of Scripture, therefore, can be seen to foresee the renewal of *this* earth, after either a cleansing fire has been applied to it or the punishing fire of hell has been imposed on the wicked.

So the new heavens and the new earth will be a renewal of *this* earth and sky, as almost all Christians and Jews have believed for millennia. Israel will be at its center. This will be the restoration of the kingdom of God that the prophets prophesied and Jesus proclaimed (Acts 1:6). Yet because God's kingdom was also present in Jesus proleptically (in advance)—indeed, in all of history after the fall, as we have seen, and in the Eucharist every time we celebrate it—we can say that before that future renewal heaven has been and will be wherever God is. Heaven is another dimension where spirit is more real—more dense—than matter. God is everywhere, and in that sense heaven can be in every place potentially, but he is more real in some places than others. Just as he was in all the world in the time of ancient Israel but more accessible in Israel, and in all Israel but with greater density in Jerusalem, and even more in the temple and its Holy of Holies, and the most real and dense on the mercy seat, so too God is more dense in saints like Francis and Mother Teresa than in the wicked. He is closer and thicker in the Eucharist than out in ordinary nature, because he said that only there would the body and blood of the Messiah be available. He is visible to the eyes of faith in nature and the Church but will be *extraordinarily* visible in the new heavens and new earth, as we will see below.

Bodies

As Jews and Christians have agreed for millennia, the new heavens and new earth will be material, and we will have bodies. Augustine said all believing men and women shall have the bodies they had in their youth or would have had if they had lived long enough. All deformities will be removed, though the martyrs may retain their wounds as marks of honor. Women will rise from the dead into spiritual bodies that are recognizably theirs and no other, but with a new beauty that shall excite praise and not lust. The flesh shall be spiritual and subject to the Spirit, but still flesh.[5]

Our spiritual bodies will have a density like nothing on the present, unrenewed earth. We will be among the "solid people" of Lewis's *Great Divorce*, where the grass in heaven is hard as diamonds. This is part of what Edwards was getting at when he proposed that matter is no substance at all but that heaven is supersubstantial, for it is the world of spirit, and spirits are the only substances. This gives spiritual bodies in heaven the capacity to eat but without the *need* for food. Augustine said we will be like the angels in the Bible who took on bodies and ate with human beings. They enjoyed the food but felt no necessity to eat. According to Edwards, human bodies in their spiritual form will assist their minds, just as bodily sickness today clogs the mind, so that on the renewed earth we will have heightened intellectual capacity. Our sharpened thinking will give us mental pleasures we never thought possible.

Kreeft has argued for our *need* to have bodies in this heaven on earth.[6] For bodies can do things no spirit can do. We are better than angels, he reasons, at many things, such as smelling flowers and tasting mangoes, because these sensations require bodies. God created the bodily senses to reveal the unique and irreplaceable delights of each particular thing in the cosmos, the "thisness" of each part of the universe. Something like the bodily senses must be in God if he created them. God the Father does not smell or hear or taste with our kind of senses, but he knows all particulars and therefore particular smells and sounds and tastes. For all of these particulars we need a body to know what God knows. That is why the resurrected body is intrinsic to the immortality of the soul and not a dispensable extra.

Bodies are also necessary in heaven for one of its greatest joys, knowing and loving other saints. As Kreeft puts it, spirits meet in human exchange, but the matter of bodies is the street corner where they meet.[7] A soul without a body is not free but bound. It cannot grasp hands or see the face of another body. And, in Kreeft's words, "the face is me." The face shows a soul's personality, whether it has chosen bitterness or gratitude. Especially the eyes. Sanctity produces a quiet glow. "Beautiful are the wise and gentle eyes of a very old woman at peace with God," but how empty by comparison are the eyes of a childish, spoiled

---

5. Augustine, *The City of God*, trans. Marcus Dods (New York: Modern Library, 1950), 838–40.
6. Kreeft, *Everything You Ever Wanted to Know about Heaven*, 90.
7. Kreeft, *Everything You Ever Wanted to Know about Heaven*, 93.

movie star.[8] These eyes will identify each of the billions of beautiful souls on the renewed earth.

Animals

What about animal bodies? Aquinas didn't think they would be in heaven or on the renewed earth, but Lewis and Kreeft think this is too Platonized and unbiblical. Psalm 36 says that YHWH saves both man and beast (v. 6), and we can recall the souls of animals who repented in Jonah's Nineveh (Jon. 3:6–10). Images of the renewed earth picture the wolf and lamb lying down together, a white horse in heaven, and the creation being set free from its bondage (Isa. 11:6; Rev. 19:11–16; Rom. 8:21). Lewis was convinced that tamed animals would be in heaven, and perhaps wild animals too, since wildness is a proper pleasure for us. From the beginning, he argued, we were to have stewardship over the animals, perhaps in anticipation of a renewed stewardship on the new earth.

Beatific Vision

Scripture and the tradition are unanimous that in the new skies and earth we will see God. This is what the tradition has called the beatific (blissful) vision. One of its primary biblical attestations is Paul's statement in 1 Corinthians 13, "Now we see as with a mirror through an obscure image, but then we will see [God] in the face" (v. 12a). This is a powerful statement, as deep as it is obscure. What can it mean?

The best interpreters say that it does not mean that we will see all of God or that we will see as God sees. Only God sees like that. Our vision will be limited because we will always be finite creatures through all of eternity. As Aquinas wrote, quoting John's Gospel, only the Messiah has the Spirit without measure (John 3:34), and only the Spirit knows the things of God (1 Cor. 2:11). We will not see anything of God with the eyes of our resurrected bodies, for God the Father does not have a body. Everything that we see of him will be through the glorified body—and eyes—of the Messiah. As Aquinas and Edwards wrote, this is why Revelation testifies that in the New Jerusalem the Messiah will be the lamp. He will enlighten the saints about the inner beauties of God.

---

8. Kreeft, *Everything You Ever Wanted to Know about Heaven*, 104.

And this, for Edwards, will be the greatest joy of heaven, seeing God through the eyes of the Messiah. God will be the life of the eternal party on the renewed earth. The dimensions and mysteries of God will take eternity to unfold, so there will never be an end to new beauties to behold. It will be utter bliss to know the saints of the ages and our old friends and family if they are among them, but those joys will be as drops in the ocean, and God will be the ocean. The sight of the Messiah in his divine nature and the sight of all that his divine nature reveals about his Father will be our greatest happiness.

This will be the way we will see the essence of God. Augustine said it will be with the spiritual—not bodily—eyes of our future bodies. Aquinas agreed that we will see the divine essence by our new intellect, not with the eyes of our resurrected bodies. Edwards called it the eyes of our souls.

Not all of us will see the same things in God. Aquinas said some will see more than others, none will see all, and some will instruct others. The angels and the saints will be ignorant of certain things. Just as our new bodies will be like the Messiah's new body but never equal to his, so too we will not be equal in our souls or minds. We will see more below about differences in heaven.

Seeing Others' and Our Sins

Aquinas said our bodily eyes in the renewed world will see the Godhead indirectly by seeing its corporal effects in the Messiah's glorified flesh.[9] That will be the primary way we see God indirectly. The secondary way will be by seeing the bodies of all the saints and all other material things (like animals and trees) in the renewed world. The glories of God will be visible in all the glorified matter of the renewed world. Edwards said that among these glories will be new and more wonderful colors! The artists among us should be excited.

Edwards was convinced from Scripture that in the intermediate state the saints in heaven now see the progress of the work of redemption on earth. For example, in Revelation 6:10 the martyrs under the altar ask when their deaths will be avenged. Why would they ask this, Edwards inquired, unless they know what is going on down on earth? But after the general resurrection, he figured, learning the past history of the work of redemption in all of its fascinating detail will comprise even more of the happiness of eternity. Was the ark of the covenant hidden somewhere?

---

9. Thomas Aquinas, *Summa Theologica*, supplement, 91.2, in vol. 5, trans. Fathers of the English Dominican Province (New York: Benziger Bros., 1948).

Where is Cleopatra's tomb? Was there a second shooter in Dallas when Kennedy was assassinated? Did Roosevelt know the Japanese were coming before Pearl Harbor? What happened to the billions of souls who never heard the gospel but seemed moved by the Spirit to embrace the True and the Good?

Here in eternity we will see, thought Edwards, how the meek inherit not only the land of Israel but also the earth (Matt. 5:5).[10] Those who have lost houses and lands and families on earth will inherit, as Jesus told the rich young man, houses and lands and families a hundredfold (19:29). They will see that the Church's failures were used by God for the good of the Church and God's glory. Eventually, Kreeft observes, this movie-to-end-all-movies will come to an end, for even the history of redemption is finite since the size and history of God's people are both finite. The movie might last several billion years, but after that it will end. Yet even then, there will be no end to seeing the infinite majesties of the Triune God. Of that movie there will be no end.

Will it be humiliating to see our sins displayed not only at the judgment but also as the history of redemption is reviewed? No, said Edwards. For we will see the glories of God's grace, how he used even our sins for later good. And seeing his mercies toward us will make us overflow with gratitude. One of the "Bright People" in Lewis's *Great Divorce* told a ghost from hell who was afraid of being seen that confessing one's sins enables one to laugh at them in heaven. "Shame is like that. If you will accept it—if you will drink the cup to the bottom—you will find it very nourishing: but try to do anything else with it and it scalds."[11] Kreeft adds that in heaven we will not hide or fear rejection because we will know, as all the other saints will know, that God's mercy and grace used everything for good and his glory. Only the lost and damned will be afraid of their sins being known.

Seeing Hell

The greatest theologians of heaven are all agreed, as are the writers of Scripture, that in heaven the saints will see something of the souls in hell. Edwards pointed to Revelation's portrait of Babylon, a type of the damned: "Rejoice over her [fallen Babylon], Heaven and the saints and the apostles and the prophets, because God has avenged your judgment by her" (18:20). At the end of Isaiah's prophecy YHWH says that on "the new heavens and the new earth that I make . . . the flesh

10. Jonathan Edwards, "Happiness of the Saints in Heaven," Miscellany 1059 in *The Miscellanies 833–1152*, vol. 20 of *The Works of Jonathan Edwards* (New Haven: Yale University Press, 2002), 395–96.
11. C. S. Lewis, *The Great Divorce* (New York: Macmillan, 1946), 61–62.

the final judgment, but only works performed in love. Diversity in rewards will be according to diversity in loves. All other things being equal, those who obey both the counsels (say, of poverty, chastity, and obedience to earthly superiors) *and* commandments receive greater rewards than those who obey merely the commandments. Unless, that is, those who obey only the commandments do so with more love. After all, Paul taught that the three supernatural virtues are faith, hope, and love, but the greatest of these is love. All that counts "for anything is faith working by love" (Gal. 5:6).

Edwards taught that different capacities (his "cups") come from different degrees of holiness. Holiness will be measured by God according to degrees of self-denial, suffering, and eminence in humility. All will have love in heaven, but some will have more love than others. All will have glory, but there will be those who have more glory than others. They will be the saints with the greatest holiness and love.

Envy in Heaven?

Won't these differences in glory and rewards provoke resentment? No, said Edwards in his great sermon, "Heaven Is a World of Love."[13] These different rewards will not raise hell, so to speak. For every saint in heaven, no matter where he or she is on the heavenly hierarchy, will be full of love. Each will have as much love as he or she can bear. Each will be beloved by others and will be lovely him- or herself, and each will see the loveliness of others with pleasure and delight.

There will be no envy because those highest in glory will have the greatest holiness and be the most beloved of the heavenly community. They will have more humility and love than others. Therefore, those lower on the scale will be delighted and honored by the love shown them by the humble lovers above them. So, as Kreeft puts it, there will be no jealousy in heaven because that is the principle of hell, and there will be no hell in heaven.

Work

Besides the joys of seeing God and the saints and the history of redemption, what else will we do in heaven? The greatest theologians of heaven don't speculate

---

13. Jonathan Edwards, "Heaven Is a World of Love," in *Ethical Writings*, vol. 8 of *The Works of Jonathan Edwards* (New Haven: Yale University Press, 1989), 375.

about too many details, but they agree that there will be work in heaven, the kind of work that is fulfilling and therefore joyful. Those with talents who never got to use them will use them to the fullest. Edwards said this will not be inconsistent with the rest that heaven promises, for the joy of meaningful work will seem like rest after the frustration they suffered from lack of opportunity on earth. They will be more active than in their times on earth, and all employment will be in the service of others. Aquinas said "higher souls" shall teach "lower souls."

This work of teaching might help unlock part of the mystery of premature deaths, especially those of children. Augustine taught that aborted souls shall rise again to have active lives in their prime. Infants shall receive the bodies of what they would have had as young adults. All these young souls, writes Kreeft, will receive all the experiences of growing in love and earthly learning that they were denied on earth. It would be God's way to employ their parents as their tutors.

Happiness

All are agreed that the renewed world will be a place of bliss, the greatest happiness. Edwards wrote that this will be the eternal wedding day for the Church and her groom the Messiah. There will be pomp and glory, entertainment and mirth for all. Somehow, even in the midst of the work and learning we just saw, this wedding feast will keep being celebrated. Perhaps this will be like ancient biblical weddings, which could last for a week or two, full of entertaining events, but at the wedding supper of the Lamb the events and nuptial joy will never end.

Among those joys and events, said Edwards, will be new beauties continually discovered and ever-new learning about what happened in the history of redemption, all the way back for thousands of years. Even now, in the intermediate period after death and before the judgment, there will be happiness for the saints, but nothing in comparison to what will ensue on the renewed earth.

Aquinas agreed. There will be greater happiness after the general resurrection at the end of the world, greater for both body and soul. The perfected body will help the soul to become more perfect in mind, which will bring elevated joys. Part of those joys will be heavenly humor. We get glimpses of this, according to Kreeft, in Jesus's irony, which surely made his listeners laugh, such as when he spoke of proud men with logs in their eyes trying to take splinters out of the eyes of others. God will laugh at repented and forgiven sins, and so will the saints. "Joy," Lewis wrote in *Letters to Malcolm*, "is the serious business of heaven."[14] It will be full of laughter.

And it will be so more and more. That is, heaven will be eternally progressive, said Edwards. That was his word not for political modernism but for the continuing increase of knowledge and happiness in heaven. Every day throughout eternity we will be seeing more of God's beauty and wisdom, not only God himself but in the Messiah's history of redemption. So our happiness will always be increasing. We will never be bored. And to spice things up, humor will abound, and more and more.

So will our freedom. Augustine remarked that whereas at the creation Adam was given the freedom not to sin, in heaven and on the renewed earth we will have the marvelous freedom of not being *able* to sin. Moderns think this is absurd, for by their lights there is no freedom without ability to do what we want, good or evil. But Kreeft observes that true human authenticity comes from doing the will of God, so that disobeying God is inauthenticity. In heaven we will have the freedom to be truly authentic, which means having the gift of *inability*—delighting in the freedom of neither sinning nor being able to sin. Kreeft compares it to those moments when we made our biggest decisions—say, choosing a marriage partner or deciding to convert—when it seemed that we had great freedom and yet that our free choices were determined by destiny. This delightful inability will be part of the happiness of heaven.

Prayer and Time

One of the most difficult promises of Jesus is that if we abide in him, we can ask whatever we will and he will do it for us (John 15:7). What of the multiplied trillions of prayers by believers through history that went unanswered? Augustine suggested that all unanswered prayers are actually answered, either with a no on earth or a yes in heaven. Besides, he argued in *The City of God*, if all our prayers to Jesus were answered on earth, we would be liable to practice piety simply for the sake of this earth rather than the next. Prayers that await their answers in heaven lead us to hope for heaven.

Kreeft says that our hopes are not in vain. All those who were unjustly denied goods on earth will get them in heaven, perhaps the persecuted at the hands of

14. Lewis, *Letters to Malcolm*, 93.

their persecutors. Heaven is the answer to those and all other faithful prayers. When God confers physical healing in the here and now, these are merely previews of coming attractions in heaven, where every earthly disease and handicap— whether physical or emotional or mental and spiritual—is healed. The upshot is that every prayer for healing for the saints is answered, but some not yet. What matters is the timing, and it is always God's timing, not ours.

The question of time in heaven is related to this question of answers to prayer. Here again Kreeft is helpful. Most of us are familiar with the concept of God being outside of time, looking at the timeline of history in his eternal present. He is simultaneously present to the whole timeline—past, present, and future. Kreeft, following Lewis, has suggested that this is like all the events in a novel being present in the mind of the author. Each event has its own present, its own time for this event. This is the time called *kairos* in the Bible. The succession of events in the novel one after another is called *chronos*. Just as the author of the novel can change an event and thereby change the way that event affects the rest of the events in the novel, so God from eternity outside time can, in answer to prayer from anywhere on the timeline, change an event and its impact. So when a Christian decides to forgive his persecutor, God will make that persecution work for the Christian's good. As the Christian looks back, it even changes the nature of the crime that the persecutor committed. Rather than an unmitigated evil, it now becomes something that mysteriously brings good to the Christian and perhaps others. As Joseph said to his brothers, you meant it for evil but God meant it for good (Gen. 50:20). This is a way that eternity can act on time and change it from the future toward the past. The higher dimension can work on the lower. Prayers of forgiveness can step outside of time by God's power and reach back to the past.

In this way, eternity includes time. Another way we can think of that is to consider the resurrection of the bodies of the saints and the succession of their acts on the renewed earth. One day there, as it were, will follow another. The second day will show more of God's beauty and power than the first day. That will be a succession of events in the time of heaven on earth. Even though this will be in eternity, it will have its own time in the midst of eternity. There will be new days, as it were, when we will meet our ancestors (if they were in the Messiah). Because eternity includes time without being limited to it, there will be other "days" on which we will meet our descendants. *Kairos* events will be followed by other *kairos* events in the succession of *chronos* within the eternity of the new heavens and earth.

Sex in Heaven?

I have left this section toward almost the end because the question seems so bizarre. Most of us would say this is ridiculous and typically modern, but Kreeft insists there will be sex in heaven. He argues that it is clear there will be men and women in heaven and that sex will affect every aspect of existence there, because sex is something we are, not what we do. It affects every part of our inner essence because it is innate and natural and affects every cell in our bodies. It is not socially conditioned or conventional or environmental but hereditary.

Human sexuality is derived from cosmic sexuality. There is love among the particles of the cosmos, seen in gravitational and electromagnetic attraction, and between positive and negative charges. Scientists can tell us *how* this works but only lovers know *why*. Cosmic sexuality starts with God, who is a sexual being, the most sexual of all beings. For Scripture tells us that sexuality is in the image of God: He created man in the image of God, male and female he created them (Gen. 1:27). This is why there will be sex in the new sky and earth, because we are close to the source of all sex. None will marry or be given in marriage *anew* (Luke 20:35–36), but existing marriages joined to the Messiah might have cosmic love we cannot presently envisage.

Intercourse on earth is a shadow of intercourse in heaven, where there is no procreation but the expression of love. Since men and women are sexually complementary and it is not good for a man to be alone, there might be specially kindred souls who enjoy the communion that comes with the opposite sex. Human beings don't eat candy while making love because they realize there is something better than the candy. For that reason sexual love in heaven will probably not involve the "clumsy ecstasy" of fitting two bodies together. There will be something far better.

Preparing for Heaven

So how do we ensure we will enjoy that something far better? Edwards said we should aim for the top. As John Gerstner put it, the American theologian was intent on riding first-class in heaven and urged all his parishioners to do the same. He said there is nothing wrong with seeking high degrees of glory in heaven. Self-love is a neutral principle, and only inordinate self-love is a sin. It is biblical and righteous to seek eternal happiness with God and to seek as much of it as we can. Jesus, he observed, prayed for his own happiness: "Father, now glorify me in your presence with the glory that I had from you before the cosmos [was created]" (John 17:5).

Edwards advised his parishioners how to get to heaven and climb to glory there. The sky is the limit, he said, and it is finally our choice what path we will take. The path to heavenly glory is uphill and wearisome. It requires us to live in self-denial and love and not to presume that earth is the place for fulfillment or complete joy. "We can't suppose that the reason why providence won't suffer men to enjoy great happiness here, is that he is averse to the creature's happiness, but because this is not the time for it. To everything there is an appointed season and time. . . . God reserves happiness to be bestowed hereafter; that is the appointed time for it, and that is the reason he don't [sic] give it now."[15] Better to seek glory in heaven and not be disillusioned when earthly happiness is frustrated. If frustration comes because our faith forces us to lose glory and possessions and family here on earth, we should take comfort that we will be rewarded proportionately in the renewed world.

He Will Make All Things New

Some Christians are afraid of heaven. They fear that they so regularly sin that God has given up on them. They should listen to Edwards the pastor, who often reassured his parishioners that while there is indeed an infinite distance between the holy God and unholy sinners, the blood of the Messiah has removed all hindrances to intimacy between the merciful God and trembling sinners: "He whose arms were expanded to suffer, to be nailed to the cross, will doubtless be opened as wide to embrace those from whom he suffered."[16]

If we are willing to be embraced by the one who wants to expand his arms for us, we will experience the renewed world that Thomas Howard has graphically depicted.

> Behold I make all things new. Behold I do what cannot be done. I restore the years that the locusts and worms have eaten. I restore the years which you have drooped away upon your crutches and in your wheelchair. I restore the symphonies and operas which your deaf ears have never heard and the snowy massif your blind eyes have never seen and the freedom lost to you through plunder and the identity lost to you because of calumny and the failure of justice. And I restore the good

15. Jonathan Edwards, "Heaven's Happiness," Miscellany 585 in *The Miscellanies 501–832*, ed. Ava Chamberlain, vol. 18 of *The Works of Jonathan Edwards* (New Haven: Yale University Press, 2000), 120–21.

16. Jonathan Edwards, "Happiness of Heaven," Miscellany 741, in Chamberlain, *The Miscellanies 501–832*, 370.

which your own foolish mistakes have cheated you of. And I bring you to the love of which all other loves speak, the love which is joy and beauty, and which you have sought in a thousand streets, and for which you have wept and clawed your pillow.[17]

Select Bibliography

Augustine. *The City of God*. Translated by Marcus Dods. New York: Modern Library, 1950.

Catherine of Genoa. *"Purgation and Purgatory," "The Spiritual Dialog."* New York: Paulist Press, 1979.

Edwards, Jonathan. "Happiness of Heaven." Miscellany 741 in *The Miscellanies 501–832*, edited by Ava Chamberlain, vol. 18 of *The Works of Jonathan Edwards*, 366–97. New Haven: Yale University Press, 2000.

———. "Heaven Is a World of Love." In *Ethical Writings*, edited by Paul Ramsey, vol. 8 of *The Works of Jonathan Edwards*, 366–97. New Haven: Yale University Press, 1989.

———. "Heaven's Happiness." Miscellany 585 in *The Miscellanies 501–832*, edited by Ava Chamberlain, vol. 18 of *The Works of Jonathan Edwards*, 120–21. New Haven: Yale University Press, 2000.

———. Sermon on Col. 1:12. In *Works of Jonathan Edwards Online*, vol. 67, edited by the Jonathan Edwards Center, http://edwards.yale.edu.

———. "The Way of Holiness." In *Sermons and Discourses, 1720–1723*, edited by Wilson H. Kimnach, vol. 10 of *The Works of Jonathan Edwards*, 465–79. New Haven: Yale University Press, 1992.

Gerstner, John. "Heaven." In *The Rational Biblical Theology of Jonathan Edwards*, 541–604. Powhatan, VA: Berea Publications; Orlando, FL: Ligonier Ministries, 1993.

Howard, Thomas. *Christ the Tiger*. San Francisco: Ignatius, 1989.

Kreeft, Peter. *Everything You Ever Wanted to Know about Heaven . . . but Never Dreamed of Asking*. San Francisco: Ignatius, 1990.

Lewis, C. S. *The Great Divorce*. New York: Macmillan, 1946.

———. *Letters to Malcolm: Chiefly on Prayer*. New York: Harcourt Brace Jovanovich, 1964.

———. *The Problem of Pain*. New York: Macmillan, 1962.

Thomas Aquinas. Supplement. Vol. 5 of *Summa Theologica*. Translated by Fathers of the English Dominican Province. New York: Benziger Bros., 1948.

---

17. Thomas Howard, *Christ the Tiger* (San Francisco: Ignatius, 1989), 151, quoted in Kreeft, *Everything You Ever Wanted to Know about Heaven*, 165.

33

God Glorified
in the Church Glorified

We have now come to the end of this story, the most wonderful story of all. It is the story of this world and of how the Triune God has used this world to redeem a people who have said yes to his eternal invitation. This has been the history of the work of redemption.

I explained in my two opening chapters that redemption involves many things: the defeat of evil, the restoration and renewal of what was destroyed at the fall, the uniting of all things in the Messiah, perfecting God's elect people, and the glory of God. We also saw what this implies for the purpose of creation. God created the world with two purposes. First, the world was made to demonstrate YHWH's goodness, greatness, and beauty. This means that *everything* in the creation and redemption's history was for the end of showing God's glory—this physical cosmos, his human creatures, the saints, Israel and the Gentiles, the Christian virtues, and even his justice in punishing evil.

A second ultimate end of the creation was for YHWH to share his goodness and beauty with his creatures, for he loves them! Both ends—his glory and the happiness of his creatures—are ultimate, which means they are goods in themselves. God has no joy in wrath, and so manifesting his justice toward the wicked is his "strange" work. But even this glorifies him, as does, far more so, his sharing himself with the creatures who want him.

These two ends are one and the same. God glorifies himself by sharing himself with his people, and they have joy in this sharing. Sharing or giving is a characteristic of God. He is a fellowship of three divine Persons who ever give of themselves to one another. So it is not that they *have* love but that God in these Three *is* love. And since his people are the Body of his Son the Messiah, when his people glorify him, he glorifies them. All the glory that goes to him he shares with his Body, sharing his glory and goodness with them. When the Son glorifies the Father by sharing in the creation and effecting the redemption, he shares his love and beauty with God's people, Jews and Gentiles. They know God by sharing in the Son's knowledge of the Father, they are holy because they share in the Son's holiness, and they are happy because they share in Jesus's joy that he shares with the Father. That joy and love are so real that they are the Person of the Holy Spirit.

In this last chapter I will first discuss what the end of this story means for the kingdom of God—that is, the question of whether the Son delivers the kingdom back to the Father. Then I will reflect on how the history of redemption reveals God's glory and brings happiness to his people.

Whose Kingdom?

Paul says that at the end of history, after establishing the new skies and earth, the Son will deliver the kingdom back to the Father.

> Since through a man came death, so also through a man [will come] resurrection of the dead. Just as in Adam all die, so also in the Messiah all will be made alive. But each in his own order. Firstfruit was the Messiah, then those of the Messiah at his appearing [*parousia*]. Then will come the end when he delivers the kingdom to the God and Father, after having destroyed every ruling principality and every authority and power. For it is necessary for him to reign until he has put all his enemies under his feet. The last enemy to be overthrown is death. For "He has subjected all things under his feet" [Ps. 8:6], When it says "He has subjected all things," it is clear that he [the Father] is excepted who subjected all things to him [the Messiah]. When all things have been subjected to him [the Son], then the Son himself will be subjected to the one who subjected all things to him, so that God might be all things in all. (1 Cor 15:21–28)

Edwards believed that whereas the Son will return the kingdom to the Father, the Son will never give up being the mediator between the Father and the Church. Nor will the Son ever give up his headship of the Church: "That relation that Christ stands in to his church, as the Father's viceroy over her, shall cease, and shall be swallowed up in the relation of a vital and conjugal head, or head of influence and enjoyment." Edwards explains the latter:

> The church now shall be brought nearer to God the Father. . . . And her enjoyment of him shall be more direct: Christ the God-man shall now no longer be instead of the Father to them, but, as I may express it, their head of their enjoyment of God, as it were, the eye to receive the rays of divine glory and love for the whole body, and the ear to hear the sweet expressions of his love, and the mouth to taste the sweetness and feed on the delights of the enjoyment of God. . . . Hereby God's communication of himself to them shall be more direct than when it was by a vicegerent.[1]

Christ will go from having "employment" ruling a "delegated kingdom . . . for a season" to greater "enjoyment" of the Father, which is "more honorable." Edwards concludes that it is fitting that the Son should return the kingdom to the Father because the kingdom doesn't "belong to the Son but to the Father, by the economy of the Trinity. 'Tis the Father that is economically the King of heaven and earth, Lawgiver and judge of all; and therefore when the Son is made so, he is by the Father advanced into his throne, by having the Father's authority committed unto him, to rule in his name and as his vicegerent."[2]

For Edwards, then, the Son is still head of the Church in eternity. He fought with blood for it, and so the kingdom that was formally the Father's (since the Father, as Jews have always seen, is the King of reality) and was delegated to the Son during the history of redemption is still the Father's but declared by him, in loving condescension, to remain the Son's in another sense. He had purchased it by his humiliation and suffering, and therefore it would be called the Son's kingdom even though formally the Father is still the King of all reality. The Father would glorify the Son by sharing his own glory with him.

It seems, then, that the kingdom belongs to both the Father and the Son. The Son will indeed deliver the kingdom back to the Father after he has subdued all his enemies and the saints are enjoying the renewed world. But when the angel told Mary that her son would reign over the house of Jacob forever, and when the seventh angel in Revelation says the Messiah shall reign over his kingdom forever

---

1. Edwards, "Consummation of All Things: Christ's Delivering Up the Kingdom to the Father," Miscellany 742 in *The Miscellanies 501–832*, vol. 18 of *The Works of Jonathan Edwards* (New Haven: Yale University Press, 2000), 374.

2. Jonathan Edwards, "Economy of the Trinity and Covenant of Redemption," Miscellany 1062 in *The Miscellanies 833–1152*, ed. Amy Plantinga Pauw, vol. 20 of *The Works of Jonathan Edwards* (New Haven: Yale University Press, 2002), 439.

(Luke 1:33; Rev. 11:15), as the Nicene Creed proclaims, it appears to mean that when the Son delivers the kingdom back to the Father, the Son's commission as delegated king will cease, and he will then be coruler of the Father's kingdom—a position he has earned by fighting for it and perfecting it.

This shows that the history of redemption is not about a final equality but an order of love in which there is humility at the top and satisfied love at the bottom. Even the final disposition of the kingdom is about the Father's love toward the Son, in which he yields his ordered priority so that the Son can share in the glory of the eternal kingdom. Headship—in love and humility—is never surrendered.

This headship of the Father, in both eternity and history, shows us two things about redemption. First, that the ancient and modern Jewish insistence that God's principal title is King is right. God the Father is King of reality, and ultimate honor and glory go to him. In our desire to honor the Son's redemption, we Christians tend to forget this. But Paul did not. Note one of his many prayers that drive the glory of Messiah Jesus and the Church back to the Father: "Glory to God whose power, working in us, can do infinitely more than we can ask or imagine: Glory to him from generation to generation in the Church, and in Messiah Jesus for ever and ever" (Eph. 3:20–21).

Second, the headship of the Father reinforces the trinitarian nature of redemption and history. God redeems us by his two hands, the Son and the Spirit, as Irenaeus taught. The three Persons have always been at work in every redemptive act of God. Too many Christians have restricted redemption to either the Son or the Spirit, not realizing that all of reality has a threefold stamp on it because it is trinitarian in both creation and redemption.

Glory to God

Let us now review the majestic story we have followed in this book. God took thousands of years to prepare the way for the Son to purchase redemption. The purchase was almost too mind-boggling to be true, which was why ancient Jews could scarcely believe it. Would the eternal YHWH live on earth for thirty-three years in a despised condition, living a life of such suffering that it ended on a cross for criminals? But then they saw the glorious aftermath, which convinced many of its truth: this same man of sorrows was raised from the dead and lifted on high to the right hand of God at the top of the universe.

This was the culmination of a remarkable history of God calling out and caring for a people he made his own. We recall God teaching Adam and Eve that sacrifice and blood were necessary to atone for sin, the early revivals poured out on Enosh and his generation, and resurrection of the body demonstrated by Enoch. Then as now, the proportion of human beings who wanted to walk in God's light was small, and things went from bad to worse. God destroyed the nascent world by a flood but miraculously preserved his little flock of Noah and his family.

After the flood God resettled the world, which in turn led to more apostasy. Most people wanted to make names for themselves apart from God's name, symbolized by their building Babel, which led to God's dispersing people to the nations and shortening their lives. Redemption started anew with the calling of Abraham, the destruction of Sodom and Gomorrah, and miracles God performed for Abraham, Isaac, Jacob, and Joseph. More miraculous interventions came for God's people in Egypt and then at the Red Sea, but not without much suffering. This continued for many centuries as God preserved his Jewish people amid threats to destroy them from ancient empires. Redemption proceeded with God's supervision of the rise and fall of empire after empire before the coming of his Messiah. And after the rise of the early Church and its persecution by the Roman Empire came what no one could have predicted, the transformation of that pagan empire by the Christian faith. Jews continued to suffer, even those who wanted to adopt the new Messiah, but the meandering and unpredictable history of redemption saw God forming a people for himself among Jews and Gentiles over the next two millennia in remarkable ways—and often against what seemed impossible odds.

Greater Than the Creation

We have seen that the work of redemption was the greatest of all God's works and was the purpose of all his other works. Redemption, which was the purchase and purification of a people, was the principle driving all God's works of providence. It was greater than even his work of creation. The new creation was more prodigious than the old creation, as much as the temple was more magnificent than the tabernacle, the renewed covenant through Jesus greater than the Mosaic covenant, the priesthood of Messiah Jesus grander than that of Aaron, David's throne outranking Saul's, and the New Jerusalem surpassing the glory of the old Jerusalem.

God's design has emerged from this history. His intent was to create a world that would provide a bride and kingdom for his Son. All of world history was directed by him to set up the kingdom of the Messiah and the marriage of his bride—God's people—to the Son. This was what all the creation, both old and new, has been laboring to bring to pass. It all started in the covenant of redemption, before the creation, the pact agreed upon by the three Persons of the Trinity before the foundation of the world. Every decree of God in directing human history came out of this original covenant between the Father and the Son in the love that is the Holy Spirit.

The End of History

This means that God is the beginning and end of all human history. As the book of Revelation proclaims at its beginning and end, God is the Alpha and Omega (the first and last letters of the Greek alphabet). As Paul put it at the end of Romans 11, all things come *from* God, exist *through* God, and go back *to* God (v. 36). And while everything else constantly changes, the eternal God of Israel remains ever the same in his character and purposes. This form of the earth and heavens shall perish one day, but God will remain forever (Ps. 102:26). All the other gods of this world, principalities and powers that have tried to imitate the God of Israel, have perished. The gods of Egypt, Canaan, and Rome have died. Allah, the Buddha, and the gods of the New Age are being exposed as vain hopes. Even Satan, the god of this world, was crippled on the cross and one day will be forever confined to the pit of hell. The God of Israel is the only creator and redeemer, and the history of redemption has demonstrated this for all with eyes to see and ears to hear.

The death of false gods has shown that history is one story. Like a huge world-class river system whose tributaries go in different directions but eventually join at its mouth, so the windings and turnings of world history finally issue in the ocean that is God. God's providence in history is like Ezekiel's cosmic wheel, which has the dazzling glory of God at its head and has turning wheels within wheels full of eyes round about, directed by the Spirit (Ezek. 1:15–20). The events of history can appear to be disconnected, Macbeth's sound and fury signifying nothing. But in reality everything in history is directed by those eyes and wheels in Ezekiel's vision. Every event in history is a link on a gigantic chain, the first link from God and the last going to God. The naked eye sees only obstacles and impediments. Redemption often seems light years away. But Scripture promises and this history has shown that just as the course of providence has redeemed God's people in the past, typically snatching victory from the jaws of defeat, so too in the future all the wandering streams of providence will unite in the ocean that is God.

History and Redemption in a Higher Order

In this book, then, I have tried to show that "history" and "redemption" mean things not normally taken for granted by those words. They should now be seen as integral to a higher order of things. Perhaps the best way to express these higher meanings, which are usually contemptible to worldly order, is to say that the higher meanings of history and redemption are counterintuitive. Let us count the ways.

1. The history of the human race is driven by the history of redemption, so the story of human history is, at its heart, the story of redemption.

2. Redemption is more than salvation, for even after being saved from sin and death and the devil, we need redemption from the *power* of sin and death in the old creation by renewal and restoration through the power of the new creation.

3. Israel is at the heart of redemption and history. As Mordechai suggested in George Eliot's *Daniel Deronda*, Israel has seeded world history with revelation necessary for redemption: "The *Shemah*, wherein we briefly confess the divine Unity, is the chief devotional exercise of the Hebrew; and this made our religion the fundamental religion for the whole world; for the divine Unity embraced as its consequence the ultimate unity of mankind. See, then—the nation which has been scoffed at for its separateness, has given a binding theory to the human race."[3] Mordechai spoke of Jewish monotheism that changed the world. This volume has focused on the Jewish Messiah who has redeemed the world. The One who embodied Israel was the redeemer from just after the fall and all through humanity's and Israel's history. He inspired her Torah and sacrifices, as Israel was the world's priest for the world's redemption. Israel's Messiah in his twofold Body continues to redeem the world through his Body's Word, sacraments, and fellowship— which anticipate the *shalom* of the renewed world to come.

4. Israel's redemption of the world through the work and body of the perfect Israelite is of the body and not just mind or heart, is visible as well as invisible, is corporate and not only individual, and is radically different from liberations promised by other world religions.

5. Israel's redemption of the world has usually been appropriated only by a remnant, just as Jesus Messiah spoke of his "little flock." The remnant is

---

3. George Eliot, *Daniel Deronda*, ed. Graham Handley (Oxford: Oxford University Press, 2014), 617.

often persecuted and usually suffers in this world. Its greatest triumphs are often in the midst of worldly defeats and opposition.

6. The story of this history of redemption demonstrates the beauty of God and his Church, but only when seen through the history of the suffering remnant.

7. In its worship the persecuted remnant transcends time, entering into the past redemptive works of Israel and her Messiah but experiencing the future *shalom* of the kingdom through its sacramental *anamnēsis*, which lifts its members out of linear time and sets them in the midst of the celestial assembly of the Church triumphant. This is the fullness of future redemption in the here and now.

The Glory of the Messiah

By these counterintuitive meanings of history and redemption we have seen that history was enacted for the glory of Jesus Messiah: God designed the world for his Son's use in the work of redemption. This was why the Father created the world *through* the Son. It was also why the Father made the Son his firstborn and why he set his throne above all other thrones. It is why every kingdom and empire has fallen and why his will be the last standing. It is why his people are redeemed and made happy and his enemies have become his footstool. It is why this world, when it has been renewed and restored, will become his inheritance.

That which glorifies the Son also shows the glorious majesty and power of the Father. What else can explain the unexplainable death and resurrection of God's people over millennia, regularly facing defeat and apparent elimination only to be saved and prospered? This has been God's way and glory, to use weakness to show strength and through that weakness triumphing over the powers of earth and hell. One day little infants will tread on the lion and adder, trampling underfoot the young lion and dragon (Ps. 91:13). This is God the Father, who conquers by a man who once was a baby and appeared as a poor, weak, and despised man. His only weapon was an instrument of torture, the cross, but by it he defeated all God's enemies through history—Satan, the Roman Empire, the repeated kingdoms of Antichrist that have tried to destroy Christians and Jews. God's enemies typically have seemed invincible until the day when they blow away like chaff in the wind or melt like fat in the fire. They disappear and come to nothing. So shall it be for every anti-Christ kingdom before the Messiah returns.

At that point God's glorious wisdom will be visible to every believer. We will be reminded of how God has so often brought good out of evil. It started, of course, when the Messiah turned the fall on its head, beginning the work of redemption just outside Eden. The progress of redemption over the millennia illustrates this divine wisdom, as time and again God brought order out of a train of confusion, frustrating the devil by turning his devices to God's glory—think of Satan's most wicked device, the crucifixion of the Son of God—and the eventual happiness of God's people.

In all this history we have seen the consistency of God's love and faithfulness to his people. These two attributes, love and faithfulness, were declared to be part of God's name YHWH when he revealed himself to Moses (Exod. 34:6–7). They continued to be named and illustrated time after time in the history of redemption. As the psalmist praised, "Your steadfast love, O YHWH, extends to the skies, your faithfulness to the clouds" (Ps. 36:5). Psalm 136 repeats the refrain, "His steadfast love endures forever." This is what the history of redemption reveals about the only true God, the God of Israel: he is a God who loves his people and is faithful to them.

Because of that love and faithfulness, the God of Israel has brought eternal happiness to his people. He has loved them with an everlasting love, and he has given people for his people and given nations in exchange for their life (Isa. 43:4). For their sakes he has given the blood of all their enemies and has given all nations that have stood in their way as sacrifices for their good. For their sakes he made the world and created angels to be ministering spirits to them. He has turned all things, even wickedness, to serve them and their redemption. As Paul said, "All things are yours" (1 Cor. 3:21–23). God has made all things for the sake of his people, the Body of the Messiah, so that they might be a happy and blessed society.

As God glorifies himself, then, the Church too is glorified. We have now seen in the course of this book what I argued at the beginning—that the two purposes of the creation have become one through the work of redemption: God's glory and the happiness of his people.

Select Bibliography

Augustine. *The Trinity*. Translated and edited by Edmund Hill. Hyde Park, NY: New City Press, 1991.

Berkhof, Louis. *Systematic Theology*. Grand Rapids: Eerdmans, 1941.

Bromiley, Geoffrey. "Eternal Generation." In *Evangelical Dictionary of Theology*, edited by Walter Elwell, 368. Grand Rapids: Baker, 1984.

Calvin, John. *Institutes of the Christian Religion*. Edited by John T. McNeill. Translated by Ford Lewis Battles. Philadelphia: Westminster, 1960.

Edwards, Jonathan. "Consummation of All Things: Christ's Delivering Up the Kingdom to the Father." Miscellany 742 in *The Miscellanies 501–832*, edited by Ava Chamberlain, vol. 18 of *The Works of Jonathan Edwards*, 373–76. New Haven: Yale University Press, 2000.

———. "Economy of the Trinity and Covenant of Redemption," Miscellany 1062 in *The Miscellanies 833–1152*, edited by Amy Plantinga Pauw, vol. 20 of *The Works of Jonathan Edwards*, 430–43. New Haven: Yale University Press, 2002.

Fisher, David Hackett. *Historians' Fallacies: Toward a Logic of Historical Thought*. New York: Harper Torchbooks, 1970.

Hodge, Charles. "The Mutual Relations of the Persons of the Trinity" and "Examination of the Nicene Doctrine." In *Systematic Theology*, 3 vols., 1:460–77. Grand Rapids: Baker, 1968.

John Chrysostom. *Homily 7 on Philippians*. In *The Nicene and Post-Nicene Fathers*, Series 1, edited by Philip Schaff, 13:212–18. 1886–89. Peabody, MA: Hendrickson, 1994.

———. *Homily 39 on First Corinthians*. In *The Nicene and Post-Nicene Fathers*, Series 1, edited by Philip Schaff, 12:233–43. 1886–89. Reprint, Peabody, MA: Hendrickson, 1994.

Muller, Richard A. "The Doctrine of the Trinity from the Sixteenth to the Early Eighteenth Century." In *Post-Reformation Reformed Dogmatics*, 4:59–140. 4 vols. Grand Rapids: Baker Academic, 2003.

Schaff, Philip. "The Trinitarian Controversies." In *History of the Christian Church*, 3:616–98. 8 vols. 1910. Reprint, Grand Rapids: Eerdmans, 1995.

Subject Index

Scripture and Ancient Writings Index